ASPECTS OF LANGUAGE

By the same author

THE SPANISH LANGUAGE

*

With W. A. Morison

RUSSIAN AND THE
SLAVONIC LANGUAGES

ASPECTS OF LANGUAGE

BY

WILLIAM J. ENTWISTLE

M.A., LITT.D., LL.D.

*Late King Alfonso XIII Professor of Spanish Studies
in the University of Oxford*

FABER AND FABER

24 Russell Square

London

First published in mcmliii
by Faber and Faber Limited
24 Russell Square, London, W.C. 1

PRINTED IN GREAT BRITAIN

EDITOR'S PREFACE

THE untimely death of William James Entwistle took from us one of the most learned philologists of the English-speaking world. He had long been distilling from his vast experience of languages reflections on general theoretical problems of linguistics, and it is some measure of consolation for a grievous loss that shortly before his death he delivered to the publishers the completed typescript of the present book. In a letter to me at the time he wrote 'My *Aspects of Language* is a complete ms, done for the tenth time'. For an editor who knew Entwistle's amazing neatness, carefulness, and power of work there remained nothing except the mechanics of proof-reading. His own text stands without emendation except for obvious typing errors. In the same letter he alluded to friends who had read his typescript 'as the range of languages is too wide for my unsupported testimony'. I would ask those unnamed friends to accept from me the grateful acknowledgement which he would have made explicit.

L. R. PALMER

PREFATORY LETTER

12 FYFIELD ROAD
OXFORD
20 November 1951

Dear Mr. de la Mare,

Many years ago you suggested this book, but I dare not hope that this is the book you asked for.

Our problem then was to find some way of commending as reasonable to small boys two languages constructed on systems so very unlike those of their own—and in their view, uniquely sensible—mother-tongue. A better linguist than I has expressed a hope of 'an elementary grammar for children, free from the usual taint of abstraction and unreality which those hardest and sanest of critics are so quick to detect and condemn'. His thought was of English, but perhaps he came up against the same difficulty that we did, namely, that the very young get on very well with an arbitrary discipline, but are perplexed by general principles which we elders fondly believe will simplify their labours. Simplification is not simplicity; simplicity is as often as not arbitrary and, on analysis, puzzling and inconsistent.

You left your barb in my mind, which has itched ever since. Something, I have felt, should be done for somebody, if not for the irreflexive young. The same notion has been in the minds of many persons since the war, and one of the problems of this book has been to keep pace more or less with the endless flow of new literature by linguists and philosophers on the topic of language. Perhaps the undertaking would have been impossible if it had not been that no two ventures agree in principles or presentation. The topic is far greater, far more interesting, than the efforts to exhaust it, and one more attempt in yet one more direction may even be welcome. There are dogmatists among language experts, but I do not hesitate to describe the present moment as one in which no dogma is imperative, but the whole matter is up for open discussion among men of good will. Language is more wonderful than linguistics; perhaps it is the greatest wonder within the reach of man.

The motion of this book is then discursive and undogmatic. It is unphilosophic, though recognizing that philosophers may have their own legitimate interest in language. It is not based on a hypothesis of the unity of the human understanding, nor yet on the assumption that there is much diversity. The savage and civilized minds are differently endowed, but they have means of entering into each other to some extent.

Thousands of languages have their independent grammars not by infinite variations of principle—which would make language-learning impossible —but by permutations and combinations of the few solutions available for each problem in self-expression. I do not find language either systematic or wholly unsystematic, but impressed with patterns, generally incomplete, by our pattern-making minds. They are not logical or illogical. They may be alogical, but those of civilized Europe and China have had logical principles stamped upon them.

No man can really know more than his own language, it is said, but I do not happen to be an Anglicist. I must use what light has been given me. A distinguished continental linguist, when asked how many languages he knew, has said that he had no obligation to know more than one, that his business was with the principles of language itself, and that there could be nothing less scientific than learning languages.

Alas, I have always felt this unscientific yearning, though wanting skill as an executant. Another might have written this book on the basis of English, but I am impressed by the eccentric position of our mother-tongue, which would have to be twisted into very queer shapes if it is to ape the methods of so many others. The experiment has been tried; I can never persuade myself that Anglo-Eskimo or any other combination is either the one or the other. Moreover, I have a certain pleasure in seeing the foreign forms objectively as they occur and as alone they can combine with each other to make human speech. I hope I have not loaded this text, and that the examples will be regarded only as they are offered, *exempli gratia*.

Among all my predecessors I find myself most in sympathy with Wilhelm von Humboldt, who sought so diligently among all the tongues of men for the common principles of expression. To offer to solve these problems on the basis of one language, be it English or French, or of one family ultimately reducible to one language, such as Indo-European, seems to me insufficient for (as it were) linguistic triangulation. I offer my suggestions, therefore, on the basis of languages known in some degree to me and separated as widely as possible in space and idiom. It is only so, I suppose, that one can reach a universally valid proposition or, at any rate, a list of the alternative solutions which have been adopted by races of men.

I am grateful to Mrs. D. R. Sutherland, Mr. A. Sillery, and Mr. R. E. Russell for having the patience to read this disquisition in manuscript, and I expect to incur other obligations as it goes through the press. I am indebted for books to Mr. C. S. S. Higham of Messrs. Longmans, Mr. D. M. Davin of the Clarendon Press, and the Secretary of the New York Viking Fund, as well as to friends and colleagues who have so kindly kept me posted concerning their achievements over thirty years. I am aware that there are many books I have not read and ought to. A scholar is no Croesus, and often a book in the hand is worth a dozen in a library. No one can read to an end the enormous literature of language, and if he is to make any contribution at all, he must lay down his book and take to his typewriter.

To you who spoke to me of this thing, or of something akin to it, I now offer it with its sins upon its head, hoping that the intelligent discussion of questions of language, without preconception or pride of intellect, may help to restore to the first place in our interest our first and solely human activity.

Yours sincerely,

WILLIAM J. ENTWISTLE

Richard de la Mare, Esq.

CONTENTS

CONTENTS

I
LANGUAGE

MAN is the talkative animal. All other definitions lead up to or away from this crucial talent for speech. Man stands erect and looks at the stars. The posture is awkward and requires a great increase of mental control. Even the fifteen degrees of difference between man and gorilla seem to require more than double mental capacity. With this increase of brain goes the increase of those frontal areas on which man depends for the co-ordination and reproduction of speech-sounds. Man invents, thanks to his opposable thumbs; but chimpanzees would be twice as inventive if they could communicate their inventions by speech. In gregariousness, sociability, or political efficiency man is perhaps less competent than wolves, bees, or ants, if we measure means and ends, but man alone can alter his polity by discussion. Man is rational; his reasons are recorded in his language along with his unreason, his emotionalism, and his subconscious urges (so far as these can be known). Man has a history; but knows it only because of speech, not merely in rudimentary forms, but as an art of oral or written record, and by means of language he knows his own history and that of animals and material things. The higher apes have most of the organs of speech, and a chimpanzee or gorilla is said to have been educated to the point of greeting Florida friends by the exclamation *Hi!* But there is no evidence that the animal made the discovery of speech for himself, nor does his conversation seem to have much variety. The apes use a visual intelligence and follow what they see. They locate sounds only imperfectly, pay no attention to speech symbols, but are capable of establishing routine reactions to sounds and understand their owners as dogs do. This understanding is of the broadest kind and easily surrendered; it is bound by routine and cannot be voluntarily reproduced.

This supreme human characteristic, however, is not due to a primary endowment of speech. The brain seems primarily concerned with the co-ordination of movements; it receives stimuli, reacts, and issues orders. The nose, windpipe, lungs, and diaphragm inhale and exhale breath. The teeth tear food which the tongue rolls round and tastes. The lips protect the buccal cavity. Only the glottis (Adam's apple) is concerned with the production of sound, either without impediment (breath) or by friction (aspiration) or by vibration of the vocal chords (voice) or by stoppage and consequent explosion (glottal stop). It is able to regulate the volume of air and even to give it definite musical wave-lengths, but the greater part of talk results from shaping the air current in the mouth by blocking or leaving more or less open the passage through the nose or by constricting or blocking the air stream between tongue and palate or at the lips. The result is a continuous emission of symbolic sounds. But, like the apes, we locate and differentiate sound with difficulty. Our sight is much keener, so that we habitually speak of *knowing* in terms of sight. We can take in much information at a glance, but the same report must be spelled out slowly in a successive or linear fashion by the symbols of language, and these have to be retranslated in some mysterious way so as to correspond with things seen. Doubtless there would be other possible systems of symbols, if we could use them, such as those vibrations which butterflies are able to transmit or the scents which a dog seems to interpret to its own satisfaction. It may be that the grossness of hearing is of particular importance for the preference given to language, since vision gathers information faster than it can be analysed and always retains too many details in the general picture. Thus *house* [haus], spelled slowly to the ear in a succession of four sound-symbols, is mentally translated as 'any house', but the sight of a house would necessarily inform us whether the building is red or grey, of brick or stone, thatched or tiled, &c. These symbols, too, are necessarily separated by broad divisions. No language uses narrow distinctions such as a musician could no doubt make with accuracy, but aims at a common measure of intelligibility, so broad that adjustments affecting as much as the whole system (as between Scottish and southern English) are overlooked in favour of broad conformities. Perhaps because of its very sluggishness, language confers the power of generalization, so that a herd of sorrels, greys, duns, roans, bays, chestnuts, piebalds, and creams, for instance, can and must be generalized as a herd of *horses*. By doing so language weaves a cocoon around our consciousness. What we are aware of are concepts and representations. It is a world into which the speechless animals have no entry, but from which we humans, no doubt, have no exit.

Thus when we *know* anything we hold the right language about it. We do not call a whale a fish in zoology, though as a means of livelihood we are as capable of going whale-fishing as fishing for tarpon or salmon. We learn to call water H_2O in chemistry, though it is not with H_2O we wash our hands. In medieval English history we learn that a manor was a social unit and the wardrobe an organ of government. We are informed by Plato that justice is the state of society in which every man receives his due. A physicist tells us that a table, or any other object we see, is a field of electrical forces. The anthropologist, anthropometrist, and linguist require us to distinguish between a community unified by some pattern of life, by physical characteristics, or by a common means of communication, i.e. between society, race, and language. In all these directions we may, and probably do, progress towards some objective truth. The physical scientists in particular are soon checked for error, though philosophers are not called upon to pay a forfeit for a misconception. Yet there is verbalism in all knowledge and no knowledge without words—the words, so far as we are concerned, of our own particular language. All true thinkers struggle to escape from the bondage of words, but a total evasion is impossible for men.

Language is an art, and the arts are best defined as languages. In each case some material—a column of breath, vibrations mathematically spaced, pigment, wood, stone, metal, &c.—is deliberately shaped as a sign of something not connatural with the material. Music may perhaps constitute an exception, if it is concerned only with the combination of vibrations for their own sake, but music has also been held to give healthy exercise for the emotions. The remaining arts are all marked by the intrinsic unlikeness of the signifier and the signified, as between certain lengths of lines on paper and natural distances, or of stone and human flesh. Each art enjoys its own advantages and conveys its own message in a way otherwise less complete, but the art of language is more universally applicable and can express more of the content of other arts. It is Everyman's Art. The poet, according to Mr. MacNeice, 'is a specialist in something which every one practises',[1] but he is not the only linguistic specialist. The poet's objective is beauty or imaginative truth or something of the kind. But the orator makes an art of persuasion from the material of breath, and the logician and the scientist specialize variously in the art of precise statement.

[1] L. MacNeice, *Modern Poetry*, London, 1938, p. 178.

The punster, the comedian, and the tragedian are preoccupied with the linguistic arts, but so also are the social climbers, the purists, and those who sink to avoid the opprobrium of snobbery.[1] The ordinary man, framing an ordinary sentence, endeavours to arrange it for some special effect, and his methods are not always unhappy. The vivid American metaphors now flooding the English language are of anonymous origin, but commend themselves by their vitality.

It is natural, then, that every man should be interested in the questions of language which flare up now and then into newspaper polemics; and it is the more natural since he renders thereby homage to the power of the spoken word. In the word lies the power to name things. According to magical thinking knowledge of the name gave power over the thing, as when Adam named and became ruler of the animals. In some cases the name had to be concealed, as that of *Yahwe* under the form *Jehovah* and those of Phoenician gods under the style of *Baal*. An enemy who learned the real name of a tribal god took the god and the tribe into his own hands. But the real strength of the name is to bring something into effective existence, even if, like *phlogiston, Aryan race,* or *the square root of minus one,* it is 'a thing which is not'. A college discussion on the evils of *nepotism* evolved the word *nepot,* and within a few minutes the *nepots*—those who presumably benefited by unfair favouritism of the kind—were being freely discussed as if they were a known social class. So *capitalism, democracy, Islam, jihad, pan-Americanism, pan-Turanianism, ninepence for fourpence,* and *Lebensraum* are examples of words of power. There are no 'mere words'. The antithesis of word and deed which Thucydides drearily reiterated is fallacious, because the word is a deed. The act comes from a formalized intention which may be expressed in one word (such as *operation Overlord*) or in many (such as an Act of Nationalization). Words may also be used to draw attention away from the deed veritably intended or to cloud the whole issue by vague or contradictory talk, but it is none the less true that all human deeds of importance have their origin in the faculty of speech.

But though the art of language occupies Everyman in some fashion all the time, the science of language earns in England scant recognition. Everyman shies away from knowledge in this matter

[1] V. Grove, *The Language Bar*, London, 1949.

if it is positive, objective, definite, and consistent. Exact analysis
has no charms for him, and the artists in words, like Plato, prefer
to make a mystery of their arts lest their depths be plumbed. The
services of the linguist, too, are rendered in association with all
secondary types of human activity, and (in times of danger) under
the seal of secrecy. Society, which values diamonds above coal and
ennobles the distiller rather than the milkman, leaves the linguist
unrewarded for his practical services and unknown in his science.

LANGUAGE AND PHILOSOPHY

As a vehicle of thought language has fallen under the severe
scrutiny of philosophers, and many of the terms used by grammarians are of philosophical origin. Both linguists and philosophers
discuss the sentence, predication, subject and object, grammar, logic,
function, form, hypothesis, affirmation, condition, meaning, and
similar topics. The grammarian also uses derivative philosophical
terms such as 'accusative case'. Case implies falling away from the
upright nominative, and the nominative names the subject (the
underlying matter) of the sentence. The verb is completed as action
or motion by the accusative (αἰτιατική), and by the well-known
identification of ends and causes (αἰτίαι) the complement of the
verb is given as the cause of the whole action. Philosophical terms
enter grammar, however, only on condition that they lie down
peaceably together. The grammarian uses them positively and cannot afford to stray into the camp of Agramante of the philosophers,
who tear them up, rearrange, discard, and supersede them. The
good philosopher for the grammarian is the dead one; the best of
all is Aristotle. None the less, the incursions of philosophers into
the linguistic field are episodes of grave importance, and especially
so at the present when their attention, after a period of distraction,
has been called to the 'profound and almost unrecognized' influence
of language. 'With sufficient caution, the properties of language
may help us to understand the structure of the world.'[1]

[1] Bertrand Russell, quoted by M. Black, *Language and Philosophy*, 1949. See
also G. Ryle's 'Systematically misleading expressions' in A. G. N. Flew, *Logic
and Language*, 1951; R. Carnap, *Die logische Syntax der Sprache*, 1934, and
Introduction to Semantics, 1942; C. Morris, *Signs, Language and Behavior*, 1946;
C. K. Ogden and I. A. Richards, *The Meaning of Meaning*, 3rd ed., 1930; A.
Korzybski, *Science and Sanity*, 2nd ed., 1941. W. K. Kneale's inquiry into *Induction and Probability*, 1949, is a good example of 'reflection on the way in which
we use words'.

Philosophers make it their business to define words, to lay down the rules for precise communication, and to discover whether signs point to realities. Psychologists, in addition, hold out the hope of knowing some day what happens in the brain. All this is of great importance to the linguist, who is seeking a new Semantics, a theory of communication to underlie his grammatical structure, and may be dissatisfied with traditional grammar. He sees in philosophy a powerful ally, but he must approach with the caution of friendly armies on the Elbe. At the last major conjunction of the sort a violent controversy arose between Wundt and Delbrück with regard to which the only certainty seems to be that the blows of the Titans did not fall on each other. They were talking of different things; the 'language' of the philosopher may not be that of the linguist, even if the former acknowledges that his business is largely 'to thrash out "what it means to say so and so" ', and even if he goes farther and binds himself to accept what we 'commonly' mean.

'Philosophy (according to a distinguished Spanish exponent) is the enemy of knowledge, that is, of the ascertained fact.' The linguist cannot deny any fact of language (such as the French subjunctive or the third person singular) and remain in office. The philosopher is bound to question realities which the linguist is bound to accept. The philosopher defines meanings and rejects those which he deems unsuitable. If he lights on a sense for which there is no word, his business is to invent the word. A considerable part of our civilized vocabulary consists of inventions by philosophers and scientists, many of them made serviceable by loss of their exact application (e.g. *energy*, *idea*). It appears, however, that the rejection of 'systematically misleading statements' in philosophy does not prevent their being directly intelligible (and even necessary) in language, as when we say 'Mr Pickwick is a fiction' intelligibly, though the expression is 'misleading in virtue of a formal property which it does or might share with other expressions' (*Logic and Language*, p. 19). The strenuous attempt of the late Viggo Brøndal to base universal grammar on Aristotelian logic (*Ordklasserne*, 1928) has coincided with the relegation of Aristotelian logic to the exclusive domain of language, and even with a furious attack on Aristotle as an impediment to the espousals of Science with Sanity.[1]

---

[1] It appears, however, that Count Korzybski's Aristotle was not the man who wrote in Greek (cf. M. Black, *Language and Philosophy*, p. 230).

R. Carnap teaches, unless I go astray in a world of horse-shoes and other cabbalistic signs, that to become logical each sentence must be rewritten. 'A thing is a complex of sensory experiences' must become 'Each phrase in which a symbol for a thing appears resembles in content a class of phrases in which no symbols for things appear, but only symbols for experiences', and 'Numbers are classes of classes of things' becomes 'Expressions of number are class-expressions of the second stage'. If this rephrasing be necessary the linguist may be tempted to say good-bye to logic, since the primary condition of his task is respect for the language-material in front of him. Yet it is probably not enough to say, with Vossler, that language is intrinsically 'alogical'. The term is too negative. Language has been savagely indifferent to much that scientists and philosophers have revealed; it has barbarously invented a superfluity of categories on the basis of superficial and magical resemblances; but for the last 2,300 years in Western Europe its grammars have shaped expression as much as possible according to the dominant system of logic. And some advance must be made in discussing the relation between signs and realities or meanings if linguistic science is to take the step forward which now seems imminent.

On the other hand, the linguist can hardly fail to observe how much philosophy is not only shaped by language, but by particular languages. For E. Sapir's conviction that Kant might have written as well or better in Eskimo there is little enough evidence.[1] The German of Kant's day was still fluid and malleable, though it had been exercised (as Eskimo has not) in Latin and French schools of thought, and even in those of Greece and England. German philosophy owes a great deal to the linguistic resource of composition, which, by naming instead of describing, brings into existence a thing. *Völkerpsychologie* is, in this respect, more potent than *la psychologie des peuples*, since one can proceed (as Wundt does) by a simple formal analogy from *Individualpsychologie* to *Völkerpsychologie*. The French idiom requires a much more analytic treatment. The discussion of the Blessed State in Aquinas's *Contra gentiles* is determined by the word *beatitudo*, derived from *beatus* which has some quite earthy connotations in Latin. Cartesianism depends on the facility of the phrase *la raison ou le bon sens*, though Latin *ratio* and *sensus* (the latter neither good nor bad, but a true

[1] E. Sapir, *Selected Writings*, Berkeley (Cal.), 1949, p. 154.

sensual report) cannot be thus identified. Locke's *ideas* correspond to a fortunate breakdown of the Platonic *idea*. If we compare

'What do we mean when we say right, probable, mind?' and

'Qu'est-ce qu'on veut dire par droit, vraisemblable, esprit?' there is, apart from the doubt about the exact correspondence of terms, a difference in the way the question is posed. Each question assumes that the terms are sufficient for discussion. The first formula asks: 'What do we (English, whose words correspond so well with things) mean . . .?' and the second 'What does *on* (*homo sapiens*, whose language is, of course, French) mean . . .?' The Chinese would eliminate person, though still supposing the adequacy of their own term, and ask baldly 'Right is what thing?', and would perhaps prove systematically misleading. Chinese philosophy consists of apophthegms, not only because the language is laconic, and laconism has been reckoned a prime virtue of style, but probably also because the relevant works were written on bamboo tablets which did not afford much flat surface for writing. If, for Aristotle, virtue lies in the mean, it was because, on the whole, the language offered him systematically equal and opposite vices for each virtue. Where a blank occurred, he wrote in *megaloprepy*, as the language permitted, though few have been able to understand megaloprepy as a virtue.[1] His logic and his grammar cover each other because the Greek language had been ceaselessly exercised in rational statements since Homer's day, and the tendency had been speeded up by the Sophists and Socrates. The weakness of the classical scheme of grammar is its assumption that *all* language is reasonable, confusing a strong tendency towards pattern with the achievement of a perfect system *où tout se tient*.

The philosopher deals with Language, but is not bound to

---

[1] A curious case of invention occurred in Professor C. D. Broad's Marett Memorial Lecture of 1949. The problem was whether there could be any motives completely unrelated to self. He distinguished self-centred motives from those which were self-regarding (e.g. the love of a mother for *her* child, or the death of a martyr for *his* religion), and proposed to call the hypothetical class of motives without regard to any self 'other-regarding'. But in English *self-* is a common prefix, *other-* is rare, and *other-regarding* is not a term which explains itself. In Greek *auto-* and *allo-* are of the same frequency, and such creations as **autobleptic* and **allobleptic* would imply each other. In Greek the lecturer's distinction would have been assured of an immortality which is much less likely in English, not for its intrinsic worth, but merely because the languages are what they are.

inquire into languages. The linguist studies languages to see whether anything may be affirmed about Language. His business is with linguistic routines; the philosopher's is with 'serious thinking'. The philosopher may call for an ideal language (with Bertrand Russell) or consider such undesirable (with Max Black), or hold that precisely defining certain terms by means of the indefinites of customary speech sets up tensions which break down (J. Holloway). In all this the linguist is interested but incompetent, as he is also incompetent to determine whether universals give classes to particulars or particulars are generalized as universals. The presence of such powerful and loquacious neighbours keeps the linguist uneasy, but not entirely unhopeful. At best he may be allowed to take over some useful category or principle of arrangement of categories; at worst he is sure to fall under a shower of new terms and routines as raw materials for his studies.

THE DIALOGUE

The universe of speech is egocentric. At the centre is the speaker (*ego*) and the listener is slightly off-centre (*tu*). The listener becomes a speaker in his turn and the axis of the universe shifts slightly, but these are the two persons of speech, and all others are objects to be pointed out. *Ego* spreads symbols in front of *tu*, but *tu* is the arbiter of intelligibility. If *ego* makes unintelligible noises or speaks Greek to the Eskimo *tu*, there is no communication and therefore no language. If *ego*'s symbols are unsatisfactory or unsatisfactorily arranged, *tu* demands a new set or a better arrangement. Since speech is a function of action, *tu*'s acts determine the sense of *ego*'s symbols to the extent that *ego* must either acquiesce or come to a new understanding.

Soliloquy, meditation, and 'arranging one's thoughts' are imitations of dialogue. They have involved in past time even movements of lips; hence the theatrical convention that the soliloquy and the read letter can be overheard. But *ego* does not speak to *ego*; he has far quicker ways of understanding himself. He soliloquizes before an imaginary *tu* and he arranges his thoughts with a view to addressing later some real *tu*.

The dialogue occurs within a frame of reference provided by circumstances and concerns some event. Sir A. H. Gardiner[1] describes speech as four-sided, with the four factors of speaker,

[1] A. H. Gardiner, *Speech and Language*, Oxford, 1932, p. 62.

listener, words, and things. The things, however, should be those of a given moment, forming an external and concrete association which we call circumstance. It is better to think of them as external and concrete, because so they are in all languages, including savage ones. Two persons may discuss the square root of minus one in an oubliette at midnight and so reach an extreme of abstract speech, but the topic is no more than the last of a long series of abstractions which began with the sum of two flints or cave-bears or the

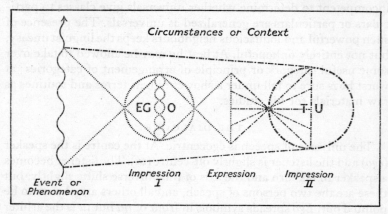

like. A square was once a pattern on the ground. If one says to another 'the unexamined life is not worth living' there has to be a context of ethical discussion to determine what is 'life', 'worth' or 'examination'. An insurance agent might be puzzled by the phrase and emend it to 'the medically unexamined life is not worth insuring'. Even so, though more concrete, his language represents the end of a complex process of civilized abstraction. That speech should be possible without visible circumstances is a relatively late development, and is achieved by the creation of contexts. The context of a discourse consists of spoken conventions which enable us to dispense with visible objects, by siting the discourse well enough to give the supplementary information that would otherwise have been derived from circumstance.

The language even of savages contains some abstraction, since they speak of some parts of circumstance and neglect others. Yet the Australian Arunta cannot count or distinguish times or identify themselves. Basque *bost* 'five' probably means 'closed fist', and counting in multiples of twenty (Basque *ogei*) was achieved by counting fingers and toes. Getting lost in the higher figures, it might prove simpler to proceed by subtraction (Lat. 19 *undeviginti*, 18 *duodeviginti*, Finnish 9 *yhdeksän*, 8 *kahdeksän*, cf. 1 *yksi*, 2 *kaksi*, and the Indo-European for 10). Chinese characters are singularly illuminating concerning the relations between concrete and abstract. 'Benevolence' is 'man plus two' (a man who thinks of another beside himself), 'happiness' is 'one mouth supported by a field', 'peace' is 'a woman under a roof' (indoors), 'home' is 'a pig under a roof' (food and shelter), 'spirit' is the skeleton of a great man, a 'great' man is one who has not only legs to obey but arms to enforce, 'father' is a 'hand holding a whip'. These written analyses are, no doubt, scholarly and sometimes whimsical. It is not exactly in that way that abstractions have been derived from objects and contexts substituted for circumstance, but the language of savages is astoundingly concrete and only fully intelligible when spoken in the presence of the objects of discourse.

Communication lies partly in what we say, partly in the circumstances. The latter fill in so much that actual speaking is elliptical, erratic, incomplete, and imprecise. Even the elliptical words may be further curtailed by substituting gestures,[1] which refer one back vaguely to the circumstances. Thus one may overhear:

A. Hullo! How's tricks?
B. So so; and the boy?
A. Bursting with energy, thanks.

The first is not a question but a breach of silence,[2] and establishes the conversation on the basis of casual familiarity. It does not seek or receive an answer, but an opening is made for *A*'s principal interest (which is known from the circumstances), and *A*, when replying with information, acknowledges the kindly intention of *B*. It is possible to say quite intelligibly 'Old what's-his-name is just bringing in the thingummy', if, at a Burns dinner, Mr. McLeod is seen piping in the haggis. It is even better to be imprecise, and to say 'my heart went pit-a-pat', 'the tray came bang, thump, crash down the stairs', or 'whiff, it's gone', because, while the circumstances

---

[1] Gesture-languages seem, however, to be translations of the spoken word or of set phrases as a whole. The Arunta are said to have a gesture-language of 250 signs. This seems to be different from the gestures which refer directly to circumstance.

[2] 'To a natural man, another man's silence is not a reassuring factor, but, on the contrary, something alarming and dangerous.' B. Malinowski, *Magic, Science and Religion*, Boston, 1948, p. 248.

would explain either these sentences or explicit statements, these expressions give an impression of the immediate event, not generalized as one which might occur elsewhere. This is the basis of the astonishing development of ideophones in Zulu and other Bantu languages which will be discussed later. When we 'speak like a book' we provide explicit contexts as if circumstances did not exist visibly to complete our meaning, and this procedure, necessary in writing, is recognized as a defect in conversation.

Grammatical and verbal completeness is thus not required of the sentence, and there is nothing to be, as older grammarians said, 'understood'. It was difficult under the old régime to say precisely what word or words were to be 'understood' since the phrase could be completed in various ways, but older grammarians, obsessed by literary contexts, did not sufficiently allow for the completion by environment. R. Lenz[1] gives the following conversation:

A. Where are you off to, Peter?
B. Valparaiso.
A. At once?
B. No. Tomorrow, by the slow train.
A. What for?
B. A matter of business.
A. Something important?
B. Yes; the sale of my land.
A. Have you a buyer in sight?
B. It seems so.
A. Well, congratulations.
B. Thanks.

This is what the linguist must accept. He is not at liberty to rewrite the sentences so that each should have subject, verb, object, and other principal parts. They are already complete and fully intelligible in the circumstances. They are even intelligible as parts of a context. Circumstance and context eliminate uncertainties which theoretically exist. Thus of eighty-four words in the fourth tone of *i* in Chinese,[2] only 'thought, will, intention' can exist in the vicinity of 'understand'. The same sound may mean 'a mountain in Shantung', 'dress', 'I' (in speaking to rulers); 'licentious', and 'hiccup',

[1] R. Lenz, *La Oración y sus partes*, 1925, p. 32.
[2] Chinese words are quoted according to the transliteration adopted in D. MacGillivray's *Mandarin-Romanized Dictionary of Chinese*, Shanghai, 1925. It is according to Wade's system, which has no special advantage beyond that of a wide diffusion. See also the pocket dictionaries by Goodrich and Soothill.

but none of these are things one 'understands'. Actually, by combining synonyms (i^4-$sz\breve{u}^1$ 'thought, will, intention') modern Chinese gives the hearer more time to identify the meaning, but these compounds are readily dissolved when no ambiguity is possible. The written language provides ninety-two different signs for i^4 so that the precise meaning identifies itself, without dependence on visible circumstances or even on context. By way of compensation, the old literary style was sparing of doublets or other helps to understanding.

Within the frame of circumstance each sentence refers to an event or phenomenon as it appears to, and interests, us at the moment of speaking. We distinguish activities and states, but the distinction is partly an illusion. 'Rome is the Eternal City' now and as things appear to us, though founded traditionally in 753 B.C., and still not so long-lived as Babylon. Damascus and Jerusalem are older and still exist, but do not *appear* to us to have the enduring quality conferred by the succession of the Papacy to the Caesars. I *am* content now, but the phrase does not prevent my being discontented in half an hour; you *are* a Grand Duke or a soldier, but a revolution may cancel all titles or you may be demobilized tomorrow. The event is not known to us in all its cosmic significance; we can only speak of what *appears* to us (represented by the waviness of the line in the diagram). Of what appears, we put into words only what momentarily interests us, as in the celebrated observation: 'What a lovely day! Let's go and kill something.' We make a mock of the objective statement 'Queen Anne's dead' because we are not accustomed to make affirmations without immediate interest; though historians have devised for such statements a measure of interest by the postulate that all historical *dicta* are, in some way, worth while. Each event is, of course, unique. 'Bear kills man' and 'Man kills bear' are totally dissimilar events. It is thus not surprising that many languages should have word-sentences which express each event by a unique construction, and all show a phenomenal residue (the verb) after analysis has gone so far as to provide names for the parties, their qualities, and their modes of action and being. The verb continues to show formidable complexities in such a language as French, though the noun has become almost an invariable unit. The Latin verb offered a complex paradigm which was simplified by analysis in primitive Romance, but the Romance languages have used these analytical simplifications to build new synthetic paradigms. It is clear that the result is not due to analytical failure, but to an appreciation of the need to discriminate between phenomena.

For the sake of simplicity we are considering the first communication of a series. *Ego*'s primary impression of the event may be derived from any of the senses, though it is most likely to be visual. It will be more agglomerative than any expression, and probably either total or of selected parts modified by all their minor characteristics. Infants, like Humpty-Dumpty, endeavour to speak in a total way, packing their whole meaning into some such phrase as *din-din*. One can take *din-din* as equal to 'I am thirsty' or 'Why don't you give me a drink?' or (in the case I have in mind) 'I want more fizzy lemonade'. The situation is unanalysed and the whole of it is expressed, so far as the infant can, in two syllables and their accompanying intonations. On the other hand, the agglomerative type of structure is common in primitive tongues. The primary impression is thus intrinsically unlike *tu*'s secondary impression, which depends on the co-ordination of a linear series of symbols. The older linguists spoke of 'inner speech-form' and 'outer speech-form' as if these had a one-to-one correspondence, and it is still deemed legitimate to speak of the mental image of a speech-sound and its actual enunciation. Whether the mind works in that way a linguist is hardly qualified to know, since his task begins with the audible sentence.[1] The disconformity between global impressions and a linear series of symbols seems to be what convinces so many that their thoughts are too rich for words. There is an act of translation involved. Impressions are collected at some point of the brain, co-ordinated, transformed into orders to the speech organs, transmitted as a series of vibrations, collected by the ear-drum, and retranslated into meaning. The various mental movements have been identified to some extent by physiologists.

Ego displays his impression to *tu* in the form of a linear symbolic expression. Any symbol that *tu* accepts is valid for communication with *tu*, and any that he rejects is invalid. *Ego* may offer any one of *man, gizon, homo, anthrōpos, czlowiek, mard, ember, mies, jên, hito, insân, adam, orang, muntu, oquichtli, runa* or *tree, zugatz, arbor, Baum, dendron, derevo, car* and so on. The relation between sound and thing is entirely artificial, and according to the language so is

[1] See, however, A. H. Gardiner, *Speech and Language*, 1932, ch. ii, 'An Act of Speech'.

the convention. Even onomatopoeia is conventional. The imitations serve, not because they are good, but because they are conventional.[1] To a Frenchman one offers subject–verb–object, and to a Turk subject–object–verb; to a Chinese attribute-substantive is the same as substantive-attribute to a Siamese or Malay. Increased stress has the effect in one language that play on tones has in another. The symbols are just symbols, valid in any agreed convention, but without conventional agreement, unintelligible.

Expression is a linear succession of sounds, and the sentence is a complete expression. It is understood, as we have seen, within the frame of circumstance or context, and we cannot presume that it has any necessary grammatical form. A sentence need not have a verb 'expressed or understood', though it must have the quality of phenomenality. It need not be a judgement. Most sentences consist of parts, and this is true even of polysynthetic word-sentences. The parts are not necessarily words, for in primitive languages we find embryonic stems which are not precisely determined for form or meaning, and in synthetic and agglutinative languages we find affixes which are significant parts of a sentence.

Tu hears the expression and is the arbiter of its intelligibility. He collects and retranslates the individual syllables as soon as they begin to be heard, and combines them for meaning. If he cannot achieve a meaning he asks for further symbols, whether in the same language or in another. He reacts either by himself becoming a speaker or by performing some action. But in either reaction it becomes plain that *tu*'s impression is not identical with *ego*'s. Their minds are somehow differently constituted (symbolized in the diagram by the size of the circles). Despite all conventional agreement, there is no perfect understanding between *ego* and *tu*. What *tu* understands, more or less in agreement with *ego*, are (1) the reference of symbols to things, which is the 'logical' or grammatical sense of the sentence, (2) an emotional supercharge represented by agreed stylistic symbols (which may be zero), and (3), since *tu* is also an artist in words, something of the event itself. He understands this in his own fashion. He may, for instance, be specially susceptible to the word *torpedoed* as having gone through the experience or as being endowed with a vivid imagination. In this third aspect of meaning, however, though it is not expressed in symbols,

---

[1] e.g. the sound of a shot is in English *bang* or *crack*, in Spanish *pum* or *paf* (the latter perhaps more appropriate to the slither of the bullet as it lands).

there is something on which the artist in words can reckon; a play of mind on mind, through language but above convention, which is presumably the secret of great poetry and oratory. There is here an aspect of language which is beyond exact measurement but can be intuitively felt. The speaker not merely conveys a logical meaning and an emotion to the hearer, but stirs the hearer to a secondary act of creation. The reactions to great literature are diverse and some of them stimulate further reactions, so that works as fundamental as the Authorized Bible, *Hamlet*, and the *Aeneid* become encrusted with added meanings, and are hard to reduce to their original intention. Nor is the original intention, say of the *Aeneid*, necessarily the highest value of a poem on which the imagination of a Dante has operated so profoundly.

ON BEGINNING TO SPEAK

The origins of language are outside the linguist's ken, and one famous circle has banned the topic.[1] The event occurred in those charming ages when 50,000 years more or less made no difference. The extreme limit of a linguist's inferences is about 5000 B.C. At the limit of knowledge he encounters the highly civilized languages of Egypt, Sumeria, Babylonia, the Hittites and Greeks, the Aryans and the Chinese, and he knows them not merely because of their advanced organization, but because they have been committed to writing. By comparing the languages of Greeks, Hittites, Aryans, and others, he may reach a supposed common Indo-European tongue, but most of his information will be about its latest developments, say, about 3000 B.C. Comparing Semitic with Hamitic might go back two more millennia, but it is difficult to do so for lack of a third term of reference between ancient Egyptian and common Semitic. But though the linguist cannot *know* such things, he need not be devoid of interest or fail to notice that there are some approximate indications.

In the first place, there was a definite beginning of speech just

---

[1] An exceptional position is that of A. Trombetti, *L'Unità d'Origine del Linguaggio*, 1905, who provides a vocabulary of thirty-six primeval words, a primeval grammar and phonology. Father W. Schmidt goes part of the way in his *Sprachfamilien und Sprachenkreise der Erde*, 1926. A. Jóhannesson, *Origin of Language*, 1949, considers mainly Indo-European and Semitic evidence. L. Stein, *The Infancy of Speech and the Speech of Infancy*, 1949, writes as a speechtherapist and anthropologist. Cf. also R. A. Wilson, *The Miraculous Birth of Language*, 1941.

as there was a beginning of lively noises when the batrachians first appeared. The varieties of noise increased with the coming of birds and great animals until the world was 'full of noises, sounds and sweet airs'. In the woods the anthropoid apes were barking, howling, screaming, and chattering, conveying messages of a kind, though not according to a code or effective apart from visible circumstances. The nocturnal uproar in the Amazonian *Urwald* has been described by competent observers.

But all this noise, though consisting partly of significant messages, was not speech. The cause seems to lie in the facial angle and the consequent absence of frontal development of the brain. The gorilla, with a brain of 450 cc., is speechless, though vocal. Sinanthropus, however, had a brain capacity of about 1,000 cc., with room for the development of cerebral areas of speech-control, and he presumably did speak. Whether he or Neanderthal Man spoke very well or found language a useful tool is open to question. Sinanthropus still lacked 300–450 cc. of the brain of Homo Sapiens and he may have mumbled like an imbecile. Or, living much alone on the unpopulated earth and chiefly employed in hunting or fishing, he may have found gestures more serviceable than noises. Noises, in the immediate presence of an object, can be used indifferently and without definite shape. A cry of fear is enough to indicate a gorilla crashing through the undergrowth and to cover any consequent action. It can be translated many ways. Language, however, requires that a specific interpretation should follow from an agreed symbolism of noises, and these can hardly have been fixed save on a hit-and-miss basis. In a scanty population there may have been many small agreements as there are in the private languages of families and children. The isolated Amazonian tribes are divided by both jungle and language. Conventions may have been forgotten and remade. The clash of one set of conventions upon another would lead to further accommodations, as the language of a foreigner living outside his country becomes accommodated to that of his place of residence and untrue to that of his birth. By far the greatest effort in language history must have been the gradual stabilization of sound-symbols, whether in one speech pattern (*monogenesis*) or in many (*polygenesis*).[1]

---

[1] We have suggested above that the arbiter of intelligibility is the hearer (*tu*) and that the symbols are wholly conventional. There are theories of the birth of language which depend on the will of the speaker (*ego*) and the suitability of the

Agriculture, craftsmanship, and ritual would enforce the use of more precise symbolization, and it is possible that 'full-fledged language' may date from the Azilian culture of, say, 15,000–8,000 B.C. In place of the drawings of mammoths and other animals, with spears planted exactly as it was hoped they would be, the Azilians used diagrams, some of them curiously like letters of an alphabet. This seems to represent a loss in art but a gain in symbolism. 'This "ideoplastic" approach in advanced races, as opposed to the "physioplastic" fashion of Magdalenian fame, goes hand in hand with the growth of the faculty of abstracting and forming general concepts out of percepts.'[1]

It is clear that primitive languages of today are separated by aeons of time from primeval or primordial language. Indeed, they are separated further than the civilized languages of antiquity, since they are only known in present-day forms or by shallow inferences about their older states. Similarly, Stone Age cultures of today are more recently known than Bronze or Iron Age cultures of antiquity, and are not to be identified entirely with the Stone Ages of archaeo-

---

symbols to express things. A list is given by L. H. Gray, *Foundations of Language*, New York, 1939, p. 40:

Bow-wow theory: imitation of objects by sounds.
Ding-dong theory: harmony of objects and sounds.
Pooh-pooh theory: ejaculations of pleasure, pain, surprise, &c.
Yo-he-ho theory: physical exertion producing vocal reflexes.
Sing-song theory: rhythmic chants and singing.
Ta-ta theory: sounds uttered in half-conscious imitation of bodily movements in some activity. Tongue gestures.

There is something of each of these in language, though exercised under the convention of the language and not intelligible until the convention is explained. Thus both Lat. *cachinnare* and Russ. *chochotát* are excellent imitations in sound of that which we imitate to our satisfaction by the word *guffaw*. Satisfaction with language leads to a great deal of secondary sound-symbolism, since some primary association (e.g. of *s* with *sweet*, *soft*, *song*) of a fortuitous kind becomes a model for other uses of the same sound (as Spenser's 'Sleep after toyle, port after stormie seas'—in which the general suggestion is of quietness though the last sibilants are attached to stormy words).

Plato held that 'a word is a tool for teaching us about reality', and Indian grammarians held that there is a 'natural connexion of a word with its sense'. Democritus and Aristotle held that words are mere symbols: 'No name exists by nature, but only by becoming a symbol.' (W. S. Allen, 'Ancient ideas on the origin and development of language', *Transactions of the Philological Society*, London, 1948.)

Many of these theories aim at explaining the origin of *words*. It is not certain that words as self-sufficient units belong to the oldest stratum of language.

[1] L. Stein, *The Infancy of Speech and the Speech of Infancy*, London, 1948, p. 179.

logy. Yet if one wishes to understand prehistoric fire-making or fish-spearing, the best plan is to watch Stone Age Bushmen or Aruntas engaged in these occupations, and if one wants to get closer to primeval or primordial language, it is advisable to study savage and barbarous language-processes. Of these there will be more said later on, but for the present stress should be laid on the extreme difficulty primitive men have experienced in getting away from obvious, concrete reality. Abstraction is impossible, though there are general names for concrete classes of objects. The system of sounds used by such a people as the Aruntas is feebly organized, and interchange of vowel with vowel and consonant with consonant makes no difference to meaning. Words as such do not exist, but there are embryonic words in the form of loosely constructed stems which agglomerate with other stems of like nature so as to express in one utterance all or a considerable part of a concrete phenomenon in all its momentary relations. These agglomerations are associated, but it is not clear that there are definite sentences, i.e. finite and complete expressions of the speaker's impression. A good deal of satisfaction is obtained from vaguely expressive sounds. There is no calculation, and sometimes no counting. The savage goes through a daily routine without resource or forethought, and has no capacity for looking beyond the immediate concrete present. He is indifferent to knowledge or invention or distinctions which do not, like those of exogamic relations, serve his purposes. Though some of his concepts are worked out (like those of the totem and relatives on two sides), most are characterized by a savage indifference.[1]

In these conditions language is a mode of action. Savage speech is brilliantly depicted in action by Malinowski[2] in an account of fishing by Trobriand islanders:

The canoes glide slowly and noiselessly, punted by men especially

---

[1] See A. Sommerfelt, *La Langue et la société*, Oslo, 1938. E. Sapir, *Selected Writings*, Berkeley, 1949, held (p. 10) that 'Language is felt to be a perfect symbolic system, in a perfectly homogeneous medium, for the handling of all references and meanings that a given culture is capable of'. Though we may *feel* that our language is perfect, at best it is fairly adequate. Its adequacy is measured, as Sapir stated, by the capacity of the culture it expresses. I find it hard to accept the allegation that 'There is no general correlation between cultural type and linguistic structure' (p. 26), though, of course, in the immense history of linguistic evolution almost any given feature may occur anywhere. But primitive languages have been habitually described from without and little attempt made to determine what the speaker himself intends.

[2] B. Malinowski, *Magic, Science and Religion*, Boston, 1948, pp. 244–5.

good at this task and always used for it. Other experts who know the bottom of the Lagoon, with its plant and animal life, are on the look-out for fish. One of them sights the quarry. Customary signs or sounds or words are uttered. Sometimes a sentence full of technical references to the channels or patches on the Lagoon has to be spoken; sometimes when the shoal is near and the task of trapping is simple, a conventional cry is uttered not too loudly. Then the whole fleet stops and ranges itself —every canoe and every man in it performing his appointed task— according to a customary routine. But, of course, the men, as they act, utter now and then a sound expressing keenness in the pursuit or impatience at some technical difficulty, joy of achievement or disappoint-ment at failure. Again, a word of command is passed here and there, a technical expression or exclamation which serves to harmonize their behaviour towards other men. The whole group act in a concerted manner, determined by old tribal tradition and perfectly familiar to the actors through life-long experience.

'Each utterance [he wrote] is essentially bound up with the con-text of the situation.' The ritual formulas used by Sommerfelt for his account of the Arunta language are also modes of action. They are not devised to communicate information about wild cats, gum trees or the like, but to work magically on or through them. For this purpose they are equipped with rhythm:

>
> *nunat albubalbuma*
> *nunat intingerama*

'Nous tous retournons, nous tous, nous nous heurtons l'un l'autre.'

The informative value of language grows with civilization, and passes from the concrete to the abstract. In the perfection of evolution it becomes possible to use the definition which French writers instinc-tively employ: 'Le langage est l'expression de la pensée.'[1]

When a community is awakened from its indifference to gram-mar, it seems to pass to a barbarous excess of discrimination. Perhaps the first stage is the word-sentence as a definitely contrived instrument of communication. The sentence is afterwards broken into major parts, which are more or less the same as parts of speech, and minor modifications are identified by analysis and either separated or associated in predetermined ways.[2] The parts of the sentence become parts of speech, that is, forms and functions tend to correspond. But, as a glance at Chinese will show, much more

---

[1] A. Dauzat, *La Philosophie du langage*, Paris, 1948, p. 9.
[2] I. I. Meščaninov, *Členy predloženija i časti reči*, Moscow, 1945; *Glagol*, Moscow, 1949.

discrimination is used than is grammatically necessary or even helpful. Grammar pululates genders, numbers, moods, tenses, and cases. Some of these are convenient, others merely baffling once the original reason for making the distinction has been forgotten. In addition to carrying forward such failures of identification as *man/wife*, *bull/cow*, &c., barbarous languages invent all sorts of categories for incompatible reasons. Thus, to take an extreme case, Bantu divides all nouns into some eight or nine categories with appropriate plurals (which are not formally related to the singulars) and then brings the whole sentence under the régime of the subject by using the class-prefixes of the subject on all significant words. This discipline satisfies some demand of the Bantu *psyche*, but the classes cannot be logically separated and the whole process (*teste* Chinese) is grammatically superfluous. It results, however, in a complex formal grammar which, like that of Sanskrit or ancient Greek, earns the admiration of linguists.

Some of this sumptuousness is lost by increasing civilization. The speed of living, thinking, and speaking is increased, and the grammatical forms suffer attrition. Their magical causes are forgotten and one only remembers, for instance, that every word in French must be either masculine or feminine as an inherited routine. The analysis of case as spatial position breaks down as more and more precise locations are found, and also by reason of the insufficiency of the spatial analysis itself. Cases come to be used with prepositions, and as precise grammatical definition is gained by the auxiliary word, the case-ending becomes superfluous. It may be usefully dropped as in English and the Romance languages. In Russian the 'prepositional case' is one only found with prepositions (though not the only case found with them!) and its proper value as a locative is wholly forgotten. It is preserved by its own robust form and by the slow evolution of the Russian language.

The linguistic habits of savage and barbarous peoples are not intimately known to us and have been described chiefly by ultra-civilized men whose mental habits are quite different, but each of us repeats the linguistic history of the race in childhood. The world we enter is not the tentative hit-and-miss world of primordial man and the whole process is immeasurably accelerated. At first the infant[1]

---

[1] A. Gesell, *How a Baby grows*, London, 1946, pp. 42–43; J. Tarneaud, *Traité pratique de phonologie et de phoniatrie*, Paris, 1941, pp. 99–103; L. Stein, *The Infancy of Speech and the Speech of Infancy*, London, 1949.

'has no language but a cry'. Then follows crowing, laughing, and smiling, and a considerable language of gestures possessed at the age of 52 weeks. After 12 weeks a baby turns his head to listen to the human voice. (Apes remain indifferent.) At about 16 weeks baby is so impressed with the possibilities of vocal noise that he practises his tongue, lips, and vocal chords in an endless prattle, without any purpose of communication. He produces far more sounds in this babbling play than he will ever need for a language. At 36 weeks he gives ear to utterances as wholes, paying special attention, it would seem, to intonation. The first definite syllables come at about 32 weeks, and are of the nature of *ta* and *da*, that is the most open vowel separated by stops. There are thus primitive syllables in human discourse which tend to be associated with things of primary interest. They begin with *m p/b* or *n t/d*, and linguistic practice on the whole would suggest that the latter is a slightly earlier attainment. Thus we hear *mama* and *dada, me* and *tu, to/ta* 'that', Chinese *ni* 'thou' *na* 'that', &c. Chinese *ma¹-ma¹* has the same sound and meaning in English and Quechua, and is not unlike Arabic *umm*; but Georgian *mama* means 'father' and *deda* 'mother'. Father is based on *t/d* or *p/b*, as Greek *atta*, Latin *pater*, Chinese *fu⁴* (*b'iu*), Arabic *abû*, Swahili *baba*, Quechua *tayta*; but Russ. *baba* means 'old woman'. It is the coincidence of first sounds with first things that has given rise to the notion that there is a 'natural connexion of a word with its sense'.

Prattle becomes meaningful when a second person (*tu*) attaches a meaning by showing a reaction which baby can then reproduce at will. As the nearest person is probably the mother, she appropriates to herself the first sounds as *mamma* or *me*, and assigns the next to the next person, *daddy* or *thou*, and after that to the background objects (*this* and *that*). An important feature is *tu*'s anxiety to understand something. This anxiety may be seen even in a dog, which develops routines based on sounds that it does not understand as speech. The results are not always what one might expect. There is said to be a mountain in Chile called *Quisapué*. Someone asked for the name of the mountain, and a peasant replied *Quién sabe pues?* 'Who knows?' (in Chilean vernacular *qui sa pué?*). Many nations are known by wrong names, as the Germans by the name of a Celtic tribe, and the Aymaraes (properly Collas) by the name of a Quechua tribe. The case of a missionary is cited[1] who wished

[1] C. K. Ogden and I. A. Richards, *The Meaning of Meaning*, 1923, p. 174.

to learn the word for table. He rapped the table and got words for tapping, hard, wood, and table. The baby gets what it wants by establishing a convention of signals, and within the family its imperfect utterances continue as a secret language long after the baby itself has grown up and become indifferent. The parents are anxious to attach meaning to any distinctly articulated syllables and they show profitable reactions. Baby notices that sounds, at first casually uttered, produce invariably certain reactions; he begins to use them on purpose.

Once a communication has been made the hardest problem of speaking has been solved. The further progress of the child has, however, some bearing on the natural order of evolution of language. After the first three months spent upon the gymnastics of articulation, the child concentrates and retains only those which it hears used by adults or other children. A period of babbling and intoning is completed in the fifteenth month, and meanwhile (between the seventh and twelfth) the child possesses no more than a few words which cannot be reproduced at will. The twelfth to fifteenth months are devoted to silent assimilation, and between the fifteenth and eighteenth the child utters comprehensive phrases eked out by gestures. Thus Mme Borel-Maisonny instances *awa* as valid for *au revoir, le monsieur s'en va, papa est parti*, &c., and (if *cṛ* means *chose sucrée*) *cṛ Fafa* means *Françoise veut son sirop*. These are word-sentences which have a magical effect on the universe, since to utter one of them suffices to produce any one of a number of services. A German child, watching brother Rudolf throw down a toy horse (*Rudolf hat das Pferd umgeworfen*), first said *olol* (Rudolf—since anything that Rudolf might do was of first importance), and then many months later *olol hoto wapa*, analysing the situation into subject–object–verb, but without much grammatical finesse.[1] The situation and the words were strictly concrete, as in the language of savages, where compendiousness is also common.

Between the eighteenth and twenty-fourth months the process is speeded up immensely because the child asks questions. At first the child regards itself objectively and not as a person. The pronoun *I* takes a long time to appear. An Arunta, when shown his photograph, recognized in it himself, his brother, and his totemic animal. His life was entirely that of his clan and he had no notion of 'self'. Numbers come much later than pronouns, but they share the

[1] E. Winkler, *Grundlegung der Stilistik*, Bielefeld, Leipzig, 1929, p. 13.

peculiarity of being eminently durable. Though not the oldest parts of speech they are usually the oldest surviving forms, because they are not affected by the affective considerations which keep shifting nouns and verbs.

An intense period of linguistic activity covers the third to sixth years, after which the process is virtually complete. The language is still grammatically unconstrued. Children act variously in learning. Some pour out expressions with much gesture and action, and gradually drop those which are unacceptable; others study quietly and only bring out phrases when they are sure to pass as current coin of speech. Grammatical analysis goes on for another seven years or so, but a whole lifetime is required for the refinements of the written tongue.

ARTIFICIAL LANGUAGES

The above analysis reduces the distance between 'natural' and 'artificial' languages. Each has to be learned and each rests on a sort of social contract. The contract is of a hit-and-miss variety for a 'natural' language and needs emendation. The nature of an 'artificial, universal, auxiliary, or secondary' language requires that there should be no change. Thus arise the Esperanto pontificate of Dr. Zamenhof and the Basic pontificate of Dr. Ogden. An auxiliary language in actual circulation would not be able to resist the drift of speech, and would proceed to divide in form and usage like other tongues. The artificial ideal is, therefore, one unyielding pattern to which all 'natural' expressions might be referred for evaluation.

The most drastic proposals for a universal language are based on the classification of ideas. These are displayed in Dalgarno's *Ars Signorum* (1661) and Wilkins's *Real Character* (1668). If all things can be listed under (say) forty categories, then words can be obtained by the same method as plants and animals are classified, by genus and species. Thus, if *de* is the category 'element', *deb* may be the genus 'fire' and *deba* the species 'flame'. Being unrelated to any language, *deba* is equally accessible or inaccessible to them all; but the proposed method presumes that the categories will remain acceptable, which is by no means certain. Moreover, since *deba* recalls nothing in anyone's experience of talking, it remains completely foreign and unreal.

The problem of babel is acute, and never more so than at present.

It has traditionally been solved by electing one national language for international use. Thus Babylonian served for international correspondence in the days of the great pharaohs, Aramaean for the monarchies of Assyria and Persia, Greek for the successors of Alexander, Latin for half the Roman empire, and Chinese for the Far East. The linguistic pattern of the world has always been simpler than the ethnological. Grammatical ease has counted for little or nothing in these elections, but the habit naturally suggests that some 'natural' language might be picked for its natural advantages and tidied up in some way for universal use. Latin had a sound and simple phonetic system, but is encumbered with flexions; hence *Latino sine flexione* might be supposed to commend itself. English is simple in construction and the fundamental vocabulary might be reduced to about a thousand words either intuitively (Simplified English) or by a systematic word-count (thousand-word English). It is phonetically untidy and has some unneeded legacies from the past; remove these, and one gets Anglic. On the assumption that Britain and America have and will hold the lead in science, international usefulness, and commerce, one reaches Basic. Attention is concentrated on the unfortunate fact that our commonest words are polysemous, i.e. ambiguous as to meaning. The Basic vocabulary, leaving orthography unchanged, selects the 845 words which will combine to give unambiguous meanings. They are not necessarily the simplest words in the language, and are mostly nouns (400 general things, 200 pictured things, 100 general qualities, 50 opposite qualities = 750 substantives or adjectives). There are no 'verbs', but the nouns are combined by 100 'operations' (verbs and adverbs), according to 7 rules. (On the same basis a *Chisic or a *Rusic are also conceivable; the selection of English depends on an estimate of probability which may yet prove to be perishable.) A complication has arisen through the interaction of English with Basic. It would be well if the 750 nouns were operated in all ways, as numbers are by mathematical signs, but in fact they are operated according to the English idiom. The champions of Basic have been stirred to prove that their language is English and have achieved notable *tours de force* like the translation of the New Testament into a sort of English. But what is gained in nationality is lost in universality. One says in Basic: *The sun is up and my umbrella is up*, but the difference between the two *ups* appears in *Il fait soleil et je porte mon parapluie*. Operators such as *get*, *put*, *up*, &c., carry with them some of the most recondite idiomatic peculiarities of the English language. By admitting derivation and technical terms the attractive figure of 850 words becomes illusory, and the total vocabulary runs to many thousands. By denying verbs Basic is opposed to the phenomenalism of true language.

Volapük, Esperanto, Ido, Novial, Reformed Esperanto, and a number of other 'universal' languages have been proposed on the basis of an *a posteriori* vocabulary drawn from various European languages with a simplified grammar. All such proposals are examined by the International Auxiliary Language Association, which has almost as much business as a comparative linguist. The international European vocabulary is of no assistance to Chinese or Quechuas, and even Europeans find the occasional irruption of Polish into Esperanto unfamiliar. The grammar of Esperanto, though simplified, distinguishes formally substantives, verbs, adjectives and adverbs, singulars and plurals, nominative and accusative cases, the tenses of participles, and it allows derivation. Comparison with Chinese shows that these distinctions are not necessary for grammar. But the strength of Esperanto, as compared with its numerous rivals, lies in its dogmatism. No change is permitted, and so the social contract persists in the same terms.

Children make up quite elaborate artificial languages for their own pleasure, without any claim to universality. It has been said that the best way to learn what language is, is to make one. The making of new languages, however, is hardly a likely solution for the problem of babel.

LANGUAGE, RACE, CULTURE, NATION

It should be said at once that there is no necessary connexion between a given language and a given race or culture or nationality.[1] On the other hand, language does imply a community of speakers. To make an abstraction of language as if it were self-sufficient is dangerously unreal. One may, no doubt, treat language (*langue*) as a generalization which becomes concrete and individual in speech (*parole*), but these are aspects of a single subject (*langage*) and cannot be realistically separated. Language exists only as spoken by some one in a community accepting the same conventions of com-

---

[1] The topic has been treated by every writer on this subject. Cf. O. Jespersen, *Mankind, Nation and the Individual*, London, 1946.

munication. The community lives somewhere and at some time.[1] It may very well be that we do not know what the time was, where the place, who constituted the community, or how it was politically organized, and in such a case the argument proceeds *as if* these factors could be dispensed with. But to treat language as a self-consistent system unrelated to speakers, and to make deductions from such an abstract proposition, involves the risk of unrealistic analysis.

The connection between language and nationality seems to be essentially modern. Its effect is practical: to insist that where there is a language there must be a nation, or where there is a nation there must be a national language. In this respect language has proved to be one of the most dangerous divisive forces of our time. It makes national claims where a language (such as Catalan or Lithuanian or Latvian) exists, even when the physical unit so created lacks the essentially national characteristic of capacity for self-defence. Linguistic irredentism claims, for instance, Transylvania for Rumania. The existence of a nation like the Finnish or Irish leads to the artificial resuscitation of the Finnish or Irish languages, the first that of a majority imposed on the Swedish-speaking minority, the second that of a small minority which the majority is urged for national reasons to obey. The breakdown of the Austro-Hungarian empire was largely linguistic, and with it was lost in central Europe a great civilizing idea: that large, self-protected bodies of men should live in one polity within a natural geographical area. On the other hand, the linguistic community of British and Americans forms a kind of super-nation, with elements of mutual understanding denied to those who talk differently.

The Greeks and the Romans took no special thought for the spread of their own languages, and their extended use was due to their political, commercial, and intellectual advantages. The Incas taught Quechua to the sons of subordinate chiefs, but otherwise

[1] Thus Frankish village-names are dense north of the Loire, but absent from southern France. As Frankish was spoken in France for only a limited period after the invasion, the linguistic facts are defined in both time and space. From this correlation W. von Wartburg could legitimately infer that the Frankish settlement was a mass-movement, not, as some historians aver, a thinly-spread Germanic aristocracy. Similar data show that the Visigoths, thinly spread over Spain before the Moslem conquest, settled densely on the land in Galicia after 711.

recognized their empire as fourfold (*Ttahuantin-suyu*). The Chinese have always been defined by a way of life, such that one of its members would be acutely unhappy when living in some other manner (e.g. among nomads), and the extension of Chinese has been due to the adoption of this mode of living by peoples formerly classified as barbarians. The Swiss are one nation with four languages. The British Commonwealth may survive as an English-speaking community or as a group of nations unified by common ideals, but it has not in the past been definable in terms of language. Once, however, the equation language = nation (though false) is commonly accepted—that is, chiefly since the end of the eighteenth century under the influence of Romantic ideas—it becomes extremely powerful, and a linguistically united nation operates with more energy than one in which translation is required or many possibly common activities are divided. An example to the point is Swiss literature. There is a certain similarity of Swiss literary productions in two main languages, but no identity of ground; on the other hand, they do not definitely belong to French or German literatures. Similarly, Finnish-Swedish writers since 1860 have not been definitely contributors to either literature. To make two cuts —the one by language and the other by nationality—is to aggravate the tendency of our civilization to fall into unrealistically tiny fragments.

The language-community may be a super-nation or a nation, a people, a tribe, a clan, or a great family. An astonishingly large number of languages serve astonishingly few needs. In a Melanesian islet six miles long there are 'two distinct and mutually incomprehensible languages'. The need of a *lingua franca* is felt among savages as among civilized folk, but the selection of a wider field of talk is disconcertingly casual. A Samoyede tribe twice changed its language in two generations; the first time it adopted a neighbouring Turkish dialect which gave only a small outlet into the world; the second time it chose Russian. The isolated families of the Amazon valley use each their own language. They also use Tupi as a *lingua franca*, though it offers no great cultural advantages, and they would make much less use of a common tongue had not a form of Tupi been recommended by Portuguese missionaries as a *lingua geral*.

No term has proved more unhappy for linguistics or mankind than the term 'Aryan race'. There was at one time hope that the intensive study of 'Aryan' tongues, myths, fairy-tales, and pre-history would reveal the 'Aryan race' in intimate spiritual detail, but the word 'Aryan' is now reserved in linguistics for those who used it of themselves, viz., the Indo-Iranian branch of the Indo-European speech-community. The physical constitution of these persons, whether uniform or varied, is now referred to another science, and it is not known how many of the Aryan speech-group were Indo-Europeans by descent, or whether the speakers of primitive Indo-European were racially alike. The known peoples and speech-communities prove to be of mixed anatomical breeds, though there are predominant characteristics in various communi-ties. Some of these arise in a secondary way from living in the same area under the same conditions of life, including perhaps the use of the same language, so that in the secondary sense of a 'breed or variety' one currently speaks of such races as the Slav, Anglo-Saxon, Latin, or Mongolian. These words call up simultaneously a vague notion of physical type and linguistic usage.

Language is a vehicle of culture but not necessarily identifiable in any cultural condition. A Russian writer who described the Lusatian culture, which extended from the Elbe to the Dnieper about 2500–1800 B.C. and was characterized by fields of funeral urns, as 'entirely Slavonic' was exceeding his evidence. The Lusa-tian way of life was agricultural; the primitive common Slavonic vocabulary is rich in agricultural terms; and that is all that can be affirmed. There is no evidence about this Lusatian speech four millennia ago. But it is legitimate to suppose that news of technical processes spread easily (in the absence of writing) as far as the boundaries of a given language, so that states of culture may be sums of linguistic integers. The occidental civilization of Europe, the Americas, Australia, and parts of Africa is expressed in many languages and enjoyed by a number of nations, and is at least available as far as each language extends, though not necessarily to each member of a nation (e.g. to each Spanish-speaking Peruvian, but not to those who speak Quechua).

In studying language we have to accept the terms 'nation' (and its synonyms) and 'culture', though we cannot, in default of evidence, make historical deductions from language alone. If there is a correlation of evidence, such as the Spanish discovery of America in 1492, the facts of language gain definition in time and place, and we can see in dated words the effects of the contact of two ways of life. Only the anatomical term 'race' cannot be brought into association with language, though in the secondary sense of a community with a certain kind of breeding it may be found that the use of a given language coincides with, and helps to stabilize, the breed.

LANGUAGE, DIALECT, IDIOM

Language is the mode of expression of some community. In the proper sense of the term, a language belongs to an organized and relatively self-sufficient community, whether it be an Amazonian tribe or a European state or a group of mutually intelligible states. It is not possible to offer a purely linguistic definition of a language. Hugo Schuchardt[1] amused himself by proving the impossibility by an account of a real or imaginary walk from Rome to Paris in search of the Franco-Italian language frontier. He began to meet French traits over the crest of the Apennines (*grand tutt paes vzein ciel*/ *grand tout pays voisin ciel*), and these features increased through Umbria and Lombardy until he found a very French sort of speech in Piedmont (*mör žust caud porterai*/*meurs juste chaud porterai*), but in Nice he found himself using more Italian than French. There was no linguistic frontier between French and Italian. But, of course, we call 'French' that which resembles a type of language fully characterized in Paris and 'Italian' a type of language proper to Tuscany and now standardized in Rome. Each language is defined by its centre, not by its circumference, and by the autonomous jurisdiction of that central standard over its dialects. The frontier between French and Italian is not a line frontier (like that between French and Spanish at the Pyrenees), but a broad band frontier, in which one standard type gradually sheds characteristics as it is dialectally metamorphosed into another. Owing to the medieval divisions of Italy this band frontier is exceptionally wide. In Spain there is a band of fifty miles in Upper Aragón where Spanish features subside and Catalan features take their place. This is a sign of old uninterrupted intercourse. From Tamarite southwards the frontier is a line traced by the parallel advance of Catalans and Aragonese in the thirteenth century. A band frontier lies between Spanish (Leonese) and Galician-Portuguese north of the Douro, and is succeeded by a line frontier of the Reconquest.

[1] H. Schuchardt, 'Über die Klassifikation der romanischen Mundarten', *Hugo Schuchardt-Brevier*, ed. L. Spitzer, Halle, 1928, pp. 166–88.

Dialects also are fully characterized at their centres and have vague frontiers, but they differ from languages in not being autonomous. Mutual ease or difficulty of understanding is not a primary consideration. Norwegians and Swedes, Spaniards and Portuguese can understand each other fairly well in their different languages, but authentic Lancashire would be unintelligible to a southern Englishman. At the centre of a dialect there is often some administrative seat or a cathedral or at least a confluence of interests which affords a focus of authority for innovations or resistance to innovations. A small system of waves reaches outward from the centre, but is broken by the more powerful waves emanating from the national centre. The authority of the latter is paramount; the dialectal capital does not aspire to be more than a point within the whole community. Under modern conditions the standard national languages have gained heavily at the cost of the local dialects, especially along lines of communication, such as the railways. Standard French has poured down the Rhône valley from Paris to Marseilles, splitting the Provençal dialects of the Alpine foothills from those of Gascony and Toulouse. Provençal, which once enjoyed the cultural autonomy of a language, though it had no single capital, is now a group of dialects; but it is possible to regard Catalan as having regained in the nineteenth century its independent rank as a language.

Below the dialect is the local idiom (*parler*) which has a certain consistency but no proper character. It may rule in a small area or be identified with a group (such as a professional body) or even with a person. In the last case what would be meant would be the individual's habitual usages (e.g. the use of *me father* for *my father* or *-in'* for *ing* in participles), not his creative use of words and phrases. It might result, for instance, through his being a stranger to the place where he lives and having shed most of the characteristics proper to the place of his birth; those that remained would distinguish his manner from that of his neighbours.

In addition to the horizontal or geographical dialect divisions there are also the vertical or social, and these have been the object of considerable study. Each group—philosophers, doctors, lawyers, tinkers, thieves, or politicians—has its own idiom, which varies from a small glossary of technical terms to a complete language. Usage is fluid by nature, but some items of private language emerge and are more widely circulated. This is particularly true of slang,[1] which owes its origin (in the sense common since 1818) to the creative urge in speech, the search for more satisfying and vigorous terms even at the cost of exactitude. Thus the Latin *caput* 'head' gave way to *testa* 'potsherd' and this has become Fr. *tête* 'head', and similarly with *jambe* 'leg (of bacon)', Russ. *zub* = Albanian *dhëmp* 'tooth' = Greek γόμφος 'peg, nail'. When so adopted a word loses its special vigour and invites new slang creations. A somewhat older sense of the word is the jargon of a class or a period. The technical language of sailors, for instance, impresses land-loving travellers, who talk for a while about *knots*, *starboard*, and *port* instead of *miles*, *right*, and *left*. When voyages were longer, this influence sank deeper. Thus in Spanish America 'tie' is colloquially *amarrar* ('moor a ship'), and 'horse' *flete* ('freight'). Soldiers who have been in India give the army such words as *char* 'tea', *cushy* 'soft, easy', *Blighty* ('Britain': a *Blighty one* was a wound that took the sufferer to a hospital in Britain), *panee* 'water', &c. Politicians *close an inflationary gap* by first depriving the public of a sufficiency of goods so that scarcity prices rule, and then depriving the public of money lest they pay scarcity prices; they speak of *collective security*, the *welfare state*, *sanctions*, and such terms circulate for a while. At a lower level is slang in its oldest meaning, viz. the cant of persons 'of a low or disreputable character'. It consists of euphemistic words ('*convey* the wise call it'), or the first syllables of dangerous words, or words in reverse, or words provided with meaningless first syllables. The object is to conduct a conversation which will be unintelligible to third parties (if not also criminal).

There are in addition the various 'pidgins' or vocabularies drawn from one language with constructions from another. The most famous is perhaps 'pidgin English', English words construed according to Chinese syntax. Various Creole languages of Spanish and French exist in which the greater part of the morphology has been shed and a large non-Romance vocabulary has been admitted. H. Schuchardt studied many of these in his *Kreolische Studien* (1882–3).

There is always some discrimination of language according to

---

[1] E. Partridge, *A Dictionary of Slang and Unconventional English*, London, 3rd ed., 1949; *A Dictionary of the Underworld*, London, 1950; *Slang*, London, 1935; A. Dauzat, *Les Argots*, Paris, 1929; R. Priebsch and W. E. Collinson, *The German Language*, London, 1948, pp. 293–9.

sex, since the topics and affections of the sexes are different. Thus Spanish augmentatives and diminutives are chiefly affective; they express aversion or contempt or compassion, and the use of diminutives for the latter purpose is especially frequent among women. The discoverers of the New World were not accompanied by women and had at their command augmentatives and diminutives which could be used to express a likeness between new objects and familiar ones. According to R. J. Cuervo American Spanish properly does not possess affective diminutives, since these resources have been used up to name new things. Conquest may set up a more drastic sexual division. The Caribs devoured Arawak men and married Arawak women in the Antilles; the result was a Carib language for men and Arawak for women and children. According to A. Hanoteau the mass of the Kabyle people, *all women without exception*, and sedentary men speak and understand only their Berber dialect, while men show a certain reluctance to write a language which (they say) is for speaking, not for writing. Arabic is the official tongue, but only those know it who have some official or religious reason for using Arabic. In Medieval Andalusia women, with very few exceptions, spoke Mozarabic Spanish and this was the language of all children for the first few years. When boys are initiated at the age of puberty among the Arunta, an important part of the instruction consists of altering their vocabulary. They are told that what they have called *x* is called *y*. The resulting vocabulary is both male and secret. E. Sapir[1] has studied the systematic discrimination of male and female speech in Yana (a language of northern California). There is no gender in the language, though a small number of verbs distinguish activities as performed by a male or a female: *ni-* 'a male goes'/*ʻa-* 'a female goes', *bu-ri-* 'a male dances'/*dja-ri-* 'a female dances'. But the principal distinction is that words are fully pronounced by men and abbreviated by women, or else they have for men an additional suffix. Thus there are doublets for the two sexes: *mô'i* 'eat'/*mô'i*, *'isi* 'man'/*'isⁱ*, *cūcu* 'dog, horse'/*cūcᵘ*, *yu-na* 'shelled acorn'/*yuʻ*, *ba-na* 'deer'/*baʻ*, *môtʻê'a* 'it is said he gives to eat'/*môtʻê*.

---

[1] E. Sapir, *Selected Writings*, Berkeley (Cal.), 1949, pp. 206-12.

II
CHANGE

It is the fact of change, 'mutability' as Chaucer would say, that makes linguistics a science, viz. an historical science.[1] The changes are seen in historical sequences such as Old English *wīf*/*wife*, *ufeweard*/*upward*, *fæ̃ger*/*fair*, *earm*/*arm* or *ēcnes*/*eternity*, *folc*/*people*, *nation*, *ēode*/*went*, in the first place as developments of speech-sounds, in the second as substitutions in the lexicon. In a strictly contemporary sense, linguistic maps show change as the co-existence of forms belonging to different stages of evolution, as *kirk*/*church*, Ptg. *outeiro*/Sp. *otero* 'hillock'. If we consider only the official language, such as literary French, we have to remember that parts of the apparently static pattern are actually in motion. The system is a shifting system. A French grammar shows a well-nurtured subjunctive, for instance, which is virtually dead in current speech.

If we question our own consciences in the matter, we may reply at first that we have not changed our way of speaking and do not intend to. A little more reflection leads us to conclude that there is a tension in our speech between the need to conserve all symbols for the sake of intelligibility and an urge to create more effective expressions. The creative urge is discussed chiefly under the heads of stylistics and vocabulary, but the conservative attitude holds for grammar and speech-sounds. They are emotionally and intellectually indifferent, and our liberty to make small changes elsewhere depends on our keeping inviolate these symbols. Further reflection, however, reminds us that we have frequently been driven to the dictionary by hearing a word pronounced in an unfamiliar way, whether by an announcer on the B.B.C. or by a majority of people around us or by some person for whose judgement we have high respect. Thus, we may have said *vágary* (= *vague*) for *vagáry* or hesitated between *láboratory* and *labóratory*.

---

[1] E. H. Sturtevant, *Linguistic Change: an introduction to the historical study of language*, New York, 1942, was rewritten as *An Introduction to Linguistic Science*, New Haven, 1947, 3rd ed., 1948. The altered title may have been a concession to those who profess descriptive linguistics, but in its first form it embodied a valuable thought.

A northern Englishman among the southern English or an Englishman resident in America is forced to make these small adjustments, not with the sense of innovating, but of conforming to an established model. The series *sawed, soared, sword* contain a long open *o* [ɔ:] and (in the second pair) a retroflex fricative *r* [ɹ] for some of the northern English, but they understand that the southern English have no real *r* at the end of a syllable. The dictionary gives *sword* [sord], which seems improbable in the vowel and the consonant, but a Scot may be heard to pronounce in this way. An American[1] remarks 'the feeling that the average Englishman would have that such words as *sawed* and *soared* are not phonetically identical. It is true that both *sawed* and *soared* can be phonetically represented as [sɔ:d]', but he goes on to say that the associations *saw* : *sawed* and *soar* : *soared* produce an impression of latent difference in the form that the first is 'zero = zero' and the second 'zero = *r*'. The difference 'heard' between *sawed* and *soared* is thus, for Englishmen, a 'collective illusion', but a psychological reality: [sɔ:d] *v.* [sɔ:-d]. In the face of conflicting testimony of experts one may decide to make no change. But whether one changes or does not change, the objective is conformity with a norm; whether there be actual innovation or not is thus concealed from us. An Englishman resident in America must change from *pavement* to *side-walk*, *autumn* to *fall*, *railway* to *railroad*, &c., and must shed specifically English speech-sounds and accentuation, but in doing so he may actually revert to older states of English. We know we have made alterations in our speaking, but we do not think we have innovated; we know that we have made them deliberately, but our will has subjected itself to common usage.

Lest these self-interrogations should seem too subjective, we may cite conditions in the commune of Vaux, which an expert kept under observation for fourteen years.[2] The commune belongs to the Franco-Provençal area. It contains 170 persons of native birth, of whom 73 are over 60 years of age, 75 over 30, and 22 under 30.

---

[1] E. Sapir, *Selected Writings*, 1949, p. 54. It may not be an illusion. The retroflex *r* [ɹ] brings the tip of the tongue into the high palate. The *d* is retroflexed and pronounced at the same place [ḍ]. The distinction 'heard' may be due to this effect on the *d* before the loss of consonantal *r*, and *sawed* [sɔ:d] might be differently formed from *soared* [sɔ:ḍ]. The effect of a retroflex *r* in my pronunciation is also felt on the preceding vowel.

[2] A. Duraffour, 'Trois phénomènes de nivellement phonétique en Franco-Provençal', *Bulletin de la société de linguistique de Paris*, xxvii, 1927.

There were also 80 strangers. In words like *abeille, vache, chasse, puce, noire,* the local dialect has a final *-i.* A very conservative family of father, mother, three boys, and a younger girl, were divided in such a way that the parents said *văşi* and the like, but the children *vache.* The girl imitated her elder brothers and they imitated a boy (intelligent, talkative, and enterprising) whose parents were not from Vaux. The father and mother never noticed this difference in their children's habit of speech. In another group the dominating personage was a young man from another region. The phenomena observed are not of innovation (though such they are within the dialect) but of approximation to standard French, and their occurrence can be traced to particular persons with qualities of leadership. The commune shows a steady drift from the *patois* towards standard French in each of its three generations. A similar drift by generations has been observed at Charmey (La Gruyère, in Switzerland), and agrees with changes in the speech of Cerniat, a village near by but completely disconnected from Charmey. The changes 'are more or less latent in the first generation, appear irregularly in the second, and expand in triumph in the third'.[1] Half a dozen phonetic laws were found in operation at the same time. There was no communal unity, but a marked difference of pronunciation according to age, and at the same time the same changes were being fulfilled in a disconnected village.

The same conclusions arise from the study of percentages adjusted to quarter-centuries in R. Menéndez Pidal's *Orígenes del Español* (Madrid, 1926, 3rd ed., 1950), for instance, in the shift $ai > ei > e$. With each period of years the percentages of the older forms are lowered and the newer forms gain, while the mid-career is a time of considerable vacillation. It seems, therefore, that the 'generation' is a real unit of measurement of linguistic change. It is true that individuals are born and die unceasingly, but life seems to create groups of those who are ceasing to be active workers, those who are fully employed, and those who are coming forward to their responsibilities, and the members of these groups look to each other rather than their predecessors or successors. At some date around thirty years the young man or woman acquires the responsibilities which continue until about sixty, and which make all those between thirty and sixty in a special sense contemporaries.

[1] L. Gauchat, 'L'unité phonétique dans le patois d'une commune', *Aus romanischen Sprachen und Literaturen (Festschrift Morf),* 1905, p. 230.

The division is clear in Homer. Achilles is a contemporary of Agamemnon and Ulysses since he is a leading chieftain on active service, but Telemachus and Laertes belong to the generations which have not attained to strength or have lost it. Nestor is a contemporary of Laertes or Anchises as to age, but, because of his abiding strength, a somewhat anomalous contemporary of the mature warriors. The women of Charmey seemed to have a more advanced pronunciation than the men, and the children adopted decidedly the new style of their mothers. The children of Vaux, however, proved to be as hardy imitators, but took as their models other children or young people.

SOUND-LAWS OR DRIFT

The most astonishing feature of linguistic change is its steadiness and completeness. A movement once initiated (it is averred) will tend to complete itself in all similar situations within one and the same dialect during the period of its operation unless prevented by some special circumstances. The drift will even continue beyond its original cause, as in the case of Castilian *c*, which has become interdental [θ] though the initial cause amounted to no more than approximating velar *k* to alveolar or dental *e i*. And this has happened to every Latin *c* before *e i*. So much for speech-sounds. When studying forms (morphology) we are dealing with two conditions, the one vocal, the other mental. The formal elements of words as sounds share in the general tendencies to change, but are more easily compared with each other and so constitute little islands of resistance to sound-change and they make easier other sorts of substitution. Thus *mens-am domin-um, man-um di-em*, and *reg-em* have as common feature an accusative in vowel + *m* in Latin, and act on that basis, though *reg-em* was originally a sonant *-m̥*. In western Romance *-s* is the sign of the plural, not only where it is proper in the accusative, but also in the nominative, and in Russian the plural cases of all nouns have been remodelled in view of the declension in *-a*. In respect of their sounds, therefore, the forms of words (morphemes) are specially rich in the kind of association which our statement of principles envisaged. But they serve to articulate the sentence and (in their absence) other syntactical devices must be employed. This change is conditioned by the attrition of the speech-sounds, and may not occur. When it does occur, a syntactical reshuffle takes place which cannot be described as in any way obligatory. In a third branch of language study (stylistics) it has been held not only that the history of changes has no certain direction, but that it is of no significance at all. Thus the question of change must be discussed on the basis of sounds, rather than forms, order, or style.

It is not of great moment whether we speak of drift (Sapir) or phonetic tendencies (Vendryes) or sound-laws (Lautgeschichte— Brugmann, &c.). The last term is convenient as stressing the remarkable regularity of these phenomena, and much depends on what one means by 'law'.[1] The 'Young Grammarians' who did most to formulate these laws insisted on their working without exception. The definition, however, by insisting on similarity of conditions and absence of opposing circumstances, provided exceptions enough to isolate each instance. No word or form is absolutely identical with any other word or form. The legislators worked in a period of rapidly advancing exact (and rather dogmatic) science and sought to establish laws like the laws of Nature, but it is open to question whether philologists understand the nature of laws in physics or biology, or whether the laws of these sciences operate in the same way. One can predict the date of the next eclipse of the sun. There is a suppressed hypothesis in such a prediction, namely, that the sun will not blow up as a nova or supernova, in which case there would be no moon to make the eclipse or earth to observe it from. But the risk of exceptional circumstances is so minute that tables of future eclipses can be drawn up with full assurance that they will occur. But one cannot predict the jumps made by electrons within the atom. Among animals one may trace a general evolutionary drift and connect it with a time-scale, but we cannot predict the rise of a superhuman race nor even interpret accomplished evolutionary stages as necessary results of causes. Biology is history, and phonology is human history. Since Man is within Nature, he obeys natural laws either spontaneously or voluntarily, and in his attempt (unique among animals) to reshape Nature he must make use of Nature. The sound-laws, phonetic tendencies or drifts are comprehensive formulas to embrace what has actually happened, and they are shaped to exclude what has not happened. Latin *fŏcus* has given Italian *fuoco* and *lŏcus* has given *luogo* and the 'law' must be shaped accordingly. The Spanish

[1] H. Schuchardt, 'Über die Lautgesetze', *Hugo Schuchardt-Brevier*, Halle, 1928, pp. 51–87.

forms are *fuego luego*, and the Spanish 'law' states that Latin *c* [k]
between vowels becomes Spanish *g*. But in saying so we have to
allow that this sonorization is a western feature, and was often
absent in Mozarabic, Old Aragonese, and Catalan. With French
feu lieu the law states that the consonant [k] was sonorized and
reduced to a fricative before it disappeared, but it will be seen that
Latin short *o* has had a divergent history in French, though it gives
consistent results in Spanish and Italian.

Nature was understood to be a vast machine and its motions and
impediments mechanical in character. They were thus without
exception automatic. The sound-laws eliminated human vagaries
from the history of language. If the law did not operate in some
instance within the conditions propounded it was supposed that
there must be an obstacle—analogy—of a mechanical type. This
was restricted to inner and outer analogy. In the first place an
association of meaning caused two words or forms to interfere with
each other's normal development; in the second a formal resemblance set up similar reactions. This point will have to be taken up
in another chapter, but for the present one must say that it is often
impossible to say which are the cogs which foul each other in language. They cannot be identified like those in a machine. *Sapĕre*
and *habēre* affect each other in Romance, though they have no
inner or outer analogy, e.g. Italian *ho so/avere sapere*. Many considerations operate other than analogy. For instance, as J. Gilliéron
often pointed out, there comes a moment when phonetic attrition
is on the point of making a word too insubstantial to mean any
substantial thing. A reaction occurs. The therapeutics of language
come into play. But it is not necessary for development to reach as
far as making words unrecognizable before laws are amended. The
Spanish of the thirteenth century shows a steady tendency to re-
impose trochaic rhythm by restoring lost final syllables though the
texts of the twelfth century were readily understood. Western
dialects, no doubt, helped this reconstruction but a mental principle was also involved. The chief error of the mechanical view is
to eliminate Man from his own speech, treating the latter as if it
were a machine independent of Man.

The announcement of laws of a rigid type has, however, been
of great advantage to linguistic study by discouraging the premature abandonment of the search for causes of effects.[1] There are,

[1] L. Bloomfield, *Language*, 1946, p. 354, speaks of the laws as 'fruitful'.

in fact, causes which operate on an enormous scale and with astonishing regularity, such as Grimm's law. It accounts for the correspondences *decem/ten, tres/three*, στείχω 'go'/Goth. *steigan*, and a vast number of others of the same type. When it was emended, it was by means of other general principles in Verner's and Grassmann's laws. So, too, Fortunatov's law of the attraction exerted by a final rising tone on a previous falling one accounts for a Slavonic accent-shift without envisaging exceptions. When exceptions do occur, the conception of law requires that they should be fully explained. They cannot be dismissed as merely sporadic, though the explanation may be unique and fitted to a single instance. The cause of a discrepancy is not limited to some analogy, but may be any of the innumerable considerations which affect human behaviour. J. Gilliéron pressed the laws to their severest and most consistent conclusions in individual cases in order to set in high relief anomalous developments and to demand an account of them. His work revealed that the wide dominion of consistent evolution is matched by another wide dominion of anomalous development, and that often the rule is exemplified in the exception!

One cause of this paradox is that a language alters by divergence and by convergence. Owing to its extensive claims a language must conciliate more or less the different usages of its dialects. It tends, too, to impose on its forms and phrases a logic of its own and to produce a more systematic result than strictly historical evolution would allow. To overcome this difficulty the suggestion has been made that the sound-laws are absolute for a smaller unit, the dialect. But a dialect is by definition not autonomous. Its frontiers are invaded by other dialects and its communal centre by the national practice. The most one can hope to find is a certain accumulation of characteristics around the dialectal focus. It has been observed, at Charmey and Vaux, that there is no phonetic unity within the dialect, but a division by three generations. While a development proper to the dialect shows steady evolution from generation to

H. Schuchardt complains that right results are obtained by possibly false premisses (*Brevier*, 1928, p. 78). There might have been premisses more false than those of the Young Grammarians, and their conception of 'Laws without exceptions' has produced, as Bloomfield suggests, results that are closely approximate to consistent. One may affirm with Schuchardt that 'there are sporadic changes', but it would lead to serious misstatement of linguistic evolution if the notion of sporadic change were introduced before the full story of consistent changes had been worked out.

generation (as I. *å*, II. *å/ao*, III. *ao* in *alå* for *aller*), there may also be convergent movements towards a standard usage, represented initially by the practice of neighbouring dialects (as in the substitution of *e* 'mute' for *i* at Vaux for final *a* after a palatal consonant).

That phonetic laws operate for a period and then cease to work is a circumstance which makes them quite unlike those of physics or even of biology. No prediction is possible since no one can know whether a tendency will continue to operate. For a time Latin *ĕ ŏ* under stress developed, first into long open vowels [ɛ:] [ɔ:], then into homogeneous diphthongs (*ie uo*)—under somewhat different conditions in each of the Romance languages—and finally by dissimilation into Spanish dialectal *ia*, and *ua uə ue*. The final establishment of Spanish *ie ue* belongs to the twelfth century, but there came a time, probably earlier than that age, when accented *ĕ ŏ* no longer diphthongized, and Basque words like *berri gorri* remained unchanged in place-names. The first Slavonic palatalization made *k* into *č* before front vowels. Its date is uncertain. The second palatalization was provoked by the rise of new front vowels from older diphthongs; *k* was drawn forward but actually passed through the palatal to the dento-alveolar position as *c* [ts]. The cause is the same in each case, but the trajectory of the second change is longer than the first. The philologist can only accept the fact and 'explain' it *a posteriori*.

Viewed from a sufficient distance the sound-laws appear to fulfil themselves over the whole language, and it might be supposed that they operated in each part equally all the time. But viewed closer at hand in Romance documents the innovation is seen to start from some initial focus and to spread slowly over the whole national area. Its history is different for each word and form. It tends to complete itself, but there are unfulfilled sound-laws to the present day; for example, that which produces French *chanter chez chandelle chambre* has not reached the dialect of the Channel Islands.

DIVERGENCE AND CONVERGENCE

In a celebrated observation the Colombian linguist, R. J. Cuervo, supposed that European and American Spanish would necessarily diverge until they became separate languages, but that it was the duty of every Spanish-speaker to combat the tendency. In fact the usages have converged. To secure 'American' material C. E. Kany[1]

[1] C. E. Kany, *American-Spanish Syntax*, Chicago, 1945.

has relied chiefly on writers of the second order or under, and there is no reason to suppose that Spanish-Americans will take as their models less than their best. Cuervo's remark was based on the typical metaphor of the day, which envisaged a family tree with branches necessarily drawing farther apart or with second cousins necessarily less closely related than brothers and sisters. Such a tree might be, for instance:

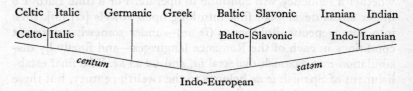

Celtic Italic   Germanic Greek   Baltic Slavonic   Iranian Indian

Celto- Italic   Balto- Slavonic   Indo- Iranian

centum   *satəm*

Indo-European

If that were a true picture, one would have to conclude that the mutability of speech would draw languages ever farther apart. But there are several causes which prevent this development. A language involves a measure of compromise. Though Spanish is Castilian by reason of six characteristically Castilian innovations, Castilian itself furthered two Leonese innovations and two Aragonese. Latin *planu-* 'plain' evolved in the north-west as **pllano* > **piano* > **pčano/pšano* > Ptg. *chão* Leon. *xano*. In the north-east there was Catalan *pla* Aragonese *pllano*. Castilian *llano* offered a compromise between north-eastern conservatism and north-western radicalism in this matter. Of the six Castilian innovations, that which transformed Latin *f* into aspirate *h* was resisted when the literary and official usage was made to conform to the language of Toledo (where *f* was current). The shift of point of balance from Burgos to Toledo favoured compromise among the Spanish dialects until after a long struggle the strictly Castilian usage gained universal support.

The separation of languages is not of the nature of a cut unless invincible natural obstacles intervene. Only the Polar ice-caps are of such a nature. The Himalayas, though not insurmountable, serve as a retarding obstacle. The oceans were estranging when small wooden ships made journeys of many months, but with rapid steamers or aircraft they serve to unite the countries on their opposite shores. Thus Spain and Spanish America were formerly more distant than they are now, as also England and the United States. In both cases, when the revolution was new, a considerable degree of self-consciousness was engendered in the young country and it is now in process of being shed. But in the absence of these special geographical and political conditions, separation is slow and unequal. The establishment of the *centum/satəm* line between Germanic and Balto-Slavonic did not prevent these two groups developing oblique cases in *-m* in opposition to the rest of the Indo-European world (*-bh*). The relations between Baltic and Slavonic seem to show a succession of periods of estrangement and approximation. A cause of change, too, may have begun to be effective in the period of common speech and have continued to work its effects in the period of separation, achieving the same or very similar results in independent territories. Thus **kw* became **k* in certain Indo-European languages, and this velar moved forward in the mouth to meet the vowels *e i* (**k̑*). Developing after these languages had attained separate definitions, it ended generally in palatal *č*. Similarly Latin *c* [k] before *e i* had moved to a prevelar or post-palatal position at the end of the Roman Empire, and continued to palatal and alveolar positions in the separate Romance languages. Germanisms in Spanish frequently show signs of passage through France at a period when French and Spanish were fully distinct. Their presence approximates the two languages.

The possibilities of change are not infinite. The immense dissimilarity of languages results from the combination of many possibilities, each rather limited in scope. Consequently it is not unusual to find recurrent causes which operate so as to produce new secondary resemblances.[1] One has good cause, in any Indo-European language, to associate *m s t* with the three persons of the verb. It appears at first in two forms: primary **-mi *-si *-ti*/secondary **-m *-s *-t*, and there can be little doubt that **-ti/t* is a kind of demonstrative. But Indo-European developed an isolated form in **-ō* for the present indicative (**bherō* > φέρω *fero*). This form is anomalous, and *-mi* was reintroduced into Old Irish *icca-im -i -d* 'heal' and Sanskrit *bhárāmi bharasi bharati*. If it were not for traces of *-ō* in an obscure Iranian dialect, there would be no evidence that this form had been known to the Aryan branch of Indo-European. Owing to loss of final syllables **bherō* became **ber* in Armenian, while **esmi* 'I am' remained as *em*. By combining the verb with the copula we get *berem beres berê*. In Slavonic there was first **berō*,

[1] A. Meillet, 'Convergences des développements linguistiques', *Linguistique historique et linguistique générale*, Paris, 1948.

then *berō-m (Old Bulgarian berǫ, with nasal vowel) by addition of -m (not -mi, which would have preserved consonantal m). The third personal ending dropped out (cf. Lith. 1 sg. dirbu 3 sg. dirba 'work'), but a demonstrative -tŭ (not -ti) was added. Hence the series became berǫ bereši beretŭ. Much later -m spread among Czech verbs and over all Yugoslav verbs. The net result of these changes is a striking convergence:

Irish	Skr.	Arm.	Old Bulg.
icca-im	bhára-mi	ber-em	ber-ǫ (≐ōm)
i	si	es	eši
id	ti	ê	etŭ

There are similar convergences due to the fact that both western and eastern modern Indo-European languages have sought to distinguish between the stem which signifies something and flexions which express some syntactical relation. Thus dico corresponds to I say and je dis, in which the pronouns are not emphatic (as in ego dico, Spanish yo digo) but merely give the personal reference. French and English converge in this respect, though their conjugations are quite different in principle. Similarly, the French 'logical' sentence and the English 'plain style' are converging tendencies, and yet another came into operation when Pushkin and Karamzin remodelled Russian literary phrases upon French precedents. European sentences, however different in origin the languages may be, can usually be construed in much the same order. It is their business to express slightly differentiated forms of one common civilization.

THEORIES OF CHANGE

The causes of change which we can observe in ourselves or test by personal contacts are so few and exerted in conditions so unlike those which may have ruled at other times that the student must call to his aid some general theory to reduce these effects to a pattern. Communes in Switzerland and south-western France maintain their isolation with difficulty while trains rush Parisians to Lyons, Marseilles, and Geneva. As a result of broadcasting the standardized voice of announcers is heard in the remotest villages. French is a highly disciplined and centralized tongue. Very little of this can have applied to the same region when Latin was the imperial language but was not required for the common tasks of life, when movement was at walking speed, and most people were illiterate. Still less do the conditions apply to that period in which the Western economy had collapsed by the Moslem blockade of Mediterranean trade, and there was no other standard tongue than the hesitating latinity of Gregory of Tours. At a still earlier time, when the Italic and Latin dialects approximated their utterance or when Indo-European was the language of a substantially united community, the norms of speech were still to be shaped. The percentages of sound-shifts which Sr. Menéndez Pidal has worked out for the tenth to twelfth centuries in Spain belong to a period of political concentration and growing linguistic unity. There was a demand for increased unity on a not-too-variable standard (with some accommodation for the habits of principal dialect groups); a situation quite opposed to the growing anarchy of the Dark Ages.

We must bear in mind, however, the observed facts for which any realistic theory must find a place. It is not in the interest of speakers that language should change; but it does. There is a certain tension between the creative demands of expression and the static requirements of comprehension; but innovations are only interesting against an unchanging background, and lose their freshness when they are absorbed as clichés into common speech. The search for novelty is stylistic and is at a minimum in speech-sounds, which can have no significance individually; yet the most striking and ordinary changes are those of phonemes. If we invoke the will, it is a will to conform rather than to dissent, and even in innovations the will is probably concerned to express latent possibilities of language, to convert *posse* into *esse*, and so still to occupy the same linguistic ground. The phoneme is intrinsically variable and is heard with a conventional inattention to detail. Thus it is an observed fact that the older generation of *patoisants* do not notice the existence of innovations in the speech of the younger. In so far as a phoneme is a point in a pattern, its usefulness in speech depends on its relative distance from other phonemes. Two speakers whose vowels are

$$a \qquad e \qquad i \qquad o \qquad u$$

and
$$a' \qquad e' \qquad i' \qquad o' \qquad u'$$

regard themselves as speaking in the same way. The displacement of a single phoneme (as from *å* to *ao*, or *i* to *ə*) may be automatically discounted by the listener, who expects that speech symbols offered to him will show a certain fluidity. Despite the will to conform and despite deliberate substitutions for the sake of 'correctness', despite also the fact that hearers can be induced to note variations with surprising accuracy and habitually recognize the 'accents' of other dialects, it is possible for changes to take place without exciting remark.

The wave theory, announced by J. Schmidt in 1872, can be reckoned among the facts of observation since it corresponds to the situation observed on all linguistic maps. It does not account for the origins of a sound-shift, but for its progress; some other means must be found for determining an initial cause. Thus Latin *f* > Spanish and Gascon *h* is seen at first to be, on the Spanish side, restricted to a narrow strip along the Basque border across the Cantabrian mountains. It had the monastery of Oña as its first known centre of diffusion. In the twelfth century the area of this sound-shift had spread over Old Castile, and Burgos is its centre of diffusion. Toledo was the main centre of opposition, supported by León and Zaragoza. Two successive waves of Castilian innovation (the aspiration of *f*, and the silencing of *h*) have advanced over these obstacles; the first has covered all Spanish-speaking lands, apart from north-western León (Astorga) and Upper Aragón, but the second has been halted at the frontiers of Extremadura and Andalusia. By combining the evidence for *étoile*, *toile*, and *mois*,[1] one has a more detailed picture of wave-movement. The centre of diffusion is obviously Paris. The three phenomena have in general a common frontier, but *mois* advances farther into Brittany, the Gironde and Lorraine than *toile*, and *étoile* extends farther into the Cotentin. There are also splashes of *toile and étoile* beyond the line where the waves 'break' in southern France, and two isolated 'droplets' of *mois*. The picture is thus very like the lines left by breakers on a sandy coast.

The wave theory does not account for the passage of *f* to *h* or the origin of [wa] in *étoile*, *toile*, and *mois*. These are respectively Cantabrian and Parisian historical matters. It shows only their spread. If a disturbance is made in water at any place, concentric waves spread out with decreasing intensity. If another disturbance arises, the outermost waves will intersect and break each other, producing splashes and ragged boundaries. If one impulse is stronger or newer than the other, the weaker and older will be the more damaged and

---

[1] K. Jaberg, Map I: 'Freies geschlossenes *e* vor oralem Konsonant wird zu steigendem Diphthong, dessen erstes Element *w* oder *ẅ* ist', *Sprachgeographie*, Aarau, 1908.

deranged. Various causes induce changes to travel faster, notably fashion, which is partly related to change of the things named. There are also concepts which are liable to continuous change because they involve a tabu (such as words for 'left', which tend to suggest 'sinister') or because they are uttered with humorous deprecation (as words for 'head'—'potsherd' in French or Italian —or 'leg'—'gammon' in Romance and 'limb' to the Victorian) or because they fall affectively short of the notion they express (as 'find', which is replaced by more vivid terms like 'invent'—come into, 'discover'—take the cover off, or 'step on' in Russian).

The wave theory is opposed to the concept of language changing as a block. The difference is partly one of perspective. A disturbance out in the Pacific may be circular, but it reaches the Californian coast in long parallel rollers which fill the whole seascape. Language shifts also tend to complete themselves and to occupy the whole scene as viewed from their end and at a distance. Thus we can rightly say that IE. $*t >$ Eng. th (thin/tenuis), IE. $*d >$ Eng. t (ten/decem), IE. $*dh >$ Eng. d (door/θύρα); and it would be vain to specify a centre of diffusion. Statements of this sort are made as if the whole language had shifted as a block, and they are valid inasmuch as the result affects the whole language. The wave picture can be obtained by setting down evidence in a spatial diagram, like that for the passive:

Eng. *be found*	ONorse *finna-sk*	Lith. *rasti-s*	Russ. *nachodíí-sja*	Tokh. *knitär(ci)*
OIrish *léicfider*	Alb. *kërkohem*		Arm. *sirim*	Avesta *pairye-te*
Lat. *afficitur*	Gk. *φέρε-ται*		Phrygian *αδδακε-τορ* Hitt. *yatari*	Sanskrit *tanyá-te*

☐ -r   ☐ -ai   ┆┄┆ reflexive pronoun

The first wave travels farthest, and is driven to the extremities by succeeding innovations. Hence the passive -tor of Irish, Latin, Phrygian, Hittite, and Tokharian is presumably the oldest device to show the passive. Later comes the change from vowel (-ti) to diphthong (-tai) in Greek and Indo-Iranian. The use of the verb 'be' or of the reflexive pronoun is later still.

A picture of words commencing in *kw- and *k̂w- might be:

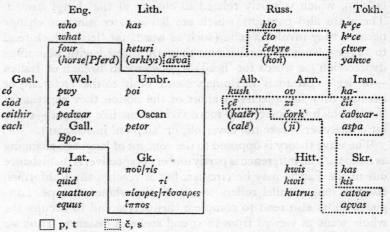

Eng.	Lith.	Russ.	Tokh.
who	kas	kto	k^{u}çe
what		čto	k^{u}ce
four	keturi	četyre	çtwer
(horse/Pferd)	(arklys) ašva	(koń)	yakwe

Gael.	Wel.	Umbr.	Alb.	Arm.	Iran.
có	pwy	poi	kush	ov	ka-
ciod	pa		çē	zi	čit
ceithir	pedwar	Oscan	(katër)	čorkʻ	čaθwar-
each	Gall.	petor	(calë)	(ji)	aspa
	Bpo-				

Lat.	Gk.	Hitt.	Skr.
qui	πού/τίς	kwis	kas
quid	τί	kwit	kis
quattuor	πίσυρες/τέσσαρες	kutrus	catvar
equus	ἵππος		açvas

☐ p, t   ┊┄┊ č, s

It will be seen that the derivatives of *ek̂wos/ek̂wa are found in the whole periphery, though changing to sibilants in the south-east. *K̂w- and *kw- remain on the western circumference (Germanic, Gaelic, Latin) and in Hittite, but a later wave of change has produced p in an inner ring (Germanic in part, Osco-Umbrian, Greek in part), with a still later t (Greek in part). There were also k-forms in Greek dialects. Borrowing has occurred in Albanian katër calë (from Latin), and horse, Pferd, arklys, koń, si, ji are novelties of diverse origin. For *kw-e/i Lithuanian keturi shows the reduction to k-e/i which is the cause of palatalization in Slavonic, Armenian, and Indo-Iranian.[1]

We have thus a picture of successive changes, but still no account of causes. Why should *kw- become p or *k-ei become č? Nothing in the wave theory accounts for these events. A previous question is whether the cause should be mental or mechanical or both or either as suits the case. As we know by experience that we wish to speak correctly and are constantly corrected by our friends for failures in pronunciation, grammar, or style, it would seem that we cannot exclude operation by the mind even in changes which, like those of sounds, may be insignificant or unnoticed. The mental operation is more evident in grammar and style. There was attrition of Latin cases so that nom. aqua and abl. aquā were no longer

[1] Entwistle does not distinguish between the labio-velars and the clusters of gutturals with w as a second element. [L. R. P.]

equipped to express a grammatical distinction. A preposition had to be employed to take the place of the sign -*ā*: Sp. *por agua*. So far the account is mechanical, but this is only one of many cases of substitution of an analytic for a synthetic mode of expression. In this sense the development is parallel to that of Latin *dīxī* > Fr. *j'ai dit*, for which no theory of mechanical attrition affords a sufficient explanation (since *je dis* also exists, but no longer covers the whole ground of *dīxī*). We have to do with a changed habit of mind. It is still more profitless to explain stylistics by mechanical causes, though style ultimately contributes to grammar.

The conflict of mentalism and materialism (or mechanism) is a live issue in the United States,[1] but the case for either view may be pushed to extreme length. 'The materialistic (or, better, mechanistic) theory supposes that the variability of human conduct, including speech, is due only to the fact that the human body is a very complex system. Human actions, according to the materialistic view, are part of cause-and-effect sequences exactly like those which we observe, say, in the study of physics or chemistry.' Chemical or physical effects are normally such as can be referred to precisely defined causes, and given a cause in operation one can predict an effect. Human sequences form complex chains which we cannot, in fact, predict. It is supposed that if we knew the precise bodily structure of an individual at all moments we could foretell a person's reactions. As we certainly have no such knowledge, this hypothesis does not lend itself to verification. The mechanist posits:

(1) large-scale processes which are much the same in different people, and, having some social importance, are represented by conventional speech-forms . . . ;

(2) obscure and highly variable small-scale muscular contractions and glandular secretions, which differ from person to person, and, having no immediate social importance, are not represented by conventional speech-forms;

(3) soundless movements of the vocal organs, taking the place of speech-movements, but not perceptible to other people ('thinking in words').

The operations of mind, on this exposition, seem to be limited to the working of 'the little grey cells', as a popular writer has it, but one misses any word for the co-ordination and interpretation of signals,

---

[1] L. Bloomfield, *Language*, New York, 1946, pp. 32 ff., 142–4.

either as received or as purposively issued. That there must be some such operation is clear from the unlikeness of all sounds (including onomatopoeic noises) to the things they express. One could shout *railway train* or *bang* all day in an elephant's ear without conveying any meaning to the animal, though he might resent the experiment as tedious and unnecessary. The 'muscular contractions and glandular secretions' act together in total operations of comprehension and volition, image-forming and emotional response.

On the other hand it seems no longer useful to go the whole way with K. Vossler[1] in his two polemical publications on language. The argument is directed against a merely mechanical account of the history of language, just as L. Bloomfield's mechanistic views spring from disappointment with Wundt's *Völkerpsychologie*. One must allow for animus. It is admitted that 'idealism' is borrowed from philosophers as a common antithesis for 'positivism', but that it does not mean philosophical idealism. Speech is creative from the speaker's standpoint, but he has not *spoken* at all if he has not been understood. What may be his thoughts, concepts, images, feelings, and acts of will are, from the strictly linguistic standpoint, unknowable; they can only be known from sound-symbols and from a certain sympathy present in the hearer as himself a creator. The well-known confusion or identity of formal with final causes turns history into teleology, to the dubious advantage of history.

In alleging mental causes it is easy to exceed one's warrant. Mechanical operations are essentially simple, but mental operations are very varied and it is quite possible for several mental causes to have one effect. There is a distinct risk of using a very small foundation of fact for too vast generalizations, such as those implied by the word *Weltanschauung*. The Spanish Jews used for 'God' the term *el Dio*. Its apparent plural *Dios*, as used by Christian Spaniards, may have been a convenient handle for controversialists, but *el Dio* itself is formed in just the same way as Italian *Iddio* (*il Dio*), which has no background of controversy. The Spanish Jews followed a Romance norm by using the accusative case, since this word is not part of their liturgical language. Spanish Christians adopted the vocative *Deus*, so frequently heard in the Mass and essential for prayer. In Old Spanish and Portuguese the use of *a* with a personal direct object was optional; that modern Spanish has opted for this

[1] K. Vossler, *Positivismus und Idealismus in der Sprachwissenschaft*, 1904; *Sprache als Schöpfung und Entwicklung*, 1905.

usage as necessary and modern Portuguese has discarded it, does
not necessarily imply a greater capacity among Spaniards than
among Portuguese to distinguish between persons and things. That
there is need to distinguish between persons as subjects and objects
is seen also in Russian and Rumanian. In Russian the distinction
of nominative and accusative singular broke down mechanically,
and the genitive was brought in (by a creative process) to carry on
the functions of the accusative. In Spanish the two sentence-orders
created a demand for a pointer to the object, when that object was
of a nature to furnish a plausible subject (i.e. personal or animate).
The idiom was established by use and wont.

The great advantage of Vossler's campaign, however, was his insistence on the place of will in the evolution of language, and with
will, of many social and historical circumstances conditioned by
this human activity. The mind may will to conform to some standard, and if the standard is in fact new it helps to spread some
novelty; it may be unobservant ('nous parlons tous la même chose',
as villagers protested to an inquirer); it may react, as in the restora-
tion of the neuter gender in Slavonic; it may attempt a new creation
for a momentary or a permanent effect; its creations may be
accepted or refused, and depend for acceptance on the general
conformity of the speaker's utterances. The mind forwards, retards
or is not exerted to control or observe change, but it is never absent,
and it receives stimuli from an ever-changing world. It tends to
impose a pattern on matter, but the patterns do not always show
the same design. Thus

Old French	*entre*	*dor*	become modern	*j'entre*	*je dors*
	entres	*dors*		*tu entres*	*tu dors*
	entret	*dort*		*il entre*	*il dort*

In this two things have occurred. The old *zero* symbol of the first
person becoming unintelligible, one group of verbs borrowed *e*
from the stem and were understood to end in -*e* -*es* -*e*, and another
adopted the pattern -*s* -*s* -*t* (from those with stems ending in *s* like
floris floris florist), and a growing demand for precision of reference
made the use of pronouns obligatory in the absence of a noun. But
this demand for precision, not effective in the more impulsive
syntax of the twelfth century, is part of a general tendency towards
unambiguous utterance which fixed the order of the sentence
(subject–verb–object) and caused emphasis to be expressed by fixed

syntactical formulas (*c'est à vous que je parle*). It can be associated with a rising standard of thinking, the influence of the Sorbonne, academic insistence on the sentence as a judgement, &c. The mechanical breakdown of English terminations in the fifteenth century was not compensated in the Elizabethan age (when variety was preferred to clarity), but the sentence was disciplined in the late seventeenth century at a time when the Royal Society was demanding clarity and simplicity for the new sciences. The breakdown of Chinese endings leads to an immense mass of homonyms in Chinese, but the need to remove possible ambiguities in speech was the less felt because there are few homonyms in Chinese writing.

For the greater number of events in linguistic history, however, the role of the mind has been passive and acquiescent. It has aimed at conformity to a standard or has been systematically unaware of details of difference. This is especially the case with phonology and morphology. Speech-sounds are essentially meaningless, so that there is no cause for mental intervention unless by reason of some association of sound. The theory of the phoneme implies systematic observance of certain expected features and systematic indifference to variations. This results in mental unawareness of variations of phonemes: 'nous parlons tous la même chose'. The morpheme (unit of formal variation of words) is meaningful but arbitrary. Morphemes entangle each other as sounds and as functions, and are thus the more exposed to the operations of analogy. They prove to be functionally inadequate in every language, and require further definition by means of auxiliaries, but these aids to precision are drawn from existing resources of the language; they are not novelties. In these two traditional fields of language study, therefore, it is possible to arrive at general statements which ignore individual eccentricities, such as that 'free accented Latin *a* has become *e* in French (*chanter pré père/cantáre prátum pátrem*)'. Not only can these statements be made in an abstract and mechanical way, but it is necessary to make them with the utmost rigour if individual aberrations are to be detected. Thus, in all rigour, Latin *apicula* 'little bee' should become French **aveille*, and Latin *fidem* 'faith' should become Spanish *he* (as it does in an obsolete exclamation). We are then made aware that French *abeille* and Spanish *fe* are deviations from the norm, and we are set to seek the reasons for these vagaries.

For this mechanical aspect of evolution we can draw on the

science of phonetics which reveals the fault-lines of language. Over
and over again, in languages which have no contact with each other,
we see the same developments taking place under the same phonetic
conditions. No particular development can be predicted, nor, once
begun, can its end be foreseen, but we can give a continuous account
of what has happened. The semivowels *y* and *w* are of the nature
of glides from vowel to consonant or consonant to vowel. They
vary in character as they are being uttered, and tend to attach themselves to an accompanying vowel or consonant; generally to the
sound which precedes them. They tend to fuse and to produce
modifications which draw the preceding vowel or consonant to the
palatal position of *y* or the labial or velar position of *w* (which is a
sound, as we have noted, with a double articulation). Hence the
disturbances labelled palatalization, labialization, and velarization.
Of these the first is the most active, since not only the semivowel but
also the front vowels *e i* cause palatalizations, and one of the commonest facts of the history of languages is the acquisition of palatal
consonants unknown to the primitive tongue. The back vowels *o u*
have velar effects, but are less distinctly uttered and so cause less
linguistic disturbance. So we can 'explain' Latin *sapiam* It. *sappia*
Ptg. *saiba* Sp. *sepa* Prov. *sapcha* Fr. *sache* as palatalizations. They are
somewhat different palatalizations, however. *Sapiam* > *saiba*/*sepa*
shows metathesis of *pi* to **ip* and a resultant effect on the vowel in
Spanish. *Sapiam* > *sappia* > *sapcha* > *sache* shows no metathesis,
but a tenser pronunciation of the semiconsonant resulting in the
ultimate disappearance of the preceding labial consonant in French.
In Latin *equus* 'horse'/Gaul. *Epo-* Gk. ἵππος, we have *kw* as a starting-
point. Since *w* is a labial as well as a velar sound, it affected the
preceding velar consonant *k* so as to transfer the sound-group to
the lips (labialization) in Gaulish and Greek. In French *mauvais*
'bad', the *u* comes from a velar [ɫ], which comes from a normal *l*
(It. *malvaggio* Sp. *malo*). The velar [ɫ] is heard in Ptg. Cat. *mal*; the
process is one of velarization. In like manner we can explain how
Chinese *fu* may come from an older *pi̯u*, *pʻi̯u*, or *bʻi̯u*, and the relation between *king*/*ching*[1] 'capital'. There is no way of predicting
results, however; Lat. *saltus* 'grove' gives Sp. *soto*, but *saltus* 'leap'
gives *salto*, Lat. *planus* 'plain' gives Sp. *llano*, but *platea* gives *plaza*
(It. *piano piazza*), Latin *locus* 'place' gives It. *luogo*, but *focus* gives
fuoco (Sp. *luego fuego*). The two Slavonic palatalizations give different results, and the second has moved velars farther to the front of

the mouth than the first. The faultiest sounds sometimes show astonishing powers of endurance.

One may also notice the relief of tensions, such as those due to
double formation of sounds. Thus *kt* implies a bunching of the
tongue at the back of the mouth against the velum, and at the front
against the teeth or gums. If no vowel is intruded between *k* and
t, there is bound to be a moment when the tongue is attached
at both back and front, and one can understand speakers seeking
relief from this excessive tension. There are three possible ways of
relief: to move the bunched tongue forward to the position of *t*
(It. *otto* 'eight'); to remove the stoppage of air by the velum ($k > h$;
Umbrian *uht*), and move the point of friction forwards as far as the
palate (Fr. *huit*); or to eliminate the velar occlusion and make use
of the similarity of *h* to *f* (*ft*, as in Albanian *truftë* 'trout'), and then
develop a labial occlusion (Rum. *opt*).

Accentuation is another common cause of change. When stress is
heavy, unstressed vowels become obscure. They tend towards the
neutral vowel *ə* as in English or Old French, which may disappear
as in English and French; they lose distinctive qualities of length,
as in Romance or Modern Greek; and the heavy stress destroys
fine gradations of tone, as in Russian. On the other hand, stress
makes the stressed vowel longer than any other, and it may exaggerate its length. The lengthened vowel then tends to split between
its more consonantal beginning and its more vocalic ending and
so develop into a diphthong, as in *lócus > lǫóco > luógo*. The
weakening of feminine *-a* in French to an unpronounced '*e* mute'
has been the cause of numerous gender-shifts which are not
paralleled in Italian or Spanish, where final *-o/a* are regularly
preserved.

In some cases one notes hypertrophy. Rumanian *opt* has passed
the point of enunciation of *t* and produced a new double occlusion.
Spanish *c* [θ] has passed the positions of *e i* in *cero* 'zero'. An object
may be made definite by pointing to it (demonstrative pronoun
developing into an article) or by some specification (by number or
by a possessive pronoun). *Mi patria* 'my country' is definite, but
Ptg. *a minha patria* shows hypertrophy of definition. French *la
vérité* 'truth' shows hypertrophy and so does Coptic *ou-me*. Since
truth is abstract and indivisible, it does not admit definition (*la*) or
particularization (*ou* = 'one' 'an') when considered as a whole,
though there are, of course, particular concrete truths (Sp. *decirle*

a uno las cuatro verdades 'to tell one the four truths = to tell someone off'.) In language, as in other parts of the human story, consequences are often greater than their causes.

Since the drifts persist so uniformly, various efforts have been
made to describe them by one general formula, and among these
the most plausible seems to be that of economy of effort. The
Pekinese have effected such an economy by losing final *p t k m*,
and by tending to reduce *n ng* to nasal resonances—this requiring
less muscular effort from the organs of speech than is required
for Cantonese or was required for the T'ang common speech of
the seventh century. A modern Englishman saves five syllables in
the first four lines of the *Canterbury Tales* by his loss of final *-e*.
As between *laboratory* and the slurred *láb'rat'ry* there is a saving
of two syllables. French has increased the number of front and
middle sounds, vocalic and consonantal, at the expense of back
sounds, economizing movements of the tongue by keeping it more
constantly in the front of the mouth. Slavonic languages have got
rid of many extra-short *i u*-sounds, thus reducing the length of
words. There may be mental economies, such as those which result
from substituting an intelligible auxiliary for a morpheme whose
proper sense is lost. Thus, Lat. *cantabo* 'I shall sing' (though it
contained an auxiliary meaning 'grow' *bhū*) became Romance *cantare habeo > cantar' ae*. French *chanterai*, Sp. *cantaré* is a new
synthesis, but there is still a trace of analysis in Ptg. *cantá-lo-hei*
'I shall sing it'. The passive voice is so purely grammatical that it
has been reconstructed many times. Scandinavian *-s(k)*, Russ. *-sja*,
Romance *se* in some cases and auxiliaries from *esse* in others are
examples of this effort towards mental easement. The notional
moods (subjunctive, optative, jussive, &c.) may lose their finer distinctions and become fused, as in Latin, or eliminated by the help
of auxiliaries. In Old Bulgarian there was a conditional auxiliary
fully conjugated for person (*bimĭ*) which has resulted in a Russian
invariable particle *by*; and it is doubtless easier to say Russ. *ja byl*
'I was' than OBulg. *byl jesmĭ* or Serbian *jesam bil*.

Against these instances of economy of effort we have to set those
of increased tension (It. *piazza* as compared with Lat. *platea*) and
others in which no easement seems to have been obtained (as the
passage of French *r* from the gums to the uvula, and the derivation
of pharyngal Sp. *j* from palatal *x* [š]). Judgements of ease and difficulty are often subjective. Thus French *u* [y] may seem easier than

Latin *ū* to Frenchmen, but not to the English who can never master it. Moreover, though progress may be from a more complex to an ultimately simpler state of language, there are intermediate stages of greatly increased difficulty. Slavonic alternated vowels and consonants in the common age. By eliminating *ĭ ŭ* in alternate syllables individual Slavonic languages created consonant-groups not present in the common tongue, and a great deal of their subsequent development has consisted in smoothing out the harsh collisions thus created. The loss of morphemes in English was not immediately compensated by a reformed syntax, and the Elizabethan Age contains much ambiguous writing. If we agree that *cantare habeo* represents economy of effort in relation to *cantabo* by substituting analysis for synthesis, we can hardly say that *chanterai* is economical for the same reason. If, on the other hand, we hold that the verb is naturally a complex of signs in close momentary association, then the process of analysis itself becomes suspect. It is not simple, but a simplification reached by abstract thinking. Primitive peoples prefer synthesis both of nouns and verbs, since that device shows the subordination of auxiliary notions most clearly. This preference persists, unless defeated by phonetic attrition. Turkish *el-ler-iniz-den* 'hand-s-your-from = from your hands' indicates perfectly the noun and the subordinate qualifiers, and is as lucid in each part as the English phrase. There is no special virtue in order, but the Turkish puts the main concept first. When fusion occurs, as in *manibus*, *rukami*, &c., forms and meanings become indistinct and interchangeable; auxiliaries are used to give more precision, and since the auxiliaries carry the sense, the flexions become otiose and wither.

The need for precision is increasingly felt in highly civilized languages, which therefore show an increasing number of auxiliaries. That is true even of ancient Greek to a large extent, despite its intricate synthetic structure. Order and auxiliary words play at least as important a role as inflexions in Greek, though order may be used most effectively to show the relative importance of words. English, Scandinavian languages, and Persian depend almost wholly on analysis. Wilhelm von Humboldt placed Chinese among the imperfectly developed languages on account of its lack of flexion, and Russian linguists classify it as 'amorphous'. If, however, the resources of Chinese are measured against the demands of civilized intercourse, they will be seen to be at once fully adequate and extremely economical. Whether this results from a steadfast avoidance of the lures of agglutination and flexion or from a process of simplification cannot be determined.[1] Chinese is 'amorphous' only in the sense of not making use of morphemes (flexions and agglutinations), but its formal rules for arrangement are eminently precise. K. Vossler asserted that the most civilized languages substitute syntax for intonation. He had in mind the syntactical expression of emphasis in Fr. *c'est à vous que je parle*, as opposed to the Eng. '*I*'m telling *you*'.

The process of attrition may go so far as to take away the substance of a word, as in the reduction of Latin *apem* 'bee' to *è*, *ef*, and this forces upon a language a task of reconstruction. It may concentrate too much difference of meaning upon too little difference of symbols, as Norwegian *bud* 'order', *bue* 'bow', *buk* 'belly', *bukk* 'buck', *bukke* 'bend', &c. It may create, as in Chinese and English, homonyms which, while not normally inconvenient in a concrete situation, are troublesome in a context and unintelligible alone.

A cause of change may be sought in imperfect imitation, and that in two ways: imperfect reproduction by one generation of the speech of another, and the imperfect acquisition of a language by persons born and brought up in another. The first implies inadvertence, the second some sort of speech-impediment.

Concerning imperfect learning by generations, we have already noted that remote French-speaking communes show dialect-groupings over sixty, over thirty, and under thirty. Despite the overlapping of individual ages, occupations, and responsibilities, readiness to welcome or refuse novelty distinguishes the generations of Laertes, Odysseus, and Telemachus. If we extend our view over the whole nation it is true that people are being born and dying all the time, and the notion of generation is more difficult to accept. Even here, however, a certain character is imposed on a period of years by the leadership of the Odysseus-group, which tends to be associated with reigns. Republics thus date styles of art or manners not by

---

[1] The first and second personal pronouns once had different forms for the nominative and oblique cases. Whether this represents some primitive declensional structure lost even in the earliest recorded Chinese or whether it is an expression of the unlikeness of pronominal agents to pronominal patients (cf. *ego/me, tu/te*) may be debated. The tendency towards declension of an agglutinative sort is notable in Tibetan, but there is little to show in which direction the current of Sino-Tibetan history runs.

their presidents, but by foreign kings: 'Victorian', 'Edwardian', and 'Georgian' are terms with a reasonably fixed value in more languages than English. However, we are not concerned with whole nations when studying the causes of change, but with particularly influential communities. The *wa* pronunciation of *foi* established itself on the initiative of the Parisian populace during the French revolution, though the tendency towards this solution was common in the eighteenth century. Paris, though large, is still a particular community in which division by generations might have reality. The communities from which the major Romance changes took their origin were much smaller than the Paris of the Revolution, e.g. medieval Burgos for the Castilian innovations of the eleventh to thirteenth centuries. There is a tendency of persons within an age-group to copy each other rather than those of another group. Owing to the large tolerance needed in a common speech, such changes go unnoticed or are at any rate accepted as within the prescribed limits. It is to be remarked, however, that changes would occur at random unless there were some principle of authority to determine their drift.

According to Henry Sweet no imitation is perfect, but every linguistic imitation is almost perfect. The first dogma gives a ground for change, the second for its gradual character. Transferring language to new individuals, notably to children, involves imperfect reproduction of sounds. These insignificant aberrations lead to organic readjustments which are consummated as major sound-shifts. The youngest generation also shows wilfulness and virtuosity. A baby practises more sounds than it finally uses in speech, and not all baby-sounds or baby-words are lost. Pet-names and secret family-words are examples of those which survive. The baby-word *atta* 'daddy' has become standard in Russ. *otec* 'father' and Alb. *at*. School-words follow: *nice, jolly, top-hole, A1, wizard*. They kill each other, but not always before they have killed the proper meaning of such a word as *nice*. Children are intolerant of anything outmoded, especially of outmoded slang; but the same fear of censure is found among landsmen at sea, who labour to acquire nautical terms that are of no real use or interest to them. Children also imitate the speech-habits of other children with excessive accuracy, despite parental reproof.[1]

---

[1] O. Jespersen, *Mankind, Language, and Nation*, London, 1946, and *Die Sprache*, Heidelberg, 1925. L. Gauchat noted that instinctive imitation by

When language is transferred to new speakers in the form of adults of another language-group, there is resistance by old prejudices to new usages. Adults, in fact, rarely learn a new language perfectly. Thus, when Latin spread in the Roman empire there was, no doubt, a Gaulish-Latin and an Iberian-Latin, each made up of Vulgar Latin with characteristic local impediments. Romanian would likewise be Daco-Latin. Bulgarian, Albanian, and Romanian may show some Thracian peculiarities (if the postpositive article belonged to the Thracians). The Min tribes may influence the Chinese of Amoy, and so on.

What is lacking in support of these propositions is objective proof. As announced by Graziadio Ascoli, the substratum theory rested chiefly on the supposed speech-impediments of latinized Celts. One could show that *ü* occurred for *u* in Romance areas which had dense Celtic populations (France, N. Italy), and *-it-* for *-ct-* where there were important bodies of Celts (Portugal, Spain, France, N. Italy). The speech-habits of transalpine and cisalpine Celts are not known well enough for these statements to be made on the basis of observations, and the changes alleged are not common to all Celts. Besides, it is clear that only the beginnings of change can have been made in the first period of romanization, and it is in this form that A. Meillet was willing to support the theory.[1] The evolution of *ü* from *u* in France, N. Italy, and Alsace, said Meillet, 'would not be a direct Gaulish survival, but the distant effect of certain acquired habits transmitted by heredity'. This statement seems more mysterious than the original doctrine. Supposing there were a Thracian habit of suffixing the definite article, and that this worked as a distant inheritance in Albanian, Bulgarian, and Rumanian, why should it break out also in the dialects of north Russia? Latins could say *ille phaselus* or *phaselus ille* 'that skiff'. When *ille* was denuded of demonstrative sense and became an article, it had to be assigned a conventional position, either before or after the noun. But the choice was open, just as was the choice between *habeo* (*de*) *cantare* and *cantare habeo* as a Vulgar Latin

children contributed greatly to the spread of new modes of articulation in Charmey, especially because the new sounds were generally (though not always) easier. Children are very ready to correct their parents.

[1] A. Meillet, *La Méthode comparative en linguistique historique*, Oslo, 1925, p. 80. R. Thurneysen and K. Vossler seem to have held similar views. See also W. von Wartburg, *Die Ausgliederung der romanischen Sprachen*, Bern, 1950, pp. 34–50.

future tense. Spanish has opted for *cantaré* 'I shall sing' and *he de cantar* 'I must sing', but Rumanian for *voi cantà*.

The strength of the substratum theory has been our ignorance of the speech-habits of the Gaulish, Iberian, Thracian, and other proposed substrata. To them, therefore, scholars may with impunity impute what habits suit their arguments. The substrata survive in the Basque of the Iberian peninsula and the native languages of America. The indigenes have proved negligible in Canada, the United States, Uruguay, and Argentina, but have remained massively in Mexico, Central America, the Andine states, and Brazil. They have contributed many words to American vocabularies, but have not influenced the development of American speech-sounds or grammar.[1] It is true that the Aztecs at first turned *señora* into *šenola*, for lack of native cacuminal *s*, palatal *ñ*, or vibrant *r*, but they later borrowed *sobrino*, *señas*, and the like. The Guaranies not only have acquired Spanish sounds for Spanish words, but continue to use the alien palatal *ll* [λ], though it has become *y* or some allied sound in the speech of most South Americans of Spanish origin. In some cases native speech-habits may have helped to retain a sound in its older form, but in no instance have they projected a new development.

The Basque substratum exists, but its relation to 'Iberian' is not fully established. It may be taken to be a survival of some form of Iberian. This form lacked *f*. R. Menéndez Pidal has shown that Latin *f* was not correctly reproduced in a narrow strip of territory hard against the Basque border, where there were no Roman schools and where romanization may have been delayed until the end of the Visigothic Era. The primitive Cantabrians used an aspirate *h* as a substitute for *f*, and the aspiration was weak and died away. Thus in special circumstances and where correction was impossible, a local aversion for *f* established itself. It spread slowly to Burgos (twelfth century) and to Toledo (late fifteenth)

---

[1] See R. Lenz in *Zeitschrift für romanische Philologie*, xvii, who argued for the 'Araucanian' origin of features of Chilean Spanish which prove often to be common to all American Spanish (the correction was given by M. L. Wagner in the same periodical, vol. xl, and by R. Menéndez Pidal, 'La unidad del idioma', *Castilla: la tradición, el idioma*, Buenos Aires, 1945). M. A. Morínigo, *Hispanismos en el Guaraní*, Buenos Aires, 1931, shows how the Guaranies acquired the alien sounds *rr f l ll*, and retain *ll* when their Spanish-speaking neighbours have lost it! On Mexican Spanish see *Todd Memorial Volumes*, 1930, vol. i, pp. 85–89. The point has been studied also by the Swedish Romanist, Bertil Malmberg. For Tupi influence upon Brazilian Portuguese see G. Chaves de Melo, *A Língua do Brasil*, Rio de Janeiro, 1946.

and became a Spanish norm in the sixteenth century. An aspirate persisted in Toledo till 1578, when the usage of the saints of Ávila caused its extinction; it continues as a sporadic aspirate in south and south-west Spain. This is no pan-Iberian development, but one due to unique and highly localized causes.

From these examples it appears that conditions affecting speech-change are always complex and cannot be referred to either sub-stratum or superstratum or any other single cause. The difficulties of adults do not affect children, who learn one language as easily as another in the proper milieu. The adult Gauls and Iberians may have had ineradicable defects in their Latin, but it was the business of schoolmasters to bring up boys in the true tradition, and the boys would be quick to correct each other's and their parents' faults. The rhetorical schools of Córdoba were good enough in the first century to support the literature of the Silver Age, and those of Bordeaux produced such elegant latinists as Ausonius. Standards are high when education is not wide. The 'best' South American Spanish is used in the Andine republics where a small number of whites dominate an alien indigenous or mestizo population. When Indians and mestizos, by force of character, thrust themselves to the front, their language is that of their white rivals. In the Plate region the use of Spanish is universal in all the social strata, and its average and norms are much 'lower'. So Iberian Latin may have maintained its high standard down to St. Isidore by relying on a select minority of the nation, whereas Catalonia and Languedoc may have developed a more popular style from the number of legionaries settled in them as pensioners. When Iberian Latin began to reach the Spanish rural communities it was still highly conservative, and the whole development of the language is rather less than that of French in the earliest French documents.

On the other hand, though education is conservative, it is also a mental adventure. There is a new scholarly vocabulary to acquire, several varieties of professional jargons, the appropriate slang of the school, &c. In optimistic ages like the Renaissance novelty is welcome; new objects and new ideas require new words and there seems even a quickening of phonetic changes. The most cultured nations are often those which, like English, French, or Chinese, show the quickest phonetic development. A community denied its cultural outlet, like the Christian subjects of the Andalusian ca-liphs, is halted in its linguistic development. Under the unvarying conditions of the steppe and desert, the Arabs and Turks show remarkably little evolution, whereas the skill needed for their livelihood is matched by the skilful structure of their languages.

The Spanish of the Americas is rich in documents concerning racial fusion. Though the standard language is virtually unaffected by the substratum, outside its vocabulary of local objects and customs, the collision of the two tongues in rural districts produces very complex patterns.[1] A huge influx of Italian workers into the Argentine produces the hybrid Italo-Spanish called *cocoliche*. The colony is large enough in Buenos Aires to have a certain corporate spirit. Yet, on examination, *cocoliche* proves to be no one dialect, but simply a process of shedding Italian and acquiring Spanish locutions by adult immigrants. The process goes on continuously for each individual, though it may not actually reach an end; the Spanish of their children is that of their neighbours. Similarly, American English is a form of English; the 'melting-pot' of races does not produce a linguistic hybrid.

The Cantabrian *h* for *f*, however, is a reminder that, for special reasons, the influence of schools may not be effective, and errors of the parents may be perpetuated by their children. Another complex of highly specialized reasons caused the reunification of the Peninsula to proceed from Cantabria in a fan-shaped extension. The prestige of Castile carried its local peculiarities (originally defects of speech) over reconquered Spain and conquered America.

The case has also to be envisaged when both schools and the social structure collapse. The irruption of the Moslems caused such a collapse in western Europe. Spain was disorganized not only by the conquest of 711, which destroyed its latinity and reduced its speech to a vernacular without prestige, but also the collapse of the Christian *imperium* of León in the tenth century. The language of the Leonese chancery was as conservative as could be suited to general understanding of documents. With the collapse of this hesitant standard, room was found for the more radical forms evolved in what had been an obscure eastern frontier. When the Mediterranean was closed to Christian shipping, French life suffered a paroxysm and emerged under Charlemagne reorientated. It came to be poised on the pivot of Paris, instead of Lyons–Marseilles, and the more radical, less scholarly language of the north became dominant.

[1] T. Navarro Tomás, *El Español en Puerto Rico*, Puerto Rico, 1948.

'The King's English', 'B.B.C. English', 'the Oxford accent', *Bühnenausdruck, Español correcto*, 'Mandarin' show that the members of a community seek to conform to some style of utterance that has authority. We are always correcting our diction from persons we esteem better informed than ourselves or from the dictionary when a doubt arises. Parkman, in *The Oregon Trail*, mentions American Indians famous for their eloquence, and Africans display the qualities of their language to critical audiences at palavers. There is no kind of society in which some few exponents do not serve as models to the mass, whether for conservation or for innovation. There is thus discipline from above, unless in times of chaos. But what is 'above' is not always the same thing. In viceregal society at Lima or Mexico City the language of the court had high prestige, the more so since the governing group was surrounded by a minority of rich landowners and a majority of Indian-speaking aliens. But in the Plate region the colonist managed his own herds and was a man of his hands. This was no place for courtly formulas but for broad country terms, and the Spanish of the Argentine, Uruguay, and Chile shows the effect of preferences for 'vulgarity'.[1] When the problem is to wrest a livelihood from unbroken ground, the man to admire is the man of his hands. At sea the admirable man and momentary superior is the sailor, who is in his element, and in a camp the old soldier's habits and expressions are copied and collected by recruits. Cervantes has given a lively picture of the acquisitions made by a student from Salamanca who was suddenly transferred to the armies in Italy. There is (if we consider 'the Oxford accent' which is so little known in Oxford) even a possibility that a certain pattern of speech be avoided when talking to the plain man, lest it seem snobbish. Indeed, all of us talk on different levels according to our audience, and a revolution may place any one of these levels on top. To its overweening bureaucracy contemporary Russia owes its considerable lexicon of bureaucratic abbreviations, such as *komsomol, gosizdat, K.S.K.*, or *K.S.U.*; and any war inundates Great Britain with initials and *V.I.P.*s. We are wrong to talk down to some audiences and to talk over the heads of others; and when we do so we are asked why we cannot say plainly what we mean—as if there were one single, simple rule.

[1] A. Alonso, *El Problema argentino de la Lengua*, Buenos Aires, 1935 (esp. p. 88 'Desvalorización de las normas'); A. Castro, *La Peculiaridad lingüística rioplatense*, Buenos Aires, 1940.

The fall of the Roman empire and the rise of the different Romance languages witnessed the collapse of a language into chaos and the reorganization of others from its ruins. Loss of control is shown in numerous personal and local initiatives, but these seem at first to work at random. A test made upon the language of Hispano-Roman stonemasons[1] reveals precocious anticipations of conditions general in Spain only at much later dates alongside developments which point to French (*auncolo/oncle, serori/* OFr. *seror, nepota/* Prov. Cat. *neboda*) or Italian (*iscolasticus*), but not to Spanish. Of course, we do not know the histories of individual masons, who may not have been Iberians, and it is hard to distinguish mere blundering from intentional effects. Another sign of loss of control is the croaking of grammarians such as Probus, with their everlasting 'don't's: *speculum non speclum, oculus non oclus, tabula non tabla, sibilus non sifilus, pusillus non pisinnus, olim non oli,* &c. The consequences are again random developments. Italian has *tavola* 'table', *sibilo* 'hiss', Sp. *silbo*, but Fr. *sifflet* (with the censured pronunciation). On the other hand, It. *occhio* 'eye', *orecchia* 'ear', and *specchio* 'mirror' are all developments of vulgar pronunciation. Neither *pusillus* nor *pisinnus* have modern progeny in the sense 'small': It. *piccolo*, Sp. *pequeño*, Fr. *petit*. Neither *olim* nor *oli* now exists. With the failure of central control the interests of communities contract and the *villa*, the diocese, or some other temporarily coherent unit covers the bare needs of living. Dialects begin to abound, since speakers have only a limited interest in wider communication. The standard language becomes irrelevant, and may even take on a high, brittle polish as in the poetry of Claudian. It must have been when the new Romance languages began to form that a definite direction was given to change, just as, when a magnet is applied, needles rearrange themselves in one direction. Some centres became more influential than others. In France there was the Île-de-France in the north, and Limoges, Toulouse, or Arles in the south. In Italy, Naples and Palermo in the south, Rome in the centre (but overshadowed by Papal insistence on good standards of Latin), Florence, and Bologna have all played their part. Dante advocated a generalized Tuscan such as he found in use in Bologna, i.e. Florentine stripped of exclusively Florentine characteristics. The lead in Spain was first taken by Cordoba and the Mozarabic dialect, then by León and Leonese,

---

[1] A. Carnoy, *Le Latin d'Espagne d'après les inscriptions*, 1906.

and finally by Burgos and Castilian. Notaries of the tenth century required a kind of Latin which could be understood without Latin apprenticeship, but they tolerated wide vagaries of pronunciation and orthography. The rise of literature introduced more definite standards, but so long as it was mostly heard by the auditors of a reader or reciter there was no insistence on single solutions for each development. Medieval manuscripts in Spanish show admixture of other dialects in the Castilian. Printed books (as Caxton knew) and the habit of reading led to a stricter regulation of usage for literary purposes, but to regulate the forms of common intercourse Europe had to wait until the Age of Steam.

A question arises whether sound-changes take place gradually or abruptly. This inquiry is not necessarily affected by the fact that substitutions (necessarily abrupt) are a common feature of language-change as affecting individuals. The strangest case seems to have been that of the Kamassi tribe of Samoyedes, who dropped their own language and learned a Turkic dialect in 1840, and had forgotten Samoyede by 1860: in 1890 they dropped their new tongue and began to speak Russian—two complete language-shifts in a lifetime.[1] In Missouri one says *Americy, Nevady, Arizony*, but the half-educated say *America, Nevada, Arizona*, and go on to *Missoura* and *praira!*[2] These are conscious modifications like other 'corrections' we apply to our speech, but whether they are conservative or evolutionary we do not know or care. They are characterized by will to conform with what we suppose to be the standard or best mode. Nor must we overlook the fact that speeds of change are very different for different languages, and that there are some, such as the Turanian group, for which reconstructed original forms can usually be found still living in some dialect. Sound-shifts have also a different history for each word or each phenomenon. When all that has been allowed for, we may still ask whether it is the nature of these drifts to be gradual and imperceptible or catastrophic.

Older scholars have preferred to think of them as unperceived and so escaping correction until their effects have accumulated and amount to a considerable difference. The passage from *cantare* to *chanter* involves (apart from the silencing of final *r*) the series $k > k' > č > š$ and $a > ä > \epsilon > e$. The second series is vocalic and may have had many minor nuances. L. Gauchat observed the

---

[1] J. Deny, in *Les Langues du monde*, Paris, 1923, p. 187.

[2] E. H. Sturtevant, *Linguistic Change*, New York, 1942, p. 79.

series $a > a\cdot > ao$ completed in three generations. But three generations, compared with the whole history of the French language, may be regarded as 'catastrophic'. On the other hand a decade constitutes unrememberable time for an individual. Latin k seems to have had a palatal nuance [k'] before the end of the empire in *ce ci*. The evolution of *ca* to *cha* dates from after the separation of Provençal from northern French. The stage *ča-* was normal in the sixteenth century but had been reached in the eleventh. The development does not seem to have been uniform but to have been spurred forward at certain times and relatively quiescent at others. The coincidence of several changes in Spanish sibilants between about 1530 and 1570 produced a sharp division between medieval and modern Spanish, and the case for a similar coincidence of revolutionary changes in Merovingian France is made by H. Muller.[1] Mandarin Chinese makes an abrupt appearance with the coming of the Mongols in the thirteenth century, when, one presumes, these strangers gave free course to changes which the T'angs and Sungs had continued to resist, at least in educated speech. From the thirteenth century, however, Mandarin seems to have reduced its rate of development. One is aware of similarly abrupt reorganizations of English at the opening of the Elizabethan Age and in the lifetime of Dryden, while Russian was reformed between the dates of Lomonosov and Pushkin (three-quarters of a century). Since language is not geology or biology, but history, we have to make a place for cataclysmic effects measured by one or two generations and not assume an imperceptibly slow gradation of change. As we have seen, speakers are capable of accepting as one phoneme—one unit of linguistic structure—sounds which are phonetically quite distinct. They do not judge as phoneticians but according to their instinct for the system. If required to listen to two such sounds in isolation they are capable of hearing a difference, but in the business of expressing themselves by sound-symbols they systematically ignore some great dissimilarities. Hence, it is not necessary to suppose that sound-shifts take place by degrees imperceptible to the human ear. Unawareness of change may be explained by systematic indifference, and by the extreme shortness of human memories concerning their own speech-habits.

[1] H. Muller, *The Chronology of Vulgar Latin* (*Zeitschrift für romanische Philologie*, suppl. 79).

THERAPEUTICS

The action of the mind in speech is probably much the same as in movement. It develops a routine and functions as if automatically, but at any moment it may resume active control, halt a motion, alter a direction or speed up a change. While we are for the most part either inadvertent or else willing to conform in our speech-habits, especially in respect of speech-sounds and grammatical devices which have no intrinsic value, there come times when a positive decision of some kind is required if some foreseen mischance is not to occur or if some imagined gain is to be made. The general effect of sound-laws seems to be one of attrition. Gilliéron therefore described as 'therapeutics' the measures taken to prevent the uttermost consequences of attrition. Since sound-laws wear down *apis* 'bee' to *ef* or *è*, remedial measures include the use of *ep* (*guêpe* 'wasp') in *mouche-ep*, the substitution of *-ette* for the unintelligible *ep* in *mouchette*, and the paraphrase *mouche-à-miel* to avoid the absurdity of calling a bee a 'little fly'. In addition there is the Provençal loan-word *abeille* in the literary language. Latin *diis* and *filiis* may be both masculine and feminine. The first is an inconvenience when one aims at placating gods and goddesses, since the latter are not specifically acknowledged. Demosthenes could say τοῖς θεοῖς εὔχομαι πᾶσι καὶ πάσαις 'I pray all gods and goddesses', but the Latin *omnibus diis* does not resolve the ambiguity. Hence the formula *diis et deabus* for liturgical use and *filiis et filiabus* for legal purposes. It is not sufficient to say that *deabus* and *filiabus* are formed on the analogy of dative and ablative cases in *-bus* in the third, fourth, and fifth declensions. The resource existed but was consciously used to meet a specific need.

Analogy, of course, plays its part. The speaker is instinctively aware of similarities of sound or of meaning which bring words together in his mind (like rhymes in the mind of a poet), and from their conjunction he creates something not wholly new; something which rather seems to him to exist among the possibilities of his language. Likeness of sound in *diebus* might help to suggest *deabus*, but there is also the sense that *-bus* is a possible means of indicating dative-ablative plurals, and there is the specific intellectual need for mentioning both gods and goddesses. Without this last cause there would be no need to bring the analogy into play. Similarly, when Lat. *fidem* had given Sp. *fe* 'faith', a further reduction to *he* or *e* would have destroyed the substantiality of the word. *Fe* was halted with its un-Castilian *f*, with some help from the liturgy as heard daily, and with analogical support of other words with *f* (such as *fiesta* 'festival', *fiel* 'faithful'). *Fidelem* > *fiel* retained its *f* to avoid collision with *fel* > *hiel* 'poison', but the expected *h* of *fiesta* appears in the derivative *infestum* > *inhiesto* 'hostile'—a word which can have no mental associations with *fe, fiel, fiesta*.

The retention of the neuter in Slavonic must be a fact of this kind. Formal analogy offers only a feeble support. Since IE. **-os* **-om* both gave Slav. *-ŭ*, masculines and neuters were about to be confused and masculine agents and patients became indistinguishable. The common Slavonic instinct, whether a general feeling or originating in some individual or group, refused to surrender its neuters. The demonstrative happened to offer masc. *tŭ* neut. *to*, and this made possible the reconstructed neuter in *-o*: *tŭ rabŭ* 'that slave'/*to lěto* 'that summer'. As for masculine nouns nothing is lost by a confusion of nominative and accusative for things, since things are properly patients of any activity and can only be used in the nominative as a kind of metaphor. But for masculine persons it is important to know whether 'Peter robs Paul' or 'Paul robs Peter'. There being no formal order of discourse, this distinction had to be effected by a case. Masculine singular patients came to be expressed in the genitive singular; later this method spread to the plural also. The genitive may have been thought of as partitive; the living patient is partly affected by the verbal activity. Owing to the one attrition **-os *-om* > *-ŭ* two therapeutic reactions arose, the one designed to conserve the neuter gender (though it had no specific mental content) and the other to continue to distinguish personal agents from patients. A somewhat similar reintroduction of a gender (the feminine) is now in progress in Norwegian. We are told the motives. There exists a distinction between masculine *-en* and feminine *-a* in western dialects, as opposed to the common gender *-en* of the capital. At present the common gender with article *-en* is used for all but about fifty words, which are held to be more Norwegian if construed with *-a*. There are obligatory and optional feminines, and one competent grammarian merely says 'we use *-a* in many words, especially in concrete words of daily life: *klokka døra lia*'.[1] The ruling is alogical rather than illogical, and is such as a living linguistic prejudice should be. The concrete

[1] S. W. Hofgaard, *Norsk Skolegrammatik*, Oslo, 1939.

feminines are very familiar words with which it is instinctive to associate the spoken -*a*. The remaining feminines are less familiar, and the speaker's instinct does not urge him to oppose for them the common gender in -*en*. Yet genders are now a completely useless burden on language and many European languages have sacrificed one of them without regret. Where gender or case is formally recorded, it is notable that the singular is more precisely distinguished than the plural.

One may discern a mental attitude in the observance as well as the evasion of a rule. A characteristic feature of Slavonic linguistic history has been the series of palatalizations. The instinct to divide speech-sounds into parallel series of 'hard' (normal) and 'soft' (palatal) sounds has come into operation at different epochs with strikingly similar results. The palatal series continually tends towards autonomy and so become normal or 'hard'. For the future of such a language as Yugoslav, in which all sounds are normal or 'hard', one can make no predictions, but in the Slavonic past one can discern a tendency to affirm the parallelism of the alphabet by new palatalizations. In Gaelic there is a similar insistence upon the parallelism of 'broad' and 'slender' consonants, the latter being palatalized. In thirteenth-century Spain it was necessary to reaffirm the trochaic rhythm of the language, threatened by the loss of final vowels in the twelfth century; many final vowels were restored by analogy and the help of conservative dialects.

Other examples of intervention can be cited. Fr. *aimer* 'love' and *esmer* 'estimate' became identical in sound; the difference was restored by using the latinism *estimer*. Lat. *hedera* 'ivy' should give *ierre*, but more substance was obtained by agglutinating the article, *lierre*. The final consonants of *cinq sept neuf* are being strengthened at present to avoid excessive attrition.[1] Latin *sitim* 'thirst' should give **soi*, but there are also *soi* 'self', *soie* 'silk' and *soit* 'so be it', all pronounced [swa]. In the central regions *soif* [swaf] is spreading without any historical justification and with the help of only the most distant analogies (*clef bœuf suif*), because the distinction is convenient. In all languages the transactions of very little verbs (be, have, do, give, come, go, know, &c.) are very complex. They preserve some very old forms such as Slav. *vědě-* Gk. οἶδα, a unique Indo-European perfect in the Slavonic group. They interfere with each other, and they suffer so much attrition as to need

---

[1] A. Dauzat, *La Géographie linguistique*, Paris, 1922, p. 99.

constant repair: Russ. *dajú* 'I give' for OBulg. *damĭ*, Fr. *je donne*
for Lat. *do*. Sp. *so* < *sum* 'I am' agglutinated the adverb *y* < *ibi*
either to gain more body or to mark the verb off from the old masc.
so 'his'; from *soy* come *doy*, *estoy*, *voy*. The modern equivalents of
Lat. *habeo/sapio*, *teneo/venio* interfere with each other, though not
over the whole conjugation.

It is possible for speakers to adopt a certain mental posture to
their whole language. The Berbers, we are told, rarely write and
then only with reluctance. 'The Kabyle tongue, they say, is spoken
but not written.'[1] A purely spoken language has more fluidity and
variety than a written one, and the Kabyle, priding themselves on
this fluidity, use Arabic letters each according to his own taste and
write what the recipient is unable to interpret. A Portuguese scholar
has spoken of expressing one's originality in spelling, and the notion
has proved attractive to both Milton and Bridges! Similarly, a
Bantu dialect is said to become something different in the act of
being written down. Its only native usefulness is in oral communication, and in this function it is conspicuous for 'its richness, flexi-
bility, expressiveness, and present living power of forming at will
and selecting suitable forms for the embodiment of new general
ideas and new objects, as well as of varieties and refinements of
those already existing'.[2] On the other hand a highly literate community impresses its literacy upon its spoken words, is shy of new
inventions, seeks precise turns of phrase, and fills out the context
of the spoken sentence so as to eliminate dependence on the concrete circumstances, on gestures, or other extraneous aids to understanding. A second sense can be built up behind the first by means
of literary allusions, to the extent that Chinese mandarins are said
to have been able to converse in allusions to the complete exclusion
of intelligent strangers who have been able to follow the obvious
meaning of the words. Without such intricate refinements, Dante's
ideal for Italian was a *volgare illustre*; not merely a common tongue
to override the dialectal differences of Italy, but an elegant and
illustrious tongue in all communications—'cleansed, fixed and
splendid', as the Spanish Academy later defined the ideal.

[1] A. Hanoteau, *Essai de grammaire kabyle*, Algiers–Paris, 1858, p. 2.
[2] A. C. Madan, *Living Speech in Central and South Africa*, Oxford, 1911, p. 9.

III

TECHNIQUES

For half a century after its first appearance in print Hermann Paul's *Prinzipien der Sprachgeschichte* (1880, 5th ed., 1920)[1] continued to be the vade-mecum of the philologist. Paul harvested the 'methodological gains' of the previous fifty years, and formulated for investigators a 'Prinzipienlehre' or body of dogmas which gave a particular shape to their collectanea. He opposed the History of Language to 'mere' descriptive grammar, and formally excluded from the category of a science any method that was not historical. His basis of experience was Indo-European, and within that field it was predominantly Germanic. Noting that there is no direct communion of minds Paul insisted upon the physical side of speech, and within this area he concentrated upon speech-sounds. Speech being a continuum of infinitely many sounds, the speaker has a sense of movement but no consciousness of individual elements of sound, and a sound-shift is uniform for all similarly conditioned instances within one and the same dialect. The sound-law, however, though working without exceptions other than those caused by analogy, was considered by him to be an historical summary, not a forward-looking law of cause and effect. Analogical pictures of the speech-process must be rejected. Our knowledge is the more scientific in proportion as it treats the activity of single factors in isolation. The true object of the linguist's study is the general manifestation of the activity of speaking rather than the effect of individuals upon each other; and the primary cause of change is the speech-activity itself.

In the same year (1880) there appeared the second edition of Wilhelm von Humboldt's *Über die Verschiedenheit des menschlichen Sprachbaues*. For von Humboldt the linguist's task was an open-minded inquiry into the nature of Language for which the evidence of the most diverse types was solicited; for Paul it was the application of a technique to a specialized field. Technique is a

[1] Priority in stating the views of the Young Grammarians may be claimed for W. D. Whitney (*Language and the Study of Language*, 1867; *Life and Growth of Language*, 1874). His work in English was, however, eccentric in an age dominated by German philologists.

methodological gain, a tool hardened and tempered, made from once lively thoughts, but capable of multiplying the results for which it is efficient. Languages were rapidly dismantled. Their constituent elements (especially of sound and form) were identified, traced as far back as records permit, and codified in historical grammars. Any intelligent person, using the method, could obtain results, and an immense pile of facts concerning languages was gathered and sifted, but not put together again. The historical investigation of single elements seen in isolation did not produce a picture of a language as it is or was. The language itself—the almost complete pattern of correspondences which makes communication possible—died on the operating table.

The notion of scientific discipline is uppermost in the title of Ferdinand de Saussure's *Cours de linguistique générale* (2 ed., 1922) and the word 'linguistique' (*anglice* 'philology', as in the encyclopedias) was normally employed by the great Antoine Meillet, for a couple of decades the moderator of linguistic debates in Europe. But in the last quarter of a century, and especially in the last ten years, books have been multiplying under the pens of both linguists and philosophers in which the title-word is *Language*. This is so even when the author's purpose has been to teach a technique or a doctrine, but it seems to be a symptom of the return of philology to the area of open discussion. The subject-matter of Language is more important than the techniques which, at any time, fill the tool-chest of Linguistics. New techniques have arisen (dialect geography, words and things, idealistic philology, synchronic description) which have proved the old definition of the linguist's function to be unduly narrow. The linguist's attention, like that of the philosopher, has been 'called to the curious fact of language', and both the philosopher and the linguist have reached a new awareness of the astonishing resourcefulness of human speech and a new desire to learn, without preconceived ideas, how it functions in the circumstantial world of phenomena. The title 'Language', with more or less additional matter, has been used by scholars as diverse as J. Vendryes, O. Jespersen, E. Sapir, L. Bloomfield, L. H. Gray, F. Bodmer, Louise Homburger, A. Sommerfelt, M. Pei, and Sir A. H. Gardiner. Their expositions differ widely in contents and exposition and offer no single doctrine. Anyone who deals with language is forced to frame some system of general ideas on the basis of his own experience, and the diversity of experiences leads to diversity of treatment. Each writer has his own perspective and experience of Language, and Language itself is greater than all.

LANGUAGE AND SPEECH

Can an activity which differs from place to place, from person to person, and from one set of circumstances to another be the object of a study which yields a regular doctrine? It was to get over this difficulty that Ferdinand de Saussure classified terms as follows:

$$\text{Langage} \begin{cases} \text{Langue} \\ \text{Parole.} \end{cases}$$

Langage is an abstract term covering all aspects of the human speech-activity. It is divided into *langue*, namely, each and every system of sound-symbols used in communication and independent of the volition of individual speakers, and *parole*, the individual act of will and intelligence. 'La linguistique a pour unique et véritable objet la langue envisagée en elle-même et pour elle-même.' It is, nevertheless, possible to have a chapter-heading 'Linguistique de la langue et linguistique de la parole'. The uniqueness of *langue* as an object of linguistic study seems thus to be denied at the same time as it is asserted. Everyone knows there are Homeric dictionaries and Homeric grammars, and similar treatments of Shakespeare, Camoens, and others. The speech of the individual is, as Jespersen pointed out, not governed by his untrammelled will or intelligence, but socially conditioned. *Ego* can only use those symbols which *tu* can understand or can be brought to understand from their context. On the other hand, the role of the individual in shaping language is very considerable, even if infinite numbers of innovations are lost. Further, language only exists when spoken, and when unspoken it is not actual but potential, *posse* not *esse*. This potentiality arises from actual speaking. 'Nothing exists in language which has not previously existed in speech.'

The principal effect of the Saussurean distinction has been to make linguistics (or, as we say, philology) a science closed upon itself. It is a system of self-consistent reasonings, sufficient unto itself and independent from any other division of knowledge. By comparison of the Romance languages we reach a linguistic system which we may call 'Romance'. It is a convenient check upon our inferences concerning this 'Romance' that Latin should be a fully recorded system, but that fact does not affect the self-consistent validity of the inferences. By comparing Indo-European languages we attain Indo-European. From our standpoint Indo-European is a term applicable to some community (*masse parlante*), if the heads of inference happen to have been contemporary in fact. If they were not contemporary in fact, the premisses continue to be valid for their conclusions. From linguistic evidence only linguistic consequences can be inferred. The linguist's sphere is sharply defined and autonomous.

Of course, it may happen that linguistic and other evidence are found entangled. The linguist may only say within the bounds of his science that *canoe* is an Arawak loan-word in European languages. It is a fact, however, that *canoe* came back with Columbus from his first voyage of discovery, and the preponderant importance of Arawak loan-words among Americana is due to the historical course of the discoveries. Even purely linguistic affirmations do not always lack correlations. If we assert that Common Slavonic lacked terms of social organization above village level, made no use of hieratic compound words apart from personal names, and had a singularly rich and uniform agricultural vocabulary, it is scarcely possible that these three statements should fail to describe a particular kind of community. It implies a society, for instance—very unlike the Vedic, with its insistence on religion and kingship and its organization for war. Where other correlations are unknown or insecure, the self-sufficiency of linguistic arguments is an important asset. But language is a social activity, linked to other social manifestations, and correlations must be made when they can. There is a risk involved in the attempt to pursue philology as an abstraction, above and independent of humanity.

By an accident of language the three French key-words answer to two in German and English. In German one may add an artificial *das Sprechen* to *Sprache* and *Rede*. In English the obligatory terms are *Speech and Language*.[1] '*Speech* is a universally exerted activity, having at first definitely utilitarian aims. In describing this activity, we shall discover that it consists in the application of a universally possessed science, namely the science which we call *language*.' Thus *speech* includes both *langage* and *parole*, while *langue* is *language*. But *language* does not have the singularity of *langue*, which was defined as each and every system of communication by sound-symbols; it is used in a universal way. The investigator's problem,

[1] A. H. Gardiner, *Speech and Language*, Oxford, 1932 (1951).

according to Sir A. H. Gardiner, is to discover 'How language enters into speech', and he himself is a 'theorist of speech'.

A later attempt to state this dichotomy brings the poles still closer together. According to G. Devoto *lingua* bears the name of the community which recognizes it, and within which the individual finds a guide and a means of effusion, but *linguaggio* carries the name of the person who has shaped it (as *il linguaggio di Dante*). He relies further on a distinction between 'institution' and 'instrument', the difference being mainly one of perspective. What we have to deal with is simultaneously *speech* and *language*, though we may view it at one time as a recognized system of symbols, at another as symbols in use for some end. In an actual investigation, as T. Navarro has pointed out with regard to the Spanish of Puerto Rico, it is not always possible to know whether a usage belongs to an individual or is part of the common fund. Between 'individual language' and 'collective language' the line of division cannot always be traced. How much Homeric Greek is Greek, and how much is Homeric? And what Homer had once said became the common property of all Greeks, though there were certain conventions about the use of Homeric terms. What had once been the personal style of Homer became a 'vertical' dialect of Greek, viz. that which was used upon the epic level. The creations of Pindar are more specifically Pindaric, but his basic dialect and his formulas became those of the choric song.

HISTORY AND LINGUISTIC PATTERN

Hermann Paul, as we have noted, distinguished the history of Language from 'mere' description, and asserted that only the former had a scientific value. Wundt attacked this principle of *Historismus* and proposed to base the study of language upon folk-psychology, but that notion is, apart from individual psychology, a myth. Another criticism starts from the standpoint of language as creation and will have to be discussed later, since it goes so far as to affirm that 'that science which considers the conditioned, practical, and technical (that is, the non-aesthetic, non-artistic, non-linguistic) aspect of language no longer merits the title of Linguistics'.[1] Less

---

[1] K. Vossler, *Positivismo e Idealismo nella Scienza del Linguaggio*, Ital. transl. T. Gnoli, 1908, p. 148. L. Spitzer holds that historical analysis is no more than a preparation for the study of Language, but he admits the soundness of the method so far as it goes.

drastic is the view of Ferdinand de Saussure which distinguishes two legitimate methods of approach to *Langue*, i.e. to the non-individual aspect of *Langage*. The one is historical (*diachronique*), the other is a synthesis either in present or some past moment of time (*synchronique*). Both approaches are scientific. There is a science of evolution which might be called *linguistique évolutive*, and a science of states which might be called *linguistique statique*. In both cases, in his view, the material is reliably objective, since neither the evolution nor the states suffer from the vagaries of individual speech (*parole*). What the synchronic method reveals is a *system* of communication by sound-symbols constituting a given language at a given time. As a result of evolutionary changes the elements constituting the system may change, but the significant pattern that arises out of their relations does not change. The two studies are radically unlike, because diachronic changes occur 'outside all intention', while the synchronic system is always 'significant'. The latter relates indissolubly two or more terms (such as *Gast/Gäste*), whereas for the emergence of a new diachronic form (*Gäste*) it is necessary for the older form (*gasti*) to vacate the needed room.

It has been held that languages are 'perfect' systems or at least completely self-consistent (*où tout se tient*). It is not easy to see how these appreciations are justified. A language consists of actualities and possibilities, and what the possibilities may be, who can judge? It is a weakness of Turkish, we have been told,[1] that it cannot form compound nouns. To vary a basic concept, especially an abstract one, it resorts to borrowing from Arabic. In Arabic the seventy triconsonantal noun-patterns afford more than sufficient devices for meeting such needs. Actually languages have to be recruited to meet new demands, so that there is often a sense of the lag between words and thought. There are redundancies in language systems. Neither number nor gender are necessary, and cases are too few to express the many relations between parts of the sentence and too numerous not to constitute a burden. It is far from established that diachronic changes occur 'en dehors de toute intention'. No doubt few speakers deliberately make a change in the system of their language, but it is hard to accept the view that systems do not slowly change. What once had a function may become a routine and then be eliminated. The Bantu classes, for instance, are distinct in their

---

[1] 'Turkish language', *Chambers's Encyclopaedia*, 1950.

singular and plural prefixes, but there is a tendency for *ma-* to spread as a common denominator of the plural. The distinctions of animate/inanimate and masculine/feminine were, perhaps, once windows on the world. Now they are confusing routines. It does not seem to be certain, therefore, that the passing of one element is compensated by the rise of another in such a way that the system remains unchanged. Within any given system there are broken arcs of former systems, not fully worked into the new design.

Both synchronism and diachronism are chronic, i.e. refer to time. Of a language with slow evolution, like Finnish, it may be possible to give a strictly synchronic account,[1] but it is less easy in a more rapidly moving tongue. The Latin pluperfect indicative (*cantaveram/-aram*), used in conditional contexts, became a doublet of the pluperfect subjunctive (*cantavissem/-assem*) in Spanish, but remained indicative in Galician and Portuguese. In the last fifty years a number of talented Galician authors have partially reintroduced this value in Castilian literary writings. On the other hand the conflict between *-ara* and *-ase* continues with fluctuating fortunes. The whole situation in present time can hardly be explained without some mention of, at least, the immediate past.

On the other hand, the diachronic exposition progresses from one state of rest to another. The second is the state of the language when the exposition ends, whether in Classical Latin or contemporary French, or at any other moment. But the starting-point is also a state, real or theoretical. The Romance languages go back to Vulgar Latin in theory; in fact their descent is traced from the Latin of the Ciceronian and Augustan Ages, which is a fully documented linguistic system in its literary aspect. The vulgar speech is glimpsed beneath the literary tongue. Similarly, the Indo-European languages are traced back to Indo-European. Our heads of inference are probably not contemporary, but in the immense perspective and in respect of their consequences, they may be assumed to form a pattern. One investigates the shifts from

$$
\begin{array}{llll}
\text{IE.} & p & t & k \\
& b & d & g \\
& bh & dh & gh, \text{&c.,}
\end{array}
\qquad
\begin{array}{lll}
\text{to Eng.} f & th & h \\
p & t & k \\
b & d & g, \text{&c.,}
\end{array}
$$

that is, from one set of correspondences to another. But though each position on these lists has been filled with a modern equiva-

---

[1] Cf. A. Sauvageot, *Esquisse de la langue finnoise*, Paris, 1949.

lent, the second system of sounds differs from the first in being unevenly spread over the mouth and in containing fricatives (*f th h*) unknown to the parent tongue. If we complete the English system of speech-sounds we find even greater divergence from the evenly distributed Indo-European system of occlusives, sonants (*m n l r*) and one sibilant (*s*). The change of system is still more marked in English grammar.

Not only the beginning and end of a language's history lie in systems, but also every intervening moment. The synchronic and diachronic perspectives must be used together,[1] if some part of the evidence is not to be veiled. But speech only allows us to say one thing at a time. In describing the growth of a language we must speak at one time about its successive features, at another about their simultaneity. Fortunately, development is not uniform, and we can conveniently carry a narrative of successive events to some date at which we review the general state attained. The history, then, alternates its perspectives, now diachronic, now synchronic.[2]

According to Paul's definition, phenomena are more scientifically determined when each single feature is reviewed in isolation. If we do so, language as a system is completely disrupted and we have only a mass of isolated observations. This mass may be called Historical Grammar, since the phrase appears on the title-pages of many classic examples of the isolating method. It will then be formally opposed to the History of a Language (G. Devoto)[3] which seeks to carry forward the account of the whole language in one evolutionary surge. Instead of alternating perspectives by calling a halt now and again for review, the analytical and isolating method will appear in one treatise, and the associative method in another. The latter will presume that the reader has already mastered the former; the second writer will take a good deal for granted, but will also add associations with other aspects of human evolution as occasion offers. The convergence of the Italic dialects upon Latin, for instance, is associated with the Roman hegemony in central and southern Italy when one considers the History of the Latin Language; but the writer of an Historical Latin Grammar will be

---

[1] W. von Wartburg, *Problèmes et méthodes de la linguistique*, Paris, 1946, p. 11.

[2] See W. von Wartburg's treatment of French in *Évolution et structure de la langue française*, Leipzig, 1937.

[3] G. Devoto, 'Una introduzione alla storia linguistica', *Archivio Glottologico Italiano*, xxxv, 1950, exemplified in his *Storia della Lingua di Roma*, Bologna, 1940.

at pains to weed Italic elements out of the authentic Latin tradition.

The notion of language as system leads to the formulation of rules for linguistic analysis.[1] Any language may be viewed from without and its features systematically arranged under the headings 'Phonetics', 'Phonemics', 'Morphology', and 'Syntax'. This is a technique which requires the presence of two parties—a trained linguist and an informant. It is not supposed that the linguist knows the language or that the informant is philologically trained, but the business of the former is to elicit from the informant facts and place them in their proper place in the analytical scheme. The resultant grammars have the great convenience of following an almost identical course and being comparable paragraph by paragraph. They are strictly synchronic, of course, since they rely on the testimony of one or a few individuals, and they aim at building up a logically intelligible pattern. But the question arises whether a language looks the same from without as from within? Is an objective analysis entirely reliable? Does it correspond to what the speakers expect their words to effect for them? The investigator is logically trained. The community from which the informant springs may be magically minded. Is it not, then, necessary first to penetrate as far as possible the structure of the society and its current notions, and then to see how these notions clothe themselves in speech?[2] The way of external analysis gives quick results, reliable with reference to the premisses of the research, readily comparable and easily assimilated by the logical mind of a civilized man. It performs important services by making an archive of facts which can be learned about rapidly dissolving savage languages. To relate language to society makes each grammar unique and some of them must follow routes unfamiliar to civilized thinkers. There is also more risk of error through accepting false premisses; but, when successful, a socialized grammar should reveal the system of communication on which a community relies.

THE -*EME*-FAMILY

A by-product of Linguistic Analysis and its severely objective and material view of language has been the sudden burgeoning of

[1] B. Bloch and G. L. Trager, *Outline of Linguistic Analysis*, Baltimore, 1942.
[2] See A. Sommerfelt, *La Langue et la société*, Oslo, 1938, for an attempt to correlate Arunta ways of thought and the system of Arunta speech.

the -*eme*-family. The suffix -*eme* is held to mean 'significant unit of
. . . in the structure of a given language'. From that follows the
phoneme, chroneme, toneme, stroneme (!), tagmeme, taxeme, lex-
eme, and semanteme with reference to sound, length, pitch, stress,
grouping, order, word-formation, and meaning. There are also
sememes and episememes. Since the structure of language is lax,
each of these units is variable, and the first four are theoretically
supposed to multiples of precise phones, chrones (!), tones, and
strones (!). There are also kenemes and pleremes invented to express in pseudo-Greek the Chinese terms 'empty' and 'full' words.

It is difficult not to suspect that the ease of composition of terms
has caused terminology to outrun thought. The concept 'unit' must
be relaxed to 'recurrent feature' or 'habitual association' in some of
the last members of the family, since it can hardly be pretended
that we know patterns of, say, meanings (semantemes) which consist of recognizable points throughout the whole language. We can
often say that a given feature or association habitually recurs, but
that is less than to affirm that it has a fixed place in a system which
we can describe in its totality.

The *phoneme* is a place in the system of sounds which a given
language employs. It is useful to distinguish between a speech-
sound as physically determined and a relative and arbitrary place
in some system. Phonemes do not extend from one language to
another, though speech-sounds physically determined may do so.
In speaking we pay attention to certain sonic distinctions and ignore
others; we ignore them to the extent of insensitiveness, and will
affirm of two demonstrably different pronunciations that they are
the 'same'. They are the same with reference to interpretation as
symbols of meaning. Difficulties accumulate when we try to define
the phonematic 'place' by physical equivalents. The variations exceed scientific toleration, and involve us in the dilemma of deciding
whether to break the phoneme into two or more, or to assign
physically dissimilar characteristics to one phoneme. None the less,
the usefulness of stating what are the 'places' of the phonological
system is such that the phoneme must be accepted even if it escapes
consistent theoretical definition. It will be discussed more fully in
the next chapter.

The classical unit of quantity was the *mora*, two of which made
a long vowel or consonant. It is readily measured. Does much
profit spring from calling the *mora* a *chrone*, a constituent part of a

chroneme? *Strone* and *stroneme* are barbarisms; they could only mean 'strewing', not 'stressing'. Stress is eminently variable, and different measures in different persons are equated in practice. Tonal languages have musical pitch as an indispensable part of the speech-sound or phoneme. These are single tones or else movements from one tone to another over two *morae*. Non-tonal languages use tone either for affective purposes or as parts of the intonation curves of phrases which may have definite significance. Thus, for instance, parenthesis is indicated in English by a lowered tone for the enclosed phrase, and interrogation by a steep initial rise and a minor final rise, or rise and fall. Such patterns may be called *tonemes*, but not to great profit. These tonemes occur where the words are not discriminated by tones.

The advantage of the term *morpheme* seems to lie in its imprecision. It refers to some significant alteration of a given word within the sentence, and is not conveniently applied to derivative processes. In a language like Turkish, *ev* 'house' and *evler* 'houses' differ by a significant element *-ler*, but as this is a suffix (*-ler/lar*) it is best so described. But in inflected languages, where fusion takes place, the morpheme may sometimes be a distinct prefix, infix, suffix, or the like, or it may be a complex of stem-vowel plus formative element. It may be convenient to distinguish Lat. *dominus/dominum* by the morphemes *s/m* which are casual suffixes, but *dominus/dominis* by the morphemes *us/is* which are stem-vowels plus suffixes. To be quite consistent in the latter case we should have to use reconstructed forms and distinguish *-*o-s* from *-*o-is*, and so reach *s/is* as casual suffixes. Internal mutations (*umlaut* and *ablaut*) are also morphematic, as *foot/feet* (*fot/foti*), *sing/sang*, Gaelic *an cat/na cait* 'the cat(s)', *na circe/nan cearc* 'of the hen(s)'. The seventy forms of an Arabic root belong, however, to derivation rather than to morphology, and even the 'broken' plurals should probably be regarded as collective nouns derived from singulative nouns and therefore as different words, not forms of the same word. That leaves among Arabic morphemes the signs for tense and person, the mutation of vowels to indicate mood and voice (*kataba* 'he wrote'/*yaktubu* 'he writes'/*duriba* 'he was struck'/*daraba* 'he struck'), some verbal prefixes, suffixes, and infixes, and the three case vowels.

The Chinese concept of 'full' and 'empty' words may be expressed by giving an extended use to the word 'auxiliary'. It is better to do so than to maltreat the Greek language again. A Chinese 'empty' word is not empty. It has its own proper meaning, and in the group (*syntagma*) it has its proper verbal or nominal or demonstrative construction. It is only in relation to other groups forming the sentence that the 'empty' word becomes partially voided of meaning, and that a verb meaning 'give', for instance, is reduced to the status of a preposition meaning 'to'. Auxiliaries have long been known as words partially voided of their own meaning to serve to place other words in a syntactical context. It is not only verbs which require such aids, but also nouns. A preposition is as conveniently described as auxiliary to its noun as a tense sign to a verb, and this recognition of occasional function does not prevent our noticing that the same words may sometimes have full independent status. To allot words to two exclusive lexical classes is probably misleading.

THE ART OF SPEECH

When a language is dissected on the philologist's table, the patient dies. This is true either of the synchronic or the diachronic techniques. By means of the latter it is possible to make neat little heaps of positively identified facts—the *p*s and *q*s of language which are not language itself. The disappointment of many well-wishing beginners is due to this circumstance; the classifications and the successions of such events bear no meaning for them. Similarly the synchronic dissecter determines 'places' within a system, just as an art teacher may determine the proportions of the human canon. The result is a diagram, not a picture. Philologists have studied languages which cannot be known in living detail, or they have compared many languages without mastering any. The cost of mastery is years of study and practice, and even then—for a foreigner—endless vigilance. If more philologists were in the habit of using the languages they dissect—writing articles, making after-dinner impromptus, conversing, broadcasting—they would be more aware of the infinity of little things which lie between grammatical correctness and idiomatic usage. It is probably for this cause that the lethal nature of linguistic techniques has passed unobserved or, at least, uncorrected.

The origin of this inadvertence may be found in the persuasion of the Young Grammarians (in Paul's words) that it is most scientific to study single things in isolation. The science might be that of a chemist when breaking down a compound into its constituent atoms or molecules. But the chemist reconstructs either the same compounds or others more to his taste, and his materials are such that they do not lose their reality in the two processes. The bio-chemist, however, conducts his experiments on condition of never letting slip that intangible and indefinable something which is life. No one procedure is more scientific than the others; the most scientific method is that which gives the closest approximation to the reality under study. So, when that reality is language (an essentially human activity associated with the performance of every other essentially human function), the most scientific account is not that which obeys a particular technique, but that which gives the truest account of this many-sided human activity.

The analytical method, however, provides positive and ponder-able facts, and these are not to be neglected when reaching after more elusive ones. It is even legitimate for a given scholar to say that the heap of positively determined facts is still too small, and to resolve to devote himself to making more of that kind of dis-coveries. A specialist may decline to go outside his specialism if his refusal is made with modesty. It has been held, however, by more than one that 'what I don't know is not knowledge'. On that plane one may legitimately complain of the older linguists that, though their winnings were positive, they failed to secure all the positive gains that were ready to be reaped. One observes, for instance, that *feminarum* becomes *des femmes*. That is a positive gain so far as it goes, but it does not go very far. Turkish *karı-lar-ın* also means 'of the women', and the order of significant parts is the same as for *feminarum*, but to reverse them (**ın lar karı*) offers no advantage of clarity, and they remain undisturbed. The significant parts in Turkish have each a definite form, and are separately interpreted as pronounced or read. Moreover, they enjoy the advantage of putting the main idea first and subordinate modifications after. In accounting for *feminarum/des femmes* and all similar developments, the linguist is under an obligation not only to say *what* happens but also, so far as he can, *when* and *how* and *why* and amid what con-current events. The positive particulars of speech have many more bearings than appear from their schematic treatment in manuals of historical grammar.

Speech is directed towards practical ends. Though it consists of conventionally recognized symbols, these are employed purposively in an act of creation. The Saussurean division between *langue* and *parole* left this aspect outside the proper business of the philologist. But since speech exists in the act of speech, and the act of speech is directed towards its ends, it is obviously possible to consider the whole problem from quite another standpoint. It is so with both O. Jespersen and Sir A. H. Gardiner, who, acknowledging the antithesis of *language/speech*, yet consider that the philologist's business is with *speech*. A more radical position was taken up by K. Vossler, who has already been quoted for the view that 'that science which considers the conditioned, practical and technical (that is, the non-aesthetic, non-artistic, non-linguistic) aspect of language no longer merits the title of Linguistics'. To the former, which he dubbed positivism, he opposed 'idealism', not so much thinking of the philosophical implications of the term, as to express his disagreement with positivism. 'Idealistic philology' was thus born with a misleading title, and other words used in the argument have also misleading connotations. One speaks of 'creation' normally as creation from nothing, and of aesthetics as having for object the beautiful. The ends at which speech aims need not be beautiful, though they envisage some transfer of perceptions (αἰσθήσεις), and the creative power is strictly conditioned by the receptive capacity of the hearer. It is possible to claim for idealistic philology more than it can actually give, but the insistence on the speaker's purposes has been a notable service to the clearer understanding of the problem.

This insistence shifts emphasis from causes to ends. The end is a cause; but while we may consider antecedent causes as outside the speaker's volition, his ends or final causes are his own. We have to consider both points of view. The obligatory use of personal pronouns in Modern French compensates for the loss of formal distinctions in the personal ending of verbs as actually pronounced, but that is not their whole story. The absence of such pronouns so often in the *Chanson de Roland* belongs to a state of mind which appreciates energetic statement above precision; their presence in modern French is due to age-long insistence on precision. 'What is not clear is not French.' The same insistence on logical clarity may be illustrated by word-order. In the *Chanson de Roland* the poet said *esclargiz est li vespres et li jurz* where a modern would say *le soir et le jour est éclairci* (*sont éclaircis*) 'the evening and the day brightened'. The old poet, concerned with the energy of his statements, puts first the most striking word; the modern speaker, concerned with logical clarity, prefers a prescribed order and uses other devices for emphasis. The systematic reduction of French vocabulary by Racine to fully significant words, and the later demand for greater lexical variety towards the end of the eighteenth century are other examples of purpose in speech, and they are connected with social manifestations of which we have adequate knowledge. The supremacy of the dialect of the Île-de-France itself is connected not only with the situation of Paris at the main northern cross-roads, but with the uniqueness of the Capetian dynasts, powerless though they were, as symbols of French unity. The logic of the schoolmen, of Descartes and of Voltaire influences the way in which the normal Frenchman envisages his language. It has been described as an 'abstract language', and it is certain that a passage idiomatically expressed in French will be more general and impersonal in its terms than a similarly idiomatic passage in Spanish.

In the reign of Charles II the Royal Society demanded clear statements in simple English; Dryden carried forward this programme by his prose-style, and the English of Swift and Pope is as logical and lucid as that of any French author. The revolution was purposive; it descended from literature to conversation (which became an art in Johnson's circle). It involved not merely a mode of polite utterance unlike that of the Elizabethans in any circle of their society, but systematic indifference to some features of the style of the Authorized Bible which, in other respects, was held up as the model of plain English. The obsolescence of biblical English is a considerable obstacle to understanding, but its familiarity discourages retranslation.

The effect of these creative intentions, when constantly following one direction, is bound to stamp upon each language a peculiar character.[1] Perhaps the actual attempts at characterization have been trivial or have shown prejudice or have been dubiously justified, but this should not blind us to the fact that a new language is, as the Emperor Charles V averred, a new soul. He had the experi-

---

[1] Among other essays in this kind of interpretation, see V. Brøndal, *Le Français: langue abstraite*, Copenhagen, 1936; E. Lerch, 'Spanische Sprache und Wesenart', *Spanienkunde*, Hamburg, 1932; H. Sten, *Les Particularités de la langue portugaise*, Copenhagen, 1944; W. J. Entwistle, 'Russian as an Art of Expression', *Oxford Slavonic Studies*, 1950. The essential proposition is that where alternative expressions are offered, the instinct of the whole mass of speakers takes one kind of alternative rather than another.

ence of passing from German to Spanish, which he insisted on using even in high diplomacy. The French use of *on* as a virtual first personal pronoun in many phrases is a significant feature. One may write it down to modesty (suppression of one's own person) or assurance (exaltation of one's person to the grade of the universal). There are difficulties in fixing on any suitable account of a fact which is obvious enough. Similarly Spanish *usted* 'you' (from 'your grace') is a courtly term surviving from elegant use in the sixteenth century; but the anecdotes of that time make it possible to interpret it as a courtesy given to others or as an assertion of the speaker's own rank. While modern French has a fixed order (subject–verb–object) from which it does not even depart for emphasis (but uses *c'est* to keep this order, e.g. in *c'est à vous que je parle* 'I'm talking to *you*'), Spanish has two normal orders: S V–O and V–O S. The first states relations between nouns, the second gives precedence to the notion of activity. Whereas in the west of Europe distinctions of time are precisely recognized in the conjugation, in the Slavonic languages the conjugation is equipped to express aspect. One cannot rely on the simple proposition that Slavonic usage reflects the original Indo-European preference for aspect, since Slavonic has created tenses to express time and has then discarded them. We are, in fact, concerned with an attitude of mind in which the continuance or completion of some action is of more importance that its reference to past, present, or future time. This emphasis may be connected with the agricultural occupation of most Slavs as contrasted with the urban precision imposed on Westerners. Chinese laconism is both a habit of mind and a necessary means of preventing monosyllabic sentences from falling out of shape. The use of ideophones by Zulus and other Bantus shows that the quality of an action is of more interest to them than its specific nature; they pass on an impression rather than a reference.

The most important consequence of Vossler's 'idealistic' or 'ideological' philology has been to enrich the notion of history as applied to language.[1] History is not the atomic analysis of the Young Grammarians, though that forms part of the linguist's task, but it is the association in one statement of *all* the facts and environmental conditions of a language at all its stages. If some of these conditions cannot be known (as in ancient, imperfectly recorded languages), the historical statement is made as fully as possible, but

[1] K. Vossler, *Frankreichs Kultur und Sprache*, Heidelberg, 2 ed., 1929.

is necessarily incomplete; but with fullness of knowledge language is seen as entering fully into all social relations.

It is more fruitful to consider the ends of speech in stylistics, semantics, and grammar, and the antecedent causes of change in phonology and parts of morphology. In stylistics we are concerned with variation for effect, and it has been argued that grammatical constructions begin with style. In Old English *ic singe* meant 'I sing' and 'I shall sing', and *ic sang* 'I sang', 'I was singing', 'I had sung', but by an attempt to imitate the style of biblical Latin (itself relying on biblical Greek and the latter on Hebrew) periphrastic tenses arose like *hwæt sceal ic singen* 'what shall I sing', *hē wæs singende* 'he was singing'. They have lost their stylistic effect and have become parts of the normal paradigm of the verb.[1] The history of the notional tenses and moods exemplifies this abundantly. The distinction between nearer and remoter possibility in the Greek subjunctive and optative declines into a distinction between nearer and remoter time within the Latin subjunctive. The urge to maintain the subjunctive at all, i.e. to distinguish beween factual and notional statements, tends to fail in French and has been quite lost in English. The future also is not a fact, like the present or the past. It is expressed in various languages by devices which all have some basis in style.

Hermann Paul thought that the science underlying syntax should be psychology, as phonetics is the science underlying phonology, but he specifically rejected the Wundtian psychology of speech. Rudolfo Lenz accepted Wundt's doctrine as the basis of his brilliant account of Spanish parts of speech. L. Bloomfield was at first strongly attracted by Wundt's folk-psychology, but later reacted as strongly. 'Since that time (1914) there has been much upheaval in psychology; we have learned, at any rate, what one of our masters suspected thirty years ago, namely, that we can pursue the study of language without reference to any one psychological doctrine, and that to do so safeguards our results and makes them more significant to workers in related fields.'[2] The suggestion that seems to emerge from Ogden and Richards's *The Meaning of Meaning*, that psychology holds the key which has dropped from the nerveless hand of philosophy, has, I think, been generally disappointed.

---

[1] F. Mossé, *Esquisse d'une histoire de la langue anglaise*, Paris, 1947, p. 29.

[2] L. Bloomfield, *Language*, New York, 1946, Preface. Delbrück professed this indifference.

The position seems to be much the same as that of language and philosophy. In so far as psychological or philosophical propositions are themselves *sub judice* it is scarcely possible for them to serve as a basis for further systematic inferences. The linguist is concerned primarily with the fact of language and that he must respect at all costs. But when the facts cohere in a pattern to which he must give a name, the linguist is very likely to borrow from the vocabulary of experts in motions of the mind. Thus the agglomerative word-group and the word-sentence of some peoples may suggest the use of Ward's *ideational continuum* contrasted with 'thought as analytic', without requiring the linguist to accept the whole of Ward's system or to refuse to look for the mental cause of, say, sex-gender in some quite different direction. Thus much for deductive psychology. Experimental psychology, if it is to be exercised on language, must begin as the philologists do, by collecting all relevant facts, and continue, as they do, by offering the hypothesis which seems to fit the facts most snugly. The experimental psychologist, no doubt, would proceed to dovetail these hypotheses, if possible, into a greater mental system, but his superstructure may be too precarious for the linguist to adopt. The latter moves in a more modest orbit of facts and proximate explanations; if he cannot always give explanations, still his facts remain facts. But he is exposed to grave error if he accounts for a mental activity without mind.

GEOGRAPHY AND REALIA

The use of geographical methods has completely transformed the study of language in both its aspects, the synchronic and diachronic. It arose from a growing sense of the importance of dialectal information. This had taken, in England, the characteristic form of a dictionary;[1] in France dialectal evidence consisted of local studies, vocabularies, and applications to the problems of etymology. Jules Gilliéron conceived the idea of making this evidence complete and definitive by covering the whole of France and placing the results on maps. He determined upon 639 points in France at which a list of about 2,000 words would be investigated, partly in isolation, partly in phrases. He selected as investigator E. Edmont, a man without philological training (and to that extent free from prejudice), but already a competent student of dialect and endowed with a keen ear. Edmont moved from point to point between 1897

---

[1] J. Wright, *The English Dialect Dictionary*, London, 1898–1905.

and 1901 according to a fixed schedule, selecting the peasant or informant most likely to give him authentic data, and, after gaining his confidence, sitting together to translate the questionnaire. Information was recorded as it was given; not retouched. It covered the essentials of vocabulary, speech-sounds, forms, and syntax; old words and neologisms, varieties of flexions of nouns, pronouns, and verbs, the forms of prepositions and adverbs, combinations showing the use of particles. It was Gilliéron's business to mark this information on maps, and later to interpret the results.[1]

A first fascicule of German maps had appeared as early as 1881, and Gilliéron's initiative was at once appreciated in that country both by Romanists and Germanists. F. Wrede's *Deutscher Sprachatlas* dates from 1926. There were shorter atlases of the Swabian dialect, and of Danish, of north Holland, Flanders, Catalonia, Rumania, the Romance and Germanic dialects in Switzerland, Corsica, Switzerland with Italy, and Italy alone, as well as numerous dialect atlases for France. The stage of inquiries had been completed for Spain when the Civil War broke out, and the present outlook is uncertain. A questionnaire has been prepared for Spanish America, and the island of Puerto Rico has been elaborately studied. A. Griera is the author of the Catalan Atlas. Proposals for an English Atlas have been approved by the Philological Society, and some of its possible services indicated by L. R. Palmer.[2] A new general atlas for France is in preparation, which will correct some flaws of the older one, give evidence of development during the half century, and preserve dialect material which may not survive another fifty years.

That there were flaws in the first French atlas is not surprising; what is surprising is that there are so few. The enormous advantages of the method were quite unforeseeable, and the pitfalls were hidden. Informants were uneasy and the learned world at first hostile. A natural love of paradox was thus kindled in Gilliéron, so that he sought opportunities to flout the reigning theories. The severe methods of the neo-grammarians have not been abolished or even weakened by the linguistic evidence, but they have been

[1] A. Dauzat, *Le Géographie Linguistique*, Paris, 1946. See also J. Jaberg, *Sprachgeographie*, Aarau, 1908; E. Gamillscheg, *Die Sprachgeographie*, Bielefeld, 1928.
[2] *An Introduction to Modern Linguistics*, London, 1936 (vii: 'Linguistic Geography', with maps for *she* and *without* in north England). Cf. also J. Orr, *Transactions of the Philological Society*, London, 1948.

transformed. In place of an arid and artificial presentation, which was all that the bookish material allowed, language could be seen moving on the ground, each constituent unit enjoying a special history. The great lines of communication, the capitals of countries and provinces, remote valleys, old boundaries, and so on, appear on the maps with startling clearness, alongside of changes of fashion, rustic confusions of sounds; popular etymologies, &c. The maps show the past alive in the present, but they can also be made to cover past time. Ancient areas, the movements of words in the Middle Ages,[1] stages in romanization and successive strata of vulgar Latin have been laid bare by J. Jud, and R. Menéndez Pidal has detected former extensions of Basque along the Aragonese Pyrenees. More ambitious still, M. Bartoli[2] has used principles inferred from modern linguistic geography to throw light on conditions in the remotest past. The law of continuous areas assures us that if *camp* is spoken in Normandy–Picardy, in south-western France and in the Alpes Maritimes, there was a time when these areas were joined over the whole of Gaul—a fact confirmed by our knowledge of the Latin origin of French. The same law can be made to assure us that if passive *r* appears in Celtic, Latin, Hittite, and Tokharian there must have been original contact between these widely severed members of the Indo-European family. The law of marginal archaism can be illustrated from the same example, since *camp* is an older form and *champ* is an innovation, possibly dating from the seventh century. The newer forms are found in the centre, the older on the frontiers. A form found at the western and eastern extremes of the Indo-European territory must be an old form. Combined with other indications of the same nature it leads to the conclusion that Latin originates in a relatively archaic state of Indo-European dialectology.

The geographical inquiries are atomic in nature, and therefore will not answer questions which depend on the mutual relations of speech. The method of translation leaves a possibility of false suggestion to the informant who may thus give an unsuitable answer, and it conceals variants. An informant may answer under a misapprehension, or his reply may be misunderstood. It has become apparent that successful interrogation depends on previous

---

[1] S. Moore, S. B. Much, and H. Whitehall, *Middle English Dialect Characteristics and Dialect Boundaries*, Ann Arbor, 1935.

[2] M. Bartoli, *Saggi di linguistica spaziale*, Turin, 1945.

acquaintance with the region. It is better not to ask questions, but to elicit information indirectly. It is better still, if one has time, to wait until the facts present themselves in the normal way of talk. Then the expressions of various persons can be compared, and differences of age, sex, education, and intelligence allowed for. The investigator needs a good ear, but even so he may have unconscious bias. Gramophone recordings are valuable, not merely for being unbiased, but because they can reproduce the dialect as a living whole, but local knowledge is needed to interpret them correctly. In any case, complete texts are needed to complete the atomic information resulting from the questionnaire, and dialect grammars may be of great assistance.

Above all, the geographical investigator must associate words with things. The best maps are now accompanied with albums of drawings or photographs to show precisely what a word denotes. Words differ because things differ, or because different social groups attach importance to minor differences of one type of thing, or because the thing is variously suggestive. The words *pot*, *plough*, *yoke* are single in an urban vocabulary, but are divided into many in the country. A pot maybe is nothing more to a townsman, but may be a *boiler*, *copper*, *earthenware pot*, in the language of peasants; for ploughmen yokes of different make have different names. The names for *bat* are numerous—*chauve souris*, *vespertilio*, *murciélago*, *pipistrello* among others of more limited range—because the animal is one to impress the imagination. From the heel (*calx*) hose extended upwards until they displaced the older word for trousers (Spanish *calzas* for *bragas*), and then differentiation set in (*haut-de-chausses*, *bas-de-chausses*) until the heel was covered by socks newly named (*bas*, Spanish *medias*). All these have their particular geographical extensions. Thus Gilliéron's movement is united to Rudolf Meringer's advocacy of the study of *Wörter und Sachen*. Both are methods that infuse realism into language study.

To complete information maps must be carried at times beyond the national or linguistic frontier. *Street*, *church*, *Saturday*, German *Zins* (*census*), *Keller* (*cellarius*), Italian *cavalla*, Spanish *hablar* and *hallar*, are all words which bear in one way or another on the history of French (*chemin*, *église*, *samedi*, *rente* and *loyer*, *cellier*, *jument*, *parler* and *trouver*). For the study of Romance languages the English and German forms have the special interest which linguistic geography attaches to the circumference of a cultural area.

At first sight the maps suggested that the notion of dialect is an abstraction or an illusion. This impression had, indeed, been gained by some scholars, such as Gaston Paris and Hugo Schuchardt, before the coming of the maps; but the maps show the lines marking identity of sounds (isophones) and of words (isoglosses) running in all directions, apparently at random. Every word, sound, and form has its own area of extension, and even the most closely related do not coincide. In France, for instance, *toile* has a narrower area than *étoile*. It came to be seen, however, that there is an art of linguistic map-reading which clears up some of the difficulties. In some instances it was found necessary to go back over the ground, since the map points were too widely spaced for tracing of boundaries, and the information of several persons was needed. Dialectology had come into being as a branch of science precisely when the dialects themselves were most severely jostled by a centralized civilization and were in process of disappearing. Mountainous regions remote from traffic were found to show relatively clear isophones. Identity of sounds is more reliable than that of words, since words are liable to many accidents of fashion, homonymy, &c. In the map of *étoile*, *toile*, and *mois* given by K. Jaberg in his *Sprachgeographie* (No. 1) the point to be illustrated is the development of a closed Latin *e* in open syllable to a rising diphthong of the nature of *wa* or *we*. The frontiers of the three words certainly do not agree at all points. They sometimes run together, sometimes are spaced apart. But they all surround a central territory dominated by Paris and Orleans. At some points the Parisian innovation has made a leap beyond the frontier. The map thus shows that a language or dialect has a focus, and that its boundaries may be either lines or bands of lines. A. Dauzat gives examples concerning Lyons. The extension for *caya* 'sow' covers only part of seven departments; words from Latin *lacrimusa* for 'grey lizard' and *anevoliu* 'slow-worm' reach the sea west of Marseilles and have a boundary running north to south; representatives of *feta* in the meaning 'ewe' are found to the west of Narbonne, and only stop short of Toulouse. For all these Lyons is clearly shown as the centre of diffusion, and the areas of expansion are connected by Dauzat with epochs of varying prestige for that city.[1]

Other examples of line and band frontiers can be obtained from Scandinavia or Spain. In Spain, for instance, the three languages

---

[1] A. Dauzat, *La Géographie linguistique*, Paris, 1922, p. 204.

are divided by sharp lines south of the bases from which the Reconquest started. North of that line the ancient dialects shade into each other over broad bands of transition. Between Catalan and Provençal there is a sharp line of isoglosses along the foothills of the northern branch of the Pyrenees in Roussillon. This lies slightly south of the medieval frontier of Catalonia, which included Rousillon, but it also connotes the change of mode of life between hillmen and plainsmen. A Norwegian scholar called the sharp transitions 'dead' and the broad ones 'living'. Perhaps the metaphor begs a question; but it calls attention to the need to ascertain causes of division.

Dialectal conditions may be too complex to be set on a map. In the parish of Aaby (Jutland) 57 per cent. were found to speak Jutish and 17 per cent. a mixed dialect; 22 per cent. spoke standard Danish, and this figure included all the landed proprietors. Incoming Swedes passed over into the standard group. Out of 131 farmers, 90 spoke Jutish and only 11 standard Danish; but the cottagers were divided on this point as 56 to 39, and workmen (gardeners) as 73 to 27. A couple of German children in another parish were found speaking a broad Jutish, and when asked where they learned it, they said they learned it at school. Their 'school' was the language of their playmates, not of their teachers or their parents.[1] Ordinary folk have a very keen sense of dialect, and enjoy proverbs and witticisms at the expense of their neighbours. Maps rightly interpreted justify their instinctive awareness of such differences.

DIVISIONS OF STUDY

The divisions of study proposed in this book include Phonology, Grammar, Vocabulary, and Stylistics. Those offered by E. Bourciez in his singularly lucid *Éléments de linguistique romane* are 'les sons', 'les mots', 'les formes', and 'les phrases'; Bloch and Trager in their *Outline of Linguistic Analysis* offer 'phonetics', 'phonemics', 'morphology', and 'syntax'. It is necessary, in our submission, for the linguist to be acquainted with the results of phonetic inquiry, but this is part of a physical and physiological science not uniquely concerned with speech. In speech and language we are concerned with the relations of sounds with a view to

---

[1] J. Brøndum-Nielsen, *Dialekter og Dialektforskning*, Copenhagen, 1927, p. 24. This book has a level-headed discussion of the nature of dialect, and a series of Scandinavian particulars, with maps.

significant utterance, and for the sake of avoiding technical terms
the chapter-heading *Sounds* is used to cover that much of phonetics
which concerns the student of language and questions affecting the
pattern (phonematics, not the ungrammatical 'phonemics') and its
evolution (phonology). Development is profoundly affected if a
language employs flexions and creates paradigms. In languages of
such a sort the study of forms, or morphology, requires separate
attention; but there are also languages without morphology, viz.
the isolating and the polysynthetic (or more strictly the holosynthetic—a type which nowhere actually exists). In others, such
as the agglutinating group, it may be better to speak of affixes than
of morphemes. For lack of native grammatical thought, it is open
to consider Bantu languages as containing verbal paradigms or as
having verbal stems with prefixed or suffixed auxiliaries. The orthography is one for the convenience of Europeans. In general, relations within the sentence are expressed by modifications of form
(morphemes), by auxiliaries and by order. Something of each of
these is present in every language, but there is an antithesis between
synthesis and analysis created by the fact that what is not expressed
by a morpheme is taken up by auxiliaries and order. The Hum-
boldtian division of morphology is of great importance for inflected
languages with fused forms; it gathers together the facts which
cannot be ignored, since they are obvious, and for which certain
explanations have to be offered on the side of sound or sense. In
the more general view taken by this book, however, the special
consequences of paradigms for sound falls within the study of
speech-sounds, and those which affect relations fall within grammar. A distinction may be made, however, between 'parts of the
sentence' which are matters of common concern and 'parts of
speech' which are numbered and defined by each separate language by its own usage.

The term *Grammar* is use in preference to syntax, because the
latter refers properly to order only. Syntax has been extended to
cover the use of prepositions and other auxiliary words, but it does
not properly refer to modifications of form. Yet modifications of
form fulfil the same functions in some languages as order and
auxiliaries in others. The word grammar covers all three resources.
It is a system of references, sometimes described as 'logical'. But
all the resources of vocabulary and of sound, form, auxiliaries,
and order, in so far as they do not constitute a system of neutral

references, are available for affective or emotional ends. This is the domain of *Stylistics*, independent of grammar, and reaching out from certain specific devices at the service of all speakers towards highly effective personal uses of language which can only be estimated intuitively.

A separate chapter is devoted to *Words*, units of form and meaning, because of their enormous importance in civilized speech. Though primitive languages may not have words in our sense of the term, but stems ready to fuse with other stems or affixes, the definiteness of civilized words is such as to cause civilized grammars to be built upon them. Phonetic transcriptions are commonly representations of words, not of the breath-groups which are the actual units of utterance; civilized syntax is order of words; the auxiliaries are 'empty' words and morphemes are modifications of words. The separate treatment of so powerful an element of communication imposes itself and divides into the two aspects of form and meaning, and includes subsidiary specialisms like semantics or onomastics, and combined sciences like linguistic geography and lexicography.

Two other chapters are concerned with methods of classifying languages and the distribution of these classes, *grosso modo*, over the surface of the earth. The first would not have been necessary if any of the existing devices for summary description had obtained general support. The second is essential to any broad study of language. For not everything is found everywhere. When monosyllables and tones turn up in a West African language they are not those of Chinese; but the very slight agglutination in Chinese, augmented considerably in Tibetan and Burmese, shades into the full agglutination of the Altaic languages, in one branch of which (i.e. in Turkish, not in Mongolian) the basic stems show a tendency to the monosyllablic. In fact the language-patterns shade off gradually into each other across vast areas, as Henry Sweet showed in his *History of Language* (1901). In some cases the cause for this typical resemblance may be traced in history. There is little doubt that African languages were carried across from nearer Asia, and it is plausibly argued that Egypt played a great part in their organization. In other cases the resemblance may be due to communication with neighbours. Whether the whole pattern is due to one common origin of language, as some aver, or to accommodations between languages, or the dominance of the greater over the less, the broad spatial succession of typical structures is one of the most striking and puzzling features of human Language.[1]

[1] Since everything but sounds is meaningful in speech, the word Semantics may be used to cover both Grammar and Stylistics (S. Ullmann, *The Principles of Semantics*, Glasgow, 1951). I have assumed the notion of meaning to be inherent in those terms and kept Semantics (the 'Meaning of meaning') for the chapter on Words where it has a special applicability.

IV
SOUNDS

THE study of speech-sounds has progressed more rapidly than other linguistic disciplines because its conditions admit of 'explanation'. The explanation results from the possibility of correlating the conclusions of two types of study, each assured of its own data. A historical study—phonology—gathers all the information available about a given speech-sound in isolation or in combination or as influenced in some way by others. A physical science—phonetics —tells us how this material is organized. The study is no less historical if the material to be explained is drawn only from the present, since 'now' is a moment in historical time. The investigator may pick any convenient moment in present or past time for a synchronic study designed to show how the elements of a given tongue are mutually related. As phonologist he gathers and sets out the facts, whether of modern English or ancient Greek; as phonetician, or with the help of a phonetician, he explains them. The explanation also is factual, and it may be urged that it does not go very deep nor tell us all we wish to know. It is both a source of satisfaction to the philologist, who finds he can treat with confidence of things of 2000 B.C., and of dissatisfaction to many others who feel that they have learned nothing essential concerning human speech. The latter includes operations of mind as well as of voice. But within their own limits both phonology and phonetics are positive sciences, and their interaction is such as to explain each other.

It has been of advantage to this branch of linguistics that psychological considerations rarely interfere. They play their part in the ordering of speech material, which is grammar, in preferences which constitute stylistics, and in the ramifications of vocabulary, but a sound as such is devoid of meaning. It is possible for sounds to gather associations, and to be deemed soft or harsh, musical or hissing, but such associations are inferred from use and wont; they are not inherent. Thus the phonologist gathers *centum*, *cet*, *hund*(*red*), ἑκατόν and *śim̃tas*, *sto*, *satəm*, *çatam*. He notes that often *k* is found in all Indo-European languages, but that in this series and all like it there is a systematic discrepancy. He posits, therefore, a

*$\overset{?}{k}$ or *k, and asks the phonetician what this may be. The phonetician replies that it is of the nature of k to be prounounced in different places of the back of the mouth (as in *kw ka ki*), and that the foremost conceivable position is palatal. The *centum/satəm* development is explained by assuming a palatal *$\hat{k}$ in addition to a velar *k in all or part of the Indo-European family. The difference between ἵππος, *equus* and κόπτω is explained by pointing to the postvelar position of *kw as compared with the mediovelar of *k.

Among relevant historical facts, of course, there are those which concern the use of sounds in grammatical and lexicological situations. It happens that the most ancient languages of our group are heavily inflected, so that both nouns and verbs appear in fixed paradigms. These paradigms invite comparison within themselves or between each other. Thus Old French

| chant | chantes | chantet |
| entre | entres | entret |

invite comparison person by person, and the phonologically correct distinction of the first person is removed in Modern French *je chante*. Similarly all but a few Russian nouns have their dative, instrumental and locative plural in -*am* -*ami* -*ach*, which was originally restricted to nouns in -*a*. French *je puis* has an *s* which comes from reducing -*te*- to a sibilant, but *je suis* (*sum*) has an *s* due to comparison between the two very common paradigms. The importance of these occurrences in our languages has led to the recognition of Morphology—the study of grammatical forms—as an independent part of grammar; but a glance at Chinese or Malay will show that morphology is no necessary part of Language, and in Turkish we find that the term, if used, must be understood in quite another fashion.

Thus, the study of morphology is of great importance for our Western languages, but has no place in universal grammar. It is, in fact, a hybrid. On the one side, it is part of the historical statement concerning sounds to say whether they occur in paradigms and how these have interacted; on the other side, flexions serve to relate parts of the sentence which would otherwise be associated by their order or by auxiliary words designed to meet this need. On the one side, morphology is a special aspect of phonology, the study of sounds; on the other side, it goes with syntax or grammar, the ordering of speech to convey meaning.

PHONETICS

Phonetics is a physical science. It begins with the physical study of sound, which teaches that sounds are vibrations within the range 30 to 30,000 per second. Some are irregular disturbances or noises and others are musical notes. Both are used in speech. As for the notes which can be used with advantage in music, they lie between 40 and 4,000 vibrations and must be spaced at regular mathematical intervals over 6–7 octaves. Human ears are not all equally sensitive, and while musicians may be able to distinguish a difference as slight as one sixty-fourth of a semitone, language is for the vast majority who have very little capacity for recognizing absolute pitch. The study of sound deals objectively with vibrations of air, but with reference to Man inasmuch as only those are considered which can be perceived by the human ear. Other vibrations, not necessarily of air, give heat, light, X-rays, and other kinds of penetration, but they lie outside the physical science of phonology. Because sound-waves can be measured, various sorts of instruments can be designed for the analysis of human speech. None of these are perfect for their purpose, since speech is addressed to the ear and no machine has precisely the capability of an ear.

Next in order comes a physiological science. This is not necessarily limited to human subjects, but concerns itself with the production of audible sounds by any animal. It is through this science that we learn that sounds receive distinctive character from the shape given by animal organs to a column of air entering (inspiration) or leaving (expiration) the body. Both of these methods are used by the human animal, but expiration is much the most common. We describe speech in terms of expiration. The air in the lungs is driven upwards by the diaphragm or midriff through the bronchial tubes. As it enters the glottis or Adam's apple it may be completely stopped (ϵ0) for a moment by a kind of lid, the epiglottis, and thereafter explode energetically, or it may force two cartileges to vibrate and produce 'voice' (ϵ1), or it may merely rasp them in aspiration (ϵ2), or pass through unchecked in 'voiceless' sounds (ϵ3) or breathing (ϵ4). The column then enters the mouth and is given a further shape by dispositions of the tongue (γ, β) or lips (α), and it may be obstructed by the uvula (δ) or allowed to pass through the nasal chamber. The physiological science leads to an applied remedial art of phoniatry, the object of which is to correct speech defects. The patient fails to produce some or all of the sounds demanded by society for intelligibility, as when he lisps or fails to use aspiration; the phoniatrist either brings the patient's use of speech-organs into agreement with common practice or, if the organs themselves are damaged, seeks some compensation.

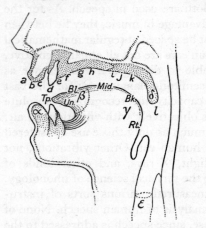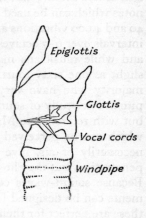

Epiglottis

Glottis

Vocal cords

Windpipe

ORGANS OF SPEECH
(lettered as in Jespersen's *Lehrbuch der Phonetik*).

MOVING PARTS

α	Lower lip.	*Tp.*	Tip.	*Bk.*	Back.
β	Front of tongue.	*Bl.*	Blade.	*Rt.*	Root.
Un.	Undersurface of tip.	γ	Back of tongue.	δ	Uvula.
		Mid.	Middle of back.	ε	Larynx.

STATIONARY POINTS OF CONTACT

a Lips protruded⎫
b Lips normal ⎬ labial.
c Lips retracted⎭
d Tip of teeth. (labiodental and interdental).
e Teeth (dental).
f Gums, alveoli or teeth-ridge (alveolar).

g Front of hard palate (prepalatal).
h Back of hard palate (medio-palatal).
i Front of velum or soft palate (pre-velar or postpalatal).
j Middle of velum (mediovelar).
k Back of velum (postvelar).
l Pharynx.

CONTACTS AND APPROXIMATIONS

o Complete stoppage (occlu-sion).
o 1 Stoppage and long off-glide (affrication).

1 Fissure opening (friction).
2 Rounded opening (friction).
3, 5, 7 Unrounded vowels.
4, 6, 8 Rounded vowels.

Phonetics is concerned only with human speech-sounds, which it defines with all possible accuracy, but also delimits broadly as distinct areas in a given system. This work is objective and does not depend on the consent of speakers. Since language begins with the agreement of a community to use certain sound signals, it follows that phonetics is not properly a linguistic discipline. It must be able to give its decisions objectively if it is to be of service in measuring and analysing so subjective a matter as language.

Since speech is everybody's business it is not difficult to test the facts about one's own pronunciation. Facing a mirror one may see whether both lips are employed (bilabial sounds) or the lower lip and upper teeth (labiodental); also whether there is a complete stoppage (occlusives—Jespersen $\alpha 0^b$), a rounded opening ($\alpha 1^b$), or a fissure opening ($\alpha 2^b \ \alpha 2^d$), or whether they stand so far apart as to have no influence on the sound. There are no English sounds pronounced with protrusion of the lips (a:) or retraction (c:), but it would be easy to make the appropriate grimaces. The action of the tongue cannot be so readily seen, but it can be felt by the simple process of forming a sound and holding it. The blade of the tongue is thin and mobile (β) and makes clear sounds against the hard teeth (d, e), gums (f) and palate (g, h); the back (γ) is thick and sluggish, and articulates dully against the soft velum (i, j, k) and back wall of the mouth (l). Generally speaking, since the tongue is used to give shape within the mouth to most sounds, the prefix 'linguo-' is not used. Without directions to the contrary one assumes that the tongue is the active organ. Its contacts or approximations are with corresponding points of the roof of the mouth, i.e. the blade (β) against the tip of the teeth (d:), back surface (e:), gums (f:) and even fore palate (g:); the middle (γ) against the high palate (g, h:) and prevelum (i:), and the back (γ) against the velum (i, j, k, l:), and the modes of articulation are occlusion (o), friction (rounded—sibilant (1)—or fissure (2)) and affrication (o1) (momentary contact in the palate or gums followed by a sibilant off-glide). Thus consonants are formed and recognized by simple experiment on oneself. Vowels involve no rasping of the breath, but are pure resonances. It is less easy to distinguish them, but a group of nine have been selected as cardinal. Anyone may test before a mirror the rising of the lower jaw which brings up the tongue from *a* to *i* or *a* to *u*, and the mirror will show that the front vowels are pronounced with the lips wide-spread, but the back vowels with rounded lips. The forward and backward positions are perceptible as tensions of the tongue. But there are also front vowels (Danish *ø*,

French *œ*, German *ö*, *ü*) and unrounded back vowels (Russ. *y*), as well as varieties of obscure central vowels (as the *a-u* of *pundit*, *pandit*).

If the whole column of air is passing through the mouth only, the sound is 'buccal', but this description is taken for granted. This occurs when the hanging skin of the uvula (δ) is pressed against the back wall of the mouth; the latter also in some persons inflated to meet the uvula, and a stoppage occurs in the entry to the nasal chamber (δo). When there is an airway, the sounds are described as nasal. Nasals owe their resonance, however, to a closed chamber within the mouth. It is easy to recognize the 'twang' of a nasal *m n* (δ2) or of an exaggerated French or Polish nasal vowel (δ3). It is less easy to note the slight nasalization of the vowel in *man* (δ1), but when the same spreads over the whole utterance it is heard as a 'nasal accent'.

It is not customary in English to drop the lid of the epiglottis upon the glottis (ϵo), though this occurs dialectally (Glasgow : *wa'er*, *bu'er*) and as part of the structure of such languages as Arabic. By clapping hands on our ears we may hear the vibration of the vocal chords (ϵ1) as an internal buzzing in voiced sounds, and no such vibration for aspirates (ϵ2) or voiceless sounds (ϵ3). The rasping of the chords in aspiration produces a certain energy in the breath-stream which will cause a piece of tissue-paper to vibrate if held in front of the mouth. By this test we may verify that English *quiet* is slightly aspirated, but French *quiète* is not.

Two groups of continuous sounds are especially important for the history of language. The one consists of the sonants *m n l r*. For these there is a stoppage in the mouth, and a way of escape through the nose (*m n*), along the side of the tongue (*l*) or between vibrations (*r*). As they are all voiced, they can make syllables without the aid of a vowel, and they tend to generate vowels for just that reason. The semiconsonants or semivowels *w y* (as in *gwa nya* / *gau nai*) consist of movements from more closed to more open or from more open to more closed positions. The direction of the movement is of the utmost historical importance, since semiconsonants precipitate changes in preceding consonants and semivowels in antecedent vowels (e.g. *folia* > *folja* > OFr. *fueille*, Prov. *folha*, Sp. *hoja*, *patrem* > padre > Prov. *paire* > Fr. *père*). Every speech-sound involves movements of this kind and consists of an on-glide, tension (more or less marked) and off-glide. In affricates the tension is

very brief and the off-glide long and sibilant. At any time the
relative importance of these three moments may change and an
evolutionary process be begun. Thus *padre*, with relaxed tension
in the *d*, became *padre* (fricative for occlusive) and so led to *paire*
(palatal fricative for dental fricative) and *père*.

Movements of speech-organs may be described with millimetre
measurements for each sound. More briefly, a set of technical terms
may be used to show which active and passive parts are used and
how they are employed. The active parts may be labelled by Greek
letters, the passive by Roman, and their relations symbolized by
numbers, and in such a case the description is quasi-algebraic. The
whole situation may be drawn, though prudence would suggest
that most of us label our drawings. H. Sweet's Romaic alphabet
was an attempt to construct an alphabet of conventionalized diagrams, and might have proved satisfactory if speech-sounds were
evenly spread, as the system supposed, over the roof of the mouth.
It failed to allow for the superior sensitivity of the blade of the
tongue and front of the mouth. It is usual to employ letters of the
Roman alphabet as far as they will go, and to acquire extra signs
by inverting or varying these letters or by using obsolete Greek or
Old English signs. Single words or letters are enclosed within
square brackets when phonetically transcribed. Ideally, one letter
should stand for each broadly distinguishable sound. But different
peoples have different powers and instincts for distinguishing
sounds, so that some require more symbols for their phonetic
alphabets than others. Moreover, sounds differ from language to
language by narrow distinctions, so that though each set is standard
in its own tongue, the different patterns do not coincide. A phonetic
alphabet, in fact, is an ambiguous script unless supported by
systematic definitions. Thus Norwegian *sol* 'sun' is transcribed as
[so:l], since it contains the standard Norwegian [o]; but one must
be warned that this *o* is intermediate between the English sounds
used in *molest* and *full*. So also Spanish *señor* is [seɲór], so long as
one remembers that Castilian cacuminal *s* is different from French
or even South American *s*.

The table on p. 104 contains some of the commonest symbols.
The front and back vowels are arranged in the table so that the
first is pronounced with a fissure opening of the lips, the second
with a rounded opening. Front vowels are normally unrounded,
back vowels normally rounded; but rounded front vowels are

familiar features of languages as close to us as German, French, and the Scandinavian tongues. Unrounded back vowels are rarer, and not many will receive enlightenment from the statement that the

	Bilabial	Labiodental	Interdental	Dental / Alveolar	Palatal	Velar	Pharyngal	Glottal	Variants
	a b c	d	d	e f	g h i j k l			ε	
	α	α	β	β	γ γ			ε	*Variants*
Consonants									
Buccal (δ0)									
0. Occlusive	p/b			t/d		k/g q/G		ʔ‖	‖ Arabic ʿ
0/1. Affricate				ş/2*	č/ĵ§				* ts/dz
									§ tʃ/dʒ
									tš/dž, č/ĵ, ǧ
1. Fricative									
Sibilant				s/z	š/ž†				† ʃ/ʒ
2. Non-sibilant	φ/β	f/v	θ/ð		ç/j	‡χ/γ		hş	‡ x § Chinese ʿ
(Labiovelar)	ʍ/w					ʍ/w			
Sonants									
Lateral				l	λ				
Vibrant				r(ɪ)			R		
Nasal (δ2)	m	ɱ		n	ɲ	ŋ			
Semi-consonants					j, ɥ	w			
-vowels					i	ʯ			

Vowels	Front	Mid		Back		Nasal vowels
	i/y	ɨ		ɯ/u		ẽ ɔ̃, &c.
	e/ø	ə		ɤ/o		
	ɛ/œ	ɐ		ʌ/ɔ		
	a			ɑ		

Examples: pin, bib, tin, din, king, gong, Arab. qaf, Glasgow wa'er; Ital. vizio, mezzo, ciò, giorno; hill; sin, zinc, shin azure; Jap. fuji, Mod. Gk. βαίνω, will, fine, vine, thin, there, Germ. ich, yes, Germ. ach, Mod. Gk. γάμος; line, Sp. llano; Sp. rango, Eng. row, Fr. rien; man, inferno, none, Sp. señor, wrong; Ital. piú, Fr. puis, Ital. quattro; ai, aw;
Fr. pis, dure, Russ. byl, Sp. uno;
Fr. été, peu, le, pot;
Fr. mère, fleur, Port, cama, Eng. but, Fr. port;
Fr. patte, pâte; Fr. bien, bon, Port. fim, um, lã.

The alphabet recommended by the International Phonetic Association is given in *Chambers's Encyclopaedia*, 1950, s.v. 'Phonetics', and in the pamphlet entitled *The Principles of the International Phonetic Association*, London, 1933.

Araucanian *u* [ɯ] is unrounded. Any higher or closer vowel may serve as a semiconsonant to a lower or more open one, e.g. in Spanish *peatón* 'foot-traveller', when pronounced as only two syllables. They may become so short as to be 'fugitive', like Common Slavonic *ĭ ŭ*, and so disappear, or may develop from nothing through the 'fugitive' stage as in Hebrew. They may lose their voicing, as in the final vowel of Portuguese *muito* 'much'. They combine as diphthongs and triphthongs. In addition, they are affected by the related features of stress, length, and musical pitch. Stress is the volume and energy of the outgoing air current. Though stresses are conventionally assigned to three grades (principal, secondary, and unstressed), languages differ greatly in the variations offered. When the range of stress is not too great, distinctions of length and pitch may become structurally significant. All stressed syllables are longer than all unstressed syllables (the syllable being centred on its vowel), but if the stress is moderate, it is possible to set up a system of relative measures and to consider them to apply, as in Greek and Classical Latin, to stressed and unstressed syllables alike. Unstressed syllables have no determinable musical pitch. So far as one can say anything about them, they show a falling off from the height reached in the stressed syllable, and are sometimes marked with accents of falling tone. The stressed syllable has pitch, and differences of pitch (level, rising, falling, compound) can be used in linguistic structure so long as they are not superseded by too energetic a stress.

The diagram of cardinal vowels is an abstraction, truest for French, but requiring closer definition for each language. In Italian, for instance, there is a system of seven vowels, none precisely in the cardinal positions: *i e è a ò o u*. Compared with French, Italian, Portuguese, or Catalan, Spanish would show a five vowel scheme: *i e a o u*. But the distinctions between *pero* and *perro*, *bota* and *jota*, though less than those of *e/ε o/ɔ* in other languages, are all the more marked within Spanish itself, and it would be an acoustic offence to level them. To make minor distinctions of this sort it is convenient to attach diacritical marks, as *ẹ* (close)/*ę* (open). These diacritics are also useful in historical statements, in which the important thing is to keep in mind a series of minor modifications. Thus Latin *æ* gave Romance *ę* and *œ* gave *ẹ*, which is the same as the outcome of Latin short *ĕ* as compared with Latin long *ē*. The diacritics help to keep in mind the likeness and unlikeness of these sounds at each stage. Additional vowel signs, however, may also be needed when two languages enter one discussion, e.g. in the case cited of Norwegian *sol* and English *sole*. The detail of vocalic nuances is extremely refined, and attempts to find 64 or 128 fixed points seem still inadequate to frame the facts. Mechanical recording shows that the same vowels in the same contexts may differ from one individual to another or from one utterance to another.

The sonants are capable of functioning as syllabic units, and when they do so phoneticians are wont to put a small vertical line beneath them, while phonologists often use a small circle. They are normally pronounced with vibrating vocal chords, but these may be wholly or partially silenced as, for instance, for Welsh *ll*. In the history of Indo-European languages the sonants have shown capacity for generating various vowels, and they can be short or long. When used with other vowels, it is sometimes convenient to regard them, as in Lithuanian, as semivowels. *L* after a vowel readily passed into *u*, as Latin *alteru-* > French *autre*. *M* and *n* may affect a preceding vowel with their nasal quality, and then themselves disappear; the vowel also may become denasalized: *Ulisipone* > *Lisbona* > *Lisbõa* > *Lisboa*. *R* is liable to be confused with *l* or *d*, and of the pair *r/l* some languages have only the one, other languages only the other.

The various buccal consonants (pronounced with the uvula pressed against the back wall of the mouth so as to prevent an escape of air by the nose) are arranged in the table in a series of correspondences familiar to us. The voiceless sound (such as *p*) results from the obstacle to the airstream, which causes an explosion or a friction, and to it corresponds a voiced sound (such as *b*) which has in addition vibration of the vocal chords. The voiced consonants may thus be regarded as in some sense secondary, and in the history of language this seems indeed to have been the case. But the correspondences need not be of this sort. In Russian most consonants fall into a normal and a palatalized order, so that the corresponding series is *p ṕ/ b b́*. In Modern Greek the voiceless series is occlusive and the voiced is fricative: *p/β*. In Swahili *p t ch k* are pronounced with outgoing breath (explosives), but *b d j g* with incoming breath (implosives). The pairs may be denoted as *p/b*, &c., though this *b* is radically unlike an English *b*; but in Zulu we must distinguish between a normal explosive *b* and an implosive *ɓ*. In other languages still the pairs may be the result of added aspiration or glottal stop. Thus Chinese distinguishes normal *p* and aspirated *p'*; casually and dialectally the normal *p* may be slightly voiced and sound to us as *b*. In Quechua there is normal *p*, aspirate *ph*, and glottalized *pp*, and so also for the other occlusives. The primitive Indo-European system was triple or quadruple: *p/b bh* or possibly *p ph/b bh*.

It is also possible to distinguish pairs by tension, as in Finnish. Finnish *tt/t* and *t/d* are different systems of correspondences, though *t* is apparently common to each; it is the relaxed aspect of the first, and the tense aspect of the second. Voiced sounds in this system do not exist *per se*, but as relaxations of others. In Mende (Sierra Leone) the opposition of 'strong' and 'weak' consonants is thoroughgoing, giving pairs like *t/l k/g f/v s/j p/w*, but also pairs in which the tense consonant has a double formation in the mouth: *kp/gb mb/b nd/l ŋg/y ŋg/w nj/y*. These consonants of double formation seem to be units and not two sounds, i.e. they are uttered once and not in two moments, so that their representation by two consonants is a reflection of European speech-habits rather than a true picture of Mende practice.

As with vowels, so with consonants, extra signs are required when making comparative or historical statements or describing particular languages. We need more signs for Semitic languages to symbolize positions in the velum and pharynx. In Hindustani there is a systematic difference between dental *t d r* (simple or aspirated) and cerebral, domal, or retroflex [*ṭ ḍ ṛ*], &c. The phonetician requires suitable signs, but the phonologist often contents himself with his ubiquitous dots: *t d r/ ṭ ḍ ṛ*. There is a similar situation in Semitic. No phonetic alphabet could embrace all the vagaries of human utterance and remain manageable. The International Phonetic Association, when it reaches phenomena too remote from European speech-habits, seems to prefer digraphs (i.e. the combination of two letters to signify one sound) to diacritics (modifications of the value of a letter suggested by marks above or below). It is pertinent to remember, however, that one of the greatest phoneticians, Jan Hus, used diacritics (in the form of points, which have later become chevrons in his own language), and that his alphabet is the most satisfactory for eastern Europe, since it has been officially adopted by the languages which use the Latin script.

A familiar sound of double formation is the labiovelar *w* of *wen*, and its voiceless mate [ʍ] of *when* (in northern English). The lip-rounding is energetic in English so that the sound is likely to be placed among labials, but less so in Spanish where the greater part of the effect is supposed to come from the friction of the back of the tongue and velum. This Spanish *hu*[w] alternates with *bw gw* in vulgar speech: *huevo* 'egg' = *buevo güevo*, whence *bueno* 'good' = *güeno*. If encountered for the first time in an African dialect *w* might have been transcribed as *[βγ]. The 'Kaffir clicks' of Zulu, Xhosa, Hottentot, and Bushman are also consonants with double formation in the mouth.[1] Those of Zulu are dental *c*, palato-alveolar *q*, and lateral *x*. They may also be voiced (*gc gq gx*), aspirated (*ch qh xh*), or nasalized (*nc nq nx*). The principle of their formation is the attachment of the tongue at two points of the roof of the mouth in such a way as to cause a partial vacuum. The release of the front obstacle causes a noise of suction, and that of the back, which immediately follows, causes an outburst of air; hence the click, located at the teeth or palate or at one side of the mouth.

The phonetic alphabet of vowels and consonants results from the much older labour of alphabet formation, and they are, like letters, an abstract inference from speech. Before alphabetic letters could be defined, analysis isolated syllables. A consonant, by definition, cannot be uttered without aid from a vowel (the fricatives are only noises in such a case), and the vowels would run into each other but for intervening narrowings or occlusions by consonants. The syllable, however, is as refractory to definition as the single vowel or consonant sign, and is not a self-contained unit of speech. No more so is the word. This is sometimes shown in spelling, as *l'enfant*/*le chat* or Gaelic *an cat*/gen. *a' chait*, but spelling is arbitrary. The unit of every utterance is the breath-group: the whole series of sounds uttered before pause for breath or for relaxation in the energy of emission of the breath-stream. There is no constancy in such groups, since they depend on the habits of the speaker and his intentions at any moment, but every utterance is made up of groups and the tenseness and relaxation of constituent sounds is determined by their position in the group. The air comes out in fullest volume at the beginning of the group and decreases towards zero at the end. It is renewed by stresses of varying intensity at intervals—usually at fairly regular intervals, such as alternate syllables—and these stresses include both those which share in the structure of words (principal, secondary, unstressed), and those which the emotion of the moment may superadd. Thus an actual utterance such as *I don't think so* may, in fact, be the group [àidṇθínkso] and *Pierre! Ôte ces fleurs qui me donnent mal à la tête*

[1] C. M. Doke, *Zulu Grammar*, London, 1947, p. 19.

would be [pjɛ̀R/ótsèflœ̀R'kimdonmalalatêt], with two groups and one semipause and three degrees of stress. We reserve this sort of transcription for languages without literary tradition, such as Eskimo, Aztec, or Bantu, and what we set down as a phonetic transcription is really a phonetic reinterpretation of the written character. This is intelligible at the cost of being faithful. So one may write:

The north wind and the sun were disputing which was the stronger.
|ðə nó:θ wind ənd ðə sʌn wə dispjú:tiŋ ˈwĭtš wəz ðə stróŋgə|.

Similarly, *les œufs* would be transcribed as [lez œ́], not [lezœ́] or [le zœ́], though it is undoubtedly one utterance and undoubtedly the [z] of the liaison begins the second syllable. In an unwritten language like Swahili 'I told him' could be written *ni ka mw-ambia* or *nikamwambia*, and the choice of the latter is a matter of convenience, chiefly for foreigners. To transcribe the languages of North America modified forms of the international phonetic alphabet are used for normal alphabetic purposes, but Aztec Nahuatl has also a long-established Spanish alphabet. Little has yet been done to investigate the natives' awareness of the meaning of parts of their word-sentences, though they must recognize stems as they are uttered and must infer relations from their order, just as we do by means of words and their arrangement. On the whole, it may be found that the breath-groups of literary languages are more complex utterances than the word-sentences of the illiterate, simply because the speakers have a mental picture of how their sentences would look. In *The Frogs* Dionysus is forced to utter eighty-six syllables on one occasion without drawing breath.

Since phonetics is a physical science, it permits measurements and experiments,[1] some of a very simple kind. The most effective instruments of research are the trained ear and, within our own language, our own knowledge of our muscular movements. The ear is important because it alone receives the full import of speech-sounds, and it fixes the limits of the study. What cannot be heard is not a factor in speech. If a machine reveals nuances not noticed by the ear, they may be the unperceived beginning of some future sound-shift, but they cannot be significant to present speakers. The argument cannot be projected into past time for lack of phonetic records, though the assumption of unperceived shifts

[1] J. Tarneaud and S. Borel-Maisonny, *Traité pratique de phonologie*, Paris, 1941.

plays a large part in phonological explanations. Moreover, speech-sounds must be so grossly spaced as to be convincing to untrained ears. The skilled investigator may perceive and demonstrate some nuance not commonly recognized, such as the peculiar formation of the *s* in *horse*, but his demonstration does not affect the social conscience, which regards every *s* as *s*. Something like speech may be obtained by rattling grains in a microphone, but what occurs within the microphone is less known than what occurs within our own mouths.

Hands clapped on the ears will reveal the vibrations of vocal chords as a buzz, which is not present with voiceless sounds. There is no simple way of observing movements of the uvula, but no doubt when air is emitted through the nose. The twang of a nasal is unmistakable, even when it lightly affects the whole discourse ($\delta 1$). The absence of this twang is equally obvious ($\delta 0$). For aspiration ($\epsilon 2$) of *h* or of *p t k*, it is sufficient to hold a piece of tissue-paper before the mouth. It will shake if there is aspiration, as in Eng. *quiet*, but remain steady if there is none, as in French *qui*. Movements of the lips can be observed before a mirror, to show closure, rounding and fissure friction and the contact of the lower lip and the upper teeth. For the tongue one must rely on awareness of movement. It is easy to produce desired sounds in slow motion and prolong the tensions.

A false palate, lightly dusted with chalk and slipped into the mouth, will show the exact area of contact between the tongue and roof of the mouth when this occurs. It shows, for instance, quite clearly the escape areas for lateral consonants. The rhino-pharyngo-scope and laryngo-pharyngoscope show action by the uvula and glottis. They are tiny inclined mirrors (at $33°$ and $11°$ respectively). The tongue has to be drawn forward to reveal the glottis. If a plug is inserted in the nostrils, a cup over the lips, and a grip on the glottis, vibrations of the nasal chamber, mouth and vocal chords can be recorded as three lines on a revolving drum. The resulting oscillations give more information than we can as yet use, since they show differences in each recurrence of the 'same' sound. The combined information also is in some way less than that which the ear takes in. Recording may be electric or photoelectric. Audible sounds runs from about *doh*[1] to *mi*[5], that is from $\frac{1}{64}$ to $\frac{1}{1364}$ of a second. The vibrations of the vocal chords are too rapid to be visible, but a stroboscope will reveal them. Thus, *doh*[2] has a vibration lasting $\frac{1}{128}$ second. The stroboscope is adjusted to $\frac{1}{127}$ second and cuts out all but one vibration in 128 of them. An oscillograph at slow speed records the length, intensity, characteristics, glides, and modes of association of vibrations, and at high speed it records sonority.

Various devices are based on the use of X-rays. Radiography gives flat images as drawn diagrams do, and cineradiography shows these images in motion. Radioscopy enables the investigator to see what takes place as movements on a flat plate. Sounds, of course, are cubically conditioned, but a necessary assumption is that secondary adjustments depend on the position determined for the central line of the mouth, whether that be observed photographically or by our awareness of our own muscular movements.

THE PHONEME

Dovetailed with the physical measurements of the phonetician are the historical statements of the phonologist. They are historical, as we have said, even when they refer to one time only. They are affirmations made concerning time and place, but those of the physical scientist are not so qualified. The particulars asserted by the phonologist are phonemes (Gk. φώνημα 'speech-sound')[1] and we are warned not to confuse them with the speech-sounds of the phonetician. One may protest that the sounds of a given speech should be called speech-sounds, the more so since the phonetician examines differences which may be too minute to play a role in any actual language. Technical terms are usually defined within the science to which they belong and the same term may be used without ambiguity in different sciences, as 'subject' in logic, grammar, and anatomy. A speech-sound in this sense may be one which has no place in any language known to us. The phonetician is entitled to pursue his studies beyond the point at which a distinction is possible in any speech. On the other hand the word phoneme tends to overflow into the domain of phonetics and to be used virtually to mean a speech-sound in broad transcription. Its popularity seems to be determined by a dislike of English usage.

[1] N. S. Troubetzkoy, *Principes de phonologie*, Paris, 1949; D. Jones, *The Phoneme*, Cambridge, 1949; F. de Saussure, *Cours de linguistique générale*, 4 ed., Paris, 1949; E. Sapir, *Selected Writings*, University of California, Berkeley, 1949, pp. 33–72.

The phoneme is a 'place' in the sound-system of a given language. Since language is arbitrary in its nature such a 'place' is also arbitrary. It is defined by the mystery of 'hearing'. We hear a *d* in *had* and *hard* and an *s* in *house* and *horse* despite the difference of formation of *d* and *s* resulting from the retroflex *r*, but an Indian hears *d* and *ḍ*, *s* and *ṣ* in his language. It is not impossible for an Englishman to hear the two *d*s and *s*s in Hindustani or to represent them to his own mind in Sanskrit, nor difficult for him to identify the retroflex sounds in his own language. While he accepts the pronunciation of a Welshman, a Scot, or another Englishman as 'the same' as his own, there is nothing of which he is more aware than what he calls a difference of 'accent'. That is to say acoustically he notices unlikeness at the same time as he 'hears' 'sameness' of sounds as they affect comprehension. Since the hearer is also a speaker, we may consider either the hearer's or the speaker's instinct in this matter, and in view of the actual difficulties of pronunciation we may describe the phoneme as a sound 'aimed at'. The main fact to keep in mind is that there is an inescapable subjective element in the phoneme. The effect of this has been to turn discussions of the phoneme in upon themselves so as to have a quasi-metaphysical twist. Grimm's law, the geographical principle that the oldest terms are found on frontiers, and the comparative method in philology are theses which can be discussed in themselves, but they are also firm bases for positive assertions, but the end of the latest study of the phoneme is a hope that 'it may prove to be of assistance towards determining the nature of the phoneme itself'.

The phoneme is a 'place' and not a point because it has magnitude. It is intrinsically variable. The variations heard in the speech of different individuals and in that of the same individual at different times when recorded electrically, prove that no two sounds are ever pronounced quite alike. To get rid of the variations due to difference of person we are advised to transcribe the usage of one person only. 'A "language" is to be taken to mean the speech of one individual pronouncing in a definite and consistent style.' But what we deduce from this study is not the speech of Mr. *X* or Mr. *Y* operating under uniform conditions, but the phonemes of English, French, or whatever language we are seeking to describe. It would be possible for the speech of Mr. *X* to stand for English (or any other language) if he were a person of uniquely mediocre genius or if it were a fact that all displacements are symmetrical. E. Sapir has pointed out that in a symmetrical displacement like

$$X: \quad a \quad b \quad c \quad d$$
$$Y: \quad a \quad b \quad c \quad d$$

the pattern and its places remain the same. But as between two speakers of English the displacements may not by symmetrical and yet the phonemes are recognized as 'the same'. A northerner's vowels and *r* are displaced with regard to those of a southerner while *l m n p t k* and *c* remain unaffected. Yet the northern vowels and *r* are phonematically the same as those of the southerner; they also are places in the pattern which constitutes English.

The phonemes are places endowed with 'psychological reality' (Sapir). Both terms are, perhaps, somewhat ambitious but we may agree that phonemes represent things on which the speaker feels he can count for the expression of a meaning, and that the hearer understands in the same sense as the speaker; they are, moreover, of such a nature that both speaker and hearer would resist a reproach of unlikeness. But it is not necessarily the case that the judgement is one of vowels and consonants at all. One of E. Sapir's informants resisted the suggestion that Sarcee *dìní* 'this' was the same as *dìní* 'it makes a sound'. When the problem was reduced to its proper terms, it became clear that these two words have different associations in the language. *Dìní* 'this' +-*i* 'the one who' or -*la* 'it turns out that' becomes *dìná·ᵃ* and *dìníla*, but *dìní* 'it makes a sound' develops into *dìnítí* and *dìníta*. There are historical reasons for the difference but they would not enter into the mind of an illiterate speaker. He was judging by association and not hearing an inaudible difference in *dìní*. In a similar fashion an Oxford amateur of language used to assert that the speech of Scottish western islanders is so pure that they always distinguish in pronunciation between *their* and *there*. If we leave aside the implication that the English are not judges of the purity of English, the allegation may be defended in two ways, neither of which recognize a difference between *their* and *there*. The words differ in their associations since *their/theirs* is opposed to the invariable *there*; and they may have such casual differences of utterance as even an Englishman may put into the phrase *there's theirs*. We have already noted that no two occurrences of the 'same' sound are identical so that a difference in syntactical use is liable to appear in enunciation though it does not count as a phoneme.

Baudouin de Courtenay treated the phoneme on two planes: physiophonetics and psychophonetics. On the one side it is the sound as 'heard'; on the other the sound as an image in the speaker's mind, a sound 'aimed at'. Prince Troubetzkoy has also spoken of the phoneme as a 'Lautgebilde' though he has insisted on its phonetic reality. D. Jones has sought to prove that it is a phonetic reality in each language and that this will appear with some adjustments of phonetic theory. The phoneme is a speech-sound in broad transcription. Since broad transcription is made up of a number of narrow transcriptions (which he seems to propose to call phones), the phoneme is, according to D. Jones, formed by a family of speech-sounds. The phoneme can be identified by various signs. It occurs alone in absolute positions, as in *ma do*, which gives us the four phonemes [m a d o]. We may find pairs of such a nature that they agree in all but one particular but differ significantly in that one. Thus *had/hat*, *rum/run*, *sin/sing* establish the English phonemes [d t m r n ŋ], and ŋ being thus established, it is recognized again in *sink* [siŋk]. Whenever we cannot find such exclusive pairs, we may work to the same effect by analogy. Reliance on significant difference leads to the defintion of the phoneme as a 'minimum unit of distinctive sound-feature' (L. Bloomfield), with the rider that differences that do not signify do not constitute phonemes. Thus *not/nature*, *tune*, *can/kin* reveal only the phonemes *t* and *k*, though we can hear differences which we caricature as *naychoor* and Mark Twain's *kyer = care*. No distinction in the system known as English is implied by these variations and they are discounted. It is admitted that there are phonemes which overlap the boundaries of other phonemes and are then to be called diaphones. This occurs in the speech of different individuals, since the habits of one overstep the limits of toleration established for himself by the other. An obvious case is provided by 'cockney' *h*. *H* is not sounded in many positions by southern Englishmen, but they insist on the aspirate in others which the more logical cockney ignores. The diaphones are also found in the speech of a single individual. Russian *e* is a phoneme which overlaps *i* in *nesëte* and *ja* in *leto* (Jones, p. 95) and French [œ] [ɔ] sometimes overlap. It is suggested that *t* and *r* may overlap in the speech of some Englishmen, and even that there may be diphonemes, i.e. phonemes which belong to two different orders, but these are set at a convenient distance in Hindustani and Japanese.

Perhaps it would be simplest not to admit the existence of diphonemes (i.e. of single phonemes which have two values simultaneously) until more evidence is available. That which is offered at present is remote and inconclusive. In Hindustani *me* may be pronounced *mẽ* without change of meaning and even without notice by speakers, but there is also a *mẽ* which may not be pronounced *me*. The awareness of the speakers in the last case and their unawareness in the first suggests the possibility of some difference in the degree of nasalization (δ1 and δ2 or δ3). Few Spaniards are aware of the occasional nasal in *mano* 'hand' and yet in *mensajero* < Fr. *messager* this nasal has become so prominent that it has made itself felt as a separate sound. Portuguese nasalization in *mim minha* < *mi mia* and Portuguese denasalization in *boa* < *bona* both imply an intermediate stage at which the nasal was very slight (Jespersen's δ1, not his δ2). A 'nasal accent' may creep over the whole of a speaker's utterance without affecting the meaning of that which he says, but it still leaves him with distinctive nasal sounds. The Japanese evidence is that *ji zu* occur in the two series *da/de/ji/do/zu* and *za/ze/ji/zo/zu*, but this does not imply that *ji zu* may belong *simultaneously* to the orders *da* and *za*. Individual words belong exclusively to one or the other. Thus *ji* 'letter' belongs to the *za* series since it comes from Chinese *tzŭ*[4], but *ji* 'earth' belongs to the *da* series since it is from Chinese *ti*[4].

It would not be prudent either to admit too quickly that a phoneme is made of atomic phones. The difference between broad and narrow phonetic transcriptions is a relative one, and does not carry with it any admissions of absolute values for the narrow transcriptions. One transcribes as narrowly as is convenient for the purpose in hand, but electric recordings show that discrimination may be carried to almost any length. The supposed 'phone' may have no existence. For aspects of the phoneme certain special terms have been proposed, such as *chroneme* for length, *toneme* for pitch, and *stroneme* (*horresco referens*) for stress, and it is suggested that these are reducible to atomic *chrones* (!), *tones*, and *strones* (!). There is little more in this than mere assertion. For length there exists a unit already established in classical grammar, viz. the *mora*. *Tones* of fixed mathematical value exist in music and of relative value in the tonal languages, but in them the tone is an integral part of the phoneme. In non-tonal languages there are patterns of tone applied to the clause or sentence. It seems there is a risk of confusing under the one term toneme (1) the pitch element intrinsic to a phoneme in such a language as Chinese and (2) the pattern of pitch used significantly in a whole clause or sentence as in English and Spanish. Among the Bantu languages the tonal pattern of the clause is important for Swahili, but there are nine possible intrinsic tones in the construction of Zulu words. There are features of stress in all languages, of course, but the suggestion that they can be measured in atomic units seems to go far beyond the evidence. Latin *vĕnī* 'come'/*vēnī* 'I came', Czech *hrabĕ* 'earl'/*hrábĕ* 'rake' differ significantly in length, but *ĕ*/*ē* *a*/*á* are intrinsically different phonemes rather than different lengths of the same one. Serbian *grȁd* 'hail'/*grâd* 'town', *gòra* 'worse'/*gòra* 'mountain', *sèlo* 'village'/*sélo* 'soirée' reveal four orders of phonemes—short-falling tone, long-falling tone, short-rising tone, long-rising tone—in which length and pitch are intrinsic features, not additional qualities. In Chinese, Swedish, and Zulu the tone is part of the constitution of the whole word, as Swed. *panter* (3.1) 'panther'/*panter* (3.2) 'oaths' (where 3, 2, 1 are decreasing degrees of stress as well as tone), Ch. *hai*[2] 'child'/*hai*[3] 'sea'. Tone may also be used with a definite grammatical value for the clause, as in parentheses, while tone, stress, and length may be used affectively. Differences of stress having significance for whole words occur in *íncrease*/*incréase*, *ímport*/*impórt*, Germ. *Wiéderholen* 'fetch back'/*widerhólen* 'repeat', Sp. *término* 'end'/*termíno* 'I end'/*terminó* 'he ended', Russ. *vórot* 'winch'/*voróta* 'gale'.

F. de Saussure approached the phoneme structurally when he considered language as composed of 'a limited number of elements or phonemes, susceptible in turn of being evoked by a corresponding number of written signs'. With reference to the speaker's mental image and what the hearer hears, he defined the phoneme as the 'sum of acoustic impressions and articulatory movements, the unit heard and the unit spoken; it is already a complex unit with a foot in each chain'. The hope of defining the phoneme in such a way that a single letter may be attached with an unambiguous sense leads to the reflection that one of the objectives of phonematic theory is to provide the basis for a rational spelling. It is of the nature of alphabetical signs that they carry with them a considerable measure of consent among speakers both by what they acknowledge and by what they ignore, and most alphabets have been at some time approximately phonemic. Tradition keeps some spellings faithful to outmoded pronunciations and the etymological principle that spelling should show the origin of a word introduces a consideration which is not proper to orthography; but there are still a certain number of alphabetical transcriptions (such as the Czech and Spanish) which express the speaker's conception of what is significant in speech-sounds and what is not, at least as well as a transcription in samples borrowed from the international phonetic alphabet. The latter may be used profitably to reveal differences of formation among sounds accepted as 'the same' in the pattern of the language.

When a European or an American scholar and a native informant sit down to give an account of an illiterate language, the resultant signs may be described indifferently as letters, phonemes, or speech-sounds in broad transcription. There is no native tradition of spelling to be taken into account and the informant has only just so much independence of judgement as his scientific collaborator allows. His information will be expressed in terms of the Latin alphabet in one of its forms. But it is very easy to forget that alphabetical analysis came late in human history. Sapir's informant in the anecdote quoted evidently thought of the whole word as a unit, keeping in mind its syntactical variants. The analysis of Chinese deals with a complex of sounds which forms the end of a word and which includes, according to our system, glides, semivowels, vowels, and final consonants. But beyond identifying the end Chinese native processes of analysis do not advance. They were only able to note another series of beginning of words, of a consonantal nature, so that each word was analysed into a beginning (when it began with a consonant) and a complex end. Those who felt that this represented the limit of analysis compatible with the special conditions of Chinese were familiar with the intricate phonetic system used for Sanskrit, so that it is hard to resist the conclusion that this distinction of beginnings and ends seemed to them proper to the special character of Chinese words.

The Japanese kana script is syllabic and is appropriate to a language of open syllables. The sign covers both the vowel sound and the consonant and also any modification of the one by the other. Arranged in five orders, the kana signs show an appreciation of the fivefold system of Japanese, and to the ordinary signs there are added others (*nigori* 'muddling') to show when primary phonemes are changed by composition to secondary values.

The system is thus an attempt to show the sound system of Japanese in its symmetry and its normal modifications. Thus there are series like *pa/pe/pi/po/pu* and *ga/ge/gi/go/gu*. But there are also series like *ta/te/chi/to/tsu, ha/he/hi/ho/fu, da/de/ji/do/zu*, and *za/ ze/ji/zo/zu*, in which changes of formation due to the association of vowel and consonant are not allowed to disturb the overriding consideration of symmetrical structure. Considerations of structure are by definition phonematic and recent proposals for the spelling known as Romagi seem to indicate that Japanese authorities find in their traditional analysis a better representation of structure than can be obtained from the Latin alphabet with its European connotations. Their design seems to be to use the Latin resources in a Japanese way. Syllabic analysis was used for Babylonian and Hittite, while ancient Egyptian, Hebrew, and Arabic identified consonants only, except for the pointing of sacred books. Even Sanskrit was syllabic to the extent of assuming the presence of *a* unless there were some sign to the contrary, and by writing consonants into each other when not separated by a vowel, allowance was made in one sign for their mutual effects.

The Latin alphabet and the international phonetic alphabet which is based upon it contain some assumptions which are not universal. It is sensitive to voicing: a *p* is not a *b*. But there are languages, such as Arunta and Quechua, in which voicing is merely accidental: a *p* may be a *b* as in *pampa/Cochabamba*. It discriminates five vowels, but there are languages which have only three and others which have seven or more. The Latin alphabet does not discriminate length as in Greek ϵ/η, o/ω, except by means of a diacritic, as if the length were not an intrinsic feature of the vowel. It has no signs for tone, represented by diacritics in Greek. The Latin alphabet does not take note of slight aspiration since it uses *p* for Eng. *pit* (slightly aspirate) and Fr. *pit*. The international phonetic alphabet also uses [p] in both cases with the proviso that the difference should be explained somewhere and kept in mind. But unaspirated *p* and aspirated *ph* are distinct phonemes in Chinese and Quechua. The distinction is found in the Greek alphabet π/ϕ τ/θ κ/χ for voiceless consonants and is a feature of Georgian and Armenian orthography. Neither Latin nor Greek offers a sign for a glottalized consonant such as Quechua *pp tt kk qq*. Thus three orders of voiceless consonants are phonemes in Quechua but cannot be represented by single letters as de Saussure wishes because

of the assumptions of the Latin alphabet, and on the other hand
the Latin distinction of voiceless and voiced (*p*/*b*) is not phonematic in Quechua. In Aranta, vacillations of orthography occur
such as *arantara*/*iruntera*/*irundera* 'son and daughter of my father's
mother's brother', *mbana*/*umbirna* 'son and daughter of my mother's
mother's brother', and *lpa*/*lba*/*alpa*/*ulpa*/*ilba*/*ulba* 'curve inwards,
return'.

The Latin script does not provide for phonemes which vary
according to tension. But this is a principal structural feature of
the Finno-Ugrian languages. Initially and in open syllables the
consonant is tense, but in a closed syllable it is relaxed, as Finn.
kukka 'flower'/*kukat* 'flowers', *tyttö* 'girl'/*tytöt*, *pappi* 'priest'/*papit*,
setä 'uncle'/*sedät*, *tupa* 'room'/*tuvat*, *vika* 'fault'/*viat*. It is true
that means have been found to adapt the Latin alphabet to this
situation, but not in the sense that each phoneme is represented by
a letter. That would have required new creations or new evalua-
tions, such as *T for *tt*/*t* *t for *t*/*d*. Similar problems of tension
arise in African languages like Mende. The phoneme shows a
regular variation from a double stop in the tense position to a
single stop in the relaxed, as Mende *mba*/*ba*, *ŋgulu*/*wulu*, *ŋgeŋge*/
yeŋge, or else it is voiced or made into a fricative as *pɛlɛ*/*wɛlɛ*,
kɔlɔ/*gɔlɔ*, *sani*/*jani*, *ndoma*/*loma*, *kpato*/*gbato*, *tawa*/*lawa*. Though
these are conditional changes of single phonemes the assumptions
of the Latin alphabet do not allow us to represent them by single
letters. Any letter chosen would implicitly exclude the casual
variant.

The shortcomings of the Latin alphabet and of the international
phonetic alphabet which is based upon it are corrected to some
extent by assigning precise values to otiose signs, by the use of
diacritics above or below letters, and by the use of digraphs.[1] But
it is doubtful if we can really attain the ideal of one sign for one

---

[1] Professor Jones has proposed a number of new digraphs in *The Phoneme* and
he has stated once again his objection to the use of diacritics. But while Hus
obtained the letters needed to express the difference between normal and palatal
sounds in Slavonic by placing a dot above the Latin letter, the modern phonetician obtains the same effect by placing a tick below the letter. The principle
seems to be the same though there may be an advantage in the latter system. On
the other hand Hus's method attained one of the objectives of phonematic theory
by forming a reasonably accurate alphabet of phonemes which has actually been
accepted by Baltic and Slavonic peoples. The modern phonetician writes *ts* and
tʃ in one sign on top of each other to represent Russian ц and ч, but this
solution is not more neat than Hus's contribution of new values to *c* and *č*.

sound. Perhaps it is wrong to speak of unconditional speech-sounds. An initial sound is conditioned by being initial and therefore tense and capable of recording differences which cannot be made in final relaxed positions. In Russian initial and medial voiced and voiceless occlusives, affricates, and fricatives can be distinguished, but only voiceless sounds are heard in final positions. In Spanish, *m ñ n* can be distinguished initially, but at the end of a syllable there is a highly variable nasal which is *n* at the point of rest. Final *m* and *ñ* do not exist. But the final *n* is pronounced in all positions possible for a nasal consonant, viz. [m] *amparo invierno*, [ɱ] *infierno*, [n] *donde*, [ɲ] *concha*, and [ŋ] *cinco*. One cannot cover the structural complexities by simply accepting three phonemes *m n ñ*.[1] To be one of the constituent sounds of a language it is not necessary to be significant. Spanish *b d g* are of such a nature that they are occlusive in tense positions and fricative in relaxed positions. It makes no difference to the sense, however, an increase of tension turns fricatives into occlusives. This may happen either when words are pronounced with special emphasis or as a personal speech habit in some consonant groups. But if all the fricatives are pronounced as occlusives by a foreigner the situation becomes accoustically intolerable; it is no longer Spanish. Thus both the occlusive and the fricative values of *b d g* must be reckoned in the system of Spanish sounds though they may be exchanged in modern (though not in medieval Spanish) without confusion of sense.

Again, though we may have identified certain phonemes, it does not follow that there may not be some other phoneme which varies over the whole identified range. In Portuguese we can identify [s] *certo*, [z] *zombar*, [š] *deixar fechar*, [ž] *gente ja*, but there is also a constructional unit *s* which has all of these values: [s] *são passar*, [z] *rosa*, [š] *aves*, [ž] *desde*. In Brazilian *s* is a phoneme which varies only from [s] to [z], but Portuguese and Brazilians have no difficulty in realizing that their units of speech are 'the same'.

In respect of their sounds languages are constructed from variable units into conventional patterns and both units and patterns are valid only for the language under discussion. A universal theory of the phoneme like a universal alphabet incurs serious difficulty in

---

[1] [ŋ] *cinco* is rejected because it does not occur alone. The word *zinc* may be pronounced [θin] or [θiŋ]. But as a variant of final *n* the speech-sound [ŋ] has as much existence in Spanish *cinco* as in English *think*.

the attempt to reduce a convention to a science. The 'places' in each system vary too much to be susceptible of simple definition or reduced with scientific precision to single letters. Letters must be used as economically as possible but they require to be supported in each language by much fuller statements. Meanwhile there is some risk that the use of phonetic signs to express phonemes may lead to excessive toleration of real differences. It is said that in one type of southern English the quality of *e* is wholly determined by length, so that *set/sate* should be written as *set/se:t*. But the conventional spelling advises me that there is a difference of quality as well as length, while the phonematic spelling proposed (even if its assumptions were true) only records length and leaves the difference of quality unexpressed. The proper business of phonetic signs is to state how sounds differ in respect of formation whether the difference is commonly 'heard' or not. If the phonetic sign is used alongside the alphabetical, we can attain greater precision by the use of two co-ordinates *set* [set]/*sate* [se:t]. If phonematic signs take the place of alphabetical signs, there is a risk of losing sight of a real distinction or of so relaxing the use of phonetic symbols that they no longer yield precise information. There is also some risk of pressing too far the notion of system by demanding a degree of symmetry which it is beyond the nature of language to give.

PHONOLOGY

For over a hundred years the traditional preoccupation of the student of language has been to trace changes of speech-sounds over the course of the years. This is the diachronic method which, at one time, was alone deemed scientific. The notion of 'science' was that of the biological sciences of last century and aimed at the production of 'laws' of development. By means of equations and the isolation of particulars, it was possible to reconstruct lost stages of language. Speech-sounds as such mean nothing and are thus relatively immune from mental interference. It was found that the sequences of changes obtained from numberless equations were uniform, apart from individual instances which could be accounted for by constructing other 'laws'. The historian of human actions once hoped to predict the future as a repetition of past events, or at least to discover general causes which would lead to determinate effects; but he now knows that humanity is too complex for this sort of calculation, that history does not repeat itself and probably has no pattern, and that the truly scientific attitude for him is to record and interpret sequences of events. The linguist deals with a portion—the characteristic element—of the human story, and his science is also one of record. But it does happen that sounds change in a remarkably uniform and total fashion, and that the phonologist has a physical science of measurement (phonetics) at hand to explain these changes to his satisfaction.[1] The same kind of satisfaction is not to be obtained from the study of grammatical changes, since they involve the notion of grammatical function, which is hard to grasp, and it is not obtainable at all from stylistics.

Traditionally this sort of study has been divided between phonology and morphology. Unless the latter term be extended to cover the whole range grammar, as in Meillet's definition,[2] it cannot be regarded as omnipresent in language. There are languages which Russian scholars describe as 'amorphous', i.e. isolating and invariable. The word does not suffer any change of form, but is associated with auxiliaries and placed in a significant order. Change of form would also seem to be ruled out by totally polysynthetic grammars, where the stems fuse into a sentence and yield meaning by order and, perhaps, some auxiliary signs. It is also doubtful whether we gain much by discussing the morphology of an agglutinative language like Turkish. There the word, as such, remains invariable (as *ev* 'house') and receives a series of affixes each of which is definite in form and meaning.

Morphology is important in the inflected languages, both in their synthetic and their analytic states, because it sets up a number of fixed patterns—parts of speech, declensions, conjugations—which are retained in the mind and subject to comparison and scrutiny. In such tongues the paradigms are convenient objective facts, and it is convenient to begin with them and ask what grammatical functions they perform. Thus morphology looks toward syntax. As regards phonology, however, these modifications set up special

[1] The most lucid short accounts are by A. Meillet, *La Méthode comparative en linguistique historique*, Oslo, 1925, and *Introduction à l'étude comparative des langues indo-européennes*, Paris, 1924. Cf. also E. H. Sturtevant, *Linguistic Change*, New York, 1924.

[2] 'La morphologie, c'est à dire l'ensemble des procédés par lesquels on modifie et on groupe les mots pour constituer les phrases.' He goes on to show that by grouping he understands 'des particules ou mots accessoires et l'ordre des mots'. In so doing he subsumes syntax into morphology, which is a convenient arrangement for the highly inflected languages he usually studied. By morphology I mean only the modification of words within the sentence.

conditions of stress and result in sound-changes that are not always the same as those of speech-sounds singly or in combination. Thus between Latin *tenére dícere* and Spanish *tenér decír* (Portuguese *dizér*) we encounter a shift of accent due to the possibility of comparing two paradigms (*-ēre/ĕre*) after the loss of the distinction of vowel-quantity, and in Latin *cantámus cantátis cantabámus cantabátis/* Spanish *cantámos cantáis cantábamos cantábais* we recognize a different analysis of the paradigm. Latin envisages as endings *-ámus -átis*, Spanish sees the stem as *cantá-*. In its phonological aspect morphology activates the working of analogy against the sound-laws.

The data revealed by linguistic geography also belong to the diachronic scale. Though existing all at one time, they do not form one system of language, but successive systems of which the earlier show as outcrops at a distance from the centre of disturbance. In a geological map London clay leads to the chalk of the Chilterns and the limestone of the Cotswolds, because the clay has been deposited on chalk, and the chalk on limestone. The pattern in space reveals a temporal scale. So English *church* and Scottish *kirk*, though both in use today, represent different phases of the development of *kyriaké*, and others are revealed by German *Kirche* and Russian *cérkov'*. The [k] of Latin *cantare* exists in modern Picardy, Provence, and Gascony, alongside French [š] *chanter*. It is often convenient to read history from the map rather than to delve down to attested or conjectural older forms, just as it is easier to study limestones in the Cotswolds than to sink a bore to the limestones under London clays. 'January' as a personal name or name of a month existed in Mozarabic Spanish of the tenth century as *janayr*, but one cannot be certain of the value of the vowels owing to the peculiarities of the Arabic alphabet; we know all about Portuguese *janeiro*, however, and this throws light on the earlier state of Spanish *enero* (from *jenuariu*—as we see from Catalan *gener*). Where historical research would only give a probable conclusion (it is probable that the Mozarabic name and month were pronounced [jenair]), the map-readings are certain.

The methods of spatial linguistics enable us to take 'map-readings' with considerable confidence where exact pointing is not possible. The map becomes a diagram oriented like a map. In a sense the whole world reveals a linguistic pattern, with primitive outcrops at a distance from the main centres of evolution in Europe and Asia. In Australia or South Africa or America we may get hints of what Indo-European must have been like before any state that we can reconstitute from the visible evidence. But just as in geology one must beware of the effects of folding, faulting, overthrusting, and uneven stratification, so linguistic map-readings show that there are many initiatives and that the tempo of change varies. Thus Slavonic languages once formed part of a group in rapid evolution while Greek and Latin remained relatively stable, as may be seen in the transformation of the verb and the early evolution of certain postpalatal sounds. Later on Latin and its Romance derivatives entered upon a period of swift evolution. At this day the Romance languages seem to be semianalytical, but the Slavonic still almost as synthetic as Indo-European itself. The initiatives of Castile and the Ile de France are the most important for the constitution of Spanish and French. Each linguistic feature has a different extension in the intermediate zone from Aragon to Rousillon, which is also affected by the initiatives of Barcelona.

The phonologist begins by setting up equations. They must be valid, that is really equal within the sound-system of each language, and preferably self-evident. The certainty of any explanation varies inversely with its length, and progress in these investigations is only possible on a basis of sure etyma. One such equation might be

Ptg. Sp. Cat. Prov. *tres* = Fr. *trois* = Sard. (Logodurese) *tres* = It. *tre* = Rum. *trei* 'three'.

As the object is to reconstruct an original form, the oldest available evidence should be used, and for *trois* we should substitute Old French *treis*. The phonologist then isolates his problems: *t* and *r* raise no questions, but the loss of final -*s* has to be accounted for in Italian and Romanian (and also in Fr. [trwa]) and one has to solve the equation *e* = *ei* (but not = *ie*). The last feature implies a closed *ẹ*, not an open one (*ę*), and the solution of the whole equation is Late Latin *trẹs*. But it happens that Classical Latin can be observed and records a difference of length, not quality (*trēs*), and that it contains a declension *trēs tria trium tribus*, where the Romance languages treat the numeral as invariable. It is clear that merely solving an equation does not necessarily reveal the whole truth concerning an older stage of language. On the other hand, it is perilous to take too abstract a view, and to regard the etymon as valid only for its consequences. Though there are strict limits to what we can

know, we are discussing actual speech as it existed in some past
time, e.g. when we conclude (from Lat. *fera*, Gk. θήρ, Russ. *zveŕ*
'beast') that there was an Indo-European word of the nature of
ĝhwēr. We do not assert merely that *ĝhwēr* satisfies the equation
fer(a) = θήρ = *zveŕ*, but that there actually existed a word of that
general nature. If it could be inspected we should doubtless learn
a number of unexpected facts, as in the case of the declension of
trēs, but what we know is at least approximately factual. The risk
of too abstract a treatment is to posit solutions which are scarcely
admissible as human speech.

Of course, the existence of Latin *trēs* removes the need to infer
its nature, and the phonologist's task is reversed. He has to explain
by means of *trēs* how the modern forms came into existence, e.g.
trēs > late *tręs* > Old French *treis* > *trois* [trwe] > [trwa]. The
phonologist is a historian, not merely an antiquarian; he is as much
concerned with effects as with causes, and his work continues into,
and is richest in, the language of our own times.

In dealing with the derivatives of Latin *centum* the persistence
of the letter *c* to cover quite different pronunciations has to be
discounted by use of the phonetic alphabet, and the equation is

Ptg. Cat. Prov. Fr. [s] = Sp. [θ] = It. Vegliotic [ĉ] = Alb. *q* [k']
=Sard. (Logodurese) *k* [k].

Latin *centum* was pronounced with a velar [k], and the development
follows the line [k'] > [ĉ] > ([ŝ]) > [s] > [θ] as the consonant
was attracted by the front vowel *e* more and more to the front of
the mouth.

With regard to the derivatives of *lucta* 'battle', the problem lies
in the treatment of -*ct*-, but there is doubt concerning the proper
equations. Italian *lotta* has developed in its own fashion by assimilat-
ing *c* to *t*, but not so French *lutte* which derives from Old French
luite. Sp. *luchă* = Cat. *lluita* = Prov. *locha* = Old French *luite*
reveal a development -*ct*- > -*it*- > -*ch*- [ĉ]. Albanian *luftë* and
Romanian *luptă* obviously represent a development -*ct*- > -*ft* > -*pt*-.
But this is only intelligible if the first stage is the aspiration of [k]
as [χ] or [h], and for this there is evidence in the west and in the
Umbrian dialect: Mozarabic Spanish *trúhta* 'trout', *noxte* 'night',
Gaulish *Louxterios* = *Lucterius*, Umbrian *uht* = Latin *octō* 'eight'.
It follows that the Italian process of assimilation or covering the
first occlusive by the second (*otto*) was one historical event, and the
aspiration of [k] in the group -*ct*- was another. As this second event

occurred in both Celtic and non-Celtic areas, it is not peculiarly Celtic as some have supposed. Since Gaelic *ochd* and Welsh *wyth* are equally Celtic, it is not legitimate to suppose that the shift from -*ht*- to -*it*- is a Celticism in Romance.

One may be misled also as to chronology. Serbian *berem* and Armenian *berem* look alike, but the former is a medieval development of the Common Slavonic *berǫ* (**berōm*), while the latter is formed from *ber* (= φέρω), with a lost final syllable, and *em* (**esmi*) 'I am'. Similarly Slavonic **berōm* is composed of **berō* (= φέρω) and *m* from a few athematic verbs; it is thus not to be compared in time or nature with Sanskrit *bhárāmi*. Modern French [trwa] has lost final *s*, but Old French *treis* shows that this was a different event in time and nature from the loss of *s* in Italian *tre*, Rumanian *trei*.

Some typical Indo-European equivalents are:

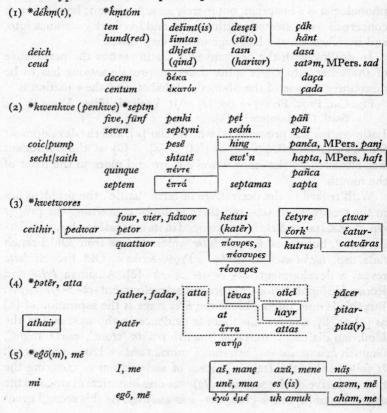

(1) **déḱm̥(t)*,   **ḱm̥tóm*

		ten	*dešimt(is)*	*desętĭ*	*çäk*
		hund(red)	*šimtas*	(*sŭto*)	*känt*
deich			*dhjetë*	*tasn*	*dasa*
ceud			(*qind*)	(*hariwr*)	*satǝm*, MPers. *sad*
		decem	δέκα		*daça*
		centum	ἑκατόν		*çada*

(2) **kwenkwe* (*penkwe*) **septm̥*

		five, fünf	*penki*	*pęḯ*	*päñ*
		seven	*septyni*	*sedḿ*	*spät*
coic/pump			*pesě*	*hing*	*panča*, MPers. *panj*
secht/saith			*shtatë*	*ewtʻn*	*hapta*, MPers. *haft*
		quinque	πέντε		*pañca*
		septem	ἑπτά	*septamas*	*sapta*

(3) **kwetwores*

		four, vier, fidwor	*keturi*	*četyre*	*çtwar*
ceithir,	pedwar	petor	(*katěr*)	*čorkʻ*	*čatur-*
		quattuor	πίσυρες, πέσσυρες	*kutrus*	*catvāras*
			τέσσαρες		

(4) **pǝtēr*, atta

		father, fadar,	atta	*tèvas*	*otĭcĭ*	*pācer*
			at		*hayr*	*pitar-*
athair		patēr	ἄττα		*attas*	*pitā(r)*
			πατήρ			

(5) **egō(m)*, *mē*

		I, me	*aš, manę*	*azŭ, mene*	*näṣ*
mi			*unĕ, mua*	*es (is)*	*azǝm, mē*
		egō, mē	ἐγώ ἐμέ	*uk amuk*	*aham, me*

Similar equivalences can be found as readily outside the Indo-European family, e.g. Finno-Ugrian:

(6) Finnish Mordwinian Cheremis Vogul Ostyak Hungarian

käte-⎫ käsi⎭	k'ed'	kit	kät	kèt	kez	'hand'
süksü⎫ süs ⎭	sokś	šəžə	tüks	⎧sòyos⎫ ⎩sùs ⎭	ōs	'harvest'
mehi(läise-)	ṁekś	mükš			mé(he)	'bee'.

(7) Semitic
Arab. ra's = Abyss. re'es = Hebrew rōš = Aram. rēš = Assyr. rēš 'head'.

(8) Chinese
Pekinese ṅien = Cantonese nĭm = Old Chinese niem' = Sino-Jap. nen 'read, think'.

(9) Malayo-Polynesian
Malay lima = Tiruray limo = Samoan lima = Maori rima = Merina dimi 'five'.

(10) Bantu lume 'man', kûa 'die', kumi 'ten'.
Kikuyu rume = Swahili ume = Herero rume = Duala ọm.
Ganda fa (Swahili, Nyanja, Zulu) = Herero ṭa = Pedi swa = Songo fwa = Duala wọ.
Swahili kumi (Nyanja) = Venda ⎧humi⎫ = Zulu shumi = Pedi šọmẹ = Duala ọm. ⎩fumi⎭

(11) Primitive Algonquin *maxkesini 'mocassin'
Fox mahkasahi (diminutive) = Ojibwa mahkizin = Plains Cree maskisin = Menomini mahkäsin.

The solution of these equations tells us nothing about times or circumstances, which have to be obtained from other sorts of record. For an illiterate language they tend to be shallow, as in the cases of Common Bantu and Primitive Algonquin. It would indeed appear from ethnographical evidence that the organization of Common Bantu was a comparatively recent event, perhaps dating from the beginning of our era. The Polynesian diffusion is dated by traditions calculated by generations, and occupied the fifth to sixteenth centuries of our era. When there is no documentary evidence, an investigator may be left with alternative possibilities. Thus the metate or stone used for grinding corn in a stone mortar, offers the equation: Nahuatl metla(tl) = Huichol mata = Luiseño mala(l) = South Paiute mara(tsi), and the investigator is left with the possibility either that the word goes back to a period before the Uto-Azteks dispersed, or that the instrument was diffused from Mexico northward.[1] The difference of date for these alternatives might amount to a millennium. On the other hand, since only the simplest

[1] E. Sapir, *Selected Writings*, Berkeley, 1949, p. 451.

equations can be solved under these conditions, the absence of proof does not imply absence of original unity. The vast number of language-families in the Americas may thus be reduced by further studies to a much smaller number, though convincing proof is hardly to be expected.

The Finno-Ugrian family is one of very slow development, except for Magyar, and Finnish forms can be quoted as approximately those of the parent speech. In Semitic, too, the triconsonantal structure is so firm that correspondences are readily noted, but comparison does not reveal conditions widely dissimilar from those of Arabic, the most conservative branch. The equations become more interesting when Egyptian is compared with Semitic, since more radical divergencies are then revealed. Thus Eg. *snb* = Arab. *slm* 'be healthy', Eg. *wdn* = Arab. *wzn* 'be heavy', Eg. *ḥq'* 'rule' = Arab. *ḥqq* 'be right'.

For this sort of study the Indo-European languages afford special advantages. They have abundant documentation at all dates, alphabetical analysis for vowels as well as consonants, and strikingly divergent evolution. On them, therefore, the whole modern science of language has been based. What is really instructive is to get cross-bearings on an ancient and unknown form by means of different recorded developments. Something that persists unchanged, like the *m* of *me*, might be ancient or modern so far as the linguistic evidence goes, but the drastic evolution of *ego* 'I' gives evidence of ancient groupings and sub-groups. Actually, *me* is probably older than *ego*, which does not appear in the two extreme language-groups (Tokharian *näṣ* and similar forms appear to develop from *mn*-). The *m*-/*t*- opposition for the first and second personal pronouns is found in the suffixes of verbs and in possessives. It also operates in Finno-Ugrian (Finnish *minä/sinä* < *tinä*, -*n* < -*m*/-*t*, Hung. -*m*/-*d*), and there is some probability of an original association between Indo-European and Finno-Ugrian. Thus *ego /me* is a good example of the truth that nothing guarantees the contemporaneity of the heads of linguistic inferences. On the other hand, there is sometimes evidence of relative chronology. Comparing the tables for 'ten', 'hundred', and 'four', we infer an original state including *k* and *kw*, attested by the western and furthest eastern languages (Germanic, Celtic, Latin, Greek, Hittite, Tokharian); a first innovation palatalizing *k* in certain circumstances and affecting a diagonal band of languages in the eastern sector (Baltic, Slavonic,

Albanian, Armenian, Iranian, Indian); a later change reducing
kw to *k* in the same region, but too late to involve the palatalization
of Lithuanian *keturi* (Albanian *katër* is borrowed from Latin); and
probably later still an evolution from *kw* to *p*, affecting part of the
Celtic, Italic, Greek, and all the Germanic areas. In the history of
Slavonic there are two palatalizations of *k g ch* [χ] separated by a
number of intervening developments, so that a relative chronology
of about a dozen stages can be adumbrated.[1] They are all later than
features common to Baltic and Slavonic.

   Studies carried to a very ancient date mask a good deal of temporal and local detail, and the resulting inferences are notably
simplified. What is remarkable is a strong tendency for a drift to
complete itself in all relevant instances so long as the evolutionary
tendency operates. The regularity of such drifts, first demonstrated on a grand scale by Grimm, was so impressive that it gave
rise to the notion of sound-laws operating with all the certitude of
laws of Nature. A sound-law completes itself in all identical cases
during the period of its operation, unless some specific obstacle
intervenes. But a study of modern languages, and particularly of
French, in which we know the original Latin position and most of
the intervening stages are recorded, makes it evident that every
case is unique. Even agreement with a sound-law is not automatic.
In a brilliant study of a village dialect conducted over fourteen
years, Duraffour was able to show that individual adoptions of
features of standard French pronunciation were due to the movements, habits, and prestige of single persons. Latin *áliquem* is the
undoubted source of Spanish *alguien*, but according to Y. Malkiel,
it is not of uninterrupted descent.[2] On the contrary, *aliquem* lost
its hold on the east and centre of the Peninsula, and was restored
from the north-west (Galicia and Western León), where it had
persisted as Ptg. *alguém*, Leonese *alguién*. This accentuation persisted to the middle of the sixteenth century, when it was replaced
by modern Spanish *álguien*.

   Sr. Menéndez Pidal's *Orígenes del Español* (3 ed., Madrid, 1950) is
of the utmost importance for understanding linguistic drift because
of its precise dating, localization, and percentaging of conflicting
forms. Thus the loss of Latin *f* is precisely located in a small strip

---

   [1] W. J. Entwistle and W. A. Morison, *Russian and the Slavonic Languages*,
1949, pp. 52–59.
   [2] Y. Malkiel, *Hispanic 'alguien' and Related Formations*, Berkeley, 1948.

across the Cantabrian mountains alongside the Basque border. This region did not initially extend so far as Burgos, in Old Castile, but it was from Burgos that the typical Castilian *h* was propagated after the twelfth century. Official Spanish, ruled by the usage of Toledo, retained *f* without vacillation until the fifteenth century. It used an aspirate *h* in that century and during three-quarters of the next, when Castilian dialects had already silenced the letter; and the loss of aspirate in the standard tongue coincided with the publication of the works of the unaspirating Saint Teresa. The aspirate was retained in Estremadura and Andalusia, where it is found even in cases in which the official language retains *f*. Words in *-air-* (Lat. *-ariu-*) and the word *vaica* obey a law which transforms *ai* into *ei* and thence to *e* in Castilian, but there is no Castilian example of *-air-* or *-eir-* after the middle of the tenth century, whereas *veiga* persisted in use as late as 1150. Different stages of development coexist side by side while the law is in operation, and it is fought out separately for each word. The Castilian *-ch-* for Latin *-ct-* spread most rapidly into Aragón and León in the official word *pechar* 'pay tax', found in an Aragonese dialect as early as 1044 and in Leónese in 1173. The loss of *n l* between vowels was substantially carried out in the Galician-Portuguese of the tenth century, but these consonants are still found in popular songs by Gil Vicente at the beginning of the sixteenth. Individuality in respect of time of change is transformed in linguistic geography into spatial differences. Thus Fr. *cha-* for Lat. *ca-* extends farther for *champ* than for *chandelle* or *chanter* in south France, but not so far in the north. In the region of Marseilles there are *champ* and *chambre*, but not *chandelle* and *chanter*; in Normandy there are *chambre*, *chanter*, and (usually) *chandelle*, but not usually *champ*. Each word has its own area because it has its own history, yet the 'law' has been substantially carried out in all but Provençal territories.

To account for exceptional instances older linguists made use of the term analogy. Two words or forms may resemble each other in meaning or appearance, and may interfere with each other's development. A convenient way of saying this is to use the form of a sum in proportion: Old French *aveir* : *saveir* :: *ai* : *sai* :: *out* : *sout* (3 pers. sg. pret.). In this series *aveir* and *saveir* appear to have the same form. Modern *je sais* may be said to follow the analogy of *je connais*, by kinship of meaning. The latter had an *s* in the stem

(OFr. *conuis*), which came to be considered proper to the first person singular. But the Spanish series *haber* (*haver*) : *saber* :: *he* : *sé* :: *hubo* : *supo* reveals the fact that at the relevant time the verbs to 'have' and to 'know' were not identical, since one had a fricative where the other had an occlusive. They were both very common words, liable to specially heavy phonetic loss in the commonest forms. In the series of past tenses *hubo* : *supo* : *tuvo* : *estuvo* : *anduvo* : *cupo* in Spanish (Ptg. *houve* : *soube* : *jouve* : *coube*/*teve* : *esteve*) we find evidence of the tendency to form tiny sub-classes of words of similar frequency in use, and to impose on them a certain mutual consistency. In general, it is difficult, when claiming the aid of analogy, to say precisely what is the basis of the analogy. *Je sais* derives its *s* not from *je connais* (the *s* of which was silent before the vowels came to resemble one another), but from all verbs ending in *s* in the stem, supported by the influence of the second personal ending in -*s*. This set up a pattern 1. -*s*, 2. -*s*, 3. -*t* which seemed convenient as 'regularizing' French conjugation.

The whole concept of analogy, as defined by the Neo-Grammarians, is too mechanical for the vagaries of living speech. On the other hand, the concept of invariable law has acquired, in the hands of J. Gilliéron and his pupils, a new value. Predict in conformity with strict sound-laws a given development; note that in fact the expected result has not occurred; and then seek to explain by all possible documentation just how the law has been frustrated. In such cases the law will be found embodied in some quite exceptional form, just as strict phonetic evolution is found only in a few 'irregulars' among the verbs, while the vast majority have been 'regularized'. Thus Lat. *fide* 'faith' is found correctly evolved in the exclamation Sp. *a la he*, which no one uses; why, then, *fe* 'faith'? It is absurd to cite analogies of *fiel* 'faithful', *fiesta* '(religious) festival', or the like. They have to defend themselves, since there exist *hiel* 'poison' (Lat. *fel*) and *inhiesto* 'hostile' (Lat. *infestus*). It is equally absurd to claim that (in Spain of all places) *fe* is a semi-erudite word. The fact rather is that when *fe* loses its *f* in *a la he* it ceases to be recognizable; there is a point at which phonetic loss has to be arrested in the interests of intelligibility. Similarly, in Common Slavonic -*ŭ* resulted from both IE. *-os -om*, so that masculines and neuters were in danger of fusing. There would, of course, have been no great harm in the elimination of a gender, but the Slavonic linguistic instinct rebelled against the risk and restored -*o* for the neuters contrary to phonetic law. There happened to be such an *o* in the demonstrative *to*, but it is not very profitable to construct the proportionate series : *tŭ* : *to* : : *rabŭ* 'slave' : *lĕto* 'year', since what we have to explain is precisely why a single demonstrative form should have gained power to reintroduce a formal gender. Gilliéron's writings are of particular suggestiveness in showing the complexity of influences at work to preserve either the seeming logic of a system or the intelligible substantiality of a word against the attrition of sound-laws.

Viewed at a distance or in general perspective tendencies appear to complete themselves within the period of their operation in a remarkably total fashion. Seen more nearly, these tendencies are found to be composed of innumerable small initiatives, none of which are precisely concurrent. Change implies divergence, but there are equally noteworthy phenomena of convergence, such as those which progressively brought closer the Osco-Umbrian and Proto-Latin dialects in Italy and so give rise to the Italic phase. 'The affinities of Latin and Osco-Umbrian are recent, the diversities are ancient.'[1] Similar convergent tendencies dominate the Spanish of Spain and South America and the Portuguese of Portugal and Brazil today. When languages diverge, they do not separate for ever like the branches of a tree, but contacts of a looser kind subsist. This is conspicuous in the history of the Romance languages, in which developments of *ce ci* and *ge gi* and of -*ct*- are independent, but obey a common trend towards palatalization. So Russian *četyre* and Sanskrit *catvāras* 'four' (and Armenian *čork'* ?) depend not merely on a late Indo-European **ketwores* for **kwetwores*, but also a common impulse to palatalize *ke* as *če*. There was still an *e* in Aryan when this process began.

The sound-laws are historical statements of tendencies, and are not the less scientific for not being mechanically based. If we are to make true statements concerning human societies they must be historical in form. Thus it is easy to understand that the operation of each sound-law or drift has its limits in time. During the whole Common Slavonic period the syllables *ke ki*, *ge gi*, and *che chi* were inconceivable. They were transformed into palatals when they occurred, so that the syllabic series for *k*, for instance, was *ka ko ku ky*/*če či ce ci*. The double series of 'soft' consonants was due to two palatalizations at widely different dates, the one giving *č* for *k*, the

[1] G. Devoto, *Storia della Lingua di Roma*, Rome, 1940, p. 67.

other *c* [ŝ]. But Russian now admits *k g ch* before *e i*. The process which gave diphthongs for short accented vowels in Romance began in the middle period of the Roman empire and came to a definite end at some Romance date which can only relatively be fixed. In Upper Aragón, as a result, Basque villages and townships which were romanized during the operation of the law show diphthongs from *berri* 'new', *gorri* 'red', &c.; but those closer to the present Basque border which were later romanized preserve the simple Basque vowels. The sound-shift which produced the palatals in *church* came to an end, and if *c* is palatalized now it gives [s] (*kinema* or *cinema*). Thus no trends can be predicted. They occur and endure and end as historical events, and explanation is necessarily *a posteriori*. The explanation consists of a demonstration of the phonetic grooves of change, and when the material is considered close at hand, it also involves detailed consideration of social influences, mental associations, reactions, and aesthetic preferences.

THE PRECEDENCE OF SPEECH-SOUNDS[1]

Discussion of the order of emergence of vowels in Indo-European got off to a false start because Sanskrit and Gothic, two of the primary languages interrogated, had only three vowels: *a i u*. Further study showed, however, that these resulted from assimilations: Skr. *a* = IE. *a e o*, Gothic *a* = *a o*, *i* = *i e*. IE. *a o* were also identified in the Baltic and Slavonic languages, discriminated according to their length (IE. **a* Lith. *a* Sl. *o*; IE. **ā* Lith. *o* Sl. *a*), though *e* was retained. Thus in comparing Skr. *bháramanas* with Greek φερόμενος it became clear that the Greek vowels were to be deemed more ancient. The vowels *e o* result from diphthongs in Sanskrit and are classified as such. When values had been readjusted there remained six vowels for Indo-European: *ă ĕ ĭ ŏ ŭ* and the neutral vowel *ə*. The matter has come up for further discussion in the light of evidence afforded by Hittite. Since Hittite *suhai* empties, sprinkles' = ὔει, *hanz* 'front' = Gk. ἀντί, ἄντα, *hastai* 'bone' = ὀστέον, the Hittite word is evidence for three (or possibly four) consonants unsuspected in Greek, but the Greek shows differences of vowels not recorded in Hittite. The consonants were provisionally designated by the signs $ə_1$ $ə_2$ $ə_3$ (with a

[1] W. Schmidt, *Die Sprachfamilien und Sprachenkreise der Erde*, Heidelberg, 1926, pp. 273–314.

vowel sign because of their vocalic effects in Greek), and these were later identified as laryngeals of the general nature of Hebrew עהא (' ẖ '). Then the Indo-European $\breve{e}$ $\breve{a}$ $\breve{o}$ were explained as resulting from diphthongs ($\partial_1 e > \breve{e}$, $e\partial_1 > \bar{e}$, $\partial_2 e > \breve{a}$, $e\partial_2 > \bar{a}$, $\partial_3 e > \breve{o}$, $e\partial_3 > \bar{o}$). Since $\partial_1 ed$ ($> \breve{e}d$) could then be considered as composed of consonant–vowel–consonant like *sed*, these laryngeals helped to lay a basis for E. Benveniste's triliteral theory of the Indo-European root. The theory allows for full roots like **pet* and reduced roots like **pt*, to which could be added full or reduced suffixes like **ek/k*, and these further enlarged by the addition of a consonant. Thus Latin *volup(tas)* 'pleasure' is from **wel-p-*, *lep(os)* 'pleasantness' from **wl-ep-*, *auis* 'bird' from **∂_2ew-y-*, *plecto* 'weave' from **pl-ek-t-*. This theory makes *e* the principal Indo-European vowel, from which many cases of *a o* are derived.[1]

Another approach to Indo-European vocalism recognizes as aristocratic words involving the alternance *e/o/-*, while those in *a* or alternating $\breve{i}/\bar{i}$ and $\breve{u}/\bar{u}$, together with onomatopoeic words involving the use of *l r sk-* or reduplication, are regarded as popular.[2] Under such circumstances what is popular is generally older. The observation is in agreement with the circumstance that the *e/o* declension is visibly the latest to be formed in the common Indo-European language.

If one takes the evidence of primitive languages, such as Australian Arunta or those of America, there is a strong case for regarding *a i u* as primitive vowels, of which *e o* are accidental variants. The neutral vowel *ə* may also be primitive. Quechua uses *a i u*, Nahuatl (Milpa Alta dialect) uses *a e i o*. In Bantu *e o* result from diphthongs, and the primitive vowels are evidently *a i u*, as they are also in Semitic. In Moroccan Arabic *e o* are sounds due to the accommodation of the three primary ones to surrounding consonants, as *kelb* 'dog'/*qalb* 'heart'. To fix the pronunciation of *e o* as two middle vowels which could be used to make significant distinctions (such as *pit/pet*, *pot/put*) would seem to have required more linguistic awareness than to fix the three outlying vowels of the vocal triangle. From the five vowels *a e i o u* have developed the mixed vowels $\bar{i}$ $\bar{o}$ $\ddot{u}$, either as a result of a tendency to shift enunciation forward in the mouth (as in French) or because of former diphthongs (as in Ger-

---

[1] E. Benveniste, *Origines de la formation des noms en indo-européen*, i, Paris, 1935; W. Couvreur, *De hettitishe Ḫ*, Louvain, 1937.

[2] G. Devoto, *Storia della Lingua di Roma*, Rome, 1940, p. 12.

man, in which the two dots are all that remains of a superscribed *e*).[1]
Unrounded back vowels like Araucanian *u* and Russian *y* are also
derivative.

The use of semivowels is virtually universal as weakening of *i u*
in contact with *a* (and *e o*, when these are present), but the full
consonantal *w* and *y* are much rarer. They are remarkably unstable.
W, which is a doubly formed sound consisting of a rounding of the
lips combined with a fissure friction between the velum and back of
the tongue, is liable to lose its rounding and substitute an occlusion
at the velum (Arm. *gini* 'wine', Fr. *guerre* 'war'; It. *guerra* represents an intermediate stage in this development), or to lose the
velar friction and substitute labiodental contact (Fr. *vin*, Russ.
vino). *Y* becomes sibilant (*ž*) or affricate (*ǰ*) by being pronounced
tensely (Lat. *iam*, Fr. *déjà*, It. *già*). The two consonants disappeared from Greek.

Concerning the sonants *l r m n*, they are characteristically voiced,
and unvoiced varieties are derivative. To some extent they are
alternatives. *L* alone exists in Chinese (Pekinese) and Nahuatl, and
r alone in Guarani, Quechua, and Japanese. *L* seems to have been
original in Bantu and Polynesian, but has passed into *r* in many of
the individual languages. In Quechua, though there is no *l*, there
is the palatal lateral [λ] (as in *llama*), and in Nahuatl there is *l*
and *tl*; in the Slavonic languages palatal *l* and velar *l* have been
systematically distinguished, though not always according to the
same principles. All specific varieties of *l* must be regarded as
secondary, and the lateral consonant allowed a wide range of casual
variation. Similarly, vibrant alveolar *r*, retroflex *r* (as in *try*), and
vibrant velar *r* (the French *r*) are variations of a single broadly conceived vibrant. *L* and *r* also permute with *d*. The nasals, too, are
broadly conceived. At the beginning of syllables *m n* are distinguished, but at the end of syllables languages tend to prefer either
m (as in Hebrew or Portuguese or Latin) or *n* (as in Arabic or
Spanish or Greek). Apart from the distinction between the nasal
pronounced on the lips and that within the mouth, there is no
other primary discrimination; the palatal *ñ* and the velar *ŋ* have
either been developed during the evolution of some language, or

---

[1] Father W. Schmidt notes that two-thirds of the examples of *ö ü* occur in the
Ural-altaic, Sino-Tibetan, and Austro-asiatic areas, which are matriarchal and,
in part, agricultural. They occur least in the Hamito-Semitic speeches (nomads)
and are secondary in Indo-European (originally nomad hunters).

they are accidental results of contact between the nasal and palatal or velar consonants.

The sibilant *s* is also almost universal, but it is generally possible to derive other sibilants from an original *s*. It was replaced by the rough breathing in Greek (ἑπτά/*septem*) and by *h* in Armenian, Persian, and eastern Polynesian (*Hawaii*/*Savaii*). There is probably no North or Central American speech without *s*, but it is wanting in some South American tongues, and it may not have been present in the original Bantu speech. The source of *s* and other sibilants in Bantu seems to have been palatalized *t'* or *d'*. The breakdown of velars or dentals under palatalization is a common cause of sibilation of some sort in the Romance and Slavonic language families, as well as in the whole *satem* group of Indo-European tongues.

Among the remaining consonants the voiceless occlusives (*p t k*) have a distinct priority. Sounds like retroflex *ṭ* in Sanskrit are later developments, and so also in all probability the distinction between velars and postvelars in Semitic (*k*/*q*). Voiceless at the beginning of a word, they often carry some voice from previous consonants or vowels in the middle and end of words, so that the action of the vocal chords is treated as indifferent in the sound-systems of many primitive languages. To fix the enunciation of *b d g* and to assign semantic importance thereto is a relatively late innovation. In fact it is not always phonetically feasible, since these sounds are liable to become voiced or unvoiced according to their contacts or position. Thus *it may*, pronounced rapidly, shows some voicing [iḑmej], and Russ. *luk* 'onion' and *lug* 'meadow' are both pronounced [luk] in isolation.

On the other hand, the original *p t k* series is amplified in some languages, such as Quechua, by aspiration and glottalization: *ph th ch*/*pp tt cc* of the traditional orthography [p‘ t‘ k‘ q‘, 'p 't 'k 'q]. The tongue forms an occlusion at the lips, on the teeth or gums, or on the velum (Jespersen's αοᵇ, βο‘ᶠ, γο ͥ), and at the glottis various events may occur: the passage may be free ($\epsilon 3$) and a voiceless enunciation result, or may be narrowed ($\epsilon 2$) to produce aspiration, or still further narrowed till the vocal chords vibrate ($\epsilon 1$), or obstructed by momentarily closing the glottis ($\epsilon 0$). The last three devices produce modifications of the simpler single explosion represented by the voiceless *p t k*.

Without affecting the glottis it is possible, as we have already noted, to make differentiations by tension, as with Finnish *pp*/*p*, *tt/t, kk/k.* Initial position is always more tense than final position, because there is more air at the beginning of an utterance, so that initial and final distinctions of tension are not necessarily marked. In Finnish it is medial tension that appears in the spelling, as in *setä* 'uncle' and *säättää* 'dispose'. In this series of distinctions voiced sounds are reckoned less tense than voiceless, since the voicing of the consonant continues the voice of the vowels, while unvoicing makes a sharper syllabic definition. Thus there arise alternations: *tt/t* and *t/d*. The voiced consonant is on the way to extinction, either by ceasing to be occlusive (*p/v*) or by disappearing altogether (*k/*o), as we have seen in examples already given. Another form of tension not affecting the glottis is double formation within the mouth. This is characteristic of some West African languages, such as Mende. In Mende there are voiced consonants, so that relaxed tensions appear as simplifications of double sounds (*mb/b nd/l nj/y*) or as voicings (*k/g, kp/gb, s/j*) or as frictions (*p/w*). Double initial consonants are also reported from central and southern American languages, but particularly strongly from those of the north-west. The Kaffir clicks are pronounced by doubly stopping the chamber of the mouth and sucking in the breath. They are proper to Hottentot and Bushman, and have been acquired by the Bantu-speaking Kaffirs and Zulus, and at least for the latter they are no part of the original system of phonemes.

There is so little use of the indrawn breath for speech that implosive *b d g* in Swahili is not likely to be as ancient as the normal explosive series.

The primitive phonemes would thus seem to be: *a i u* and possibly *ə*; *w y*; *m n*, with some tendency to be mutually exclusive; *l/r* as alternative possibilities; *p, t, k,* and *s*.

The history of all languages that can be followed over a long period of time shows that voiceless occlusives become voiced, and voiced occlusives break down and provide affricates or fricatives. Sometimes the cause is relaxation; as in *sapere* > OSp. *saber* [b], MSp. [ƀ], Fr. *savoir*; standard Spanish *agua* 'water', vulgar *awa*. A *p* without stoppage of breath at the lips is [φ]—an indistinct sound which appears in Jap. *fuji*—and this often leads to a sharper definition by bringing the teeth into contact with the lower lip (*f*). Similarly *v* derives from relaxed *b*. The principal cause of breakdown, however, is palatalization. This word covers a number of different mechanical proceedings, but depends generally on the position of *y*-sounds towards the front of the hard palate. *E* and *i* cause palatalization because their position is like that of *y*; but the semiconsonant operates more powerfully on a previous consonant than do the vowels and is effective in instances where they are inert. The effect of *yod* (anything that partakes of the nature of a palatal semiconsonant or vowel) is to drag towards the front of the mouth older velars. When they are pronounced in the high palate, an untenable situation is created: either a long and perceptible sibilant off-glide is heard and the consonant becomes an affricate [č ĵ ŝ ẑ] or contact is lost and there is only friction [š ž s z]. Dental and labial sounds are pronounced further forward in the mouth than the *yods* and are drawn backwards towards the palate, as in Sp. *sabio*/Fr. *sage*, Sp. *sepa*/Fr. *sache*, Russ. *déti*/Pol. *dzieci* 'children', Russ. *ródina*/Pol. *rodzina* 'birth-place, family'. These backward movements are rarer than the forward ones, and the latter may pass the palatal area of *yod* because of the mere impetus of the change: *Caesar* (*Kaiser*), It. *Cesare* [č] (which is a palatal), Fr. *César* [s] (which is dental), Sp. *César* [θ] (interdental). With the exception of *s* and consonantal *w y*, all affricates and fricatives seem to derive from older occlusives, and among these the voiceless series *p t k* seems alone universal.

It is not to be inferred from the above argument that primitive languages today have simple phonetic structures. Some do, others offer numerous 'difficult' sounds. No doubt, for a child all speech-sounds are equally easy, since he produces many more than are required when simply exercising his vocal muscles, but double-stopped or modified sounds may be legitimately considered more complicated than simple continuous or momentary ones. A simple phonematic system in eastern Polynesia is obviously the result of loss of consonantal resources. Nor is it implied that palatalization and fricativization may not be examples of the easier way of enunciation. They bring together distant sounds or relax tenser ones. But they also add new phonemes to the system, and these are on the whole less adequately distinguished and more liable to change than those that preceded them. Thus, in the example of *Caesar* cited above, *k* and *e* are doubtless separated by a considerable distance in the mouth, and it is an easement for the tongue to pronounce them in one place; but the resulting accommodation has proved unstable and given different results in the different Romance languages.

SPELLING

Spelling has already been considered, to some extent, in the discussion of the theory of phonemes, since one of the objectives is to produce a consistent orthography, but it also needs examination for itself. In all historical periods the evidence used by the linguist must be inferred from written signs. It is no longer a question of an optimum representation of sounds constituting the language, but the actual values of orthography at various times. A single sign has often a succession of different values, sometimes rather subtly distinguished. Minor distinctions concealed behind a symbol may ultimately cause major linguistic changes.

There is a difference of medium between written marks addressed to the eye and sounds spoken for the ear. The most direct visual impression is made by pictures.[1] Hence picture-writing has a wider dispersion than the alphabet. It has the advantage of admitting composition in one language and reception in another, but it is restricted to concrete objects and simple situations. When complex communications are attempted, as in the Mexican annals, the signs must be accompanied by a tradition of interpretation. But such may also be true of an alphabet. Arabic classics were taught by master to pupil. Though the pupil was often a distinguished scholar who read Arabic freely, the important activity was to protect the tradition of interpretation. Between *bough* and *bow* there is a difference only to the eye. The meaning of *bough* (and the difference between several *bows*) might be conveyed more directly by a drawing, though it would be read, in the absence of an interpreter, as *bough*, *branch*, or *twig*. The picture-message, in fact, corresponds to a number of different oral sentences which have the same broad effect; the picture is understood totally. But we also take in totally whole phrases or sentences, and the more gifted absorb whole paragraphs of written words. We are so little dependent on details of spelling that we frequently leave uncorrected errors in proof which the understanding has comprehended simply.

Egyptian hieroglyphs are beautifully stylized pictures. An alphabet of twenty-four consonants was developed, but the best communication of the notions of *eagle*, *chick*, *owl*, *leg*, *donkey*, &c., lay in the

---

[1] D. Diringer, *The Alphabet*, 2 ed., London, 1949; cf. an American Indian picture-letter to the President of the United States in E. H. Sturtevant, *Introduction to Linguistic Science*, 3 ed., New Haven, 1948.

drawings themselves. After the addition of such symbols as the crowns of Upper and Lower Egypt, human figures in action, parts of the body, constructions, &c., there was a great mass of words best represented by drawings, and these drawings were artistically most effective on the walls of great temples. Hence the ancient Egyptians, though they developed and used a consonantal alphabet, made its role subordinate, and it was left to less artistic, more utilitarian foreigners to use systematically an alphabet of sketchy consonantal symbols. The Sumerian pictograms came to represent on the whole single syllables, into which the language seems to have been readily analysable, and this syllabic script was adopted by Babylonia, Assyria, Persia, and the Hittite nations, though evidently less suitable to them. The scholar's first task in Hittite is to determine whether the sign he studies is syllabic or consonantal. The Sanskrit alphabet is syllabic, but has elaborate devices for reducing the syllable to a consonant or showing another vowel than the normal *a*. Japanese writing is syllabic and well adapted to the indigenous part of the language.

It was with the Greeks that vocalic signs began to appear. Vowels depend simply on resonance due to the cubic capacity of the mouth-chamber and they are much more difficult to define than consonants. Hence the spelling of vowels is always inadequate, even in so simple a language as Spanish. Diacritics are used by many languages for greater precision, though they may fall (as in French) into disorders of their own.[1]

Spelling consists of substituting the signs of sounds for the direct visual picture, so that these will be picked up as sounds by the reader. It is an indirect method and open to misinterpretation as sounds change, whether because the reader belongs to a different dialect or to a different time. We may thus understand why the Chinese persistently preferred the picture. Unlike the Egyptians their pictures were evocatory rather than pictorial. While the Egyptians drew recognizably a duck and eagle (and arbitrarily omitted a third sign) for *p'w* 'be in front of', two Chinese signs combine to make a third without being obviously pictures of two objects. This gave a first great class of words like *ming*[2] 'bright, clear' composed of the signs of sun and moon and expressing their common denominator. When this sort of pictorial analysis of the

---

[1] See, for instance, A. Lombard, 'Remarques sur le *e* moyen du français', *Mélanges Dauzat*, Paris, 1951.

abstract broke down, the Chinese combined a sign of some existing word with a sign expressing its class of meaning. Thus min^3 is a picture of a cup. It was once pronounced '*miɒng* and served to recall the sounds of *mɒng*' which is now *mêng*[4] 'eldest, first'. This *mêng*[4] is represented by the cup picture and the picture of a child, to indicate the class of idea involved. Add the sign for dog, which is credited with all unpleasant qualities: the word is *mêng*[3] 'fierce, violent'. For five-sixths of Chinese characters we thus have phonetic information which was very nearly true at the time of the character's formation. But for all Chinese characters we have direct visual evidence of meaning, independent of dialect or century or even language. They have to be learnt as complete symbols, but then can be read for meaning but not sound as accurately in Japanese as in Chinese, or now as in the time of Confucius. A great deal of time is occupied with memorizing 6,000 necessary characters and getting some acquaintance with others. But the time is not sensibly greater than that wasted on learning English spelling and the various spellings as far back as the days of King Alfred, while English orthography teaches us nothing about (say) French.[1]

The first object of an alphabetic system is to represent the sounds of which speakers are conscious. It may be said that, where there is no perturbing effect of tradition, early spellings give the broad transcription or phonemes of the language. But alphabets are in fact usually handed on from one language to another, and their letters have sometimes the sacrosanctity due to use in a Bible, Quran, or other religious classic. If this traditional obstacle is not too heavy, a new alphabet may be constructed from an old one, as Slavonic from Greek, by adding new signs and omitting those that are not needed. The new alphabet is thus still a substantially correct representation of the sounds of which speakers are conscious. The Arabic alphabet uses dots (diacritics) and has been extended for Persian, Turkish, and other tongues by additional dots over or under standard forms of letter. With the Latin alphabet, however, the pressure of tradition has proved heavier. Late Latin *ca co cu/ce ci* and *ga go gu/ge gi* have been accepted in all Romance languages with two sounds for *c* and two for *g*. What is deemed abnormal was the occurrence of the values *k g* before *e i*, and the problem was to devise signs for this abnormality. Superfluous signs in Latin were *j v h q y k x* and the digraphs *ph ch th*. These signs might be re-

[1] B. Karlgren, *Sound and Symbol in Chinese*, Oxford, 1932.

employed, so that, for instance, Czech *k* is distinct from the affricate *c* [š], and the two pronunciations of Late Latin *c* have two different signs. Similarly, *x* was the sibilant [š] in Old Spanish, since that was the sound which resulted from Latin *x* [ks]. But the non-Latin sounds proved hard to accommodate. Either existing Latin letters had their use extended to serve a new purpose or did so when doubled (as OSp. *fegga* for *fecha*), or a Latin letter written as a digraph with one of the otiose letters (e.g. *ch*) served this purpose. When one counts in the high degree of ambiguity about the values of *c* and *g*, the digraphs proposed for each non-Latin sound (chiefly new palatals) ascended to half-dozens in a Romance language like Spanish, and to dozens in such a language as Czech, which borrowed its alphabet from Germany, which borrowed from Romania. In the case of *ch*, the additional otiose letter was used to signify an affricate in Old French and Spanish (sibilant in modern French and Portuguese), but the retention of the velar [k] in Italian. In the preliterary stage Romance orthographies show many different initiatives, but the demands of literature enforced a greater uniformity, and the spelling of the *Chanson de Roland* or the *Primera Crónica General* is largely stabilized.

In Czech there was a chaos of digraphs until the end of the fifteenth century, when the great phonetician and religious reformer Jan Hus doubled the capacity of the Latin alphabet by allowing the addition of single points. These points have mostly become chevrons. They gave an alphabet in agreement with the Slavonic sentiment for 'hard' and 'soft' doublets over the whole series of consonants, and they have served to provide rational transcriptions for Slovene, Croat, Lithuanian, and Latvian, as well as some simplification of Polish. The chief defect of the system is that *ch* was accepted from German as a single letter, which it virtually is in manuscripts and Gothic print. Slavonic languages using the Cyrillic character can be transcribed, thanks to Hus, into Latin letters which represent the Slavonic consciousness of language, and this is done by all scholars who have serious business with these languages.

With the Renaissance came a vast flood of new Latinisms, and a new orthographic principle, viz. that of preserving, as far as the modern language allowed, the Latin or Greek etymon. The Romans themselves had introduced new letters and digraphs to make Greek words at home among them. At that time the early medieval spellings had fallen into disorder by reason of late medieval sound-changes. Thus the phonetic principle applied only in part; in another part the letters were purely traditional, and in yet a third they were supposed to have etymological value. Languages with copious literature have a strong motive for halting their orthographies so as not to make reading of older texts too difficult. When this is done, the word is no longer read as spelled, but absorbed as a familiar unit.

Some languages have discarded the etymological principle and returned to the phonetic value of letters. Simplification of others has been proposed. Drastic proposals for reform are commonly unsuccessful because they involve too great an upheaval all at once, but it is possible to introduce new and more rational spellings at intervals, especially if the authority of some guiding body can be employed. Such changes are from -*our* to -*or* in American English (on the authority of Webster) or the reduction of *th* to *t* in German (on the authority of the German Ministry of Education), or the elimination of the digraphs *ph th ch* by agreement between Portugal and Brazil.

Orthography rarely indicates tone. In Greek the tonal marks were added only in Alexandrian times and were unknown in the Classical period of the texts commonly studied. The use of tonal marks in Lithuanian or Yugoslav is restricted to scholars. Scholars may indicate tones on Chinese characters by means of little circles, but these do not appear in current print. The Romatzyh proposals indicate tones by conventional insertion of alphabetical signs. The effect is eminently bizarre. Similarly, stress is rarely expressed in orthography, though it is so partially in Italian and adequately in Spanish, and signs for length are not found in Latin (outside school grammars and dictionaries). But these elements of tone, quantity, and stress are of the highest importance and misuse results in complete misunderstanding. The fact is that national alphabets are devised for those who are already sure of the language they speak, *especially in its most significant aspects*, so that the most important information may be omitted from orthography. Those who suffer from this failure are chiefly foreigners who may not know, for instance, which of seven syllables of a Russian word they should stress, though well aware that the whole phonetic structure of the word is governed by the stressed syllable! The presence of phonetic, traditional, and etymological concepts within one language is eminently confusing for foreigners and natives alike (since the latter may wish to eliminate any dialectal peculiarities they may have but can find no guidance in the spelling), but is less destructive of understanding than uncertainty of stress, or of tone and quantity in tonal and quantitative languages.

V

GRAMMAR: FORM AND FUNCTION

GRAMMAR is the construction placed by mind on the unorganized materials of speech. It is a system of reference which determines the relations between the parties to an event and the circumstantial details of the event itself. With the affective value of symbols it is not concerned; grammar is a formal science, not a branch of aesthetics. The tools at the speaker's disposal are order, auxiliaries, and formal alterations of words.

That grammar is arbitrary seems to become evident as we consider opposite ways of effecting the same end. No one device can be deemed more natural than another. Each event, for instance, is unique, and it is quite natural to report it uniquely and massively. This way leads to the word-sentence, to synthesis and polysynthesis. It is also possible to observe in each event a number of parties and circumstances which appear in other events, to isolate these and to attach to them all the signs which will determine their mutual relations. The expression is then made up of masses in their relations to each other. But it is equally natural to discriminate not only the main concepts but also the relational concepts. The first way is that of the synthetic and agglutinative languages, the second that of the isolating and analytic. In French and other Romance languages we have a mixed economy. The parties to the event are treated analytically, but the event itself is recognized as a complex and is expressed synthetically. That has occurred despite the fact that the Latin tenses were often broken into combinations of separate words which expressed both verbal concepts and modified relational concepts. A synthetic conjugation has been reconstructed, partly by the chance that the relational symbols have followed the main stem and so have lost their separate identity, but partly also no doubt as the result of some obscure feeling that the verb, the specifically phenomenal element in the sentence, should be complex like the event itself.

One may predicate a quality concerning a substance by means of the order subject-predicate (SP), as in Arabic *Allāhu 'akbar* 'God is great', or the order PS, as in Samoan *ua amiotonu le alii* 'just

(are) the chiefs—the chiefs are just'. In Chinese the attributive
adjective precedes the substantive and the predicative follows, but
in Malay the attributive follows and the predicative follows after a
pause. In Russian orthography this pause is marked sometimes by
a dash, though the attributive adjective precedes the substantive
and has a different declension from the predicative. It is also possible to point from the subject to the predicate by weakening a
demonstrative pronoun in Chinese and Arabic or to state predication as an event by weakening some verb meaning 'exist', 'become',
'created', 'stand', or the like. Similarly, when the sentence is composed of subject, verb, and object (SVO), the order may be SVO
as in English, French, or Chinese, or VSO as in Gaelic *bhuail iad
am bord* 'they struck the table', or VOS as in Spanish *batió la
retirada todo el ejército francés* 'the whole French army beat a
retreat', or SOV as in Latin *Balbus murum aedificat*. There may be
two or more of these orders in one language, both customary but
with slightly different implications, or the order may in fact be
indifferent since modifications of the form of words establish the
relations sufficiently. Clearly it is not so important what the convention may be as that there should be a convention. Speaker and
hearer must be in agreement concerning the symbolism of order
or auxiliaries or formal changes applied to the word.

Though this statement of the speech situation discourages search
for principles of universal grammar and it might be supposed that
arbitrary devices have no rational limits, the fact is that variations
are surprisingly few. It is not necessary to call into the discussion
propositions concerning the unity of the human intellect. The urge
to classify all objects as animate and inanimate, or as masculine and
feminine or in more elaborate divisions, is directly opposed to the
tendency to disembarrass language of these distinctions. The Bantu
presumably finds his classes an aid to understanding reality, but
the Englishman finds his historic genders a mere embarrassment,
while the Frenchman or German retains genders scrupulously, but
to no logical purpose whatever. But there are two considerations
which limit the power to vary grammar. First, though the eyes
report events massively as totals, speech reports are linear successions of symbols. The line allows positions to be distinguished as
before or after but not as beside, above, and below, or round about.
It follows that, in the case of subject, verb, and object referred to
above, the possibilities are exhausted by SVO, VSO, VOS, SOV,

and the instance in which order is immaterial. Similarly as subject and predicate or substantive and attribute, we have SP or PS, AS or SA, but no more. With language, as with hearing or light, variation is limited to a narrow spectrum beyond which no effects are registered. The light-waves do not serve for hearing and the linear form of speech imposes strict limits upon the expression of experiences felt as wholes. What gives rise to the amazing variety of grammars is not that individual problems admit of an infinity of arbitrary solutions, but that no single solution has a necessary connexion with any other. Thus, though attributive adjectives are akin to genitive cases and relative clauses, the solution applying to the adjective does not necessarily apply to the genitive or relative. One says *white horse* but *Houses of Parliament* (as well as *John o' Groat's house*), *my words* but *the words* (*which*) *I used* (Chinese *wo³ so³ -shuo⁴ -ti hua³* 'I what-said words'). The origin of relative pronouns is commonly a question or a pointing; for adjectives there are about five possible sources. These are, in fact, not numerous causes of variety, but since they have no necessary connexion with each other, the permutations which arise are multitudinous. Languages can be learnt because at each moment the alternatives are not infinite. They are in fact comparatively few and they commend themselves to us as possible alternative solutions of the given problem. But languages are very difficult to acquire, especially with any degree of perfection, when they present a total mass of solutions different to those of our mother tongue.

The gap between the total or, as we might say, global impressions derived from our senses and the successive or linear expressions of speech has not gone entirely unnoticed. Babies, as we have seen in the first chapter of this book, are accustomed to attempt a compendious form of utterance by which, for instance, *Lo* means anything that Rudolf is doing at a given moment or *din-din* has a value of any form of words implying the immediate need of a drink. But such global forms of expression are only successful as a result of an excessive effort of comprehension on the part of fond hearers and they are too often not understood at all. In the heat of action, too, words and cries are uttered and prove stimulating though not intelligibly organized. What organization they have is borrowed from the speech of calmer occasions. In these the unorganized global sort of utterance is represented by interjections which may or may not be intelligible in form. An interjection stands for everything that the situation inspires in the way of fear, surprise, astonishment, urgency, or any other emotion. It is not properly part of the sentence but parallel thereto; it is a pro-sentence. Our inability to give a total global expression to our feelings in a given case is probably the reason why we so often complain of the poverty of language. But it should be remembered, on the other hand, that if we were not compelled to analyse in linear detail our experiences it is extremely unlikely that we should have any notion of their riches.

The three grammatical resources of order, auxiliaries, and formal change are to some extent alternative, especially as regards order and form. Relations expressed by form can make order indifferent or give it a place in stylistics. Lack of formal distinctions in grammar makes a correspondingly heavier demand upon word-order. Auxiliaries are used in all languages. They may be placed before the stem which expresses a substantial notion or after it. In the latter case more often than in the former they tend, as postpositions, to fall into the principal word and to become formal changes of that word. In a language which uses suffixes to express subordinate and relational notions it is not always easy to determine whether to treat the postposition as a form (morpheme) or as an independent word. Basque *gizon-a-ri* 'to the man' is described as receptive or of dative case, but should *gizon-a-gabe* 'without the man' be described as of the privative case or as a noun accompanied by a postposition *gabe* = 'without'? In Estonian there is a sociative *maja-ga* 'with a house' and a caritative case *maja-ta* 'without a house'. The point at which the declension is closed differs according to individual judgement and depends chiefly on an estimate of the sufficiency of the suffix. Thus Basque *gabe/bage* 'without' has enough substance to stand by itself and is usually reckoned a postposition (= preposition in English word-order) and not the suffix of a privative or caritative case. The analysis of a language like Turkish is especially difficult because of the use of suffixes for all purposes—case, postpositions, derivations—coupled with the fact that these suffixes are always such as could stand alone. There is a similar difficulty with a Bantu language like Swahili. The verbal prefixes are formally sound enough to stand alone and their spelling as part of the verb is due to foreigners only. So written they are morphemes—formal changes applied to the basic stem. If they were written separately they would be auxiliaries.

With regard to the alternative between form and order no language operates with complete purism. The celebrated Dr. Marshman said in 1814 that 'the whole of Chinese grammar depends on position'. If we allow also the use of auxiliaries, the statement is very nearly exact. But even in Chinese there do exist some genuine morphemes, shown to be such by loss of tone or other transactions of tone and stress: *la* of perfected action, *mên* of plurality, *ti* of adverbs, possessives and relative clauses, *tzŭ* and *êr* used as supports for nouns. These agglutinative elements are more conspicuous in Burmese because of the voicing of initial consonants in the second part of a compound noun. The language is monosyllabic, but there is a perceptible declension by suffixes, as sg. nom. *lu* 'man', gen. *lu-i*, dat. *lu-a*, acc. *lu-ga*, abl. *lu-hma*, &c. In Tibetan the suffixes lack even the formal conditions of independence, and the language is semi-agglutinative. At the other extreme, though grammatical devices of forms may make order unnecessary to understanding, they are often accompanied by fixed or normalized orders. In Japanese the cases are marked by particles after the noun and in Turkish by suffixes which may be compounded to any desired length, yet these languages follow a prescribed order with the verb at the end. An Old English sentence can often be read by its order with little attention to its flexions (as many an undergraduate has learnt):

pā āstāh hē on scip, and oferseglode, and cōm on his ceastre 'and he entered into a ship, and passed over, and came into his own city'. (Matthew ix. 1.)[1]

It is often possible to do the same in modern Russian. In Old Bulgarian the existence of flexions allowed a writer to place words in a spontaneous order, i.e. as they were of interest to himself. But even so associated words come together and there is nothing like the hyperbaton of

ultima funestā concurrit proelia Mundā,

which is a literary device quite alien to ordinary speech. Flexions undoubtedly open the possibility of separating words in this fashion without quite losing sight of their relations, but the practice depends on the written word, since such a manner of speaking could hardly be used without great confusion or at least trouble to hearers. The

[1] Quoted in J. Delcourt, *Introduction à l'étude historique de l'anglais*, Paris, 1944, p. 44.

spoken orders were fewer and less twisted than the written and eventually gave place to the SVO of French, Spanish, and Italian, and the VSO of old French and Spanish.

Whether the auxiliaries—by which I mean every sort of relational word—are placed before or after the main stem and whether they are kept separate or fused as agglutinations or flexions, they give rise to groups of substantive and subordinate symbols generally dominated by an accent. *Ille phaselus* and *phaselus ille* 'that skiff' are groups dominated by one accent. They correspond to expressions like Fr. *le cheval*, Rum. *calul*, of which the first is analytic and the second synthetic, but both are pronounced without interruption of the breath and brought under a single control. Similarly *manibus* and *by hands* are uninterrupted breath-groups in which the separate symbols are fused or kept separate according to the conventions of the given language. Corresponding to *-bus* is the Homeric *-φι*, which is treated as an agglutination rather than a flexion and probably at one time had autonomous status. *I shall go*, Ch. *wo³yao⁴ ch'ü⁴*, Swahili *nitakwenda* (*ni-ta-kwenda*), Fr. *j'irai*, Sp. *iré* (*ire habeo*), Latin *ibo* (*i-bo*), Turk. *geleceğim* (*gel-e-cek-im* 'come shall I') are all groups of primary and subordinate symbols bound together by sense and accent and entering into relations with other similar groups of symbols to form sentences. If a Greek term has to be used for such I should prefer συντάγματα ('that which is put together in order') to any pseudo-Greek formation in *-eme*. With fusion and agglutination some of the associations are permanent, but even so there are others which are not, such as *in excelsis* 'on high', Ἰλιόθι πρό 'before Ilium'. In analytical or isolating languages the associations are more temporary and variable, but the sentence advances in all cases from group to group just as utterance progresses from breath-group to breath-group.

When groups are considered, the difference of structure becomes less important, though not irrelevant, and we notice that all groups are modified to enter into syntactic relations. Moreover, it becomes possible to compare parts of the groups, as Turkish *ev-ler-den*— 'house-s-from = from houses'. The notion of group is taken farther at times. One might even equate *hippopotamus = river-horse, philanthropist = lover of men*, Nahuatl *nipetlachihua* = 'I-mats-make = I make mats'. A relative clause is a kind of compound adjective, considered as a group, and so we are not surprised that the relative clause should precede the noun in Chinese or take an article in

Basque. In *Graecia capta ferum victorem cepit* 'conquered Greece conquered her crude conqueror', *capta* is equivalent to 'captured, though captured, after being captured', &c. The use of participles for clauses is frequent in Turkish and in Old Bulgarian, Latin, and Greek. In fact when sentences tend to be all on one level (paratactic construction), qualifications have to be introduced by participles or other forms of the non-finite verb. The series of groups closes with the end of the sentence, but there are languages like Eskimo, in which the whole sentence may be one word (holophrase). It is made up of stems which can be identified and compared to the words of more analytical languages, but which cannot stand alone without support.

Syntax is the department of linguistics deputed to take care of meaningful changes due to order and to the use of auxiliary words. Morphology is concerned with meaningful changes achieved by formal patterns. Syntax and morphology, then, cover some of the same ground. The word 'grammar' is here chosen to cover both methods of determining relations within the sentence.

FORM AND FUNCTION

Languages offer us forms which are often extraordinarily dissimilar and the grammarian states what are the functions of these forms, i.e. what they do. One may say 'the lark sang blithely' or 'the lark sang in a blithe fashion'. The function is adverbial in either case, since it consists of adding modal particulars to the verb, but the form is adverbial in the first sentence and nominal in the second. There is a discrepancy to be noted between parts of the sentence and parts of speech. In an argument of this sort the forms presented are so various that the discussion can only proceed by function, and it might seem easiest to make a universal grammar of functions and then ask how each language gives them form. But there is difficulty in stating what are functions of speech or what are the parts of the sentence. The principles of the categories would have to be discovered by way of logic or psychology or in some empirical fashion resulting from a complete knowledge of all languages. The method defeats itself. No one lives long enough to know more than a very little about language or about anything else. Besides the deluge of facts overwhelms the power of discrimination. If the functional categories are logical, the student must counter the claim that language is alogical. If they are psychological, it seems far from certain that psychologists are at peace or that their systems are permanent or relevant to grammar. There remains, too, the greatest difficulty of all, namely the positive nature of language studies. A form is a thing in grammar but a function is a speculation. Every form has to be explained whether it is logically or psychologically justified or not, but a grammarian is not called upon to explain a function if it does not exist in a given language as a form. The article must be assigned a function when it exists. In a language without articles there is nothing to say concerning this function of definition.

The historical succession of forms in grammar has to be noticed but the historical method is less rewarding in this department than in phonology. It is important to note that Latin *manibus* has become *por las manos* in Spanish but there has been no change of function. *Manibus* itself consists of *manu+bus* (*bhos*) and the semiautonomous case-ending had values that included those of Spanish *por*. Similarly history notes that Spanish *ire* comes from *ire habeo* (*hae*) which originally had the special sense of obligation still found in *he de ir* 'I must go'; *ire habeo* replaced Latin *ibo* and *ibo* consists of *i+bo*, in which *bo* had an original sense of growing into something (Gk. φύω). The changes of form have been considerable, but the changes of function have been minute and the end is as the beginning.

What is more important is to study the system of references as it exists at one time. Even functions may not be absolute but exist relatively to some system. The notion of system is central to synchronic linguistics. It is certainly the impression of speakers that they speak systematically. Children readily invent bits of language which they have not learnt, though they often suffer correction for doing so. Our understanding reaches out beyond our positive knowledge of words and expressions and we are able to put a novelty into its place and to appreciate it for its novelty. As a system a language exists *in esse* and *in posse* and authorized persons, such as poets, do from time to time call possible speech into actual existence. It follows that the business of the grammarian is to expound the system of his language.

The most rotund affirmation concerning system has been that 'chaque langue forme un système où tout se tient'.[1] But as we have

---

[1] Cf. 'Jusqu'à présent il a été souvent affirmé qu'une langue est un ensemble où toutes les parties se tiennent et l'on a beaucoup évoqué les catégories qui formeraient le fondement de la structure d'une langue. Seulement on a négligé

seen, attempts to complete the system by analogy are not always successful, though they ought to be if the system were as consistent as dogma suggests. In addition to the reigning mode there are relics of discarded systems which are labelled 'irregular'. They are commonly found in the most familiar parts of a language and have persisted because of their very familiarity. Latin *locus*/pl. *loci* corresponds with the classical system but *locus*/*loca* is labelled heteroclite. It answers to another analysis of the situation according to which a plurality of places might not be a number of points but a collective expression of place. Gender at one time no doubt was part of a genuine attempt to give to speech an order supposed to be found in surrounding nature, divided into animates and inanimates or males (agents) and females (recipients). But the validity of these distinctions was lost, though the genders remain when their forms have not decayed. They can hardly be accounted part of the same movement as that which has caused French to insist more and more on a fixed word-order and to replace emphatic stress by syntactical devices like *c'est à*. We find rather a succession of movements towards systematic expression, each discarded in its time but leaving débris behind. A better account of the grammatical state of affairs is therefore that of Ch. Bally:[1] 'La vie et le langage nous donnent, dans une égale mesure, l'image d'une organisation, plus exactement, d'une chose qui tend à s'organiser sans jamais y parvenir tout à fait.' Linguistic functions, of which we have spoken above, are parts of this never complete organization; they never quite attain exact definition.

CLASSICAL GRAMMAR

It may be profitable at this point to glance at the history of grammatical thought in the Greek world. Systems of grammar have been evolved at various places and times as a result of a high degree of literate civilization and often in relation to some revered text, such as the Vedic hymns, the Hebrew Bible, the Quran, or the Homeric poems. That which affects our tradition most intimately is the grammatical system evolved by the Greeks, applied later to Latin, and then with more or less sufficiency to most European

de verser au débat le témoignage concret que doit apporter l'étude descriptive d'un état de langue donnée' (A. Sauvageot, *Esquisse de la langue finnoise*, Paris, 1949, p. 7).
[1] Ch. Bally, *Le Langage et la vie*, Zürich, 1935, p. 29.

languages. Like all the other original systems it was based on a single language and its universal validity came to be assumed in the course of time. It so happened that an analysis of Greek proved to be also a fairly satisfactory analysis of Latin, a language of the same stock and in about the same stage of development. A grammar of Latin could be carried on with some adaptations to the grammars of the neo-Latin languages, and further application to Germanic or Slavonic, though involving considerable violence, might seem to be worth making in order to preserve the unity of grammatical thought. Greek grammar was as much prescriptive as descriptive. Modern grammars set out to be descriptive only, but it is to be remembered that authoritative descriptions acquire the value of counsels of perfection. Classical grammar, whatever its defects, has the importance of having shaped in cultured use the more civilized languages of the West. It has also supplied the common terminology of linguistics. This may be dismissed as out of date, but it has not really been replaced by any other set of terms generally accepted. The situation is rather that some classical expressions are rejected and others retained, while the allegation of the inadequacy of the system as a whole has not progressed so far as to present more than sketches of any other system.

Probably the most remarkable feature of Greek grammatical thought[1] is the slow development of the system from Protagoras in the fifth century B.C. to Dionysius Thrax (second century B.C.) and Apollonius Dyscolus (second century A.D.). When the examination of Greek began, the language had already passed through its savage and barbarous stages and its use for impressive poetry was on the wane. Its business was to convey information and to persuade— the business of civilized prose. It was a vehicle for philosophic and scientific thought. When the study of grammar reached its most complete formulation Greek had become a *lingua franca* for the known world and a language of scholarship. It was natural that the criteria of grammar should be logical whenever possible, and it is instructive that they could not be kept on the logical plane, despite its attractiveness. The terms are sometimes logical, sometimes formal, sometimes metaphorical, and sometimes arbitrary, but the tendency is to stress wherever possible the reasonableness of the grammatical system. This is far removed from the magical purposes of the Arunta chants cited by A. Somerfelt in *La Langue et*

---

[1] G. Murray, 'The beginnings of grammar', *Greek Studies*, Oxford, 1946.

la société (Oslo, 1938) or the automatic speech reflex of action as illustrated by B. Malinowski (*Magic, Science and Religion*, Boston, 1948).

The Logos, as a 'stream of expression', was divided into μέρη λόγου, which were as much parts of the sentence as parts of speech. Among the first to be recognized were ὄνομα/ῥῆμα, the name of some thing and a statement about that thing. This ὄνομα was rather a subject than a noun and the ῥῆμα included all that might be predicated of the ὄνομα. From another point of view they could be thought of as ὑποκείμενον/κατηγορούμενον, the subject and predicate of logic. The tendency was to make each sentence into a quasi-logical proposition: *John is good, Is John good?* (answered by a judgement, *John is good*), *John runs = John is running*. At first the need for more parts of speech was not recognized except for the σύνδεσμος 'ligament' and ἄρθρον 'joint'. The first was not quite a conjunction and the second not only an article. In the same way later distinctions were gradually introduced. The preposition is defined simply by its place before the noun. This is an abiding source of inconvenience, since many languages place 'prepositions' after the noun as postpositions. Definitions of case, person and mood are similarly thoughtful, if at times too ingenious. The case of the subject (ὄνομα) is naturally a ὀνομαστική; that with which the action of the verb was completed and which might be thought of as in some way the final cause of that action was called causal (αἰτιατική) the genitive as denoting class, the dative as a case of giving and receiving. *Ego, tu, ille*—the two persons of the dialogue and a third who intervened—were compared to the three masks or actors of the Greek stage. The infinitive was the verb form without limiting characteristics. Objecting to the term dubitative for what we call the subjunctive Apollonius preferred a term meaning subordinate, while what we call the optative was classed as the form of prayer (εὐκτική).

That the Latin translations of these terms are far from apt and that they are spoiled by the legal twist of the Roman mind is well enough known, but in the end they have become a mere set of names convenient for their stability over many centuries. It does not greatly matter that a subjunctive may stand in a principal sentence or that the *casus accusativus* means the case of accusation. It is more troublesome perhaps that *sententia* should suggest a formal judgement or proposition, but it also can be treated as a mere name for a grammatical feature. The state of terms has been modified by changes and additions and they have come to be identified with parts of speech rather than, as at first, with parts of the sentence.[1] As applied to languages of structure radically unlike Indo-European this causes difficulty, because though the sentence is divided into parts, it is not possible to recognize the customary parts of speech. There is no formal difference between one Chinese word and another though we may probably distinguish *nominalia*, *verbalia*, pronouns, numerals, 'empty' words, and conjunctions. Classical Chinese also used distinctive end words to close the sentence and indicate the general sense in which it should be taken.

SOME MODERN SPECULATIONS

Under modern conditions it cannot be simply assumed in the classical manner that grammatical categories are valid, but it may still be held that there is such a thing as universal grammar. The term seems to have been used first by James Harris in his Hermes (1751) and it came naturally in an age which postulated the unity of the human intellect. If one puts forward such a view now, one cannot be unaware of the immense variety of expressions of this supposed unity of mind. It is with this variety in view that J. Vendryes says 'it is not false to claim that there exists only one human language, fundamentally identical under all latitudes'.[2] From that starting-point it is easy transition on to assert that there must be a universal grammar, though its terms and conditions have still to be discovered.[3] To satisfy this definition grammar would have to be true, not only of a language at a given time (synchronism), but at all times and of all languages (panchronism) and the problem is how to make assertions of this degree of validity. Grammatical categories as such would have to be a fixed quality of language and the principle of categorization would be inherent in every language, at every time and in every place.

On the other hand the same facts support the denial of universal grammar by equally high authority. 'No logical scheme of the parts of speech—their number, nature, and necessary confines—is of the slightest necessity to the linguist. Each language has its own scheme.

---

[1] R. H. Robins, *Ancient and Mediaeval Grammatical Theory in Europe*, London, 1951.

[2] J. Vendryes, *Le Langage*, Paris, 1921.

[3] L. Hjelmslev, *Principes de grammaire générale*, Copenhagen, 1928, esp. p. 78.

Everything depends on the formal demarcations which it recognises.'[1] Still Sapir admits that no language wholly fails to make a distinction between noun and verb, with some means of distinguishing between concrete concepts and the activities or events in which they play a part. Nor perhaps is it seemly for a linguist to proclaim the total uselessness of attempts to provide a systematic basis for this part of his studies. It might still be possible to urge that the human mind, without showing complete unity in its way of reacting to circumstances, nevertheless does not exceed certain limits of diversity. The grammatical discussion will then not reveal a universal grammar but it will show individual grammars constantly applying the same or similar conclusions to the same or similar needs. The universality of grammar would appear in the way in which individual grammars overlap and intersect, never departing far from a kind of spectral band imposed by the limited powers of the human mind.

In the classification of function it is difficult to find a starting-point. When the argument has progressed some distance under its own logic, it begins to be hard to see a resemblance between the structure proposed and any actual language system. At every step one must beware of erecting some convention into a principle.

A bold attempt on a logical order of grammar was made by the late Viggo Brøndal and is serviceable as a *reductio ad absurdum* of this method.[2] He accepted Aristotle's four parts of speech and rejected all later Greek and Roman grammar. These categories he renamed *relatum* (R), *descriptum* (D), *descriptor* (d), *relator* (r). When each related element has been related and each described element described, i.e. with the assemblage of RDdr, the sentence is complete. The *relatum* of language corresponds to the logical category of substance and finds its pure expression in proper nouns; the *descriptum* corresponds to quantity and has its pure expression in numerals; the *descriptor* with quality and is pure in adverbs; the *relator* with relation and is pure in prepositions. The primary parts of speech are thus proper nouns, numerals, adverbs, and prepositions. Other parts of speech come from combining two or three of these four essentials and the whole scheme can be represented by concentric circles of 1, 2, 3, and 4 of these terms, the union of the

---

[1] E. Sapir, *Language*, Oxford, 1921, p. 125.
[2] Viggo Brøndal, *Ordklasserne*, Copenhagen, 1928; *Morfologi og Syntax*, Copenhagen, 1932.

four constituting the phrase. Ingenious as the scheme is, it has the defect of not being intelligible without constant reference to the author's text, since his primary categories are so strange. It is alien to the historical development of Language itself. Adverbs are commonly derived from nouns. Numeration is absent from very primitive languages. Prepositions are so recent a part of speech that they are not yet fully developed in the Homeric poems or in Old English. Paradigms show certain parts of speech developing together and obviously associated in the minds of speakers but they are split by this classification—which puts possessives in a different circle from personal pronouns, separates verbs from verbal nouns, and adverbs of number and manner from the simple adverbs of the first class. The whole effect is bizarre.

The logic invoked by A. Sechehay[1] is of a more Cartesian and less Aristotelian sort. It lies within ourselves, the speakers. The parts of speech are connected with outward reality by being translations of categories of our imagination. The method followed by the author is *a priori* and the point of departure is the language of children. Baby's one-word phrase is taken to be a predicate with the subject evident in the surrounding circumstances. The two-word phrase is either subject–predicate or principal–complement. Both are equally justified by children's practice and the difference would lie, if at all, in a pause between subject and predicate which is absent from the principal–complement group (as in Malay). The categories of imagination are somewhat variously translated into parts of speech because the process is affected by our momentary needs. It is easy to identify the noun as the proper expression of the subject and of entities, and the verb of events. The transitive verb is incomplete by nature and requires an object to complete its meaning. The principal complements are adjective and adverb, though the adverb suffers as a grammatical category by being made into a rag-bag for all words which cannot be assigned to prepositions, conjunctions, interjections, or the other parts of speech.

F. Brunot[2] attempted 'a methodical statement of the facts of thinking, considered and classified in relation to language, and of the means of expression corresponding to them'. His approach shows resolute preference for function as determining form. But the basis for defining function is to be neither philosophic nor

---

[1] A. Sechehaye, *Essai sur la structure logique de la phrase*, Paris, 1926.
[2] F. Brunot, *La Pensée et la langue*, Paris, 1922, p. viii.

psychological nor sociological, but an induction from the habits of one language (French). Not all the parts of his work have titles but the scheme includes (1) names of beings, things, and ideas, together with consideration of gender and number, determination by articles and representation by pronouns; (2) actions, which include verbs and their subjects, complements, and bearings; (3) circumstances and modes of place, time, and reference to our judgements or sentiments; (4) characterization of beings and things by adjectives; (5) relations, both logical and non-logical (particles).

Analysis of French does not make for so much dissatisfaction with the traditional terms of grammar as does the examination of English (in which so many of them have become atrophied) and Chinese (in which there are no formal distinctions at all). Working chiefly on a basis of English and Chinese as a corrective to Latin grammar, Otto Jespersen produced a highly original and suggestive scheme which he attempted to reduce after his wont to quasi-algebraic formulas.[1] He allows grammatical explanations to run from function to form or from form to function, though his applications seem in the main to be functional. However, in general terms, given a form, the grammarian looks for a function, and given a function, he looks for a form. From Wilhelm von Humboldt he accepted the distinction between 'inner' and 'outer' form, which gives the symbolization $I > o$ and $o > I$ as the expression of the linguist's task. The words are not wholly desirable. They seem to imply that the mental process before words are actually uttered has the same linear nature as the sentence itself. Form and function are both objective in speech.

The Russian philologist I. I. Meščanivov probably does better when he distinguishes parts of the sentence from parts of speech.[2] It is their disconformity which causes the grammarians' difficulties.

According to Jespersen in morphology the movement is from form to function and in syntax from function to form; the type of exposition used thus depends on the structure of the language to be explained. One function may have many forms and one form may have several functions. The sentence is composed of word-

---

[1] Otto Jespersen, *Sprogets Logik*, Copenhagen, 1913; *Philosophy of Grammar*, London, 1924; *Language*, London, 1922; *Die Sprache*, Heidelberg, 1925; *Analytic Syntax*, London, 1937. The last of these works explains his system of symbols.

[2] I. I. Meščaninov, *Členy predloženija i časti reči*, Moscow, 1945; the Russian theories are given in the preliminary matter of V. V. Vinogradov, Moscow, 1947.

groups of which the principal are subject (S), verb (V), object (O), and predicate (P). The indirect object is presented by an italic capital (*O*), so that *he gave her a ring* is of the type SV*O*O, and *he is angry* of the type SVP. With the help of small letters, numbers, brackets, and marks of various kinds it is possible to reproduce schematically all sorts of sentences.

More significant is his theory of the three ranks. This takes into account subordination within the group. The groups are divided into 'junctions' (as *a furiously barking dog*) and 'nexuses' (*a dog barks furiously*). The junction is a group requiring fulfilment to become a sentence but a nexus may be a sentence or part of a sentence. The three ranks are formed by the primary, secondary, and tertiary words of each group and are specifically named 1 junction, 2 adjunct, 3 subjunct, and 1 nexus, 2 adnex, 3 subnex. The point is that in *a barking dog/a dog barks* there is evidently identity of situation and details, but in the former case the group lacks the finish as a communication, which it possesses in the second. It is from the three gradations that Jespersen obtains his parts of speech: substantives, adjectives, pronouns, verbs, adverbs. They may be found functioning in all ranks but they have also their proper places, since substantives are characteristically primary, verbs and adjectives characteristically secondary, and adverbs characteristically tertiary. If primary, a substantive may be attended by two subordinates. The finite verb is always secondary and may only have a tertiary attendant. There is trouble in this system when an adjective functions as a primary and the usual question arises whether an adjective may be distinguished from an abstract noun. The relative clause is connected with its antecedent in the same way as an adjective, and indeed clauses may be of any rank and function in the same way as single words.[1]

One other discussion of this problem remains still *sub judice*. L. Hjelmslev's *Principes de grammaire générale* (Copenhagen, 1928) was issued rather as a programme than as a conclusion. It is now not only under the author's own reconsideration but also that of an

[1] E. Hermann, *Die Wortarten*, Berlin, 1928, recognizes thirteen classes of word: (1) activity word, (2) process word, (3) state word, (4) living-being word, (5) immaterial thing word, (6) material thing word, (7) appurtenance word, (8) property word, (9) circumstance word, (10) word of relation, (11) word of conjunction, (12) word of thought relation, (13) mere appellation. 1–3 correspond to verbs, 4–6 and 13 to substantives. There is a lucid summary of this discussion in W. E. Collinson, 'Syntactical Theory', *Transactions of the Philological Society*, 1941.

international body, which presumably lessens the prospect of a conclusive result. As a programme it asserts rather than demonstrates the universal application of grammar as suitable for all languages, places, and times. It envisages not a synchronic statement confined to the system of a single language but a panchronic system to be deduced from a study of all particular languages. The study is to be based on form. For this purpose there 'must' exist a descriptive logic which forms an integral part of psychology (p. 19). Functional categories are the essential part of any grammatical system, which represents the possibility or the sum of possibilities of combining one notion with another. The semanteme expresses a notion and the morpheme expresses relations between notions. Hjelmslev's work contains a full appreciation of grammatical thinking in modern times up to the date of publication but its theses are still to be proved.

PREGRAMMAR?

The word pregrammatical already exists to describe the unorganized language of children. A German-Swiss child who says *Bub bei* (*Bube bein*) has conveyed a message of some sort about its own leg. If it has just been hurt the message is probably of the nature of 'my leg is sore'. But the message is not organized. It is an attempt at German but lacks all the relational resources of German, and it is capable of several interpretations. Such language is pregrammatical and so is much that is uttered under stress of violent emotion.

The question that arises here, however, is somewhat different. Grammars have arisen only in highly civilized communities to account for languages in which precision and logic already played an important part. They have expressed more or less adequately the instincts of the speakers of those languages. For at least four centuries before Aristotle the Greeks had been accustomed to using language principally for such kinds of communication. But is it certain that language has always been used thus? Can we not see that some societies show savage indifference to details, while others show a barbarous delight in differentiation? Civilized languages show traces of savage indifference in, for example, the opposition *bull/cow* when the language has subsequently gained means of relating males and females of the same kind. They show over-elaboration in using categories of gender and declension to no known purpose. For gender it is possible to suggest a valid cause in the system of magical correspondences common in barbarous tribes. For such there may be a real association between women and water (*aqua*) or a city (*urbs*, πόλις). The child (*Kind*) and a wife (*Weib*) are neuters, not logically, but because of their superficial resemblance to things without the power of action. These are grammatical categories which cannot be accounted for by logical analysis. Though they are not beyond the range of psychology they correspond to a sort of psychology which does not exist in civilized nations and which is unintelligible to them. The existence of such features in the most civilized grammars forces our explanation to take two or more levels. The system of a language embalms the relics of forgotten systems.

It is in this sense that I should suggest the use of the word pre-grammar. Just as prehistory is history without documents or a dated time scale, though it has its own types of evidence and approximate clock, so pregrammar might refer to those types of organization which are insufficient from the standpoint of civilized grammar, either because they are not in fact fully organized to convey definite information, or because they convey information which has no civilized value. Chinese, which is fully equipped for every sort of civilized communication, makes no use of most of the formal categories devised for the Indo-European languages. It must be evident that a great deal of our grammatical armature is in fact unnecessary and had its reasons in some very different mental climate.

The categories of civilized grammar have been applied to un-civilized languages with a certain amount of success. What the native view may be does not appear. It is in the nature of things that such a view cannot be expressed. The work has in fact been a kind of translation directed by civilized students such as missionaries or linguists. A native form *x* corresponds to a civilized form *y* (often a Latin form); from which we assume that *x* has the category of civilized (Latin) *y*. But where we can compare two civilized grammars, such as Latin and Chinese, we find that this sort of argument does not hold. If a Chinese syntagma is translated by a Latin pluperfect, it does not follow that the pluperfect is a category of Chinese grammar. Chinese grammarians would at once resent the suggestion, and might proceed to decompose the Latin tense into Chinese 'empty' words.

A grammar should have some relation to a people's way of life and thought. If the Australian Arunta,[1] for instance, make no provision for the future, do not calculate, and cannot distinguish between themselves and their relatives of the same degree, then it is not much use to compliment them on a sense of futurity so fine as to require two futures, or to discuss their numerals or their personal pronouns. One should look for something within their experience, such as a sense of incompletion and of the place and actions of speaker and hearer. Primitive societies often have complex grammars. The multiplicity of forms might be due to capacity for making more subtle distinctions than we do, or might be due to indifference and lack of specialization. The Arunta do not differentiate vowels or distinguish between voiced and voiceless consonants, nor do they insist on the precise limits of syllables. Thus *ra = era = ara = ira* and *nku = ngu = anku = unku = ingu = ungu*. They use no gender. Their basic stems are gerundial, i.e. indifferently nominal or verbal, and as they usually form parts of agglomerations, they seem unfinished in themselves. There is no definite subordination of suffixes to principal stems. The suffixes are also principal stems in their own right, and the union of stems and suffixes seems to be temporary. This is so unlike agglutination in the Turkish fashion (which depends on a strict differentiation of principal stems and relational suffixes) that it should not be called by the same name but by some other, such as agglomeration.[2] The notions conveyed by the Arunta stems are all highly concrete, and refer only to visible persons, places, activities, and objects. Though translation may introduce abstract terms these are foreign to Arunta thinking. To some extent the grammatical process has consisted in disentangling the undifferentiated masses of pregrammar.

It is not to be supposed, however, that the linguistic student can

---

[1] A. Sommerfelt, *La Langue et la société*, Oslo, 1938.

[2] W. K. Matthews, *Languages of the U.S.S.R.* (Cambridge, 1951), p. 67, n. 3, notes that the 'agglutination' of Papuan as described by A. Capell, 'Word-Building and Agglutination in South-Eastern Papua', *Bulletin of the School of Oriental Studies*, ix, 1937–9, is quite different from Turkish agglutination because it is concerned with 'the amalgamation of units which are for the most part semantically sufficient'. He does not draw the conclusion that a different term is needed to describe the different process, though 'amalgamation' is suggested by his wording. 'Agglomeration', gathering as in a ball of wool, is an attempt to mark the chaotic nature of the process, which is so unlike the tidy logic of the Altaic languages. It is a sign of grammatical indifference.

identify features of language with phases of society as illustrated by anthropologists, and to associate, for instance, a given grammatical feature with the matriarchate. Language does indeed record all that a community thinks, but not always as grammar. A notable instance is the distinction between *yang* and *yin* in Chinese popular thought. It opposes a light beneficent male principle to a dark hostile female principle. But the Chinese have never been moved to divide things into two genders and the distinction remains only in thought and words. The totem system is of great importance to the Arunta. It has given rise to a complex vocabulary of relationships which distinguishes the two sides of the family with great exactitude. An Arunta can define his relationship to any other Australian native by means of the totemic lineages. But the matter has to do with vocabulary not grammar. A similar exactitude in the Latin family terms (*patruus* father's brother/*avunculus* mother's brother and the like) and the complete system in Quechua shows that at one time exogamy was significant for these peoples and has left its mark on the language, but not specifically upon grammar. The determination of positive grammars in conformity with the habits of thought and life of savage peoples is a task full of difficulties, but the investigator should be warned not to attribute the logical categories of civilized grammar too readily, simply by the way of translation.

Correlations between grammar and society are offered in W. Schmidt's *Sprachfamilien und Sprachenkreise der Erde* (Heidelberg, 1926) with special reference to the languages of southern Asia and the Pacific islands. Differences of this sort are most energetically rejected by E. Sapir,[1] whose views were conditioned by special competence in the American-Indian field. Our self-consciousness of speech is an interesting psychological and social phenomenon, he held, but has very little to do with the question of form in language. Language is felt to be a perfect symbolic system in a perfectly homogeneous medium for the handling of all references and meanings of which a given culture is capable. Language is a perfect symbolism of experience.

The word 'perfect' is one to be applied with hesitation to any human condition. The imperfect communications achieved by speech are a common cause of regret by artists and criticism by

---

[1] 'The Nature of Language', *Selected Writings*, California Univ. Press, Berkeley, 1948.

linguists. The experiences of communities of speakers differ, and their language-patterns are affected accordingly. Abstract terms are rare because they are rare in the communal experience. Whether the language contains means for the ready creation of such terms or not, they are characteristically absent from primitive speeches, and their absence is a bar to higher intellectual achievement. The sense of the immediate and concrete prevents the same communities from expressing even concrete activities in general terms, but the presence or absence of the thing referred to, the places occupied by the speaker and hearer, and the physical peculiarities of the object, may all have grammatical expression in the discourse. Grammar, in such circumstances, is directed towards different ends than those envisaged by the Graeco-Roman grammarians and commonly applied in civilized societies, ancient or modern.

AUDIBLE AND VISIBLE GRAMMAR

Though philologists stress the paramount importance of audible and customary speech, it is difficult to reproduce this with complete phonetic accuracy. We break up breath-groups into component words: for *aiftgou hom* we write (and think) *I have to go home*. We do not set forth a paradigm *aiftgou, yuftgou, histgou*, &c., and infer that English, like Hausa and Coptic, conjugates its pronouns. That is not the awareness we have of language in a literate society. We do not occupy ourselves with *lom/dlom/dezom* in French but with *l'homme, de l'homme, des hommes. Chat* and *chatte* conform visibly to the rule that the feminine is formed from the masculine by the addition of *e*-mute; audibly, however, *ša/šat* differ because the masculine ends in a vowel and the feminine in a consonant. The visible plural is a suffixed *-s*; there is no audible plural sign before a word beginning with a consonant, but there is *z* before one beginning with a vowel. This plural prefix *z-* is recorded by investigators of folk-tales and folk-songs, where it often appears autonomously, without grammatical justification. The audible declension of *œuf* includes *œ̃nœf, dœzœ, trwazœ, saŋkœf*, &c., in which *-fs* is sounded *-f* when the number has no sibilant, but is wholly lost when there is the sibilant pluralizing *z*. But for *neuf œufs*[1] there is, perhaps, no colloquial pronunciation, since there is no grammatical justification for *nœfzœ*, and *nœfœf* is an intolerable cacophony. J. Orr reports that a grocer could not be induced to say to

---

[1] J. Orr, *Le Français moderne*, xix, 1951 ('Les œufs de Pâques . . . et d'été').

him anything but *neuf beaux œufs* (*nœfbozœ*). There is no option about recording the audible grammar of an illiterate speech, but scholars divide it as much as possible into verbal units; for a literate language we must follow the written form, not merely because that represents the awareness of the speakers, but because it offers a standard of reference for the inconsequences of oral practice. Thus the plural of *œuf* is *œufs*, with a suffixed -*s*, and to this we can refer, by a system of conventions accepted by all Frenchmen, both *z-œ* and *œf* and *œ z-* (before a vowel). Grammars of modern European languages on a phonetic basis were attempted in W. Viëtor's series 'Skizzen lebender Sprachen'; but, though they were based on the word, not the word-group, they failed to reproduce the native-speaker's awareness of his language. It is quite possible that literacy has encouraged, by giving cover to, greater spoken irregularities than are commonly encountered in the speech of illiterate communities. These are often curiously stable in their basic stems and their particles.

VI
GRAMMAR: THE SENTENCE

ORGANIZED grammar is based on the sentence and the sentence is essentially predication.

This view does not entirely commit us to belief in Wilhelm von Humboldt's thesis of the primacy of the sentence over the word. The term word may be understood in various ways, and if it is stretched to include cries and spontaneous utterances, these may well be anterior to the sentence proper. These utterances form groups of significant symbols not unlike the breath-groups of phonetics, but whether they are properly considered as organized sentences is open to doubt. It is from the organized sentences, however, that we deduce the fully organized word. The function of a single word in one language is played by two or more in another and in some of them, such as those of the Altaic group, a single word may play the part of a whole clause elsewhere. One cannot give the same account of what constitutes a word in languages of totally different types though the sentences of each are, as the definition requires, complete expressions of the speaker's intention within the frame of the given circumstances. The organized word thus comes after the organized sentence, and it is with this latter that the grammarian has to do.

To employ the term 'predication' of something so alogical as speech is perhaps awkward, but it is sanctioned by tradition and there is no other term equally convenient. It means only that something is said (P) about some subject (S), not always in the form 'S is P' but more often and characteristically SP, e.g. *John runs*. The predicate is termed ῥῆμα = ('a saying') by Aristotle and the subject ὄνομα or τὸ ὑποκείμενον. A thing which can be singled out for predication is to that extent named and is a noun; it may be said metaphorically to underlie the statement (ὑποκεῖσθαι 'underlie'). At this stage we are dealing with the gross Subject and gross Predicate as in the division into two parts of 'The boy/stood on the burning deck, whence all but he had fled'. The gross subject (S) includes all that goes to define itself, as *the boy*, *the brave boy*, *Casabianca's boy*, *the boy who was the hero of this poem*. All that constitutes the subject (S) or noun (ὄνομα). Similarly the gross predicate (P) includes not only the verb but all its complements and modifiers and may be *stood, stood firmly, stood during the battle of the Nile, planted his feet stoutly, gave heed to his father's orders*, &c. The distinction so far lies between the nominal element in the sentence, which names something that might enter into other sentences under other circumstances, and a phenomenal element proper to the particular occasion and never precisely to be repeated.

The phenomenon itself may be the subject of the sentence as in *pluit* = 'it rains'. *It* can only refer to the activity of raining. In Chinese *hsia⁴ yü³* 'down (descends) rain' the order is that of predicate and complement and there is no fictitious subject *it*. Similarly in Malay *di-chium-nya dan ditangis-nya oleh bonda-nya akan anak-nya itu* 'there was kissing and weeping over it by her'[1] the subject is the activity presented by the verb and this feature leads to the conception of the Malay verb as nominal. In Bantu almost all verbs have a suffixed *-a* which seems to have factitive value, as if, for instance, *okoa* 'save' were 'cause saving'. From the consideration of such cases some theorists have concluded that the noun is the fundamental part of speech. But in the absence of any part of speech specialized to denote phenomena any word has a phenomenal value, and is to that extent verbal. To answer the question 'are you going away' by *yes* or *not I* is as phenomenal as to say *I am going* or *I am not going*. Since all speech is about specific events, it has been, on the other hand, concluded that the fundamental part of speech is the verb. The oldest historical or social conditions we encounter show stems which are not specifically either verbs or nouns but may better be called gerunds. As soon as these receive the additional symbols which permit them to function within the sentence, the group becomes either nominal or verbal and a line of separation is drawn which is not easily transgressed.

In (S) *the boy/stood on the burning deck* (P) it is easy to see that *the burning deck* might under other circumstances be the subject of a predicate, e.g. *the burning deck/gave way*. Hence ὄνομα 'subject' was readily transmuted into ὄνομα 'noun'. The various parts of speech may be further identified by predication: A substantive because it is habitually the whole or part of a subject, an adjective because it can be predicated of a substantive (*the burning deck/the deck was burning*) but not a substantive of an adjective (thus *green*

---

[1] R. O. Winstedt, *Malay Grammar*, Oxford, 1913, p. 65.

was my valley is PS, not SP), an adverb because it is a predicate of the noun of the verbal activity (*burns fiercely/the burning was fierce*), a pronoun because it offers general reference for some noun. The pronoun stands for anything that can be named, i.e. a noun or adjective or adverb; hence the great variety of types assembled under the heading of pronouns and the doubt whether adverbs are not pronominal in some of the simplest forms. The finite verb remains as the residuum of analysis, when all possible nominal elements are segregated.

By way of compensation there is a tendency in most languages for the verb to resume the whole sentence within itself by means of affixed pronouns. Even though modal, spacial, or temporal conditions of the event may be given separate expression outside the verb there usually remains within it a sufficient number of phenomenal marks for the expression of a unique event. The separated symbols are sometimes discovered to be not autonomous for lack of accent or loss of fullness which they would possess in their autonomous states. Even in isolating languages the verb is a complex of pronouns and auxiliaries subordinated to the main verbal concept. Probably in the majority of primitive tongues the verbal complex is rich in elements designed to express the event in its whole complexity of precepts and shades of action. This richness is indiscriminate.

Though the parts of speech are to be inferred from repeated predications, their number and stability in any given language is determined by form. Where there are formative obstacles to passing from one part of speech to another, the permanence of distinction is inevitably greater than in the absence of such obstacles. In English we readily make a substantive into an adjective but not so readily an adjective into a substantive. In Spanish the opposite conditions apply; adjectives have suffixes to distinguish them from corresponding substantives but may be substantivated by simply prefixing an article. In Chinese there are no formal divisions of any kind, yet verbs and nouns are sufficiently well distinguished since they do not transgress more than a certain distance over each other's frontiers, and there is a similar semantic frontier for pronouns, conjunctions, and (in ancient Chinese) particles which end the sentence. Numerals also—which are special kinds of nouns (substantives or adjectives)—never pass into other parts of speech. The number of parts of speech differs with different languages and depends on accepted semantic limitations which may be reinforced by specialization of forms. Their relations seem to be determined as possible subjects and predicates of each other. Thus 'the black man runs his race swiftly' contains the possibilities 'the man is black', 'the man runs', 'his running is swift', 'a race is run'.

When a language is rich in grammatical forms, the parts of speech are considered on a formal basis and the problem is to assign reasons for the differentiation. *Hard/hardness*, Germ. *hart/Härte* name a quality. What makes the first of each pair an adjective is its reference to a substantive and its capacity as an attribute to take the gender of the substantive. But when the adjective is used predicatively it is invariable. It then differs from the substantive by absence of gender. A French adjective in such a position continues to show the generic condition of the substantive. A Russian predicated adjective is invariable for case but varies for gender and the whole declension is in fact known, though not normally used. The distinction of the predicative and attributive adjective is still based on form, but is such that the former uses a nominal declension (mostly in one case) and the latter uses an extended declension with a suffixed definite article (which no longer has the function of definition). Similarly *he grieved = he was sorry, to flower = to be in bloom*, Germ. *er ruht = er ist ruhig = er ist in Ruhe* 'he is resting'. What is formally a verb in one set of sentences becomes analysed as copula+substantive or adjective in others (not without minor semantic distinctions) according as part of the verbal activity or state is differentiated and named. In such languages as German and English the part of speech that emerges is identified by its form and syntax.[1]

EVOLUTION OF THE SENTENCE

The fully organized sentence has the quality of completeness within its circumstances or context which is not necessarily present in all utterances. Apart from the example offered by B. Malinowski of the expressions exchanged in the excitement of communal fishing in the Trobriand Islands, he reproduces a more leisurely statement which seems less a complete expression of the impression made by an event than successive aspects of the same as they catch the eye of the speaker.

[1] M. Sandmann, 'Substantiv, Adjektiv-Adverb und Verb als sprachliche Formen', *Indogermanische Forschungen*, lvii.

Tasakaulo	*kaymatana*	*yakida;*	*tawoulo*	*ovanu;*	*tasivila*
we run	front wood	ourselves	we paddle	in place	we turn

tagine	*soda;*	*isakaulo*	*kau'uya*	*oluvieki*	*similaveta*
we see	companion ours	he runs	rear wood	behind	their sea-arm

Pilolu.[1]
Pilolu

This, as it were, episodic quality seems to be present in examples of Arunta incantations quoted by A. Sommerfelt:

garra	*toppatuna*	*ilinatarala*	*tula*	*naria*
beast	break back	we two	we wish	to kill (*tu-*) it.

'we want to kill a beast whose back we have broken'

larra	*tjilatjila*	*kula nara*
river	white	perhaps is it there?[2]

From this sort of spontaneous speech in which the sentence is never certainly brought to a full stop, it would seem to be an advance when we come to the word-sentence, or holophrase. For in that stage at least the unity of the sentence is recognized. Languages using word-sentences are to be found on either side of the Behring strait. They might be called holosynthetic; but an extended transcription of Eskimo such as appears in A. Fick's *Die Haupttypen des Sprachbaus* shows sentences composed of agglomerated words as well as fully articulate word-clauses. The presence in one word of many relational elements constitutes polysynthesis, as in most of the American-Indian languages, and with more precise grammatical discipline it becomes agglutination of the Turkish type. Languages like Eskimo and Koryat, however, are liable to offer a word-sentence or holophrase sufficiently often to justify calling them holosynthetic.

Thus Koryat presents such a phrase as

nakomajn'ytamjun'n'ybolamyk

na	*ko*	*majn'y*	*tamjun'*	*n'yvo*	*lamyk*
they	now	greatly	deceive	continuously	us

'They are always lying to us.'[3]

Chukcha: *tymyngyntorkyn*

ty	*myngy*	*nto*	*rkyn*
I	hands	out	(active sign)

I hold out my hands.

[1] B. Malinowski, *Magic, Science and Religion*, Boston, 1948, p. 232.
[2] A. Sommerfelt, *La Langue et la société*, Oslo, 1938, pp. 82, 87.
[3] I. I. Meščaninov, *Členy predloženija i časti reči*, Moscow, 1945, pp. 21–33.

A characteristic of such sentences is that they must depend as much on the position of stems for their syntax as the words of an isolating language like Chinese. There is nothing else to show how the phrase is to be construed. In the first instance the order is SVO and in the second SOV, the first as in English or Chinese and the second as in Turkish, Japanese, and often in classical Latin. The stems within the word-sentence seem to be relatively stable. If the words are taken out of their syntactical context and made to stand alone they may change. Thus *siko* 'ice' corresponds to *sikumineq* 'piece of ice' and *-mineq-* corresponds to *-mineř-* in *sikumineřpâịt* 'many pieces of ice'. P. Rivet's example *takusariartorumagalua- nerpâ*?[1] 'do you think he really intends to go and busy himself with that?' is analysed into the words *takasar[pâ]* 'he is busy with that', *iartor[poq]* 'he is going to', *uma[voq]* 'he intends', *[g]aluar[poq]* 'he does so but', *ner[poq]* 'do you think he', â (interrogative 3rd person). But once the stem has assumed its construct form it continues to function unaltered. Within the sentence it would seem that syntax consists in the order given to invariable elements. Some of these seem to be specialized as euphonic and others may be auxiliaries, but the latter are not so easy to distinguish as Chinese empty words.

In another language of north-eastern Siberia, Gilyak, there is polysynthesis but not holosynthesis and there is the beginning of specialization of the predicate. Thus we analyse after Meščaninov:

Gilyak: *urlanivx tĭokŭudĭ*

    urla   niux   tĭo   kŭu-dĭ

    good   man   fish   hunt (predicative suffix).

Their incorporation of the adjective and substantive which make the noun-subject and of object and verb which make the predicate and the final particle belongs to the verb proper. The relations of the parts of such compounds are various. Gilyak *n'an'yn'nivx* 'hunter' could be translated 'the man (*nivx*) whose trade is in animals'. In Chukcha *tan'kljavolja kora nimyrkynen* 'the good man will kill the stag' the order is SOV, the object is distinct, but the subject is formed of an adjective and substantive fused to make a compound noun. Nouns of that sort occur in English, as in *philanthropy*. In Basque the relative clause is treated as a noun and given an article applied to the whole and in Chinese it carries a suffixed -ti which is also used to form possessives and adverbs. In *wo³ so³*

[1] *Les Langues de monde*, Paris, 1924, p. 597.

-*shuo*⁴ -*ti hua*⁴ 'my said words = the words I said', the relative clause is treated as a unit and enclosed between the possessive pronoun and its substantive.

In the Mexican (Aztec) or Nahuatl language the subject is clearly distinguished, but the verb and its complements still form a block (incorporation). Thus *mepampo?powa* 'weeds agave rows' consists of *me*[λ] 'agave'+*pami*[λ] 'rows'+*po?powa*, and λ*e·kʷepo·ni* 'bursts from the action of fire' includes λ*e*[λ] 'fire', λ*ašoči?i?kʷilowa* 'paints or engraves something (λ*a*-) with flowers (*šoči*[λ])'.[1] The nouns included in the verb complete the notion of the verbal action either as expended on an object or recipient, or is completed in a certain manner. As the last example shows, if the completive noun is absent its place must be taken by a particle λ*a* or *tla*, as in *nitlaqua* 'I eat something (*tla*)', *nitetlamaca* 'I give someone (*te*) something'.[2]

Another unresolved group results from the fact that the adjective is predicated of its substantive. In Japanese, Korean, and the Yana Indian language of North America, the adjective is conjugated.[3] A somewhat similar cause in Bantu leaves only about fifty 'genuine' adjectives; all others are formed by a relative or possessive construction. Not all Japanese adjectives are conjugated and their history is obscure but in *baka na kodomo* 'the foolish child' *na* is from *naru* 'to be'. The predicated idiom is *ano kodomo wa baka desu* 'that child is foolish'. In Korean the greater number of adjectives are present participles of verbs, as *kŏmta* 'to be black'/*kŏmŭn* 'being black = black', *súita* 'to be sour'/*súin* 'sour'. Though the adjectives of Turkish are not considered to be conjugated, the fact that the copula is a suffixed particle causes them to be in fact conjugated when forming part of the predicate. The same treatment is given to predicated nouns: *bu kitaptir* 'this is a book', *bu kitap büyüktür* 'this book is big' (-*dir* 'is').

It would be tempting to construct a hypothetical history of the evolution of grammatical discrimination, starting from the word-sentence which represents the event in its unanalysed complexity and ending with the complete differentiation of parts of speech and

---

[1] B. L. Whorf, 'The Milpa Alta dialect of Aztec', *Linguistic Structures of Native America*, Viking Fund Publications in Anthropology, vi, New York, 1946.

[2] E. Cassirer, *Philosophie der symbolischen Formen*, i, Die Sprache, Berlin, 1923, p. 239.

[3] Sir G. Sansom, *Historical Grammar of Japanese*, Oxford, 1928, pp. 98–109; A. Eckardt, *Koreanische Konversations-Grammatik*, Heidelberg, 1923, p. 38; E. Sapir, *Language*, Oxford, 1921, p. 126, n.

the emergence of invariable words. The complexity of many primitive grammars suggests this treatment and the suggestion is reinforced by the precedence of synthesis over analysis in the history of the languages best known to us. This theory seems to appeal to Russian philologists within whose immense country there are all the intermediate types postulated by the theory. But there is the usual difficulty in affirming that a modern primitive state gives a true picture of the primitive condition of a civilized tongue. As in anthropology, the modern savage condition is no more than a hint towards the reconsideration of the life of our own savage ancestors. There are also linguists of high repute who deny any correlation between social language structure.

A more serious difficulty is offered by the Sino-Tibetan languages and especially by Chinese. They are on the whole monosyllabic, isolating, and invariable, and they present no evidence of having been at any time fused into word-sentences. The few agglutinations they show may as well be due to the decay of independent words as to an earlier agglutinative condition. The personal pronouns once differed for case (subject–object), but this is a realistic distinction and offers poor support for a theory of lost declensions. The relatively well-nourished declension of Burmese nouns obviously consists of an invariable monosyllabic stem and an affixed independent particle. Some Tibetan combinations of consonants require the aid of a fugitive vowel in pronunciation and it is clear that the phonetic structure of Chinese words was formerly much more varied and complex than in Mandarin of today. Tibetan verbs still show some internal vowel mutations. But when all is said there is nothing to prevent our thinking that the languages of the whole Far Eastern area may have developed from autonomous stems without passing through any fusional stage. On the other hand our knowledge of the Sino-Tibetan family is still very inadequate. It can hardly be relied on in detail for conditions (other than syntactical) before the fifth century of our era.

TYPES AND ORDERS OF SENTENCES

The Hamito-Semitic languages distinguish with exceptional clearness between the nominal and verbal sentences. The former put two nouns into a predicative relation, the second being either a substantive or an adjective. The verbal type concentrates attention on the act or state. Thus

NOMINAL (SP) OEgypt. *ynuk*/*neb ymat* = 'I (am)/the Lord of Graciousness' (ScP)

        Arab.   *Zaidun*/*walladun* = 'Zaid (is) a boy'

VERBAL (VSO) OEgypt. *sedem sekhti heru* = 'The peasant hears the
voice' (SVO)

        Arab.   *kataba Zaidun* = 'Zaid wrote'.

In addition there is the mixed nominal–verbal sentence in which the
subject comes first but the predicate is a verb (SV): OEgypt. *yau*/
hau = 'old age, (it) advances', Arab. *Zaidun kataba* = 'Zaid, (he)
wrote'. For this order and the double expression of the subject (by
substantive and by suffixed pronoun) compare Lat. *Balbus scripsi-t*
(SV), *Balbus scripsit librum* (SVO), *Balbus librum scripsit* (SOV)
'Balbus wrote a book'. As we have already seen, other orders may
be habitually employed for the same relational effect, as Turk. *bir
kuştur* (Pc) 'it is a bird', Gael. *tha an la fuar* (cSP) 'the day is cold',
bhuail iad am bord (VSO) 'they struck the table', Samoan *e lē aoga*/
ona (PS) 'it is useless'. Since the predicate may comprise the verb
and object or recipient, we may take P = VO and state that normal
orders are SVO, SOV, VOS, or OVS and that more than one may
be used as a norm in a given language. Thus in Old French and
modern Spanish the verbal sentence is as common as the nominal
or mixed, but in modern French and English only the nominal and
mixed orders are normal. Hence any other order becomes available
for emotive expression, as *green was*/*my valley* (PS) which differs
from *my valley*/*was green* not as a system of references, but by
affective suggestiveness. To preserve an order syntactical devices
may be used such as the French *c'est* in *c'est à vous que je parle*.
This formally satisfies the required order SVO, but in reality serves
to place *à vous* in a position it would not normally occupy.

To these affirmative sentences questions and exclamations conform according to the conventions of each language. The true
nature of the question is seen best in Chinese which keeps the same
order as the assertion. The question is an incomplete assertion for
which the speaker lacks some particular unknown to him (determinative question) or requires the solution of a doubt or alternative (dubitative question). Typical examples are (in translation):

DETERMINATIVE: 'My things are *where*?'—'Here'.

DUBITATIVE: 'He *is*—*is not*—here?'—'*Not here*'.

    'This affair *is urgent*—*not urgent*?—'(*It*) *is not urgent*'.

Thus the question contains most of the material of the answer and is most logically expressed in the order of the answer. This is achieved in modern French by the form *Est-ce que*: *est-ce qu'on dîne ici?*—(*On dîne*) *ici même*. The need for this formula comes from the fact that French and other similar languages have used the device of inversion to express interrogation, and the inversion is transferred to the words *est-ce*. In German inversion is used not only in questions but also to denote subordination, in conditional clauses when there is no conjunction, &c. In Germ. *er tat, als hätte er mich nicht gesehen* 'he acted, as if he had not seen me' the principal clause has the order SV and the subordinate or conditional clause the order VSO. Questions may also be constructed, with or without inversion, by means of particles such as Chinese *ni¹*, *mo¹*, Russ. *li*, &c. When a language does not use tones to construct its words, a rising tone is sufficient to indicate a question: *So this is Oxford?* Tonal patterns are used with more energy in exclamations, for which also particles are available in many languages.

The copula (c) ἔστι[1] has been of immense importance in Western philosophy since it turned mere existence at some place (*Dasein*) into being (*Sein*) and led to judgements concerning a nature of things. The Greek Eleatic philosophers held that the basic form of every valid utterance was a logical judgement about being. The Latin *sententia* is such a judgement. The result for grammar was the mistaken view that all sentences were regarded as ultimately nominal; that *John runs* contains the judgement *John is running*, and that a question invites a judgement in reply, &c. This is erroneous. Even such a sentence as *God is good* is a judgement in speech but a progression from one concept to another within the frame of some circumstances or context. Within the frame of the religion of Dionysus (in Euripides' *Bacchae*) it would be a false assertion; though offered as a permanent truth of the Christian faith, it is spoken phenomenally concerning a momentarily important event in the outside world or in the speaker's mind. Philosophy has flourished as well in languages without a copula, and nominal sentences are perhaps more logically construed without one. Thus in Chinese the change of order indicates predication: *hao³ jên²* 'good man'/*jên² hao³* 'man is good'. In Malay, where the attributive adjective follows the noun, the copula is represented by a short pause. In Russian print there is sometimes a dash. Both Chinese

[1] E. Cassirer, *Philosophie der symbolischen Formen*, Berlin, 1923, i. 289.

and Arabic make use of former demonstratives (Chinese *shih*[4], Arabic *hūwa*, *hīya* 'he, she'). Alternatively the notion of existence may be refined upon, as in the double copulas of Spanish and Basque, and so on with other quasi-auxiliaries.

In theory a language plentifully supplied with flexions or agglutinations should be independent of word-order, but this does not seem to occur in fact. The violent hyperbata of literary Latin do not seem to have had a place in everyday Latin speech. At most these resources permit the speaker to utter his words in the order of interest of the concepts they symbolize. There is some discrepancy between the logical and the spontaneous orders, but in each case there is a definite expectancy created by the orderly habits of the particular language. These habits may go so far as to include fixed order, though the position of each part of the expression is also strictly defined by symbols. Thus the places are fixed in Jap. *watakushi wa hon wo yomu* 'I may read a book', though *wa* is the suffix of the absolute subject and *wo* of the object. Similar fixed orders prevail in Turkish and in Quechua,[1] though both are highly agglutinative, and each word is grammatically determined by its suffixes.

A distinction between paratactic and hypotactic construction has important grammatical sequence. Parataxis places all sentences on one level and is distinguished by its lack of subordinate conjunctions. Hypotaxis uses conjunctions and relative pronouns to produce subordinate clauses, which are treated as separate clauses with finite verbs. The paratactic construction is the earlier and involves less discrimination. It is common, for instance, in Arabic where an author is cited (*qāla Ibn Ḥayyān* 'Ibn Hayyān said') and what he said is then continued in his own words on the same level of discourse. The Arabic relative is a demonstrative pronoun and the clause a separate predicate of the antecedent. Similarly *the man who came yesterday said so* may have a more strictly colloquial form like *the man—the one who came yesterday—he said so*. Hypotaxis is, however, sufficiently familiar in our Western languages to be used in everyday speech.

Parataxis, on the other hand, does not remove the demand for subordination; the situation is that, since subordination cannot be expressed by a finite verb without creating a new sentence on the

---

[1] Turkish SOV; Quechua OVS (Sir C. R. Markham, *Quechua Grammar*, London, 1864, p. 59).

same level, it must be expressed in some other way, by means of a participle agreeing with a noun or by an infinitive complement of a verb. Hence early forms of language, including Indo-European, show a remarkable efflorescence of participles. In Finno-Ugrian it is the infinitive which is developed so as to show many forms and cases; in Turkish there is a considerable use of suffixes to give similar effects. When no attachment can be made within the sentence, words are placed in absolute position, the noun and adjective being united by some conventionally selected case: ablative in Latin, genitive in Greek, nominative in English, dative in old Slavonic, locative in Sanskrit, &c. As a result of the development of conjunctions in the modern Slavonic languages the participles have lost almost all their cases and remain only in certain petrified forms. The hey-day of participles and similar usages is thus intimately connected with the archaic paratactic construction.

RELATIONS BETWEEN SUBJECT AND PREDICATE

The passive sentence (*the wall was built by Balbus*) exemplifies a dilemma concerning the subject of the phrase. The topic of conversation is *the house*, which occupies the place of the grammatical subject. The source of the action is *Balbus*, whom we term the 'logical' subject. Our expressions are typically active, and it is the agent who seems to us the real subject. But though the notion of 'logical' subject clears this difficulty in one way, it does not cover all the anomalies concerning the relation of subject and predicate. We are so accustomed to regard the subject as the cause of an action that we are somewhat embarrassed when the form of sentence prevents this being grammatically true, but we do not notice instances in which the subject is not a cause or agent but a patient.

We have already remarked that the predicate itself may be the subject of a sentence. It has been suggested that the verb should normally be regarded as the subject of the Malay sentence: *datanglan anak-nya minta duit* 'there came (there was a coming by) his son asking for money = his son came to ask for money'. The fact that a verb contains within itself the name of its activity makes this possible, and counts for such grammatical but unreal distinctions as *to walk* (V)/*to take a walk* (VO). As between active and passive the Chinese verb is neutral. There is therefore no need to discuss in Chinese the problem of the logical subject of a passive verb. But there are events such as natural phenomena which have no subject.

Pluit 'it rains' has no subject other than the rain itself. The Greek ὔει Ζεύς is the poetical expression and does not reveal a veritable agent, such as 'the sky' or 'the sky god'. Similarly emotions and thoughts come to us not through our own agency, as Latin *paenitet me* 'I regret', obsolete English *methinks* (*me* is dative). This usage is much developed in Gaelic *tha an leabhar aig an duine* 'there is a book at the man = the man has a book (cf. Lat. *est mihi liber*, Russ. *u menja brat* 'by me (is) a brother = I have a brother'), *tha fios agad* 'there is knowledge to you = you know', *tha gradh agam ort-sa* 'there is love at me on you = I love you'.

With an intransitive verb the subject is as much a patient as an agent. *I walk* is as much 'I cause my walking' as 'I experience my walking'. *I die* is definitely not the causative situation that *I speak* may be. It is only when transitive verbs are used that the distinction arises, and some languages have opted to regard the subject as agent, while others have regarded the subject as patient. This results in the so-called 'passive' construction of Basque sentences: *d-oa* 'it goes', *d-u-t* 'it have I = I have it'. The same usage occurs in Georgian and other Caucasian languages and several languages of South America. The agent is then distinguished from the nominative by a suffix (Basque *-k*): *ura d-ek* 'he is (*d-* = "he")', *ni-k d-akusa-t* 'I see him (*ni* "I"+*-k* of agent, *-t* "I", *d-* "him")'. In Caucasian grammars the corresponding case is called the ergative. But it is to be noted that the final position within the verb of the pronominal subject is also a feature of our own languages, and that the active subject has a suffix *-s* (perhaps originally demonstrative) in *Balbu-s aedifica-t*.

The most complex picture of relations between subject and verb is presented by the Caucasian languages. Their association with each other is still a matter of inquiry. The 'logical' subject is, in turn, the named subject of an action (nominative case) or the actor (ergative), or the person interested in the action (ethic dative), or the human instrument of a passive verb (genitive case augmented by a postposition meaning 'by means of'). At the same time the 'logical' object changes case from dative (as recipient or object of action), in the first instance, to nominative in the other three. The same languages show the greatest amount of pronominal representation of the parties within the verb, so that exemplification of these relations can wait till we reach that topic in the section entitled 'The Verb as Microcosm'. It is sufficient at present to call attention to the difficulties underlying the notion of a subject (τὸ ὑποκείμενον), especially when, as is inevitable from the standpoint of our west European languages, we consider the subject to be the party from whom the action proceeds.

PLACE: TIME AND MODE[1]

What can be named and abstracted from a particular context must be placed when introduced into other contexts. The residual phenomenal aspect of the sentence is characterized by time and mode. Hence a dominant trait of nouns, taken in their widest sense as *nominalia*, is indication of place and that of verbs (*verbalia*) is indication of time and mode.

We must not think, however, of abstract Euclidean place in the first instance but of an active something somewhere such as squatting here or standing there. From this arise the nouns of 'here' and 'there', and also 'one' and 'another', 'I' and 'you', 'now' and 'then', the last by a metaphorical extension from location in place to location in time. In the concrete world of some primitive races, where stems are gerundial since the situation is never logically analysed, the special frame of an event must be precisely reproduced upon each occasion. Thus the Kwakiutl Indian of North America would find the phrase *the farmer kills the duck* unintelligible. He would require additional pointers to say whether *the farmer, invisible to us but standing behind a door not far away from me, you being seated yonder well out of reach, kills that duckling which belongs to you*, or the farmer, *who lives in your neighbourhood and whom we see over there, kills that duckling that belongs to him*.[2] To make an intelligible communication it is not only necessary for this Indian to state whether something stands here, there or yonder, by him, by you, or by someone else, but also whether it is in sight or invisible, and to this set of localizations Eskimo adds position to the north, south, down under, in the sea, and so on. It is a simplification when places can be reduced to three, as in the Somali suffixed articles: -*a* for what is immediately near the speaker, -*o* more or less distant but usually in sight, and -*i* unseen though known to the speaker in some fashion. These distinctions may be

[1] See the discussion in E. Cassirer, *Philosophie der symbolischen Formen*, Berlin, i, cap. iii.
[2] E. Sapir, *Language*, Oxford, 1921, pp. 97–98; L. Bloomfield, *Language*, New York, 1946, pp. 259, 470.

transferred to the more abstract notion of time in such a way that -*a* indicates present time and -*o* distant time whether past or future. Kikuyu (A. W. McGregor, *A Grammar of the Kikuyu language*, London, 1905) uses the same system. The demonstrative positions are 'near', 'distant', and 'previously mentioned'. Could they be interpreted on the analogy of Kwakiutl as originally 'palpable', 'visible', and 'invisible'? Applied to time, the scheme gives near, distant, and remote past, and near and distant future. The distinction between past and future is indistinct even in English, in which the 'now' of the present is opposed to 'then' of past or future.

Among the gestures used by a child before it can talk there are demonstrative movements away from the child's own body. Pointing significantly to itself seems to come later. Thus we must allow a high antiquity to demonstratives and especially to *that* (Gk. τò, Russ. *to*) from which *this* (Russ. *êto*) may have developed. The threefold position is found in many languages though not in English, e.g., Lat. *hic iste ille*, Span. *este ese aquel*. With these go the primary adverbs of place *hic, istic, illic*, and *aquí, ahí, allí*, and (with the notion of movement added) *huc* 'hither', *hinc* 'hence', &c. The pronominal adverbs or adverbial pronouns offer logical difficulties in grammar books because they adhere to demonstrative pronouns semantically and formally and have little to do with adverbs of manner of later formation. By way of metaphor they can express also notions of time as in Lat. *hactenus* 'up to this point/up to this time', because time is not observed by eye or ear and cannot be expressed without a mediating concept.

The definite article is a demonstrative which has lost the value of a pointer and merely distinguishes some one thing from the remainder. There is a threefold suffixed article in Armenian which has both a local and a personal possessive value: *manuk-s* 'this child, the child beside me, my child', *manuk-d* 'that child, the child beside you, your child', *manuk-n* 'yonder child, the child beside him, his child'. The possessive pronouns probably derive from this triple form of the demonstrative, both as applied to nouns and to verbs. The personal endings -*m(i)*, -*s(i)*, -*t(i)* of Indo-European verbs are possessives of the action of the verb: 'my loving, thy loving, his loving', &c. The same is true of the Turkish and the Quechua and Aztek verbs. An important step forward in abstraction occurs with the personal pronouns proper. The notion of place, which still adheres to the possessives, is fully converted by them into the notion of person. Savages like the Australian Arunta have no notion of personality and are capable only of considering themselves as parts of a family group. In that group they occupy certain spaces which are duly identified, but the forms translated by personal pronouns should probably not be given a personal value. With the fully developed notion of personality *me*, *thee*, *he*, emerge as entities independent of location in space, though the connexion of *thou* and *that* with *tu* and *to* is still apparent.

Place must be assigned to substantives in relation to the activity represented by the verb. These places may be symbolized by case-endings, by the use of auxiliary words or by position, but they are all manifestations of the grammatical category of case which is an essential concomitant of substantives. The cases are divided into the three 'logical' cases (nominative, accusative and dative), the adjectival case or cases (genitive, possessive, or attributive), and the spatial cases (locative, ablative, and accusative of goal of motion). I cite the divisions which suit Latin grammar, but it is possible to refine upon them as in Finnish so as to include distinction between rest and motion, to denote association or lack, and the passage from one place to another. The nominative may be merely named (inert) or may be the sign of an agent (ergative) and the action may refer to the whole of the named subject or only to part (partitive). The case may be metaphorical, like the instrumental, which is usually expressed as an ablative (the cause of a given effect) or comitative (an accompaniment of a given action). For these refinements see the discussion of the substantive as a part of speech in the next chapter. It is important to note here that they exist even in languages which have no case-suffixes, because it is of the nature of substantives to take up a given place with regard to the verb.

The cases are all ultimately places. The 'logical' cases situate the subject, object, and recipient (or indirect object—SOR). Most Indo-European substantives have a suffixed -*s*, as in Lat. *dominu-s* 'lord', which has been explained by the demonstrative *so* (Gk. ὁ). In modern Bulgarian the suffixed article is most commonly used after the nominative form since that denotes the concept which the speaker has most interest in emphasizing. A suffixed -*to* in Russian picks out nouns for emphasis and is more often than not attached to the subject. The accusative in -*m* may be another demonstrative. Both the accusative and the dative complete the action of the verb by a sort of pointing, by denoting the end of the action or the recipient. The adjectival cases serve to state the relation between nouns, whether of possession or material or in some other fashion. The abstract relationships are extensions of spatial notions by means of metaphor or analogy. Those pronouns which take the place of nouns naturally have case signs and in many languages adjectives receive case endings by way of concord.

The notion of place is associated in Mende with the parts of the speaker's body, 'man considering himself the central point around which all local relations are determined'.[1] Consequently, *hu* 'in', *ma* 'on', *mba* 'on top of', *mbu* 'underneath' are classified in Mende grammar as parts of the body. They are used as postposition, as *nya bu* 'underneath me'. Parts of the body have also given rise to numerals which are counted in some African languages by touching various limbs or organs. In Ewe numbers are reinforced by touching the fingers in specified ways; in Nuba there are appropriate gestures, and in Bakairi one cannot reckon beyond three unless the right hand touches objects at the same time as the left hand counts. In British New Guinea numbers are reckoned by touching the wrist, elbow, shoulder, neck, left breast, chest, right breast, right side of the neck, &c.[2] Enumeration is thus in the first place demonstrative, and the systems of numerals depend on parts of the body. The quinary system uses the fingers of one hand and counts with the other, the decimal system uses two hands, the vigesimal two hands and two feet. Individual objects have their own classes for numeration, as in our hunting and herding terms. The notion of number as order in progression is a very late development, but it is possible for communities without mathematical notions to keep count of such numbers as interest them. The absence of one animal from a herd of 400 or 500 beasts is at once noticed in the same way in which any one animal may be picked out and lassoed. The senses of colour and mass are acutely developed for the significant animals, while other animals and objects are treated with indifference and at most distinguished as units or masses. Flocks of sheep are sometimes estimated by the number of black sheep present, it being assumed that the ratio of white to black is constant.

[1] K. H. Crosby, *An Introduction to the Study of Mende*, Cambridge, 1944, where the author quotes Schoen, *Grammar of the Mende Language*, London, 1882.

[2] E. Cassirer, *Philosophie der symbolischen Formen*, Berlin, 1923, i. 183–5.

Each event is unique not merely in its frame of space but also in its time and mode of action. The verb, which is specialized to represent phenomenal elements in a situation, has complex signs for time and mode. Both are intrinsically difficult conceptions and the paradigms of verbs are widely different between one language and its neighbour. The notion of time as chronological succession does not exist for some primitive peoples, who are concerned with more concrete notions: durative and momentary activities, those which are repeated or consist of phases and those which are done once for all, those which are completed and those which are either incomplete or not specifically defined. These distinctions shade off into others which have to do with modes of action. The most important of these is the distinction between facts and notions, and of notions there are many kinds. All grammars show an active indicative in opposition, either in the paradigm itself or by means of auxiliaries, to other moods and voices, such as the subjunctive, the optative, the jussive, the quotative, the middle, the passive, &c. Among notions we must include the future. In the most concrete sense the future is remote from the present just like the past, and the chronological series consists of *then-now-then*. But the past has been a fact, whereas the future is a mere notion associated variously with desire, will, obligation, emotion, and incompletion. These are modes of activity.

THE VERB AS MICROCOSM OF THE SENTENCE

Owing to the expression of time and mode of action the verb is necessarily a complex structure. This is true even of the invariable monosyllabic languages of the Far East. Though they have no paradigms and it would be wrong to reconstruct them on the European model, the auxiliaries required to make the verb adequate to the expression of particular circumstances should be counted as part of the verb's form. There are sometimes tonal transactions between the verb and its auxiliaries and probably difference of stress to constitute a veritable group. When, however, to the symbols of time and mode the verb adds pronominal elements which represent within itself the various nouns, then the verb becomes a miniature of the whole expression. This happens in various degrees in many languages. The common basis of the practice, however, must be an instinct in favour of keeping the verb complex enough to deal with the multifarious nature of events. It

is on such an assumption that we may explain the numerous reconstructions of the verbal paradigm after its forms are worn down and
analytical substitutes have been created. Analysis of an essentially
complex situation is, to some extent, unrealistic. New verbal syn-
theses arise, especially when the new material is suffixed, because
it is then pronounced with expiring breath and is liable to lose its
identity. But suffixes (as in Turkish) may retain their identity. The
return to fused conjugations so many times in the history of the
Indo-European languages must be due not merely to phonetic
decay, but also to a feeling in favour of verbal synthesis. So *dicam*
became *dicere habeo* and then *dirai*, though *homo hominem* both
became *homme* and *homines hominibus* became *hommes*. For the
noun analysis was accepted, for the verb it was refused.

The case most familiar to us is that of the restitution of the subject by a pronoun in the verb, as *Balbus aedifica-t* (in which -*t* is
the subject pronoun, Balbus). In our European languages the
incorporation of the object or recipient is not so often exemplified.
But we have in It. *a rivederci*, Sp. *defendiéndose*, Ptg. *vejo-o* 'I see
him' *disse-m'o* 'he said it to him'. The pronouns accompanying a
verb are enclitics or proclitics in the Romance languages. Though
they may be written separately, they are in fact dependent on the
stress accent of the verb and form a single block. So Fr. *j'y suis, je
m'en souviens*, incorporate adverbial pronouns in the verb (*ibi, inde*).
In Spanish *le dieron a la señora el primer asiento* 'they gave the first
seat to the lady', *le* = *a la señora*, the recipient; and in *los tesoros
del imperio los empleaba en sus gustos* 'he employed the treasures of
the empire on his pleasures', *los* = *los tesoros*, the object. In these
sentences, then, though nouns are present in the appropriate cases
of the recipient and object, they are represented pronominally in
the verbal complex along with the representation of the subject by
a suffix. It is a situation which many languages carry through with
an excess of logic.

In Basque, for instance, the verb has pronouns to represent the
subject, object, recipient, and the male or female sex of the person
addressed. The gender of the subject is found in the Russian past
tense and for all Semitic and Hamitic persons except the first. In
Swahili *ni-li-mw-ona* 'I saw him' the subject is *ni* and the object *mu*.
These particles fit the class of the nouns they refer to, so that the
nouns of a sentence are, as it were, in apposition to the class-
prefixes of the verb. In Magyar different pronominal suffixes are

used according as the verb has a definite object or not, as *lát-ok* 'I see'/*lát-om* 'I see (it)'. These principles are used in Quechua to mark transitions from one pronoun to another in forms corresponding to Latin *ego-te/tibi, tu-me/mihi, ille-me/mihi, ille-te/tibi*. Thus *munani* 'I love' becomes *munayqui* 'I love thee', *munasunqui* 'he loves thee', *munahuanqui* 'thou lovest me', and *munahuanmi* 'he loves me'.

The most complicated of all verbal pictures is that offered by the Caucasian verb. 'I gave you my horse' is expressed by elements corresponding to 'I to-you my-horse it-to you-I-gave'. If V is the verb, s the pronominal subject, o the object, r the recipient, and p the prefix, the north Caucasian verb has the following eight possibilities.

	Intransitive:	sV	spV
		srV	srpV
	Transitive:	osV	opsV
		orsV	orpsV^{1}

Combined with nouns in their shifting cases for the subject and object, we are offered the choice of the following Georgian translations of 'the father writes (wrote) a letter' or 'a letter is written by the father':

ACTIVE:

Pres.:	*mama*	*ts'er-s*	*ts'eril-sa* (nom.+present tense+ dat.)
Aor.:	*mama-m*	*da-ts'er-a*	*ts'eril-i* (ergative+aorist+nom.)
Perf.:	*mama-s*	*u-ts'eri-a*	*ts'eril-i* (dat.+perfect+nom.)

PASSIVE:

	mam-isa-gan	*i-ts'er-eb-a*	*ts'eril-i* (gen.+instrum. suffix+ passive+nom.)[2]

In these Georgian verbs the object is not represented. The subject is suffixed and the prefixes have to do with tense or voice. The case of the subject varies with the tense and not with the speaker's thought.

---

[1] G. Dumézil, *Études comparatives sur les langues caucasiennes du nord-ouest*, Paris, 1934, p. 156.

[2] F. N. Finck, *Die Haupttypen des Sprachbaus*, Leipzig, 1910, p. 134.

VII

GRAMMAR: PARTS OF SPEECH

THE number and description of parts of speech depends on the grammar of a particular language. They correspond partly to the parts of a sentence and are partly determined by the forms and usages of the given language. Hence in the definition of parts of speech as we have inherited them from Classical grammarians sometimes 'logical', sometimes formal criteria are used. The latter, of course, come under the criticism of logicians, but they cannot be neglected in the account of a particular language. If, for instance, a language is so constructed that substantives are each of single gender but adjectives are of several genders so as to agree with the substantives, then it is of no relevance to hold with Viggo Brøndal that the adjective has no justification in morphology, logic, or syntax. Its cases in Latin or Greek are those of the substantive but it has the additional formal property of varying gender which is not possessed by substantives. In the absence of such formal criteria, as in English or Chinese, a given word may be both adjective and a substantive, e.g. Eng. *good* = Ch. *hao*^{3} (OCh. *kung.*^{1} . . . *ch'iu*^{2} *hao*^{3} *yu*^{2} *Chu*^{1} 'the duke sought good [relations] with [the state of] Chu', where *hao*^{3} is a noun).

Even in the absence of external marks, however, it can, I think, be affirmed that the distinction between certain parts of the sentence are respected by the parts of speech. There is a broad difference between nouns and verbs, the former abstracted from particular circumstances and named so as to enter into any context, the latter specialized by accompaniments which fit them to express the individual phenomenon. The verb may produce a verbal noun of action or agent but these retain their verbal properties in large part. The noun covers substantives, adjectives, adverbs, and may offer a basis for the creation of conjunctions and prepositions. But between noun and verb there is a frontier, marked by morphemes in many languages and by associations in English. Thus one may say 'my hand'/'I hand (it)' in English, but 'my hands' and 'he hands' have different morphemes in -*s* (i) plural, (ii) third person singular, and 'he handed', 'he will hand', 'he would have handed' &c., are verbal combinations quite alien to the noun. The original Indo-European stems were probably capable of becoming either nouns or verbs and English words have sometimes become by attrition stems of this sort. But the licence to convert nouns into verbs is now much more restricted than among the Elizabethans and the associations of noun and verb are so different as to distinguish two words in any such usage. In Chinese, with still less formal obstruction, the noun and related verb are often differentiated by initial or tone though employing the same written character. The character is concerned with meaning and marks the semantic connexion of the noun and verb. The difference of tone or initial suggests the use of some ancient derivational device such as the consonant inserted after the initial in Siamese. In the case in point hao^3 is a noun (adjective adverb and sometimes substantive) and hao^4 is a verb.

Within the category of nouns, pronouns and numerals generally have a distinctive character. The latter are special kinds of nouns, late in development, but once evolved little likely to change. The pronouns are specialized to general reference. They can be made precise by means of a substantive, adjective, or adverb, which is evidence of their affiliations; but it is doubtful whether there are any pro-verbs. There are, of course, verbs like Eng. *do*, *get*, Fr. *faire*, so weakened that they may take the place of any other previously used. The examples given by R. Lenz refer to the presence of marks of time and mode in the *absence* of the verbs of this weakened kind, as in Mapuche: *Tefachi manshana küme-i* 'these apples are good', in which *-i* is the sign of the indicative and there is no verbal stem; *chum-vem-la-ya-vu-n?* 'why should I not do so?' (how thus not [future imperfect] I). The Mapuche of the Araucanian Indians is polysynthetic like so many other American languages, and the reference of these particles may be to the sentence as a whole. The case is remote and difficult to assess.[1] The verbs omitted are only the simplest, the copula and the verb of undifferentiated action.

In addition to nouns and verbs a category is constituted by the particles. Their function is abstract: to link words or sentences, to locate parties to an action, or to indicate how an expression is to be taken. Being abstract they are recruited from more concrete parts of the lexicon and their derivation can sometimes be seen. Often,

[1] R. Lenz, *La Oración y sus partes*, Madrid, 1925, p. 318.

however, they resist analysis. In inflected languages they are to be found among the *indeclinabilia*, and with them is it often convenient to take adverbs, which are nouns or adjectives petrified in some particular case. In an agglutinative language it is more difficult to say how particles should be dealt with because the definition of the word itself becomes more difficult. If the word is defined as the stem, then all suffixes are particles to be explained separately. A practical difficulty results in the excessively long alphabetic list of particles which comes from this treatment. If the word is defined as a stem with a certain number of commonly recurring endings, others being treated as postpositions, the material of grammar becomes more easy to handle though the division may be somewhat arbitrary.

NOUN

Substantive (Germ. *Dingwort*). The substantive is prominently the name of a thing. One substantive may be predicated of another or placed in an adjectival (genitive) relation to another, but a substantive cannot be predicated of an adjective or be adjectivally related to an adjective. That the adjective (*Eigenschaftswort*) names quality is certain, and in so doing it names a 'thing' and overlaps the territory of abstract nouns, which are also names of qualities. The difference, when grammatically effective, is that an abstract noun has the capacity of a noun to be the subject of a predicate while the adjective continues to be characterized by the function of referring to some substantive. Thus Sp. *bello* cannot be subject of a predicate like *la belleza* 'beauty' except on condition of becoming formally a substantive by acquiring an article, *lo bello*. English *good* becomes a substantive as *goods*, *the good*, or *goodness* and is in each case formally differentiated from the adjective in *a good man*.

It has also been suggested that the category of substantives should be split because of the existence of proper nouns like *John* or *London*. These are completely arbitrary, mere tickets, and once lost they cannot be recovered by any sort of inference from the rest of the language. It is true that there are many persons called *John* but they have not on that account any characteristic in common apart from being male and probably English-speaking. We may also pluralize proper names as *Ciceros*, *Cæsars*, *Babylons* but only by generalizing them as common nouns equivalent to orators, autocrats, and sinful cities. Proper names classify themselves uniquely and do not need classifiers where these exist, as in Bantu or Chinese. The first and second personal pronouns refer to proper names. Proper names certainly constitute a special class of substantive, but we should not exaggerate the rational character of common nouns. Looking from one heap of sand to another, we can pronounce the word 'sand' in the second case if we know it from the first; but if the word 'sand' escapes our memory no process of inference from the language will restore it.

A characteristic of substantives is to fall into classes. Some of these are determined by the relations of the things expressed, as in the -ter class of the family in *pater*, *mater*, *frater*, θυγάτηρ or the Slavonic *-mnt class of young animals. In Chinese the class is indicated by the unit for estimating individuals, i.e. by lengths, hides, pieces, heads, roots, branches, tails, &c.[1] The classification seems to be merely formal in the Indo-European declensions, where Gk. χείρ 'hand' is in a consonant class and Lat. *manus* in a *u*-declension. The beginnings of declensional difference are seen in Nahuatl or Aztec, in which the singulative suffix differs according to the phonetic and other features of the noun: *teotl* 'god', *oquichtli* 'man', *totolin* 'bird', *pilli* 'rider'. The plurals differ in agreement with the singulars, but there is no development of a paradigm of cases. In Indo-European these formal classes seem to be successive in development. The oldest state is that of the consonant stems to which the case suffixes are directly added, as χήν χῆνα, &c. 'goose', θήρ θῆρα 'beast'. Then came a fashion for stems ending in the vowels *i* or *u*, as in *ovis* 'sheep', *manus* 'hand'. Some of the older consonant stems were transferred, as OBulg. *gǫsǐ* 'goose' *zvěrǐ* 'beast'. A vowel stem due to a suffixed -ā was evolved with a collective meaning, but it contained by chance the influential word *ǵwṇnā* 'woman' and probably on that account became predominantly feminine. Thus Lat. *locus* 'place' has a plural *loci* and a collective *loca*, but these collectives have been driven out of the Romance

---

[1] Classification by enumerators occurs all over the Far East (in Malay, Japanese, Korean, &c., as well as in Chinese), but the Chinese set of fifty classifiers seems to be the most complete and has spread to languages which have borrowed heavily from Chinese. A second and more subtle sort of classification occurs in Chinese writing so as to distribute all Chinese words (verbs as well as nouns) among 214 classes. These are fewer than the original number of 'radicals', and many of the classes are sparsely populated. Important ones are man, woman, hand, heart, eye, mouth, spirit, (skeleton), flesh, words; tree, bamboo, grass, grain, metal; clothes, silk (thread and a cocoon); horse, god, board, fish, insect; sun, roof, mountain, cart, walking, disease, eating.

languages other than Italian and the collective is identified with
the feminine singular: *lignum* 'wood'/*ligna* has given Spanish *leño*
'a piece of wood' and *leña* 'wood in general'. This declension in -*ā*
took case endings directly, but like other vowel stems it was liable
to fuse the end of the stem with the case-sign and so produce the
compound endings characteristic of our languages. Lastly comes
the device of declension by thematic vowel *e/o* in *dominus domine
dominum*, &c., with a variant in *i-e/i-o* when the thematic vowel
was added to a stem vowel. Further transference from old declensions to this new type produced such results as Russ. *zveŕ* 'beast',
which is declined as if in -*io*-. Any declension might have words of
any sort and the declensional endings have no reference to gender.
But there were fortuitously in each declension prominent words
which tended to assimilate others to their class and to force less
successful words to migrate. As the result of 2,000 years of such
reshuffles Russian declensions now express distinctions of gender,
though gender itself is not a concept that deserves preservation.

Classification by *genera* (genders) crosses that by declensions in
Indo-European languages and is at least so far rational as to commend itself to a wide variety of communities in Europe, Asia,
Africa, America, and Australia. The approximate reasonableness
of the system leads to a succession of attempts to reshape it partially
or wholly by the use of new criteria. In Spanish, for instance, the
feminine is used of things which are round but not long, with the
result that sometimes the larger object is feminine; it is used of
towns in Spain whatever their final vowel because of the key-words
ciudad 'city' and *aldea* 'village' (but in Chile settlements are masculine because of *pueblo* 'a settlement' and mountains are masculine
because of *cerro* 'hill, mountain'); trees are masculine but their
fruits are feminine because of the collective sense of that gender.
In Russian, as we have noticed, declension and gender have been
brought into agreement, though neither is necessary, except for
'natural' masculines, i.e. titles and offices normally held by men.
The loss of final -*a* in French has led to much reshuffling of
genders in a more or less reasonable fashion.

Primarily gender has nothing to do with sex unless, perhaps, in
the Dravidian languages. The names of animals which are of social
or economic value according to sex are simply different: *man/
woman, son/daughter, bull/cow, ram/ewe*, &c. To the primitive mind
they were different things and only later was the attempt made to

relate them according to their kinds. Thus Lat. *socer/socrus* have become Span. *suegro/suegra* 'father- and mother-in-law', and Span. *carnero/oveja* have become in some parts of South America *ovejo/ oveja* 'ram/ewe'.

The first distinction in Indo-European seems to have been between the animate and inanimate genders.[1] This proposition cannot be asserted on the faith of the ancient Hittite tongue (which has only a common and a neuter gender), because it is clear that even at so early a period a gender had been lost by attrition. It is to be grounded rather on the fact that the feminine is so obviously linked with the history of the collective ending -*ā*, which gives neuter plurals and, because of **ĝwn̥nā* 'woman', feminine singulars. The distinction between animate and inanimate was magically conceived. Moving things were considered animate and inert objects inanimate. The same object might be classified as animate or inanimate according to its appearance at a given time: thus *ignis* is masculine and *Agni* a Sanskrit god, but πῦρ, *Feuer*, *fire* are neuter; *aqua* is animate (feminine) but ὕδωρ, *Wasser*, Hitt. *watar*, *water* are inanimate. Little things and objects of affection were classified as inanimate, such as *das Weib*, *das Kind*, μειράκιον 'darling', *Cæsarion*, *Danilo* (neuter in termination but with a 'natural' masculine concord). In the nature of things an inanimate was likely to be the object of an action and required no subject suffix. Thus Lat. nom. acc. *castrum/* nom. *Dominus* acc. *Dominum*. This observation has led to other similar results. The reduction of both **-os* and **-om* to -*ŭ* in Common Slavonic made it difficult in a language without fixity of order to say whether 'Peter robbed Paul' or 'Paul robbed Peter'. The solution was to use the genitive singular, possibly with the justification that an action performed on a human being affects him as an object only in part (partitive genitive), while in another part he reacts. In Rumanian the animate object is preceded by *pe* < *prae*; it is acted on, not determined wholly by, the action. In modern Spanish *a* is used if a human object is a recipient. In all these cases the common ground is that a human object of an action is not inert nor wholly governed as neuter things are. Grammatical usage with regard to animals varies since they are not on the same plane as persons in real situations.

The Hamito-Semitic languages have no distinction of animate

---

[1] A. Meillet, 'La catégorie du genre et les conceptions indoeuropéennes', *Linguistique historique et linguistique générale*, Paris, 1948.

and inanimate but of masculine and feminine. The feminine gender is the innovation, as may be seen in the non-grammatical distinction of *abu* 'father' and *umm* 'mother'. Its source was the collective suffix *-at*. The 'broken' plurals of Arabic are also collective in original meaning and they take feminine singular concords. The collective *-ā* of Indo-European had singular concords in Greek like the feminine *-ā*, and the neuter plural concords of Latin are a later innovation.

It seems rather to have been in the Dravidian languages (which formerly extended to central Asia but are now mostly confined to southern India) that gender and sex were associated. The notions implied by sex are, however, multiple. In general the male is superior and the female inferior. The grammatical status of goddesses offers, under such conditions, a problem. The distribution of genders is different in each of the languages of this family.

Classification by *genera* need not stop at two or three divisions. In the Slavonic treatment of animate objects a difference was made between animals and humans and still subsists in Czech. In the north Caucasian languages the classes extend to eight and have probably developed from four or five. The basic distinction is not between animate and inanimate but between rational and irrational. We then get five classes:

A. Rational: I. males
                II. females
B. Irrational: III. individuals (animals or things)
               IV. collectives
              [V. relative substantives][1]

The classes are revealed by their concord pronouns in the verbal complex. In the dying Tunica language of Louisiana there are six classes:

A. Animate: (*a*) human   I. male
                         II. female
          (*b*) non-human III. male
                         IV. female
B. Inanimate: V. integral things
                         VI. continuous things[2]

[1] G. Dumézil, *Introduction à la grammaire comparée des langues caucasiennes du nord*, Paris, 1933.
[2] M. Haas, 'A grammatical sketch of Tunica', *Linguistic Structures of America*, New York, 1946, p. 358.

The development of such classes is most remarkable in Africa. African languages show a general preference for operating with prefixes. Among Coptic prefixes there are some which represent agency (*ref- sa-*), abstraction (*měnt-*), action (*čin-*) and place (*maěn-*), all of which are found as grammatical prefix-classes in Bantu. In Coptic the singular and plural have distinct prefixes, as *prōme* 'the man'/*ěnrōme* 'the men'. In Bantu singular and plural prefixes are different for each class. The Bantu system thus offers distinct pairs of singular and plural prefixes, arranged by classes which offer an approximate analysis of the world of things. Inconsistencies are numerous. Twenty-one prefixes are recognized by C. Meinhof and nineteen by Sir H. H. Johnston.[3] The Swahili noun prefix classes are as follows:

I. *m-/wa-*. Rational beings.
II. *n-/n-*. Most animals, but also individual things and some abstract nouns.
III. *m-/mi-*. Animates, including such things as have the appearance of animation by spread or motion.
IV. *ki-/vi-*. Inanimates, but also small or defective humans.
V. *ji-/ma-*. Constituent parts of larger entities.
VI. *u-/n-*. Masses (collectives). The plural may represent the mass of which the singular is a fraction.
(Originally singular *lu-*, which connotes extension.)
VII. *u-*. Abstract. No plural. Originally *bu-* (collective).
VIII. *ku-*. Verbal noun and infinitive. No plural. Often used elsewhere of place.

In Bantu generally *pa-* and *mu-* are also used of place and *gu-/ga-* are augmentative.

Gender has been lost in the course of modern English history and in the languages of western Europe it is a meaningless routine. It is not found in many savage languages nor in the highly civilized languages of the Far East. It is therefore evidently unnecessary, but it can be used to discipline the sentence by concords, to permit *hyperbaton* and to give aesthetic variety, e.g. in the alternation of masculine and feminine rhymes in French verse. The third gender (neuter) was defended in Slavonic when it was on the point of disappearing, and a third gender (feminine) is being reinforced in

[3] C. Meinhof, *Lautlehre der Bantu-sprachen*, Berlin, 1910, p. 38; Sir H. H. Johnston, *A Comparative Study of the Bantu and Semi-Bantu Languages*, Oxford, 1919, p. 31 (has a list of preprefixes also). See also the specialized grammars such as E. O. Ashton, *Swahili Grammar*, London, 1947.

modern Norwegian for a limited number of words on the ground that they 'sound better' with the feminine suffixed article.

That grammatical number has nothing to do with enumeration is seen in an idiom like Germ. *drei Pfund Fleisch* (not *Pfunde*) 'three pounds of meat'. To enumerate, all one needs is a recognizable unit of reckoning; this is accomplished in Chinese by means of the numeral adjuncts or enumeratives: i^1 *k'uai⁴-ch'ien²* 'one dollar', *san¹ k'uai⁴-ch'ien²* 'three dollars'/*ch'ien²* 'money' (in general). In Russian usage *odin* 'one' is an adjective, two to four take what was originally a dual ending but which is now construed as a gen. sg., and over five the numbers are nouns followed by the gen. pl. These distinctions are arbitrary and do not essentially aid enumeration.

The distinction between 'one' and 'many' is a residuum of many realistic distinctions but it is relatively clear and has sometimes found clear and uniform expression (Sp. -[e]s, Norw. -[e]r). But the veritable distinction is not as stated, but between 'unity' and 'many'. There are units composed of many numbers, such as a town-council, so that the speaker hesitates between *the council has resolved* and *the council have resolved*. In *sand* the units are too small to be perceived; a unit must be singularized as *a grain of sand*, while *the sands of the sea* refer either to uncountable grains or to the various beaches above or below water. From a unit of many members, such as Russ. *gospodá* 'gentry', *noblesse* 'gentlemen', singulars can be obtained by the use of singulative suffixes, as *gospodín* 'a gentleman'. There are objects which form units in the singular such as *lignum* 'a faggot of wood', and collective units in the plural *ligna* 'wood in general'. Russ. *brat* 'brother' has a collective plural *bratja* (cf. Gk. φρατρία). In Germ. *Mann*/*Männer*, *Leute* there is a plural of units and a collectivity, and the same happens in Lat. *locus*/*loci*, *loca*. (On numerals see pp. 202 f. Enumeration and plurality are not always treated alike.)

Under more realistic conditions the number of plural types increases. In Kwakiutl reduplication is used to show the presence of a given object here and there or of many kinds of particular objects. The objects may be massed, or successive, or reiterated. In Tagal *mag-súlat* 'many writes' > 'writes often', so that the plural notion passes into that of a frequentative verb. In Nuba there is a distinction made between things that are units and things that are composed of parts. There are several forms of the plural in Quechua, designed to correspond with several different situations, though

-*cuna* is the ordinary form: *runacuna* 'men' *runaruna* 'crowd', *aylluntin* 'member of a family (*ayllu*), considered collectively', while no plural sign is used with numbers: *chunca punchau* 'ten days'.[1]

A difficulty is also created when a singular word can be used generically of a class. Thus *man* may be used of a class in *man wants but little here below*, and we may say *a man wants* or *men want* in the same sense. The definite article is used in both a particular and a general sense in the Romance languages; Sp. *el hombre* is either a particular man or any representative man, and in the last sense it is equal to *un hombre* (any one representative man).

The plural would seem to originate not in enumeration but in savages' incapacity for number. At some point their powers of reckoning give out and they speak of an indeterminate multiplicity. Above *one* there are well-known groups of doublets, such as eyes, feet, arms, legs, parents, &c. These offer support for the dual number, applied to things in pairs. The dual falls into confusion when there are two things not paired, e.g. the eyes of two different persons. In some Oceanic languages a claim has been put forward for a trial number, but the grounds are somewhat insecure. There are few obvious triplets, and the trial forms adduced have been explained as due to incorporation of the number *three*. Even a dual may suffer such incorporations, as in Lith. *mu-du* 'we two'.

In any system of expression the relations of parties to the action must be defined and, as we have seen, this definition is in terms of place, real or metaphorical. There are, however, two alternatives open to the speaking community. Either the noun may be separated from symbols of relation and these possess their own autonomy, or else to the noun-stem there may be aggregated all or enough affixes to determine its function in the sentence. The first way is taken by the isolating languages and apparently also by the holosynthetic. Since language types are never pure the assertion is made with the usual reservations. The other device is used by flexional, agglutinative and agglomerative languages, and by polysynthetic tongues which stop short of the word-sentence. The device employed is suffixation. In an agglutinative language like Turkish and an agglutinative-polysynthetic language like Quechua all grammatical relations are expressed by postpositions, and it may be held in consequence that all relations have their proper expression. Some relations, however, are much more important and common than

[1] Sir C. R. Markham, *Quechua Grammar*, London, 1864, p. 22.

others and these may be brought together in a declension of cases. Custom puts a definite end to the number of cases in Finnish and Indo-European, the former at fifteen or sixteen, the latter at eight. The difference is due to a subtler discrimination of space-relations in the Finnish declension. Still further distinctions in Magyar and the north Caucasian languages make one doubt whether the notion of casual declension should be dropped in favour of a theory of suffixation in general. On the other hand the sixteen Finnish cases are not all equally fundamental and the most common Turkish and Quechua relations can be brought into paradigms for comparison with Indo-European. Georgian cases have also been reduced to seven essential cases from a possible nineteen to twenty-four in Caucasian. The 'empty' words suffixed to the Burmese noun have also been listed as nine cases. The end of the flexional Indo-European declension is placed at the point where fusion of suffixes ceases and a new positional device operated by prepositions is employed. Despite the structural difference of languages it is thus possible to compare them with regard to the more important cases (see p. 198).

Of these cases the vocative stands apart. It does not form part of the sentence but is a quasi-sentence in apposition to the statement proper. It therefore has no sign, but is the pure stem of the word. The other cases are more or less ideally employed in the different languages. A notable feature is that the dual and plural may be less complete than the singular. It is not so in Basque, Georgian, Turkish, Burmese, or Quechua, in which the singular signs for case serve also in the plural, but in the fused Indo-European declensions the oblique cases of the plural and dual are much less perfectly evolved than in the singular. (Gender also may be less important to speakers in the plural than in the singular. In Russian all declensions but one have been reformed upon the model of the $\bar{a}$-declension for oblique plural cases). Homeric -$\phi\iota$, -$\theta\epsilon\nu$, -$\delta\epsilon$, Lith. -pi, and the alternative between m and bh in oblique cases of the plural show that the paradigms were not rigidly constituted at the time of separation of the Indo-European tongues.

Adjective and Adverb. There appear to be five sources of adjectives: (1) (2) By *fusion* of substantive and attribute a compound term is formed which is a noun different from all other nouns; as *Vale of Whitehorse, Casablanca, demijohn, forecastle,* Abkhaz *ciywe-c'ikwe-r* (subst.-adj.) 'the little rat', Tunica (Louisiana) *'ónilapú*

Singular

	Greek	Latin	Russian	Turkish	Finnish	Burmese	Quechua	Georgian
Nominative	θήρ	dominus	stol	ev	talo	lu	runa	..
Inert	..	..	..	..	..	..	..	mama
Accusative	θῆρα πόλιν	dominum	stol	evi	talo(n)	lu-go	runacta	..
Ergative	..	..	..	..	..	..	..	mamam
Genitive	θηρός πόλεως	dominī	stola	evin	talon	lu-i	runap	mamis
Dative	θηρί πόλει	dominō	stolu	eve	talolle	lu-a	runapac	mamas
Ablative	..	dominō(d)	[stola]	evden	talolta	lu-hma	..	..
Instrumental	..	..	stolom	..	..	lu-hmang	runahuan	mamit
Locative	..	..	stole	evde	talossa	lu-hma	..	..
Vocative	θήρ πόλι	domine	..	..	..	ō lu	a runa ya	mama

'good people'. It is possible for a substantive to qualify another substantive and perform a function of an adjective as in *manslaughter*. Instead of fusion there may be juxtaposition with the adjective in the first place: *White House, Blue Boar*, Ch. *hao³ hua⁴* 'fair words', Germ. *der braune Tisch* 'the brown table'. In all such instances, whether of fusion or juxtaposition, the differential comes first and excludes all other combinations of the same substantive. They also exclude the unqualified substantive itself, for as the Chinese paradox says 'a white horse is not a horse'. When a substantive is performing the functions of an adjective it may be attached simply or placed in a genitive or attributive or constructive case (Basque *Gernikako arbola* 'a tree of Guernica', *abeŕiaren etsaiak* 'the enemies of the country': *-ko* attributive, *-en* possessive), or be given the form of an adjective. In Spanish *medio Sevilla* the lack of concord is a sign that the expression is regarded as one compound noun.

(3) By *apposition*. In this instance the substantive precedes and the adjective follows: Siamese *nam yen* 'cold water', *nam ron* 'hot water', Malay *rumah burok* 'a shabby house'. This has been described as a 'logical' form of expression in opposition to the 'impulsive' order of *shabby house*. The general class is first stated and then the particular quality on each choice or distinction is built. The subsequent adjective, however, carries with it the notion of the antecedent substantive and is commonly made to agree. For instance, Basque *mendi gorri-a* 'hill red–the = the red hill' becomes *mendia gorria* 'the hill–the red (hill)'. In the Bantu languages there are about fifty adjectives of the appositional type and they repeat the prefixes of their substantives, as Swahili *m-tu m-dogo* '(human) man (human) little = the little man', *kiti kidogo* 'the little chair'. The adjectives of this list are of primary and obvious qualities like big, little, good, bad, few, many, raw, bitter, soft, male, female, &c., but for those which require a subtler mental effort other kinds of adjectivization are used.

Since the appositive adjective implicitly includes its noun when used attributively, it is to such that we must probably assign the origin of concord. The predicated adjective is such as might be predicated of any noun but the attributive adjective implies its antecedent substantive. Thus *le cheval blanc, la maison blanche*. But concord once initiated from whatever cause spreads to all attributive adjectives and even to those in the predicate: *ver erat aeternum* 'the spring was eternal', *le cheval était blanc*. A distinction is made in German between the attribute with its concord *der braune Tisch* and the predicate without concord *der Tisch ist braun*. In Russian and the Slavonic languages the principle of concord was accepted for both types of adjective, but the closer association of the substantive and the attribute has led to the use in such instances of the definite form: Czech. *bohatý človek* 'rich man', *človek je bohat* 'the man is rich'.

(4) *Possessive* construction. The substantive is regarded as the possessor of a quality, as in Arab. *ṣāḥibu 'ilmin* 'master of learning = learned', *dhātu ḥusnin* 'possessor of beauty = beautiful', Swahili *kiti cha mti* 'a wooden chair' cf. *kiti cha Hamisi* 'Hamisi's chair', *mti wenye miba* 'a tree possessing thorns = a thorny tree'. In Coptic also there are comparatively few true adjectives and the genitive sign *ĕn* is employed between noun and adjective: *ourōme ĕntšōb* 'a man of weakness = a weak man'. The construction is well known from the Hebrew Bible.

(5) *Predication*. The adjective is always implicitly predicated of its noun and in some languages it is expressed predicatively. In Bantu this is effected by the *o* of relation as in Swahili *mw-ezi u-ja-o* 'the month which comes = the coming month', cf. Sp. *el mes que viene*, Fr. *le chat qui rit*. This usage is found elsewhere in Africa, as in Coptic *pran etouaab* 'the-name which-is-holy = the holy name'. In Japanese, Korean, and the Yana of north-west America the adjective is generally conjugated, i.e. formally predicated of its noun as Jap. *ashiki hito* 'a man who is bad = a bad man', *ashikarishi hito* 'a man who was bad'.[1] In the languages of the north-west Caucasian group attributive adjectives carry the termination *-ō* or *-na*, which are those of gerundives, and the construction is therefore equivalent to a relative clause.[2]

According to Jespersen's theory of the three ranks the verb and adjective are of the second rank and the adverb is conveniently explained as of the third. With such a formula it is easy to understand how the adverb comes to modify adjectives and verbs, but the theory of ranks is unfortunately itself difficult to justify. A reproach has been levelled against this category that it is too miscellaneous. There are in fact a number of primitive adverbs which

---

[1] Sir G. Sansom, *Historical Japanese Grammar*, Oxford, 1928, p. 109.

[2] G. Dumézil, *Études comparatives sur les langues caucasiennes du nord-ouest*, Paris, 1932. p. 56.

by reason of their highly generalized type of reference associate with pronouns. In addition there are the adverbs which are recruited from nouns, whether substantives or adjectives. They also have fuller forms obtained from *syntagmata* which include a substantive, as *frequently/with frequency, often/on many occasions, mildly/in a mild manner*, &c. Such *syntagmata* frequently become petrified as simple adverbs, as Latin *magnopere* 'greatly', Sp. *magníficamente* 'magnificently' (*-mente* 'mind'), Germ. *freundlich*, friendly (*-lich* 'a body' as in *lich-gate*), *likewise*, It. *tuttavia*, &c.

In languages with unvarying words adjectives and adverbs may carry no external mark of difference, as in Eng. *strike hard, play fair, drink deep*, Ch. *man⁴ -man⁴ tsou³* 'walk slowly = to be careful'. They may differ for incorporating languages since adjective and substantive may form a compound noun, but an adverb or adverbial phrase lies within the body of the verb. It is in fact a complement of the verbal activity, which it details more fully in respect of direction or manner. Thus an adjective may be in the accusative case as completing the verbal action (Gk. μεγάλα ἁμαρτάνειν 'to sin grievously', Russ. *dobro* 'well') or the locative as metaphorically 'in' some manner (Pol. *dobrze* 'well'), or any other case, usually in the singular but often in other numbers (OBulg. *meždu*, 'between' is a dual; Russ. *takim obrazom* 'thus' is an instrumental singular). The adverb is distinguished by its restriction to one case and consequent indeclinability in flexional languages.

Gradation. When two objects are compared it is in respect of some positive quality which would naturally be represented by an adjective or adverb. The difference between them is measured from one of them as basis of reference, and it may be reinforced by some emphatic adverb. Thus Chinese *pi³* 'compared with' leads to formulas of the type '*x* compared with *y* is big (or some other named positive quality)' or '*x* compared with *y* is very (*hên³, kêng¹*) big'. The type '*x* measured from *y*' leads to the use of the ablative in Latin (genitive in Greek) and the correlative *min* 'from' in Arabic. *Than* and *quam* are also specialized to such measurements.

In the series *beautiful, more beautiful, most beautiful* the adjective *beautiful* remains as the name of a positive quality but it is accompanied by adverbs of increasing energy. The same is true of Fr. *plus beau*, Sp. *más bello*. Antonio de Nebrija rightly denied in 1492 the existence of degrees of comparison for Spanish adjectives. *More beautiful* and *plus beau* imply comparison between two objects not between two qualities. One form of the superlative is concerned with comparison between one object and several others. In that instance the object must be distinguished by some singulative sign such as the article, as *le plus beau, el más bello*; the rest of the group is that from which (ablative, Gk. genitive, Fr. Sp. *de*) the superlative object is distinguished. The other type of superlative is an emphatic commendation of one object among several, or all, as in *most beautiful*, Sp. *hermosisimo* (It. *-issimo*), Ch. *kêng¹ hao³ -k'an⁴*. But in some languages positive suffixes have become specialized for comparisons and are applied to the adjectives and adverbs. Such are Gk. -τερο-, -ιστο-, Skr. *-tara -tama*, Lat. **-iōs (-ior -ius) -issimus*, Eng. *-er -est*, Arab. *akbar al-akbar*. These imply superior degrees of the quality represented by the adjective. With the analytic method inferior degrees may also be shown (Eng. *less, least*). This is something of an inversion of realistic usage, and is not permitted in Basque. In the Caucasian languages a comparative case has been specialized for nouns. Comparisons of equality ('*x* is as big as *y*') are always of positive grade.

It is obvious that more than three degrees of comparison are possible. Augmentatives and diminutives may be graded to any required scale and are applicable to substantives as well as to adjectives. As for the latter, R. Lenz[1] worked out series for 'big/little' and 'good/bad' in Chilean Spanish, the former offering *requetegrandazo, regrandazo, grandazo, regrande, grande, grandecito (regular), chiconcito, chicón, chico, chiquito, chiquitito, chiquichicho.*

Numerals. Numerals are nouns of a specialized kind; when once set apart for the purpose of numbering they are not likely to change. The process of numbering does not begin at once. 'One' is an adjective and means 'sole' in Lat. *unus* (< *oinos* cf. Gk. οἶος 'sole'), Russ. *odin*. 'Two' is connected with the observation of pairs and is a dual. Numbering thus begins with 'three' but proceeds with difficulty. 'Five' is a closed fist or all the fingers of one hand; it is the basis of the quinary system in use among some primitive peoples. The Latin digit IV shows subtraction ($4 = 5-1$), as IX shows that $9 = 10-1$. 'Six' is in Sotho 'one over', i.e. the count is transferred from the left to the right hand. In Finnish *yhdeksän* $= 10-1 = 9$, *kahdeksan* $= 10-2 = 8$ (cf. Lat. *undeviginti* $20-1$ $= 19$, *duodeviginti* $20-2 = 18$); Finn. *seitsemän* 'seven' as well as *-deksan* are of foreign origin. The native Finnish system stopped

---

[1] R. Lenz, *La Oración y sus partes*, Madrid, 1926, p. 126.

at 'six' *kuusi*. Lat. *octō* 'eight' is an original dual and goes back to a time when the number was imagined as 2×4. There is a similar relation between Swahili *-ne* 'four' and *-nane* 'eight' (*na* 'with, and', with $4 = 4+4 = 8$).

Because of the slow advance towards mastering the abstract notion of number, smaller numbers sometimes form a group. Thus in Russian 'one' is an adjective and takes the same case as its noun. Two, three, four are treated as small numerals and make a group with the substantive in the genitive singular (originally in the dual and so proper to the adjective *dva*). From 5 to 20 the number is a noun symbolizing a group of so many things and the things constituting the group are expressed in the genitive plural. The collective sense is expressed by neuter forms (*dvoe, troe, četvero*, &c.) which are substituted for cardinal numbers in certain expressions, as *nas zdes' troe* 'there are three of us here', *u menja dvoe časov* 'I have two watches'. Apart from 'first' and 'last' the ordinal numbers are of a more intellectual type and are inclined to be lost in oral use, cardinal numbers being substituted, as in *Louis XIV* (*quatorze*). 'Second' means 'following'; it is not numerical but spatial in origin. 'First' and 'second' are diverse in most languages from 'one' and 'two'; the regular count begins with *three/third*.

The variation of the Slavonic noun is due to the adjectival nature of the 1 and 2 (extended in some languages to 3 and 4), and the genitive case to the collectivity expressed by other numbers. In other tongues numbers above 'one' take the plural as implying 'more than one'. But since grammatical number is not based on numeration it is still reasonable to leave the noun unaltered after a numeral: *four hundred pounds* = Germ. *vier hundert Pfund* (but Sp. *cuatrocientas libras*).

Pronouns. Pronouns are words of general reference. They originate in the sweeping gestures of children before they can speak and as demonstratives are probably older than language. The arm points away from the child towards the second person of the gesture dialogue, or to a third or to a place of any sort. When translated into sound these words may also refer to some quality or description, as in *that man*, or (by extension of the spatial notion) to some time. Thus pronouns are a kind of vague naming and as such they are attached to the class of nominals, but their function may be that of substantives, adjectives, or adverbs of vague reference (place, time, or manner). The objection made against this category, that it is too vague and is a rag-bag of unclassified particles, can hardly be sustained in view of its essential function of general reference. Nor can it be sustained for linguists in view of the undoubted formal interrelations of words of this kind.

In a concrete frame of circumstances the general reference becomes specific. The speaker points to *that* (table, chair, manner of acting, thought, &c.). Without such a frame the pronoun requires an antecedent in the context, since otherwise it bears no precise meaning. In a general way pronouns may be said to require antecedents either in the frame of circumstances or in the context of the phrase; they are used for these antecedents, whence the term 'pronoun'. *I* and *you* refer to any speaker and listener, but can only be determinate when the proper names or the verbal persons of speaker and listener are known. *There* is any place at a distance from the speaker; the speaker's position must be known and the reference to some particular place determined by an antecedent in fact or context.

It has been claimed that there are some pro-verbs. Since pronouns are found by compensation in the verbal complexes of many languages, for very simple verbs the verbal stem itself may not be expressed but only the accompanying pronouns and signs of mode. It is not clear that the pronouns in such instances constitute substitute-verbs. Owing to a special development in several African languages pronouns may be conjugated. Thus in Hausa 'I' is, when used alone, *ni*, in the present *ina*, perfect *nā*, past *na*, object *ni*.[1] Thus *tanā* = 'she (present)' appears in *tanā chin abinchī* 'she is eating her food', *inā zūwa* 'I am coming', *na tafi* 'I went'. The source of this usage is in the African use of modifying prefixes as compared with the Eurasian preference for suffixization. In Semitic and Ancient Egyptian the balance between prefixation and suffixation is about equal; but in Coptic, pronouns and the various signs of mode (mood, tense, &c.) are prefixed and fused together while the verbal stem remains unaltered. Alterations of the verb occur because of following nouns or pronouns, and there is a qualitative form to express passive or intransitive notions, but the business of conjugation is done by the prefixes. Thus Coptic *aujne-ouh̄llo*[2] 'they did ask an elder' is composed of *a* sign of the perfect+(*o*)*u* third person plural+*jne* 'ask'+*ou* indefinite article+*h̄llo* 'old man'. When

[1] F. W. Taylor, *Hausa Grammar*, Oxford, 1923, p. 19.
[2] M. Murray, *Coptic (Sahidic) Grammar*, London, 1911, p. 29.

the pronoun and modal signs are formally separated from the verbal stem they give rise to the apparently conjugated pronouns of Hausa. The verbal complex, however, still remains and it is still the verb which is truly conjugated. The complex is written as one word in Swahili *aliwauliza* 'he (*a*)+did (*li*)+them (*wa*)+ask (*uliza*)'.

Translated into sound the demonstratives show a (not exclusive) preference for dentals, especially *t*. The second personal pronoun is often related to the third, *tu*/τό, Ch. *ni³*/*na³*, Finn. *-t*/*tuo*. *S* appears to be a variant of *t* in Indo-European *-s(i)*, Finn. *sinä* 'thou'. For the third person Chinese uses *t'a¹* which also means 'other'. *Le* occurs as the Samoan article, *al* in Arabic, *ha* in Hebrew, m. *pe-* f. *te-* pl. *ne-* in Coptic. *K* is demonstratively used in Arab. *hākā* 'there', &c.

It is not necessary for the interrogative pronoun to differ from the affirmative, but there is often some convenient degree of specialization. In Chinese it consists of a change of tone: *na³ i¹-ko⁴* 'which one?'/*na⁴ ko⁴* 'that'. In Indo-European the opposition is made between **t* and **kw*, and indefinite pronouns resemble interrogatives save for intonation. Relative pronouns were recruited much later—from demonstratives as in Greek, or from interrogatives as in Latin and English. From demonstratives also come the possessive pronouns as exemplified by the Armenian 'articles' *-s -d -n* and the verbal suffixes *-m -s -t*; from these come the personal pronouns *me te eum*. There is a tendency to parallelism in three ranks, though five are theoretically possible, viz. *ego, tu, hic, iste, ille*. Only *ego* and *tu* are persons of the dialogue and the positions of *hic, iste, ille* are estimated with reference to the speakers. The third position is understood as distinct from both speaker and hearer, and in some languages is out of sight. R. Lenz speaks of transition from a third to a fourth person in Araucarian Mapuche:[1] *elufi* 'he whom we are speaking about goes to another'/*eluayen* 'he to whom we are speaking about another goes'. But it seems that there are no true third personal pronouns in that language, and these 'persons' denote relations of nearness and distance among demonstratives. The order is often triple *I you he*/*this that that (yonder)*/*here there there (yonder)*/*now then*/*hence thence*/*hither thither*/*where whence*/*when then*, &c. In English the notions of an object 'remote from the speaker' includes both position near the hearer and position remote from both; hence the triple system breaks down. In Latin we find

---

[1] R. Lenz, *La Oración y sus partes*, Madrid, 1926, p. 237.

1. ego hic   hīc   hāc   nunc iam
2. tu   iste istīc istāc
3. is   ille illīc illāc tunc tum, &c.

qui, quis, quantus/tantus, qualis/talis, quam/tam.

In Sanskrit *atas*, *tatas*, *yatas* 'hence, thence, whence', *atra*, *tatra*, *yatra* 'here, there, where', *ittham tathā yathā* 'in this way, in that way, in what way', *kutas* 'whence, why', *kutra*, *kva* 'where, whither', *katham* 'how', *kadā* 'when', *tadā* 'then', *yadā* 'when, if'. In Malay *ini/itu* distinguish 'this' from 'that' and *sini/situ* 'here' from 'there'.

A weakening of the demonstrative gives the definite article. Its function is merely to signalize an object, not to point to it. In many languages there is no such article; its uses differ in each. It may be prefixed or suffixed (as in Rumanian, Bulgarian, Albanian, and Basque). The indefinite article is obtained by a weakening of the number 'one'. There are many kinds of hypertrophy of the article, such as Fr. *la vérité* (truth being unique does not need to be signalized; the function of the article is to mark absolute abstraction), Coptic *oume* 'truth' (*ou-* is the indefinite article). *Un homme*, *l'homme*, and *les hommes* are three ways of expressing man in general, which was done more logically in Old French by using the simple general substantive *homme* (MFr. *on* in *on dit*). Fr. *les ténèbres* = Coptic *oukake* (*ou* = 'a') = *darkness*. In Common Slavonic the definite article became attached to the adjective as a suffix (**ios*); then, fused with the case-endings, it lost its special function. Thus the attributive adjective in Russian carries a definite article whether the sense be definite or not. Similarly the adjective carries a prefixed article in Albanian, while the substantive is defined by a suffixed article: *ftua i mirë* 'a good quince'/*ftoi i mirë* 'the good quince'.

Relative pronouns are missing from many languages. In Homeric Greek they were still properly demonstratives, as in

οἶος σὺν λαοῖσι, τοὶ Ἰλίῳ ἐγγεγάασιν

'alone with the folk—those (= who) were born in Ilium'.

In English their origin is interrogative: *the man who said so was mistaken* from *the man—who said so?—he was mistaken*. In Chinese and Basque the relative clause is treated as an attributive adjective. In Chinese *ti*[1] is used for the relative phrase, for the possessive and for the adverb. In Basque the relative clause is treated as an appositive adjective and given the article -*a* to show concord with the noun, as in *aita gure-a, zeruetan zauden-a* 'our Father which art in heaven'. In Bantu the clause is predicated of the noun by means of the '*o* of reference': Swahili *watu wa-na-o-soma* 'people, they are (reference) reading—people were reading'. In Turkish a participle is used: *bir verir adamdir*—'he is a man who gives' (*verir* is the aorist participle of *ver-mek*). So with Lat. *vidit duas naves stantes secus stagnum* 'he saw two boats standing (or, which were standing) beside the lake'. In the paratactic constructions of Old Norse we find principal clauses in such positions: *Atli hét maðr; han var sonr Arnviðar* '*A* was the name of a man; he was the son of *A*'. In such conditions, in fact, the relative of a modern language must be either a principal clause or participle; and even in literate speech the relative has a somewhat bookish effect.

Neither possessive pronouns nor subject pronouns attached to verbs involve the full implications of personality. The notion of person, as distinct from position in space, is found in disjunctive forms. With them a realistic difference is noted between the subject or source of action and the object and recipient, i.e. *ego/me, tu/te*. *Me* and *te* are not parts of the declension of *ego* and *tu*, which are different words, notably in the first person. This distinction is made in the unvarying languages of the Far East.

	Ancient Chinese	Burmese	Miri (N. Assam)
1.	*nguaa/nga	nga-ga/nga-go	ngā/ngōm
2.	*ńźiwo/ńźia̧	nin-ga/nin go	nā/nōm

Since there cannot be a plural *ego et ego*, nor *tu et tu* without change of person addressed, it follows that *ego* and *tu* have no proper plurals. *Ego et tu* is an inclusive form and is naturally a dual (*we*), while *ego et alii* is exclusive of *tu* and requires a separate plural word (*nos*). Such analogical formations as the Russ. *my* 'we' are strictly contrary to the facts. The inclusive and exclusive plurals of the first person find expression in many languages, e.g. Quechua *-yeu/nchic*. Fr. *nous autres français* excludes the hearer as being of some other nationality. From that form is developed *vous autres* though *vous* alone suffices to exclude *je* and *nous*. It is strictly hypertrophical, but in Sp. *nosotros vosotros* the words have evolved so as to eliminate *nos* and *vos*, having now no exclusive connotation.

The personal pronouns form narrow groups of declensions, very primitive in type and mutually influenced. *Me te se* tend to share the same flexions, and *nos* and *vos* form an interacting group. In

Hamitic and Semitic the disjunctive pronouns are obtained from the verbal suffixes by means of an emphatic prefix, e.g. Arab. *-ta -ti* 'thou'/ *anta anti*, Coptic *-f/-s* 'he, she'/*ĕntof ĕntos*.

These pronouns are on the whole highly stable, but they are liable to be disturbed by notions of courtliness. The first development is that of the 'plural of majesty': *nos* then means 'I and those I stand for' and *vos* 'you and those you stand for'. Hence Fr. *vous*, Eng. *you*, Russ. *vy* have become singulars. This use of *nos* 'we' is more restricted and is still actually majestic. *Vos* is formal, *tu* informal; and if *tu* is used outside its proper domestic sphere it becomes insulting. But *vos* can also be insulting as suggesting an exclusion from intimacy; it is so among Spanish Jews. It may also become an insult if superseded by higher terms in formal intercourse. These are nouns of respect, such as Spanish *vuestra merced* or Portuguese *Vossa Excelência* or the feminine third personal pronouns which refer to such nouns: Germ. *Sie*, It. *Lei*. A convention may arise, as apparently in Sweden and certainly in Brazil, in which the precise ground of respect should be stated: Swed. *vad tycker professorn B.*? 'what is your opinion, Professor B.?' Ptg. *o senhor doutor*, *o meu amigo vem*, &c. In Chinese *kuei*[4] 'honourable' refers to your things and *pi*[4] 'mean, poor' to my things, as *kuei*[4] *hsing*[4]? '(what is your) honourable name?', *pi*[4] *hsing*[4] *Yang*[2] '(my) poor name is Yang'. In Malay the pronouns have been largely eliminated by expressions of rank, and in Japanese and Korean they have been incorporated into the conjugations so as to make several degrees of respectful address. Owing to this development there are no less than seventeen Korean conjugations. For 'you' in Japanese there are paraphrases which mean literally 'that side', 'prince', 'honourable friend' (for inferiors or members of the household), 'elder', 'master', another 'that side' (for use in law courts), 'thither' (to inferiors), and 'august sir' (now disrespectful in speech).[1]

Concord. An advantage secured by the intrinsically unnecessary complexities of grammar lies in the possibility of binding the sentence by means of concord.

The simplest of these is merely phonetic and consists of harmony of vowel between the stem of a word and its suffixes. This practice is best represented by Turkish among the Altaic languages and

---

[1] W. M. McGovern, *Colloquial Japanese*, London, n.d. pp. 83–85; H. Plaut, *Japanese Conversation-Grammar*, Heidelberg, 1926, p. 148.

Magyar among the Uralian. The concord is less elaborate in Finnish on the one extreme and in Manchu at the other. It is absent from Korean and Japanese. The vowels are arranged in two series (as *a/e*) or four (as *ı/i/ö/ü*), and the suffixes are made to conform to the vowel of the stem: Turk. *bakacaklar* 'they will look', *gelmiyecekler mi?* 'will they not come?'. Each word and its attendant particles is thus distinguished: *hasta olduğumdan gelmedim* 'because I was ill I did not come', *düsdüğümden yürüyemem* 'because I fell I cannot walk'. Vowel harmony has been found in African and American languages also. When a monosyllabic stem may take a considerable number of suffixes, it is clearly an advantage to have a device to show how far the construction extends.

Concord of substantive and adjective and of subject and verb seems due in the first place to apposition and in the second to replacement of the noun in the verb by means of pronominal elements. The former refers to number, gender, and case and the latter to number and gender in the languages which distinguish gender in their pronominal suffixes. It hardly affects person, because the first and second persons singular and plural are properly pronominal in speech, but it is possible to have sentences like *ego Balbus dixi* in which the subject is emphatic and in absolute position. When, however, thanks to concord, the mutual relations of substantives, adjectives, and verbs are put beyond doubt, then a stylistic device is placed in the hands of authors, who gain freedom to distribute more freely the words of a sentence, as in Lucan's *collă diu grauibus frustrā temptată lacertis* ('after long trying in vain to catch his neck with his massive biceps'). The concords of gender, number and case associate *collă temptată* and *grauibus lacertis*, while in *quod tam lentă tuas tenuit patientiă uires conquerimur* ('our complaint is that his sluggish patience has restrained your forces') the concord of number is used for literary effect.

With the further development of *genera* or classes in Caucasian and Bantu and the presence of several pronominal elements in the verb still further effects of precise reference are no doubt possible. It is not for such stylistic ends, however, that Bantu prefixes are employed, but to place the whole sentence in each of its parts under the regime of the noun subject. Thus in Swahili '*watu wa*kaenda *wa*kam*w*amsha *wa*kasema, Zimwi amka' ('the people went to awaken him saying, "Zimwi, wake up"'), all the words of the first phrase are in the personal class denoted by *wa-*, while *-mw-* is the pronoun of the object and refers to Zimwi. The success of Bantu among African languages may be attributed to its meeting two demands: for a classification of objects of daily experience in such manner as to appeal to the African mind, and for a strongly nominal discipline in the sentence to make all references clear.

A language without concord must keep close together the words intellectually associated and for that end it must establish a firmer control over word-order. The same degree of control may arise from fixed sequences, as in Turkish, or from stylistic considerations of clarity, as in French, but these instances do not imply necessity. The necessity is greater when, as in Chinese, the language is monosyllabic, and each syllable bears an individual meaning. This creates a tension which cannot be prolonged, and a complex sentence must be built from the ground up by using syntactical units which are intelligible in themselves. They enter into larger combinations by virtue of the fact that a complete syntagma or clause may function as subject or object or attribute or adverb. In combination the word-group has an outer construction different to that which exists within its members. But the correlations which are obtained in other languages by the arbitrary signs of concord are achieved in Chinese by an intense intellectual discipline of the phrase.

To express the sentence 'Please tell me whether the teacher I engaged for you yesterday is good',[1] the Chinese distinguish the short main clause (*ch'ing*³ *wên*⁴ '[I] beg to ask whether') from the long object clause. This is construed as follows:

1. I yesterday for-you engaged (subj. advb. recipient. vb.).
2. whom (I engaged for you yesterday) (relative suffix *ti*).
3. the teacher (whom I engaged for you yesterday) (substantive, attribute).
4. (the teacher whom I engaged for you yesterday) good, not good? (subject clause, alternative predicates).
5. Please tell me (whether the teacher whom I engaged for you yesterday is good) (principal clause, object clause).

Russian experts classify Chinese as an 'amorphous' language. The term is supposed to mean 'without morphemes' and should be something like 'amorphematic', but the sense is already inherent in the traditional term 'isolating'. But amorphous, in the sense of

---

¹ P. Meriggi, *Journal de psychologie: psychologie du langage*, Paris, 1933.

'formless', is a term eminently unfitted to describe the precise shapeliness of a Chinese sentence and would be better discarded.

THE VERB

The verb is equipped for phenomenal expression. It is the residuum of the sentence after the discrimination by analysis of all nominal elements. Since the event is always unique, though it may partially resemble other events, the verb is always complex. In isolating languages like Chinese each contributory phenomenal element is identified and expressed by its own word symbol, but the word-group subsists as a syntagma, e.g. $k'o^3$-i^2 $chü^4$ $chao^4$ $t'a^1$ 'you had better call him' ('permit go call/him'). It is this sense of the complexity of the verb, added to the accident that analysis was achieved by suffixed elements, that caused a reconstruction of verbal paradigms in the Romance languages. In English the verb retains a considerable part of its conjugation. In Russian the verb has lost many forms at different epochs of the history of this language and predecessor (Common Slavonic), but compensation has been sought by associating two words—a perfective and an imperfective—to constitute jointly a full paradigm. In more primitive languages verbs are often of very great complexity owing to the effort made to include within the limits of one word the many particular features of each single event. In the agglomerative languages of Australia, where particles are not grammatically specialized but function by virtue of their intrinsic meaning, several different particles may give the same effect in English translation, e.g. the effect of past or future. The speaker has not attained these abstractions but envisages various pasts and futures, or events completed and events still incomplete, and uses living stems to express them. In the agglutinative Turkish type of expression, the subordinate signs are fully specialized, but they are massed behind the verbal stem in considerable numbers, as Turk. *gel-mi-ye-cek mi-siniz?* 'will you not come?'

The verb is fitted to show how an activity or state is related to the subject and other participating objects by voice and the insertion of pronominal elements in the verb; to express the particular manifestation of the activity envisaged (aspect), the time of the event (tense), and how the speaker regards the action (mood). Tense is, properly speaking, absent from the languages of communities which have no sense of the succession of moments of time, and it is of reduced importance where the aspects of completeness or incompletion are of more interest to speakers than chronology (as in the Slavonic languages). Tense and aspect thus compete against each other for a place in the paradigm of the verb. The preference we Westerners have for tense is probably due partly to the influence of European modes of life, which depend on the clock, and not, like the agricultural, on the completion of operations, and partly on the realization that aspects are too numerous to be adequately presented without the aid of auxiliaries. Aspect is as much a part of the west European verb as tense, but its expression is to be sought among the adverbs and particles which accompany the verb. In Semitic the numerous derived forms of the simple stem allow for the expression of aspects of action, while each several verb is conjugated according to temporal aspects rather than time. The subjective element of conjugation (mood) is carried to different lengths by different languages. There is usually a distinction between facts and notions, but notional subdivisions may be carried to various degrees according to the different linguistic idioms.

Primitive stems are, as we have seen, gerundial in nature, i.e. not specifically nominal or verbal. They appear in the vocative of nouns and the imperative of verbs, as *Balbe, dic* 'B., speak'. The vocative stands outside the sentence and is addressed to only one possible person, the hearer. Therefore it needs no grammatical sign to give it direction. The imperative is also addressed to only one possible hearer, and is an enunciation of the bare idea of some action. The presumption is that the action, being announced to the listener, will be performed by him—an assumption which may be unwarranted and therefore rude. The most that is required by the imperative is a sign of plurality when there are more hearers than one: as *fer/ferte*. The suffix marks plurality not person, for which there is, in the circumstances, no need of definition.

From this primitive survival in the vocative and imperative it is an unwarranted deduction to suppose that primordial speech consisted of summons and orders. The same bare stems occur in compound nouns like *Christopher* (Christ-bearer). *Christo-* is the bare thematic stem and is not marked as an accusative because there is no need to do so in this compound. Greek φερέ-οικο-ς 'house-bearer' is not a command to a snail to carry its shell, which would be absurd, but two bare stems combined with a declensional sign attached to the whole group. When the suffixed pronouns are removed, the item appears in the present and aorist indicative of Indo-European verbs in *es-mi es-si, es-ti*, &c., *bher(-o) bhere-si bhere-ti*, *(e)bhero-m (e)bhere-s (e)bhere-t*. The pronouns are those of the possessive order ('my being, my bearing, &c.') and possibly should be thought of as originally local ('being here by me, being there, being yonder'). In this analysis the gerundial (noun-verb) nature of the verbal stem is evident. The same sort of analysis unites Turkish *ev-im* 'my house' and *der-im* 'my saying = I say', Quechua possessive and personal sg. 1. -(n)i, 2. (y)qui, 3. -n; pl. 1. -nchic -yeu, 2. -(y)quichic, 3. -ncu. A measure of specialization is found in Finnish *käte-ni -si -mme -nne*, 'my, thy, our, your hand(s)', *ole-n -t -mme -tte* 'I am, thou art, we are, you are', but the principle is the same; the pronouns are possessive and are attached to an undifferentiated stem. In Finnish the third person singular of the verb has no pronoun and in the third plural the sign is of plurality only. In Lithuanian also the third singular and plural forms are without flexion, and in Old Bulgarian the endings -tŭ -(n)tŭ are probably to be regarded as demonstratives added after loss of third personal suffixes. In Arabic the pronominal suffixes attached to nouns are sg. 1. -(n)ī, 2. masc. -ka fem. -ki, 3. masc. -hu fem. -hā; pl. 1. -nā, 2. masc. -kum fem. -kunna, 3. masc. -hum fem. -hunna as well as dual forms, and those attached to verbs (aorist or perfect tense) sg. 1. -tu, 2. masc. -ta fem. -ti, 3. masc. fem. -t; pl. 1. -nā, 2. masc. -tum fem. -tunna, 3. masc. -ū fem. -na. Though there has been specialization by function, the kinship of the verbal and possessive suffixes is still apparent.

Symbols for person, number, and gender or class intrude into the verb by the way of pronouns. Gender and number may also come from the verb-adjective and verbal noun, as in Russ. *on byl, ona byla, ono bylo, oni byli* 'he, she, it was, they were', since *byl* represents an original past participle. But person, number, and class are not properly verbal concepts; they are proper to nouns. They are permanent notions which apply to a variety of situations. Their place in conjugation—which is a big one—is due to the tendency in many languages to compensate for the abstraction of nouns from the whole word-sentence by means of pronouns attached to the verb, so that the verb is not merely the phenomenal residuum of the sentence but also its microcosm. Different languages offer different degrees of compensation, from none in Chinese, to the presence of symbols for subject, object, recipient, and interlocutor in Basque. The truly verbal modifications are other than these.

Relation of Activity to Parties: Voice. As we have seen in the last chapter, the verb itself may be the subject of its own sentence. Such phrases are common in Malay, in which the named parties are related spatially and adverbially to the verb. Expressions akin to these are present verbs with no real subject, such as those concerning natural phenomena (*pluit* 'it is raining'), and verbs of emotion (*taedet me* 'it wearies me'). They are well developed in Slavonic, as Russ. *im chorošó živĕtsja* 'they live comfortably' ('to them well is it lived'), *mne chóčetsja spat'* 'I want to sleep', *móžno est'*, *skól'ko ugódno* 'you may eat as much as you like'. Similarly the parenthetic use of *byválo* and *býlo*, *ja býlo skazál* 'I was going to say', *on byválo govoríl* 'he used to say'. Compare Lat. *sic itur ad astra* 'this is the way to the stars'. In Gaelic knowing, possessing, feeling, and all kinds of emotions 'happen to' persons, as *tha fios agad na thubhairt e* 'you know what he said' ('there is knowledge to you of what he said'). This passive attitude is frequently encountered in savage languages of South America. Savage man apparently feels that most events are not due to his volition. Subjects may be forced upon such constructions as in Gk. ὕει Ζεύς 'Zeus is raining = sends rain', Sp. *amaneció Dios* 'God dawned = brought the dawn'. Emotional verbs in English now have personal subjects as if the person himself were the cause of his emotion, as *I regret, I need* (Lat. *opus est mihi*, Russ. *mne nádo*).

In Chinese the verb is neutrally placed towards all parties: it is active in *t'a¹ tso¹ shên⁴ -mo³* 'he does what = what is he doing?', passive in *p'an²-tzŭ shih⁴ mu⁴-t'ou³ tso¹ -ti* 'the dish is made of wood', without subject in *hsia⁴ hsüeh³* 'it is snowing'. As we have seen, the subject of a sentence may be the cause of the activity, or the patient, or someone interested, or an instrument. The relations between parties and events are complex in reality and the treatment of the subject as agent in our grammar involves much unrealistic simplification.

An intransitive verb records an activity or condition affecting only one party. A transitive verb represents an action as passing from one party to another.

The intransitive verb involves certain realistic difficulties. There is nothing to show, apart from the nature of the activity itself, whether the subject is agent or patient. In many languages the pronouns which denote the patient (object) of a transitive verb are those which mark the subject of the intransitive. Basque is the standard example, but the construction is common in the Caucasus and in the Americas. Further, it is difficult to imagine an activity proceeding from a subject to nowhere. If the intransitive is a verb of motion, the end of the motion completes the action, as in Lat. *Romam ire* 'to go to Rome'. Every verb implies the name of its own activity, so that an intransitive verb may have for complement a cognate noun, as *to dream a dream, to run a race, bonum certamen certavi* 'I have fought the good fight'. If the cognate object is qualified by an adjective, the latter may be expressed and the substantive omitted. From that situation we derive adverbs which are nouns in the accusative case. In the absence of any other complement there is the fact that the subject of an intransitive verb is affected by his own activity: *I walk = my legs are put in motion*. From this comes the use of middle and reflexive verbs which replace the bare intransitive and clothe it with some personal interest: Lat. *proficiscor* 'I set out', Gk. εὔχομαι 'I pray, make vows', Sp. *irse* 'go away'. Sp. *olvidar* and *olvidarse de* mean 'to forget', but the former is a bare fact, the latter suggests somebody's interest in the event. *Dicunt = dicitur = on dit*. Fr. *il se trompe* 'he is mistaken', not that he deceives himself but that the mistake concerns the erring person as object. Intransitive-transitive verbs are also numerous, as Gk. κλαίω 'wail/bewail'.

It is with the transitive verb that a distinction develops between the active and the passive voice. There are languages like Basque which have only one voice. It is hardly right to call it passive since there is no active opposed to it; and indeed the Basque verb directly expresses the activity. The passive voice is a grammatical device to invert the order of ideas of the corresponding active, as *John did this/this was done by John*. An action involving more parties than one may be viewed from various angles, but as regards its source the passive inversion is unrealistic since *John* continues to be the 'logical' subject. This lack of realism is reflected in the precarious tenure of the passive in our European languages. The oldest form in -*r* is found only at the limits of the area, in Celtic, Latin, Phrygian, Hittite, and Tokharian. For Sanskrit and Greek a new passive was evolved by lengthening the final vowel of the active into a diphthong. In the Scandinavian and Slavonic tongues another passive was derived from the reflexive pronoun; in Armenian by specialization of verbs in -*i*-; in German and English by the use of auxiliaries *be*, *sein*, *werden*; in Romance by use of the verb 'to be' with its synonyms and by the reflexive -*se*. The forms in -*r* and -*mai* were middle voices, indicating the interest of the subject in the action, and the passive voice is laboriously constructed of middle and miscellaneous symbols. The reflexive *se* of Romance has also a middle sense and tends to eliminate true analytical passives in *esse, stare*, &c.

Aspect and tense. While our west European tenses are arranged to express time of action (past, present, and future) with intermediate points like the pluperfect and future perfect, they still express aspect to some extent. *He came* refers to a completed action, *he was coming* to an action with indefinite past duration, and *he has come* to an action with a bearing on the present situation. *He is coming* and *he comes* differ by a nuance of continuous action in the first instance. Future time does not exist and must be expressed by some implication from the present: *he is about to come, on the point of coming, going to arrive, will come* and emphatically *shall come*. In present time these are aspects of immediacy, motion, will, and obligation to which it is possible to add becoming (Germ. *werden*), growth (Lat. *ibit* [cf. φύω 'grow']). Since the future is a notion, not a fact, it may be expressed by a notional mood as in Spanish *cuando venga* 'when he comes'. The English translation shows that the future may also be treated as a simple extension of the present.

In the Slavonic languages the fundamental concept is one of verbal aspect. A perfective and imperfective verb are associated in such a way as to cover the time scale too. The crucial point is that a perfective verb in the present tense, i.e. one which has a definite conclusion of action, has its end in future time. The past perfective is concluded in past time and the past imperfective is continuous or undefined in past time. The present imperfective refers to present time, the present perfective to a definite future time and the periphrastic imperfective future to undefined future time. Thus while the scheme is essentially aspectual it gives also temporal effects.

Time in Chinese is expressed by adverbial phrases and the verb remains unaltered: *wo³ ch'ü⁴-nien² lai²-ti* 'I came last year', *t'a¹ ming²-tien¹ lai²* 'he will come tomorrow'. The word *liao³* 'finished' (weakened to a suffix -*la*) is attached to verbs to denote completed action. *T'a¹ lai²-la* means either 'he has come' or 'he is here', since the completion of a past action results in a present condition. For the future, *yao*[4] 'want, will' serves; and *chiu*[4] 'then' indicates either the immediate past or the consequential future. In Tibetan time may be inferred in effect from voice, not tense: 'all my brothers have been killed by the Tibetans' = 'the Tibetans have killed all my brothers'. The Tibetan verb, though it belongs to the mono-syllabic Sino-Tibetan type, is not invariable, but admits prefixes, suffixes, and internal mutation: *'bar-ba* 'burn' (intransitive)/*spar-ba* (transitive); *'gum-pa* 'kill' (present)/*bkum* (past); *'geṅs-pa* 'fill' (present)/*bkaṅ(s)* (past)/*dgaṅ* (future).[1] In Swahili the prefix -*me*- can express either a past action or a present state, as *a-me-rudi* 'he has returned, he is back'. Other prefixes are *li* perfective, *ta* future, *na* continuous and of present time unless there is an indication of some other (*ni-na-soma* 'I am reading'), *hu* repetitive or habitual.

The most elaborate provision for expressing aspects is made by Semitic, the Hamitic system being somewhat simpler. Arab. *katab-a* 'he wrote' is perfective, and *ya-ktubu* 'he is writing' is imperfective. Strictly speaking these are different forms of the basic stem and therefore different words. From them come derived verbs with double consonants, lengthened vowels, or with certain prefixes. With these aids the verb expresses intensivity, reciprocity, causality, reflexive action, passivity, and the conative aspect. The ninth verbal form is, somewhat surprisingly, specialized to verbs of colour or bodily defects. Though the functions of the derived forms are thus defined with some precision, their applications to particular verbs are, to our view, sometimes strained. In a sequence of verbs the time is fixed by the principal, and dependent verbs may be undefined. In Hebrew tenses combined according to special rules of sequence; in Coptic there is a specialized consecutive tense in *ĕnte-*.

In Indo-European two forms of the same root were associated to mark aspect, as *leipo-* imperfective/*lipo-* perfective. The third member of the mutation (*loipo-*) gave the noun of the verbal action and sometimes the perfect tense *leloipa* 'I have left'. The series are often incomplete, but they generally show *e-* grade for continuous action, zero-grade for momentary acts, and *o-*grade for nouns. By the introduction of the *s*-aorist a new mode of expressing com-pleted action was created; in opposition to the present it became a past definite tense. A past indefinite or imperfect tense arose independently in the individual languages; thus a general shift from aspect to time took place in conjugation. It is a remarkable

---

[1] J. Bacot, *Grammaire du tibétain littéraire*, Paris, 1946, pp. 50 ff.

feature of modern Slavonic languages that they have re-established aspect as the basis of the verbal system though tenses were sufficiently developed in Common Slavonic. Among other distinctions of aspect were -sk- for inceptives (*florescere* 'to begin to flower'), -si- for desideratives, -va- for iteration (in Slavonic), &c. These suffixes lacked body and consistency; they were liable to be fused with stems and pronominal suffixes. They were also insecure in their complication, e.g. the -sk- of Latin inceptives gives an Armenian past tense (*sireçi* 'I loved').

Time tenses offer the advantage of a simple, though highly artificial, pattern of conjugation, whereas aspects are too numerous for any measures of prevision. An activity may be seen in many perspectives, and if divisible into parts there may be preferential treatment for any one. Thus duration or momentariness, iteration or singleness of action, completion or lack of definition, state or activity, causation, the definite beginning and the end of an action, motion, will, obligation, tendency, abstraction and timelessness, desire, conation, immediacy in the past or future, are all among aspects of the verb and are most intelligibly expressed by specialized auxiliaries. The presence of formal symbols of aspect in early and primitive languages is doubtless due in part to the relative unimportance of time in primitive society, but their incompleteness to failure to envisage all the complexities of aspect. Under heavier demands for nuances of expression makeshift arrangements were made, and these have proved to be unstable in European languages, with the result that the aspectual paradigm has been abandoned and the simpler but more sophisticated paradigm of tenses has taken its place.

Moods. While voice and aspect are objective parts of the grammar of the verb, mood is subjective. It records the attitude of the speaker to his own statement, and this is primarily a distinction between what he puts forward as fact (whether it be true or not) and what he puts forward as notional. In some languages this distinction suffices and the indicative is opposed to the subjunctive, though it is also feasible to eliminate the subjunctive, as English has done, or to have never developed this aid at all. In such cases the distinction between fact and notion, if necessary to the communication, will be carried by auxiliaries proper to the various classes of notions for which expression is sought.

The imperative is often classed among moods but, as we have

seen, it stands outside the finite paradigm. It is the expression of
a concept without verbal or nominal specialization, which assumes
that the hearer will accept the command announced without quali-
fication. Similarly the infinitive is not a mood, but a verbal-noun
in a conventionally selected case. It functions as a mood only in
such constructions as the Latin accusative and infinitive, in which
subordinate clauses are expressed in the subjunctive; in such constructions it constitutes a quotative mood, since the speaker puts
forward a statement as not resting on his own authority. The same
effect is obtained in Tunica (Louisiana) by the low tone at the end
of a phrase;[1] the modal sign is the intonation.

There is thus in use everywhere an indicative mood for what the
speaker affirms, and a number of other moods may develop during
the history of each separate language to express various sorts of
non-affirmation. A negative affirms that something **is not**; it is then
indicative in mood. If used to deny a notion, it is associated with
the appropriate notional mood. In this respect the most interesting
aberration is in Finnish in which the negative itself is conjugated:
olen 'I am', *en ole* 'I am not'. In Japanese there are also negative
conjugations of both verbs and adjectives. The phenomenon to
which attention is called is the negation itself. On the other hand,
affirmations may be made with varying degrees of reserve. The
assertion may be left open to doubt, as in *what is the time?—it will
be about two o'clock*, Turkish *-miş-* in *para çok sever-miş* 'he is very
fond of money I think'.[2] In this the verb is equipped to express
what appears to be true or what is probably true.

By using suitable auxiliary verbs and adverbs it is, of course,
possible to mark the difference between what is asserted as fact and
what is put forward as a notion for discussion. In such a case the
verb itself remains unchanged. But there is widespread support for
discriminating between facts and notions by some easy and simple
symbolism. In Swahili the sign is the opposition of *-a* to *e*: *piga*
'beat'/*upige* 'that you may beat' *sipige* 'do not beat', *ni-som-e* 'am
I to read?' (dubitative). In Spanish the formulas are *a/e* and *e/a*, a
simplification of the distinctions shown in Latin: *ama/ame*, *debe/
deba*. Similarly in Arabic *yaktubu* 'he writes' is opposed to *yaktuba*
'he may write'. With the distinction between the factual indicative

---

[1] M. Haas, 'A grammatical sketch of Tunica', *Linguistic Structures of America*,
New York, 1946, p. 340.
[2] A. C. Mowle, *The New Turkish*, London, 1942, p. 60.

and notional subjunctive many languages rest satisfied. Discrimination of notional moods may, however, be pushed much farther, and these distinctions, having no support in concrete circumstances, tend to be impermanent. Thus the subjunctive has satisfied the demand for a polite imperative in the modern Latin languages. The speaker announces not a fact but a notion of an action with the implication that the listener may carry it out. This is less crude than the positive command or possibly unwarranted assumption implied by the imperative. In Arabic, however, a vowelless jussive mood (originally -*i*) is used for this purpose: *yaktub* 'let him write'. Notions may be distinguished as nearer and remoter, Gk. subjunctive and optative. Nearness and remoteness are also attributes of time, and in Latin the old optative mood has given past tense to the subjunctive. Since wishes are remoter than commands, wishes even in present time are expressed by the Latin past subjunctive; conditional and concessive constructions in Latin use these remoter tenses when the concession or condition is not assumed by the speaker to be facts. The dubitative use of the subjunctive in some languages corresponds to a dubitative mood in others. The optative of Greek is also a potential, but in Turkish a distinction is made between *gele* 'that he may come' and *gelebiliyor* 'he is able to come'. The necessitative mood of Turkish (*gelmeliyim* 'I must come') is one in which mood and aspect are hard to distinguish.

To deny a notion is different from denying a fact and may lead to specialization of negatives as in Greek *οὐ*/*μή*, Armenian *oč*/*mi*. Assertions are more frequent in principal clauses and notions in subordinate clauses; for instance, with relation to a verb of emotion and the clause defining its cause. The cause is not asserted as a fact though the emotion of joy, fear, &c., or the quality of obligation is so asserted. The accusative and infinitive construction is a quotative mood since the speaker does not take responsibility for the subordinate affirmations. Clauses subordinated to the infinitive are expressed with still less liability to the speaker in the remote optative or past subjunctive. The future in a principal clause may be implied by some present tendency or obligation, but in a subordinate clause it is expressed as a mere notion. This common connexion between notional and subordinate clauses has given ground for the name subjunctive, but the mood occurs also in principal clauses. The name must be construed as a mere technical term.

Verbal nouns. Since the verb contains within itself the name of

its own action, a verbal noun may be expressed syntactically without change of form in Chinese, and a verbal adjective may be
obtained by using the suffixed word *-ti*. The Indo-European *e/o*
mutations provide a noun with stem in *o*: φέρω 'I bear' φορός
'bearing', φόρος 'what is borne, tribute', and from these nouns
φορέω 'I convey'. In agglutinative and polysynthetic languages there
is considerable traffic from verb to verbal-noun and from verbal-
noun back to more complex types of verb. In the paradigms of
Indo-European the nominal forms in use are evidently late and
derive from the finite verb. There are adjectives in *-nt-*, *-ndo-*,
-wos/us- *-to-*; *-mo-*; and petrified cases which give infinitives. The
latter develop independently in each language. In the Balkan languages the infinitive has again gone out of use. It is marked in
Bantu by an abstract prefix *ku-*, as *kupika* 'cooking, to cook', *kufa*
'dying, to die', but other verbal nouns of a concrete type are
obtained by the use of an *-o* of reference: *mwendo* 'journey',
mwendeleo 'progress'.

The development of infinitives and participles would seem to be
connected with an increase of complexity in sentences which were
still of the paratactic type, i.e. which did not admit the presence of
any but principal statements. Under such conditions subordination could only be achieved by attaching participles to qualify
substantives within the sentence—the participle admitting its own
complements because of its verbal nature—and by using the infinitive. This form has been most energetically evolved in Finnish, a
language with five infinitive stems for each verb, these being used
in several cases. Only the third stem admits of all cases, the other
four being conventionally limited to one or two. Thus *saa* 'he
receives' has infinitives as follows: I. *saada*, translative case *saadakse*;
II. inessive *saadessa*, instrumental *saaden*; III. *saama* (used in
almost all its cases); IV. nominative *saaminen*, partitive *saamista*;
V. adessive plural *saanut*. On the other hand Finnish is poor in
participles. The use of the Finnish infinitive may be illustrated
from John viii. 56 where the inessive II. form *nähde-ssä-nsä* 'in his
seeing' is used: *Abraham teidän isänne iloitsi nähdessänsä minun
päivääni*[1] 'Abraham your father rejoiced in-his-seeing my day—
your father Abraham rejoiced to see my day'. The infinitive could
have been translated 'when he saw'. So Finnish *kaskea poltettaessa*
'the forest in-its-burning = while the forest was burning'. The

[1] C. N. E. Eliot, *A Finnish Grammar*, Oxford, 1890, p. 189.

use of participles to avoid subordinate finite verbs is often seen in Greek and Latin, as *Romā captā abiit Alaricus* 'Alaricus departed after he had taken Rome', ὣς ἄρ᾽ ἔφαν ἀπιόντες 'thus they said as they went away', ἐπὶ νηῶν βάντες ἀπέπλεον 'they boarded the ships and sailed away'.

With the development of subordinate finite clauses the need for verbal-nouns other than the infinitive has largely disappeared. Participles have become adjectives and in their verbal functions they have been reduced to a few stereotyped forms in Russian, as *skazav* 'having said', *védši* 'having come', cf. Fr. *passant, passé*, Eng. *going*. Some participles have become substantives, as *futurus* > *future*, Russ. *búduščee*, and others remain as isolated survivors, like Russ. *vedomo* 'indeed, obviously'. There remain with the verb chiefly two forms, the invariable gerund and the infinitive; and of these the infinitive tends to be eliminated in Balkan languages.

In theory an infinitive may have complements but should not have a personal subject. The personal subject is that of the governing verb, and a finite tense should be used if a new subject is introduced. But the practical convenience of the infinitive is great and subjects have been attached to it, e.g. Spanish *al venir yo* 'at my coming'. In Portuguese the infinitive is conjugated with personal suffixes when the subject is other than that of the principal verb. Examples are *passei sem me verem* (*ver*) 'I passed by without their seeing me', *ao chegarem os fugitivos à planície, um dos desconhecidos estava ali* 'when the fugitives reached (*chegar-em*) the plain, one of the unknown men was there'.

By using nominal forms of most verbs and confining conjugation to a few primitive verbs classed as auxiliaries, the Basque language avoids the full affects of its complicated and fused paradigm. Thus *erori* 'fallen' has an attributive case *eroriko* 'of falling' and a locative *erortzen* 'in falling': whence *ni erortzen naiz* 'I am in-falling = I fall', *ni eroriko nintzake* 'I would fall', *ni erori naiteke* 'I could fall'. With *ikusi* 'seen' there are formations such as *ikusten dut* 'I see it', *ikusiko/ikusiren dut* 'I shall see it'. Flexion is limited in these instances to the auxiliaries *izan* 'been' (*za*) and *eduki* (*u*) 'had'.

PARTICLES

IN addition to the noun and verb Aristotle recognized two other parts of speech, one to link expressions and corresponding to conjunctions, the other described as the article. The latter is too indistinct to be identified; the article as we know it is a weakened demonstrative pronoun. Conjunctions perform a necessary service in grammar. They are recruited from nouns which have passed through the adverbial stage (of fixity of case) and often through the prepositional as well. Prepositions = postpositions and adverbs thus enter into this class of particles but in their simpler forms resemble pronouns of general reference. In flexional languages they are indeclinable, and they differ from later adverbial and prepositional formations by the circumstance that no original process of declension can be identified. Among particles there are also expletives to indicate in what general sense a sentence should be taken. They are numerous in Greek, where they occur after the opening words of the sentence or after words singled out for this degree of definition. They were reduced to the single form *že* in Old Slavonic. In classical Chinese the expletives are numerous and are placed at the end of the sentence. Their precise values are not yet ascertained. Some simple exclamations—those which have no grammatical skeleton—are also to be reckoned among particles. The group is thus heterogeneous by definition, though usually easy to identify in any given tongue.

Prepositions are so called from their place before the noun in ancient Greek, but in many languages they are placed after the noun and must be called postpositions. In Homeric Greek they had still not acquired their function of relating the noun to the sentence and were of the nature of adverbs further defining a relation which was already generally stated by case. Thus Ἰλιόθι πρό conveyed the meaning 'At Ilion—in front'. The adverb was separated from its verb and construed ambivalently with the verb or the noun. It was thus, like the German separable verbal prefixes, related to the system of prefixes. The Homeric ὅτε Ἴλιον εἰσανέβαινον Ἀργεῖοι 'when the Argives went up to Ilion' and νήεσσ᾽ ἡγήσατ᾽ Ἀχαιῶν Ἴλιον εἴσω 'he led the Achaeans in ships into Ilion' illustrate the use of the prefix both with the verb and separated from it. Because the relation is defined in general spatial terms by case, and particles are used only for confirmation and precision, a particle may accompany any suitable case. It did not 'govern' a case in Homer's day; in later Attic εἰς Ἴλιον would be construed as if the case was determined by the preposition. Later prepositions formed from nouns are distinguished by requiring the genitive case, i.e. the case set aside for associations of nouns.

Whether primitive prepositions have a nominal origin is not certain. They form certain series of apparently related forms, of which the most elaborate in Indo-European is in *per/pr-: per peri pro, prae, para, pri. This has the appearance of a rudimentary declension but does not answer to accepted models. Other groups are apo/epi, ex/*iks (Russ. iz), ot/do, ab/ob, &c. Ambi- is related to ambo 'both'.

In Semitic the genitive case in -i is used for relations between nouns and for nouns which follow prepositions. In languages which use postpositions the analysis is much more difficult since it is not easy or always possible to distinguish a postposition from a case suffix. In fact there is a certain unreality in the attempt to do so. Both prepositional and casual relations are often concerned with position in space, which is the fundamental characteristic of nouns as such. The Bantu system of locations is not highly developed.

In Chinese these relations are expressed by verbs before the noun and nouns after. The syntagma has its own syntax: it is composed of a verb and its object, or a noun in relation to another noun, or verb+noun+noun. The verbal idioms are such as (give) to, (reach) as far as, (oppose) toward, (abide) at, and the nouns include spatial concepts like inside, outside, above, under, middle. Thus (give) to me becomes to me when the auxiliary surrenders its proper meaning in favour of some principal verb; (abide) at the town's outside = outside the town, heart's inside = within the heart.

Under paratactic conditions, in which every verb is principal, only a few simple conjunctions are required to connect nouns with nouns and clauses with clauses. This class of words has been increased by the demands of the civilized sentence for hypotaxis (subordinate phrases). Recruitment has been from other parts of speech and chiefly from both primary and secondary prepositions. The means of conversion are usually quite simple, as Fr. jusqu'à (preposition) and jusqu'à ce que (conjunction), Eng. on the grounds/ on the grounds that.

Gestures reduced to sound-symbols account for the expletive particles. In many languages words are accompanied by a more or less definite code of gestures, such as shrugging the shoulders, moving the hands, touching the fingers in succession, raising the eye-brows, &c. These show in what way the spoken words should be taken: whether ironically, didactically, with indifference, and so on. It is an advance towards intelligibility if such movements and the corresponding varying of tones of the voice are replaced by sound-symbols, which without any precise logical value may yet offer a clue to the general situation. In so far, however, as they are not conjunctions, clauses united in some specific relation, or marks of emphasis upon some word, these signs lack a suitable use and are liable to disappear. The speaker's intention is conveyed still more precisely by explicit symbols, though with loss of the subtle play of those nuances which give charm to ancient Greek style.

VIII

WORDS

A WORD is an autonomous unit of thought and sense. It 'results from the association of a given meaning with a given group of sounds susceptible of a given grammatical employment' or is 'a complex of sounds which in itself possesses a meaning fixed and accepted by convention' or is 'the smallest thought-unit vocally expressible'.[1]

Though a word is no more than a somewhat shifty hummock on the contour of a breath-group, though it is embedded in the sentence and its unity has to be defined for each separate language, though there are languages which have no words in our sense either for completeness of form or precision of meaning, and though the meaning of meaning is an unresolved problem in both linguistics and philosophy, the emergence of words as counters of thought is of the utmost importance. Because of it language studies have been inverted and made to turn on words, not the sentence. Syntax is the arrangement of words in a sentence. Etymology seeks the 'true account' or at least the origins of words. Morphology is defined as treating of morphemes, significant addition, or variations of words. Phonetic transcriptions are divided into words. Lexicography traces the history of meanings of words and arranges them in the most convenient sequences. Semantics deals with meanings, derivation with secondary word-forms. Words are entered on linguistic maps even when sounds or phrases are to be studied, because it is found that these vary according to the words that compose them. Words and things are studied in a special branch of linguistics and others are concerned with particular sources of words, such as personal and place names and names of particular classes of objects.

Words also attract the attention of non-linguists. Philosophers study certain words and attempt to impose on them meanings which they assert to be common and which are either incapable of confusion or are a guide through words to reality. The philosophical

[1] A. Rosetti, *Le Mot*, Copenhagen–Bucharest, 1947, has a full bibliography and is a summary sketch of the subject. Cf. L. H. Gray, *Foundations of Language*, New York, 1939, p. 146; A. Meillet, *Linguistique historique et linguistique générale*, Paris, 1921, p. 30.

interest in language is almost wholly confined to nouns, chiefly to abstract nouns. Sentences are rewritten by philosophers or language itself is replaced by metalanguage, but the symbols of metalanguage are a sort of words. The interest of the ordinary man can easily be aroused in words, which he collects for a dictionary, an atlas or even for his own pleasure.[1] A word, and especially a written word, has power. It is a *logos*; it sums up what we know or think, or it carries the seeds of action. Words have quality also and range from neutral to highly expressive. In short, though the proper study of languages lies in the sentence with its constituent sounds, its scheme of relations, and its expressivity, there is ample reason for treating separately questions relating to words.

The incomplete significance of primitive languages arises from their excessive concern with the concrete. Circumstances to be analysed require abstraction, and of the smallest degree of abstraction such communities seem to be incapable. In those conditions 'words are practically unintelligible unless one knows the situation in which they are spoken'.[2] According to another author, Bantu words become something different when they are written down, and a Kabyle Berber stated that his language was spoken, not written. But Bantu and Kabyle are relatively civilized modes of expression with relatively stable values for their words. The concreteness of Australian Arunta expressions is beyond the comprehension of a European. *Minta* 'one' and *tara* 'two' are, it would seem, not numbers but vague expressions of place. *Unta* 'you' properly means 'one lying down'. *Alirra* 'child' is 'one walking or appearing in front'; *talpa* 'moon' is 'something stable (*ta*) which returns (*lpa*)'. The units of thinking are such vague concrete notions as *na* 'sit, exist, be', *ka* 'cut, point, head', *ra* 'be in front, appear, become', *nga* 'permanent attitude', *tja* 'piercing, tearing movement'. A Bantu monosyllable such as *-ti* seems to indicate any doing, saying, acting, or thinking, and no precise sense can be attached to *-tu*. In the polysyllabic languages of America there is less of this indetermination but words are still not fully defined in form or meaning. In the word-sentence of Eskimo or Chukcha they are stems to be combined with other stems. If they stand

[1] The pleasure of word-hunting and word-lore can be experienced by readers of E. Weekley's admirable books of essays, such as *Words and Names, Words Ancient and Modern, More Words Ancient and Modern, Something about Words, The Romance of Words, The Romance of Names*.
[2] A. Sommerfelt, *La langue et la société*, Oslo, 1938, p. 125.

alone, they sometimes need a prop or take a different shape. Their meaning is generally gerundial and they are ready to serve as nouns or verbs according to the exigences of the phrase. The Quechua unit is also characteristically a stem requiring completion in some specific context and endowed with a gerundial meaning. If nouns, they may stand alone without a prop, but that is not their normal condition. They require a context to give them definition.[1]

These languages provide evidence for the real existence of stems, i.e. of significant units prepared for entry into some context but not complete in themselves. Stems are not fictions or abstractions. On the contrary they seem to be remarkably resistant in poly-synthetic tongues once we classify them by their construct forms. These do not seem to vary as much as the words of inflected lan-guages, though they may require props or change their vowels and consonants if abstracted and placed in unnatural isolation. Within the word-sentence their apparent invariability and their reliance on order for relationship sensibly diminishes the distance between the polysynthetic and the isolating types of language. Variations caused by fusion and inflexion on the other hand may lead to our considering stems which are artificial. Thus *Balb*- is an artificial stem for *Balbus* forced on us by the fusions in *Balbi*, *Balbo*, *Balbum*, *Balbe*. But the stem originally ended in the thematic vowel o/e to which the suffixes of case were added. In Greek one can see this stem as $log\ {}^o/_e$- without too much difficulty. In the very old con-sonantal declension ($\chi\acute{\eta}\nu\ \chi\eta\nu$-ός 'goose') the stem is firm and real. It is in fact a word. *Ovi-s* 'sheep' and *manu-s* 'hand' are also examples of real stems which are fairly stable, and so is *reg*- in *rex* (*reg-s*) 'king' and *reg-o* 'rule'. For some stems we have to make allowance for the vowel mutation of Indo-European, as $*pet$-$/pot$-$/$ pt-${}^o/_e$- 'fly'.

What is artificial in Indo-European linguistics is the conception of a root. The root is put forward as the lowest common denominator of a whole family of words; it may be prepared in various ways as stems to take the relational suffixes of declension and conjuga-tion. It is not asserted that the root existed as such but only that it is the meeting-point of all the inferences that can be made from a family of words. To what reality the root may correspond is

---

[1] The gerundial treatment is exemplified in H. Galante's vocabularies to *De priscorum Huaruchirariensium origine et institutis* (by F. de Avila) and *Catechismus Quichuensis* (by B. Jurado Palomino, 1646).

essentially unknown. All the stages of Indo-European we can describe make use of stems, but we can only look at the end of a long historical process whose beginnings may be ten times as far away as our earliest evidence. The notion of roots is a necessary artifice to cover knowledge which we cannot accurately attain.

Among words incomplete in meaning should be placed the Bantu ideophones.[1] They have poor relations among our interjections— utterances, vaguely expressive of feeling, which do not form part of the sentence for lack of precise sense and are 'interjected' between intelligible phrases. Since they complete the meaning of verbs, ideophones are also like our adverbs and they occupy places often filled by our nouns. They are in fact a separate part of Bantu speech, designed to give an impression of a situation in a general way by completing a predicate in respect of manner, colour, sound, or action. They are expressive but not intelligible, like a baby's expression *to go bye-bye*. Thus Zulu *godu* is used of going home, *klebu* of redness and of tearing cloth or paper, *pheshe* of flashing past, *baxu* of hitting with a whip, *gham* of a sudden appearance, *cikithi* of being quite full, *babalala* of falling on the stomach, *bacalala* of lying prone and watching for something, *gombolokoqo* of turning inside out, which can also be expressed by *gumbulukuqu*. Since *boklo* refers to hitting on the back or ribs, and *hunu* of cutting an animal's ears, the Zulu says *wa:mbokloza wamuthi boklo* (*boklo boklo*) 'he hit me "biff" in the ribs' and *ngizoyihuna amadlete ngiyithi hunu* 'I shall cut its ears'. These are both examples of the formation of a regular word by derivation from an ideophone; but such a practice is exceptional. It does not occur with *khace* which refers to darkness: *kumnyama khace* 'it is pitch dark'. In English an intelligible metaphor 'pitch' has the expressive effect which is the primary characteristic of an ideophone.

In general it would seem that primitive words are incompletely defined for form or sense. They are not always primarily conveyers of a logical meaning. They refer to strictly concrete notions and are only fully comprehensible in the material situations in which they are spoken. Under such conditions there is not much incentive to avoid homophony or synonymy. A sound defined by its circumstances need not differ from one defined by quite different circumstances. Different expressions of the same circumstances are equally well explained by the visible event. Though much of Chinese

[1] C. M. Doke, *Zulu Grammar*, London, 1947, pp. 255-70.

homophony is due to phonetic decay it is hard to think that so very many homonyms could arise without a high degree of original homophony. In spoken Chinese they cause surprisingly little embarrassment. Most alternatives are excluded by the situation itself. Should any confusion arise, an explanation is asked for and a second term is offered. Sometimes reference is made to the written character or to an unambiguous context. But on the whole the written character has nothing to do with spoken Chinese, which solves its own problems by word of mouth. Probably the chief effect of the written language has been negative, viz. it has not itself fallen into confusions due to homophony because of its distance from actual utterance and thus has not provided an impulse to obviate these difficulties in speech. A verbal context has so less power than material circumstances to explain the sense of our expressions, that a phonetic Chinese script is soon plunged into difficulties by homophones.

The process of comparison of Indo-European meanings possibly gives undue favour to the wider and vaguer, but it is also possible that these ancient stems had the formal and intellectual incompleteness we find in primitive tongues. For Greek δρῦς 'oak' δόρυ 'spear', Breton *derv* 'oak', Russ. *dérevo* 'wood', Eng. *tree* we posit a word or stem of general meaning like 'tree' or 'wood'. Similarly since the congeners of *beech* include a word for oak (Gk. φηγός), we have authority only to say that the original word must have meant some large tree like a beech or oak. The comparative method enforces this degree of indefiniteness just as it enforces too much definition when we treat of paradigms, but it is also possible that a certain incompleteness characterized the primitive Indo-European tongue. The stems are ultimately gerundial since they give indifferently nouns or verbs, though there is a notable degree of specialization in the use of the mutation $e/o/-$, by which the e grade is used for continuous tenses, the zero grade for perfectives, and the o grade for nouns: Gk. τέμνω 'I am cutting', τέτμηκα 'I cut', τομός 'cutting', τόμος 'a cut, slice'.

WORDS AS UNITS OF FORM

In the isolating languages of the Far East words are isolated and invariable. They are monosyllabic in the Sino-Tibetan and Mon-Khmer groups but mostly disyllabic in Malayo-Polynesian.

It seems that the monosyllable is unsuited to express more than a limited range of substantive ideas. Its use for primary verbs of action or state is not challenged and it serves also for some simple nouns. But the monosyllabism of a language like Chinese is eluded in various ways. The hearer needs time to grasp the speaker's intention. That time is presented in writing, but in speaking time has to be gained in other ways. A first device, suitable for particular objects, is to give a hint of the way in which the object is measured. The 'numeral adjuncts' or enumeratives of Chinese, fifty in number, warn the hearer that he has to do with something pertaining to man or woman, or made of wood, bamboo, or metal (the sign is 'gold'), or measured in lengths or pieces, or characterized by hide (animals), or respectability (gentry) and so on. Thus in i^1-$t'iao^2$-lu^4 (one [twig] length of road), $t'iao^2$ is sufficient indication that the listener is not to expect 'deer' or 'green' or 'dew' or 'official income' or an 'egret'. The device is used in Malay, Korean, and Japanese and in the last two it contains both native and Chinese units of measure. It is not unknown in Europe, where a unit of measurement may be placed before a material object, but in no language is the system so complete and strictly applied as in Chinese.

A second device is to place together two words with the same or similar sense, the meaning being that found in both. Thus $huan^1$-hsi^3 or hsi^3-$huan^1$ (double joy) means 'joy' or 'pleasure', $jên^4$-$shih^4$ (double know) means 'to know, cognition'. Two words may be used to give more precise definition, as $ming^2$-wu^4 (bright intelligence) 'talent, genius', $ming^2$-pai^2 (bright clear) 'to understand', or $tien^4$-pao^4 (lightning message) 'telegram'. More complex structures also exist. There are also monosyllables which merely receive a supporting prop, such as hai^2-$tzŭ^3$ 'child', $hsiang^1$-$tzŭ^3$ 'box'. When the context makes clear what the object is, one may omit one of these words, e.g. i^1-ko^4 $hsiao^3$ hai^2 'one (piece) small child'. The monosyllabic character of Chinese basic words is thus not in doubt, but the actual speech uses words of two or more syllables to express most concepts. Even 'mother' and 'father' are so expressed: mu^3-$ch'in^1$, fu^4-$ch'in^1$, though mu^3 and fu^4 refer to primary concepts and are readily used alone.

From the above it is clear that there is only one kind of derivation possible for a monosyllabic isolating language, namely juxtaposition. Fusion is prevented by the separability of the parts of the compound word. The device of juxtaposition is effective enough to provide Chinese with all the scientific and philosophical terms it requires. The only necessity is time enough to choose the terms and to determine what sense they are to take. Otherwise several different solutions may be offered for the same problem of expression.

A sequence of monosyllables each expressing a particular concept would be unintelligible for lack of interrelations. Chinese vocabulary therefore includes 'empty' words, viz. words which have their proper sense but are partly avoided to help to relate other words. These 'empty' words form little syntactic groups with their principals and are fully construed as such; they then enter into relations with other similarly constructed groups to form the sentence. Hence the suggestion that the isolating languages should be called 'grouping languages' (*lingue aggruppanti*, *langues groupantes*). The only objection to raise is that all languages form *syntagmata*, but the process is certainly a significant one for Chinese. It is also characteristic that Chinese readily places such groups in absolute position, since otherwise it would not be tolerable to construct a long sentence of monosyllables. Finally, it must be admitted that some of the 'empty' words have lost their tone and are veritable agglutinations. There are more of these in Burmese, which has what may be described as a declension. The suffixed particles become voiced (e.g. *ko/lu-go*). In Tibetan the agglutinative process is still more marked.

As for the dissyllabic isolating languages of Malaya and Polynesia, they show a certain capacity for derivation by means of affixes and there is less reason why juxtaposition should not develop into fusion. Thus there is juxtaposition in Malay *orang hutan* 'man of the wood, aboriginal' but fusion in Samoan *vaitusi* 'ink' ('water'+'write'). There is also a limited amount of derivation by affixes in Malay: *kata* 'saying, utterance'/*pěrkataan* 'a saying, word', *kunchup* 'closing' (of a flower)/*kěmunchup* 'sensitive plant', *guroh*/*gěmuroh* 'thunder', *gigi*/*gěrigi*/*gěrigis* 'serrated' (*gigi* 'teeth').

In an agglutinative language like Turkish the 'full' and 'empty' words of Chinese correspond to words (or stems) and suffixes. The suffixes have the phonetic consistency of words, which is not the case in the semiagglutinative or semiflexional languages of the Finno-Ugric group, but they do not occur as autonomous words and their dependence is accentuated by vowel harmony. As a result of vowel harmony, suffixes differ formally from the stems by being capable of variation, as Turk. pl. *-ler/lar* in *evler* 'houses'/*çocuklar* 'children', *sicağim* 'I am hot'/*soğuğum* 'I am cold', -*im*/-*im*/-*um*/-*üm* 'my', &c. The stem is a word in *ev* 'house' but only a stem in *sev-* 'to love', since the verbal stems do not appear separately. The distinction of verb and noun seems generally held: *ser* 'head'/*ser-mek* 'to spread on the ground'; *sev-mek* 'to love' *sev-im* 'I love'. Turkish stems are mostly monosyllabic, but comparison with Mongolian suggests that they were originally longer: Turk. *dağ* 'mountain'/Mongol *dabaga* 'mountain pass'.

To the noun or the verbal stem one must reckon in a Turkish word all possible combinations of relational suffixes. Thus *ev* 'house' implies the existence of *evi evin eve evde evden evler*, &c., with the suffixes of declension, and *evim* with those of possession. There are also derivative suffixes such as give *evli* 'married = having house', *evermek* 'to give in marriage', and by fusion one gets *evkadini* 'housewife'. These constitute new words. But Turkish seems to have made little use of its powers of derivation, being content to borrow from Arabic or Persian the words which played no part in the life of pastoral nomads. In more recent times there have been heavy borrowings from French and Italian. In Quechua (polysynthetic and agglutinative) derivatives are freely made by the fusion of basic stems (*Pachacamac* 'Creator'); suffixes lack phonetic sufficiency.

The most remarkable feature of Turkish and, in general, of agglutinative languages is the power of piling suffix on suffix. The principal concept is sufficiently defined by going first, and what follows is subordinated. The order of succession is prescribed and is slightly different from the order used in Mongolian. A new series may be built upon the basis of some derived form. Thus there is no difficulty in interpreting *sev-in-dir-il-me-mek* 'not to be made to love one another'[1] or *düş-düğ-üm-den* 'from my having fallen, because I fall' (*düş-mek* 'to fall'+*dük* of the past participle+*üm* first person possessive+-*den* ablative of cause). By this means subordination is obtained through participial constructions and the sentences themselves are all on one principal plane.

Though the Turkish word is equipped with suffixes which entirely account for its syntactical relations and might dispense with order, the Turkish sentence is in fact strictly bound, the verb being last. The same happens in Japanese despite the suffixes of case and the full conjugation of verbs. In Japanese and Korean the

[1] Cited by G. Murray, *Greek Studies*, Oxford, 1946, p. 174.

adjective is conjugated. In Turkish the predicated adjective is in effect conjugated because the verb 'to be' is a suffix, as *soğuk-tur* 'it is cold'. Not merely the adjective, but any predicate is thus conjugated in Turkish, e.g. *bir kuştur* 'it is a bird'.[1]

The Bantu group of languages may be classed as agglutinative but with reliance on prefixes rather than suffixes. The unit of meaning is a stem initially incomplete. When of two syllables it is complete as to meaning (*-lima* 'hill' *-toto* 'child') but incomplete as to form since it requires the prefixes of its class: Swahili *kilima* '(thing) hill', *mtoto* '(human) child' or *kitoto* '(thing or diminutive) child'. Monosyllables are felt to be incomplete as to form and meaning. As to form, they carry their prefixes when dissyllables drop them in the flexions of verbs. As to meaning, *-tu* in *mtu* 'man' and *kitu* 'thing' derives meaning from the prefixes themselves.

The words of the two flexional families are very different. Those of Semitic are unusually easy to define. They are each one of the recognized forms of a three-consonant root, since each of these permutations may be inflected to express relations within the sentence. This system is more rudimentary in Ancient Egyptian, Coptic, and Berber, and in the eastern branch of the Hamitic family (between the Nile and the Red Sea) there is evidence for a system based on two consonants only. Thus with the immense provision of permutations for each three-consonant root there is no need in Semitic to develop the word-building processes characteristic of our European languages.

In languages of European type words imply the whole of their paradigms, the declensions of nouns and the conjugations of verbs. Though this may make for an enormous mass of forms where there is a number of declensions and conjugations, there is a definite limit to the number of shapes a word may take. The postpositions of agglutinative languages are unlimited. When they retain their phonetic identity, as in Turkish, this causes little inconvenience, but when as in Quechua they are themselves phonetically insufficient, the task of analysing a polysynthetic mass is arduous. The European word is a contour on the line of speech which varies at the end and occasionally in the middle: *foot feet, hand hands, bid bade bidden, vinco vici victus, πείθω πέποιθα ἔπιθον, dominus domini domino, lego legis legit*, &c. Initial variation is much less common. It is characteristic of the Celtic languages, e.g. Welsh *Bangor/ym*

---

[1] Examples from A. C. Mowle, *The New Turkish*, London, 1942.

Mangor, gardd/dy ardd 'thy garden'. But initial changes are for the most part effected by prefixes which make new words from old ones. There is only one infix *-n-*: *iungo/iugum* 'yoke', so that the mutations which are part of the being of a single word are generally suffixed.

But a characteristic of these suffixes is their insufficiency. Consonant fuses with consonant and vowel with vowel, and vowels and consonants mutually interact. Suffixes may be parts of the stem as *ov-i-* 'sheep' or relational as *ovi-s ovi-m* or derivational as *ovi-lia* 'sheep-fold'. With the rapid evolution of the Indo-European languages they readily lose their identity as in *oves*, which seems to have as stem *ov-*. Hence the assertion that our stems are theoretical; the true stem requires so much reconstruction. The relational signs are brief and arbitrary and they are readily lost. The Latin *-m* was silent and Romance *ove* was reinforced to give it substance in *ovicula* 'little sheep, sheep'. While *-iculu/a* had substance enough to serve as a diminutive, its reason for existence is not so plain with us. President Harding's misnomer *normalcy* is a famous example of such confusion, since the required suffix was *-ity* (normality) and *-cy* is detached from *-ancy, -iency*, or *fan-cy* (*-sia*). False divisions of words have occurred at all times in the history of our family of languages.

At any time some of these suffixes are dead and others still active. New words are formed from the active suffixes, but the quiescent ones are not recognized as suffixes and are not used to modify basic nouns. The list of suffixes in use seems a haphazard affair compared with the ample provision shown in Semitic or the clear association of form and meaning in Turkish, but they have the effect of placing every word in a family which is partly realized and partly *in posse*. Dictionaries list the words which have reputable authority behind them, but not necessarily all the words in use and still less the potential members of a family. Yet if one of these is spoken hearers have little difficulty in identifying the basic concept and the particular nuance intended. It is a frequent experience to understand a word never heard before or to think of a word and find it has no support in the dictionary.

Successful innovation calls into existence words which are *in posse* and therefore in agreement with the genius of the language. Resistance to innovation or welcome varies considerably at different periods. In highly creative epochs new words are welcome for their freshness. There are times, like the early Renaissance, in which the welcome is limited to useful and necessary terms. In the later Renaissance new words were sought out for their dignity or their relation to the resources of Latin, but care was taken to give them an appearance in conformity with current linguistic taste. In the late Renaissance words were called into being for merely decorative purposes and not necessarily designed to become part of the normal language of speakers. In all cases, however, the word was understood by its place in the family group and by its agreement with the expectations of the hearers. Our languages, therefore, though their methods are disorderly, are well equipped to expand and meet new needs.

The study of word-formation (*Wortbildungslehre*) occupies a considerable part of historical grammars, though it is not often possible to get beyond an arbitrary catalogation of symbols. There is an easy path from derivational affixes to relational ones, e.g. from -*si*- as a desiderative suffix to its use as the suffix of the future tense. On the other hand the variability of words due to the effects of fusion has relevance to the problem of the phoneme when the variation is reduced to vowels and consonants. From Welsh *pen* 'head', *dy ben, fy mhen* we obtain a variable phonetic unit p-/b-/mh- which has no effect on the significance of the word. From Polish *noga* 'foot' *nodze* (dat. loc.) we get an equation of meaning nog- $=$ $nodz$- or a variation g/dz without significant effect. Since Common Slavonic times (the tenth century) gi has been reintroduced so that g and dz are considered to be separate sounds, but in the earlier period dz or z was the sound necessarily assumed by g before e, i. The fusional character of our languages is thus a principal cause of the complications of phonematic theory.

THE MEANING OF MEANING

'A word is created to express thought. What is the relation uniting it with the idea it symbolises? Up to what point do changes of meaning reflect a history of thought?' Thus Arsène Darmesteter[1] defined in 1885 a series of problems which affect philosophers, linguists, psychologists, and sociologists alike, and which linguists are best equipped to approach in the last form. Their positive science is suited to observing changes, though change is not, as Darmesteter seems to suggest, the most important consideration

[1] A. Darmesteter, *La vie des mots*, Paris, 1946, p. 25.

concerning meanings. The need for change may be limited to words themselves and imply little or nothing concerning thought or society. Classification of observed changes of meaning was carried to so high a pitch of perfection by Michel Bréal in his *Sémantique* (Paris, 1897) that no definitive advances have been registered later nor even seem to be in sight. But his work leaves the primary problem unsolved, namely, how do arbitrary noises mean anything and in what way do they correspond to anything? We are here, as Darmesteter observed, faced with a problem of creation, and specifically of artistic creation. The medium is quite unlike the object and it is generally held that the results are inadequate. Since the 'attention of philosophers was called to the remarkable fact of language', they have scrutinized meaning with more and more fervour in the hope of reaching some understanding of reality. They have the right to reject or rearrange meanings if it helps their purpose. This right is not given to the linguist, though he may have to thank philosophers for the verbal acuteness of their discriminations and may have to accept their verbal preferences if these establish themselves in the common language. He is concerned rather to set forth the meanings normally or exceptionally attributed to each word and to understand how they come together in one place. He must know whether they are continuous or discontinuous and whether comprehension is due to reference to some dominant sense or is no more than the sum of all the contexts in which a word appears. In the series

$$\text{A} \quad \text{B} \quad \underbrace{\text{C} \quad \text{D} \quad \text{E}} \quad \text{F}$$
$$a \quad b \quad x \quad p \quad q,$$

in which *a* and *b* are words corresponding to realia A and B, but *x* corresponds fully and uniquely to C D E , while *p* and *q* correspond to aspects of F but not completely nor uniquely, the philosopher is concerned with the aids or obstacles to a true understanding offered by the words *a b x p q*, while the linguist is concerned with the historical causes leading to disconformity between the sign and the thing signified: why *x* should have assumed a wide range and why F should be represented only by aspects.

The classical solution of this problem lay in finding τὸ ἔτυμον, the genuine nature of the word which was also supposed to be its first sense. Thus Isidore of Seville entitled his encyclopaedia *Originum sive etymologiarum libri*. In would-be *etyma* consonants counted for little and vowels for nothing at all and as historical statements the *etyma* are hilarious rather than instructive. Of such are γυνή 'woman' from γονή 'offspring', ἄνθρωπος 'man' from ὁ ἀναθρῶ[ν ἃ ὄπω]πεν 'one who looks up at what he sees', St. Isidore's association of *sol* and *solus*, and the famous *lucus a non lucendo*. But it is worth remembering that the objective was not history but definition of essential meaning and that the last-named recognized by chance a real relation, viz. *lucus* is a clearing in a wood and hence a wood with open spaces. It comes from the root *leuk/louk-* (cf. *lux lumen luceo*).

The modern science of etymology is a strict analytical discipline designed to reveal the oldest possible forms of words and the tree of their genealogy. The arrangement may be under the *etymon*, as in R. Trautmann's *Baltisch-Slavisches Wörterbuch*, or under the primary words of a language, as in A. Walde's *Lateinisches etymologisches Wörterbuch*. In the former case it is possible to set down hypothetical forms not greatly differing from those in use in the Baltic tongues and so to keep the exposition in the historical order of succession. In the latter case the *etyma* are conjectural and are discussed at the end of each article after the available evidence is placed on record. In the introduction to his *Etymological Dictionary of the English Language* (1898), W. W. Skeat laid down ten canons for those who would explain the formation of English words.[1]

This science is the basis of all sound historical linguistics, since it establishes sure equations and refutes false or 'popular' etymologies. On the basis of information supplied by etymology it is possible to trace the development of the sounds of a language, and where sure equations cannot be established, as in Sino-Tibetan, investigation reaches a dead end. But this modern science contributes more to phonology than to the understanding of meaning. There is no similar assurance from the comparison of meanings though some of the secondary ones disappear when the oldest evidence is considered. The best that can be done is to offer as general a range as possible in order to include as many as possible of the subsequent acceptations. The modern science of etymology does not, and does not profess to, offer an answer to the problem of the meaning of meaning.

This is a problem of name-giving, since even verbal activities are named. There is some evidence to show that names are given

[1] Article 'Etymology', *Encyclopaedia Britannica* (11th ed.).

in an off-handed fashion with little regard to propriety. Thus the
American 'robin' is a bird of the size of a thrush with a faint red
flush on the breast and a habit of hopping round gardens. There
is no real robin in the U.S.A., but in calling their native bird a
robin the settlers cannot have been influenced by a wish to express
its real nature. The conditions present were the absence of true
robins, a slight resemblance of colour and habits, and welcome for
a bird which resembled in some way those of the old country. In
the northern parts of South America the condor is called *galli-
nazo/aza* 'big male or female hen'. *Gallo* 'cock' was excluded on
sight, for the drooping attitude of the birds is more hen-like, and
they have no crest or wattles. Apart from those facts there is no
propriety in the word. *Tanks* as armoured vehicles were so named
because the word gave no indication of the thing. It is also our
practice to describe our emotions incompletely and sometimes by
their less important part. We sit at table to partake of a substantial
meal but sit *behind* a table to administrate. We go *to* the counter as
clients and *behind* the counter as dealers or by favour of the dealer.
Between what is sold *over* the counter and what is sold *under* the
counter there is an ethical difference left unexpressed.

   Our words are at times marked by evasiveness, misdirection, and
furtiveness. ' "Convey" the wise call it' said Autolycus concerning
theft and rogues. Lest when we speak of the devil he should come
we refer to *Old Nick*, *Auld Clootie*, Rum. *necuratul* 'the sloven',
Sp. *el Pecado* 'sin'. The host of the damned or the ancient gods of
the earth are called *brownies, the little people, the good folk*, or OSp.
estantigua 'the ancient host', and the furies in Aeschylus' play
change their name at Athens to *Eumenides* 'the kindly ones'. Since
knowledge of the name gives power over the thing, it was important
to conceal the name of a god. *Baal* 'lord' and *Melkarth* 'prince of
the city' are titles only; *Jehovah* is written with the vowels of
Adonai to conceal the true name, which seems to have been *Yahweh*.
For similar reasons a Chinese emperor's name was made taboo
during his lifetime. A Polynesian chief can put out of use any word
and decree the employment of another. There are also words
proper only for chiefs. In Australia the initiation ceremonies are
said to consist largely of instruction that what has been called one
name is really known by another, and this information is kept
jealously for adult males. The name of a dangerous animal is
avoided. *Bear* means no more than 'wild beast' (Lat. *fera*) and in

Slavonic the word is attenuated to 'honey-eater' (Russ. *medved'*). The *wolf* is the beast that tears (Lat. *vellere*) but the same account is given of *vulpis* 'fox'. Since evil omens come from the left, that name is constantly changing: *sinister, gauche, izquierdo,* εὐώνυμος 'of a good name'.

The effects of fashion, prudery, deprecation, and humour combine to keep vocabulary unstable. When the *calceae* (Fr. *chausses*) began to extend up the leg from the heel (*calx*) in the form of tight hose, they drove out the older loose *bracae* (Fr. *braies*) and could be divided into *haut-de-chausses* and *bas-de-chausses*. The loose *pantalon* superseded the *haut-de-chausses* leaving only the *bas* as stockings. In Spanish *calzas* remain, with *calzado* for 'shoes' and *medias* for stockings. Our Victorian grandparents did not think legs nice, and preferred *limbs* clad in *unmentionables*. The word *arm* originally meant 'shoulder-joint' (Lat. *armus,* Gk. ἁρμός 'joint'), but Fr. *bras,* Sp. *brazo* is from *bracchium* 'the lower arm'. Words for 'foot' are steady except for Russ. *noga* ('claw'), but those for 'hand' vary: *làmh, manus,* χείρ, *ruka, dorë, jeřk', kara*. The cause of change was probably dissatisfaction with the expressiveness of the term; words for 'find' show the same dissatisfaction: *invent* (come into), *discover* (take the cover off), Russ. *nachodit'* (step on). Fr. *jambe* 'leg' must be connected with *jambon* 'ham', and Sp. *pierna* with *pernil* 'hog, ham'. Words for 'head' are unstable: *caput, cabeza* (little head), *tête* (potsherd), κεφαλή, *krye, golova* (skull, bald head). The humorous effect of Russ. *golova* is continued in *noga* 'foot' (from 'claw') and *zub* 'tooth' (from 'nail', cf. Alb. *dhemp* 'tooth', Gk. γόμφος 'nail').

Thus the etyma of words tell us much of their history and sometimes suggest the speakers' motives but they do not enlighten us on the subject of true natures of things. On the other hand the etymologizing habit goes far beyond the limits set by scientific investigators. Speakers arrange their words in classes according to their apparent resemblance, which may or may not be historically valid. Popular or folk etymology enters at this point and converts Fr. *écrevisse,* for instance, into *cray-fish,* or *samblind* (semi-blind) into *sand-blind* 'afflicted with partial blindness, in which particles of sand seem to flow before the eyes!' There is constant reference back to the supposed or real *etymon* to determine the 'real' sense of a word. Each class of words enters into relations of sound and meaning with other classes, so that a word's meaning must be defined from synonyms, antonyms, and habitual contexts. For instance, *great* is defined as reference to *grand, huge, magnificent, well-born, intelligent* and with reference to *little, petty, humble, poor, stupid*; it has also to be known in such combinations as *great heart, great-aunt, great Anna, great awk, Great Missenden, great-souled, greatcoat, the great unwashed, the great, great traitors*.

The meaning of a word can only be the sum of its contexts. Etymology cannot do more than help towards an historical statement which will show that some meanings are older than others. Each word presents a spectrum of meanings, but it has been suggested that these can all be placed under the rule of a dominant meaning. This would seem not too difficult in the case of words referring to concrete objects and happenings. *Cat, wild cat, great cats, cat-walk, cat's cradle, catamount* can no doubt be referred to the dominant *felis domesticus*, though the second excludes the domestic variety and the third excludes all true cats, while the fourth is probably learnt by most as a technical term independent of the notion of cat. With *table* more difficulties arise. Speakers are not troubled by the physicist's two tables, the one for his papers and the other a field of force, nor by the metaphysician's inquiry how we know a table is a table. But in *table, groaning table* (heaped with food), *littered table* (with papers on it), *table of contents, time-table, laid on the table of the House*, and other contexts part of the meaning derives from *tabula* 'a board' while other parts refer to a 'smooth flat slab or board with legs' (Gk. τράπεζα). In fact there are two dominant meanings, the one derived from the Latin *tabula* and the other from the substitution of *tabula* for *mensa*. Similarly, J. Orr has shown that some meanings of French *aimer* are due to Latin *amare*, others to *aestimare*, OFr. *esmer*. Spanish *venir con una explicación* implies an attempt to impose an explanation, *salir con* implies improvisation. These are distant consequences of a distinction between 'coming with' and 'coming out with'. Prayer-Book English uses *prevent us in all our doings* ('go before' = 'help'), but in present-day English *prevent* means 'hinder'. The older context is no longer found in colloquial speech. On the other hand, we speak of *reaching* a *lowered target*, though a target lowered below the butts for checking hits cannot be reached by any marksman. But with the more abstract types of words doubt concerning a dominant meaning increases. An adjective is conditioned by its substantive, as *black face, blackboard, Black Maria, black Monday, black disaster*.

Both are parts of a compound noun and incomplete in themselves, and if 'a white horse is not a horse', it is not 'whiteness' either. For *nice* the *etymon* is Lat. *nescius* 'ignorant', whence OFr. *nice* 'foolish, simple'. From that come, according to *Chambers's Dictionary*, 'foolishly simple, very particular, hard to please, fastidious, marking or taking notice of every small difference, done with great care and exactness, accurate, easily injured, delicate, agreeable, delightful'. That such a list of meanings lacks a dominant sense is evidenced by the unlike senses of the abstract nouns corresponding to the adjective: *nicety* and *niceness*.

Sometimes a word may be defined by its opposites. A *good baby* is not a *disobedient* baby; but, since babies are not morally responsible for their actions, one cannot speak of a vicious baby. A *good man* is not a *vicious* man, though he might be disobedient to authority for good reasons. Contrariwise, a *silly child* is not the same as a *silly man*. The first is presumably *acting* silly, the other is silly by character. The difference lies in the presumption that character is still unformed in the child, but fixed for an adult. The context determines the meaning of these adjectives.

That it is an error to attempt to reduce all the meanings of a word to one dominant seems to be proved by Fr. *occuper une place* and *occuper un ouvrier*.[1] Two quite different operations are involved; but there is a middle term *s'occuper d'une œuvre* to make the transition. It is related by metaphor to *occuper une place* (from to 'occupy a seat' with to 'occupy oneself with a piece of work') but literally, by change of person, to *occuper un ouvrier*. *Occuper une charge* is literally of the same form as *occuper une place*, but it is impossible that *charge* could in this context have the sense of a 'load'. The meaning of the words shifts along a spectrum according to the context. This shiftiness has caused *courtisan* and *courtisane* to diverge subtly but definitively. The triconsonantal roots of Semitic languages formally forbid explaining identity of sound and difference of sense by homophony, but the series of meanings are hard or impossible to relate to a dominant: e.g. Arab. *kalaba* 'spared, sewed, barked like a dog' or *kalb* 'dog, pivot of a mill stone, hook, streak on a horse's back'. In Arab. *ghamma* 'screened, covered, veiled, hid, was unintelligible, musician, was hot, had long hair, was abundant' we have another such spectrum with a possible dominant sense of 'covered', but with extremes which are far removed from each other.

[1] Ch. Bally, *Le langage et la vie*, Zurich, 1935, p. 97.

On the other hand the analysis of situation may be carried to different degrees of detail. The variety of possible things is, according to Locke,[1] always greater than means of expression in a vocabulary. Density of vocabulary varies according to the interests of the speakers and of the society they belong to. The Javanese are said to have ten ways of standing and twenty of sitting.[2] In exogamic societies degrees of blood-relationship are expressed to four generations in either direction and on both sides of the family. A relic of that state is found in Lat. *patruus* 'father's brother'/*avunculus* 'mother's brother'. But the usefulness of the distinction was lost, and Sp. *tío tía* It. *zio zia* were drawn from Gk. θεῖος/θεῖα, which described both, while Fr. *oncle tante* Eng. *uncle aunt* represent an improper generalization of *avunculus* and *amita*. Germ. *essen* and *fressen* occupy the same space as Eng. *eat*. Unhappily we have cause to distinguish *kill slay slaughter murder massacre decimate annihilate liquidate execute exterminate*, &c. These words occupy, with their antonyms, an intersecting range or semantic area[3] of such a nature that while some of them exclude others there are intersections throughout the group and an area is thereby defined.

In accordance with the diagram on p. 10 sentences refer to events and words to 'things' in the events. For the sake of pictorial convenience the event was shown externally, but it may be an event of the mind and its 'things' may be things of the mind. 'Material objects and sensible phenomena are not the only things to which we can refer; we can talk equally well about abstractions, about feelings or about creations of the imagination. . . . A sample of genuine speech which does not deal with some 'thing' is impossible to conceive.'[4] The things are not illusory since they can form part of different sentences, and the same sentence can, on different occasions, refer to different things. But they may be unreal as

---

[1] J. Locke, *Essay on the Human Understanding*, iii. 3, sect. 2–4.

[2] E. Cassirer, *Philosophie der symbolischen Formen*, Berlin, 1923, p. 148.

[3] A combination of the notion of semantic area with etymology is the foundation, as I suppose, of E. Juret's *Dictionnaire étymologique grec et latin*, Mâcon, 1942. Our traditional rules of etymology refer to, say, 3000 B.C., a period when occlusive consonants formed three or four orders (*p b bh ph*?, &c.) and vowels and diphthongs were mutually exclusive. But this phonematic condition is not universal, and when Greek and Latin words are collected in semantic areas, they show correspondences of sense not predicted by traditional etymology. These may be due to some older phonematic arrangement less differentiated than that of the time of the dispersion of Indo-European speakers.

[4] A. H. Gardiner, *Speech and Language*, Oxford, 1932 (1951), p. 22.

centaur or their reality may have been gathered slowly from their contexts. Thus Monsignor Knox is surely at fault in treating *righteousness* as a 'meaningless token'.[1] The contexts he enumerates are 'with regard to man, innocence or honesty or uprightness or charitableness or dutifulness or (very commonly) the fact of being in God's good books. Used of God, it could mean the justice which punishes the sinner or, quite as often, the faithfulness which protects the good; it could mean also the approval with which God looks on those who are in his good books.' But these contexts define and bring into being a 'thing' which could be predicated of both God and man (though in ways which differ by the difference of their natures), which is inclusive of certain other predicates and expresses them as a certain kind of God-man relation.

The meaning as the diagram shows (p. 10) is different from the thing meant. The meaning is part of the expression but the thing meant is part of the event. Sir A. H. Gardiner has insisted on this distinction and on the purposive nature of meaning. It was a word at first used only of persons. The speaker intended something and aimed at producing an effect by means of symbols concerted with the hearer. The French *veut dire* and Spanish *quiere decir* show this role of the will; while *significare* has a demonstrative value, as of a meaning which calls someone's attention to something. F. de Saussure's account of *signifiant/signifié* was perhaps intended to give the same impression, but it suggests rather too much the two sides of one abstract notion. The meaning of *religion* is distinct from the 'thing-meant' *religion*; the former is purposive pointing, but the latter is a thing 'which could create saints and inquisitors'.

With the assertion of 'things' the linguist enters into the field of other specialists, though he is not, as a linguist, bound to produce proof of the existence or define the nature of things. It is enough that things have sufficient objectivity to serve for reference in discourse. There is an intense philosophic debate on meaning now raging; it seems to pass by or over the linguist's problems.[2] It

---

[1] R. Knox, *On Englishing the Bible*, London, 1949, p. 10.

[2] M. Black, *Language and Philosophy*, Cornell, 1949; A. G. N. Flew, *Logic and Language*, Oxford, 1951; R. Carnap, *Introduction to Semantics*, Harvard, 1948; R. Carnap, *Meaning and Necessity*, Chicago, 1947; C. K. Ogden and I. A. Richards, *The Meaning of Meaning*, London, 1923; A. Korzybski, *Science and Sanity*, New York, 2 ed., 1941. S. Ullmann, *The Principles of Semantics*, Glasgow, 1951, deals with the whole meaningful aspect of Language from the standpoint of philology.

by-passes formal speech for it admits that this may be valid for its own purposes within its loose structure. The stricter language of philosophy is a separate idiom which does not seek to take the place of ordinary conversation. Philosophy passes over the linguist's problems in logical positivism when it construes words as logical terms and occupies itself with metalanguage. Claims to replace grammar within its own field by some other science were made by Messrs. Ogden and Richards; they proclaimed in *The Meaning of Meaning* that psychology was ready to deliver a new science of symbolism. The fundamental situation is represented as 'thought or reference' in relation on the one side to a 'referent' and on the other to a symbol. The referent is the result of interpreting signs, past interpretations being lodged in the thought as 'engrams'. If the thought is adequate to the referent and the symbol is correctly chosen, then the symbol is true of the referent. The philosophical difficulties of this account of interpretation are expressed by M. Black (op. cit., pp. 195 ff.). The first Canon of Symbolism is that 'one symbol stands for one and only one referent'. This may be a desideratum, but it hardly agrees with the polysemic nature of language. The attempt to satisfy this canon is made by the author's invention of Basic, the vocabulary of which is as far as possible *monosemic*; but Basic is not an actual language, but a deformation of English.

INCREASE OF WORDS

Basic stems are those which at the limit of vision cannot be resolved into simpler stems. The limit of vision is in many instances very close to the present time. In other cases words of a specially atomic type, as in Chinese, offer sturdy resistance to decomposition. In the most favourable examples—the Indo-European and Hamito-Semitic speech families—our knowledge goes back some 5,000 years to stems which cannot be analysed into combinations of other stems (though they may be reduced to roots), but which must have been affected by formative processes extending over the 50,000 or more years of unknown linguistic history. Of that period we have only adumbrations in the study of roots or the theory of the formation of stems. These roots and solutions are abstractions taking the place of some probable real condition which cannot be adequately brought into focus. Yet another approach to this problem is to gather basic words into semantic areas. The formal resemblances then brought into view include some which traditional etymology has hitherto disallowed.

But in addition to basic stems every language has taken measures for the increase of its vocabulary by means of word-building or borrowing or shift of meanings. Word-building is carried out by composition (juxtaposition or fusion), by mutation, and by derivation (with the use of prefixes, infixes, or suffixes). Shifts of meaning include extention or restriction of sense, shift from one sense to a neighbouring one, substitution, metaphor, and petrified clauses. Most languages use most of these resources, but they show highly characteristic preferences for one device or another.

The invariability of the Chinese word would seem to make additions to the lexicon difficult, but in fact the language is infinitely resourceful. This is due to the facilities for making juxtaposed compounds. Two or more words may be placed together to give a meaning which is *that* of them both singly (i^1-*shang*^{1} 'clothes'), or in which one serves as a prop (i^3-*tzŭ* 'chair'), or the sense is derived from the common characteristics of the two constituents without being wholly present in either (*ming*^{2}-*pai*^{2} 'understand' from 'clear' and 'white'), or there is a syntactical relation (*ming*^{2}-*wu*^{4} 'talent, genius' from 'clear'+'notice', 'understand'; *ho*^{2}-*shi*^{3}-*lan*^{2}-*tzŭ* 'laundry-basket' from 'basket for washing clothes in a river'). There is no fusion in these Chinese compounds, though there may be transactions with regard to tone and stress. With these resources at hand Chinese is not required to use derivational techniques. On the other hand, Chinese has not hesitated to borrow from other languages, especially during the hasty period of acclimatization of Buddhist vocabulary. The condition imposed is that the foreign words be divided into Chinese syllables (*p'o*^{2}-*lo*^{2}-*mên*^{2} *chao*^{4} 'Brahmin religion', *o*^{1}-*mi*^{2}-*t'o*^{2} *fo*^{2} 'Amitabha Buddha', *lo*^{4}-*han*^{4} 'arhat'). Not all the syllables of the original are preserved (as in Amita(bha) Budd(ha) just cited).

In other languages of the Sino-Tibetan group the alphabets are of Indian type and writing is continuous not only throughout the word but throughout the whole line. It is thus not at once obvious whether Burmese *yedwin* 'will', *kyetma* 'hen' or *pongyi* 'priest, bonze' is monosyllabic or dissyllabic, whereas Chinese *t'ao*^{3}-*fan*^{4}-*ti* 'beggar' is revealed as monosyllabic by the isolating nature of the script. There is a certain amount of derivation visible in Burmese, Tibetan, and Siamese, with the use of a characteristic device:

infixing a consonant after the first consonant of a word. Variations
in words denoted by a single Chinese character probably result
from an archaic use in Chinese of this derivational device.

While no language is without resources for the increase of
vocabulary, some put restrictions on their native processes. Among
these the most prominent is perhaps Turkish. The Turanians who
dwell on the steppes of south-western Asia follow a mode of life
which involves great skill and precision in herding, horsemanship,
camping, and so on, but which has not changed over the centuries
and falls within strict limits of civilization. Their kin who have
conquered Asia Minor at first destroyed the urban civilization for
which they had no use, and then confined their interest to war and
government. The higher terms of culture they were content to
borrow from Arabic and Persian, and those of modern mechanical
civilization and commerce from Italian and French. Thus Turkish
native resources remain much what they were upon the open
steppes. There are some fusions such as *kurukluyildiz* 'comet'
(*kuruk* 'tail' *yildiz* 'star'), *sonbahar* 'autumn' (*son* 'late, end'+Pers.
bahár 'spring'). There are also some derivatives like *kurt* 'worm',
kurtlanmak 'become maggoty, be agitated', *kurtlù* 'maggoty, uneasy'; *kurşun* 'lead, bullet', *kurşūnī* 'lead-coloured', *kurşunlamak*
'to cover with lead'. This failure to develop native resources is not
something inherent in agglutinative languages, since composition
by fusion is readily used in tongues as geographically remote as
Finnish and Quechua: Finn. *sanakirja* 'dictionary' from *sana*
'word'+*kirja* 'book', *merenkulku* 'navigation' from *meri* 'sea'+
kulku 'march, course', *pantinantaja* 'mortgager' from *pantti* (Germ.
Pfand) 'mortgage'; Quechua employs fusion and suffixes: *puma-
cancha* 'lion-house' from *cancha* 'place, enclosure', *camani* 'to
create', *camac* 'creator', *Pachacamac* 'creator of the world', *camasca*
'creation', *camarini* 'to prepare, arrange'. The Turkish phenomenon
is one of instinctive restriction.

A parallel is offered by Latin and the Romance languages and
by English since the Norman Conquest. Horace's mockery of
sesquipedalia verba expresses the Augustan aversion from such
compounds as Ennius was willing to employ and which form a
considerable part of the Greek lexicon. Derivation tended to be
restricted to the use of prefixes and a limited number of lively
suffixes, and the limits of parts of speech were not to be lightly
overstepped. The demand for uniformity made by the modern

Latin languages imposes limits on their welcome to foreign words. It is relatively simple to adapt to Spanish uses either French or Italian words, but hard to pass on English vocabulary, which remains strange in form and refractory to Latin types of word-building. Composition is a resource reluctantly used in French but freely in German, Dutch, and the Scandinavian languages. It was also common in old English from which we have such survivals as *sword-bearer*, *sixtyfold*, *neighbourhood* (OEng. *nēa-wist*), *island*, though we have lost *ǣrist* 'resurrection', *eorþ-fæst* 'firm in the earth', *rīp-tīma* 'harvest' (reaping-time), *siġe-fæst* 'victorious', *tēon-rǣden* 'humiliation'. This loss was redeemed by a notable readiness to accept first French and then Latin words instead of attempting native compounds, and to use these foreign elements with native freedom: from *false* we have *falsely*, *falsehood*, *falseness*, as if the basic word were native English, while from the native *husband, yeoman, outlaw* we have obtained *husbandry, yeomanry, outlawry* by means of the French suffix -*ry*. Other such suffixes are -*ess* -*age*, -*ance* -*able*.[1] English-speakers have shown since the Conquest an extreme willingness to accept foreign words from any quarter, coupled with, on the whole, an aversion from the method of composition. At the same time we have an unusual wealth of formative elements, since we draw on English, French, Latin, and Greek for our derivations.

In the Common Slavonic tongue there was a notable lack of those compounds which give solemnity and elegance to Vedic Sanskrit and Homeric Greek. There was no lack of capacity to form them. Russ. *medved'* 'bear' ('honey-eater') is of the required type. Slavonic names in heathen times were compounded like those of ancient Greek (*Svjatoslav*, cf. *Agathocles*), and Christian Greek treatises were turned into Old Bulgarian with no hesitation about transcribing the Greek compounds (*archangelŭ*) or translating them into Slavonic equivalents (*jedinojestistvinŭ* = ὁμοούσιος 'of like being'). The earlier lack of compounds was probably due to the preoccupation of the common Slavonic folk with the primary business of agriculture and hunting, while at the same time their political and religious organization remained undeveloped or lost such elaboration as it may once have had as part of the Indo-European community.

Composition. The simplest kind of composition is total reduplica-

[1] F. Mossé, *Esquisse d'une histoire de la langue anglaise*, Paris, 1947, p. 93.

tion or gemination, as in Samoan *ti'eti'e* 'put', *tumutumu* 'top', *tusitusi* 'writer', *fa'amaumau* 'disappear', Quechua *ccapaccapalla* 'very cheerful', *cusicusi* 'spider'. Some specialization occurs when the gemination has semantic value, as for adjectives of colour in Samoan *sinasina* 'white', or to distinguish a collective from a plural composed of individuals as in Quechua *runaruna* 'crowd'/*runacuna* 'men', Chinese *jên²-jên²* 'mankind', or the adverbial use of *man⁴-man⁴-(ti)* 'slowly'. Gemination is found in English and similar languages chiefly in ideophones with change of initial consonants from voiceless to voiced or of vowels from front to back, as *huggermugger*, *hurleyburley*, *willynilly*, *sing-song*, *tick-tock*, Sp. *tiquismiquis*, *trochemoche*. As an affective device we find it in *wearily wearily*, *dear dear* for 'most wearily', 'very dear'.

Less naïve is partial reduplication. The initial is reduplicated with the aid of a conventional vowel in Lat. *sisto*/*stō*, Gk. ἵστημι 'stand', τίθημι 'put'. In this instance the effect seems to have been to give an impression of continuous action in present time. Gk. πέπονθα 'I have suffered' shows reduplication with the vowel *e* to make perfect tenses from noun-stems. In Mexican Aztec (Nahuatl) some plurals are formed by partial reduplication, as *teotl* 'god'/ *tetêo* 'gods'.

Juxtaposition is the formal method of the isolating languages such as Chinese. The resultant sense is due either to the common mean of each part, or to the separate contribution of each part. In the latter instance the principle is that which we have noted for adjectives. An adjective+noun or noun+noun makes a compound word which is not the same as either of its parts. *The White House* is a unique building in Washington and so is *La Casa Rosada* in Buenos Aires. But *a white house* is different from all houses not white and from all white objects not houses; jointly the two terms make the name of a new class of things. The two words may be in some syntactical relation, as Malay *orang utan* 'man of the woods' (genitive), Sp. *vaivén* 'agitation' (*va y viene* Fr. *va-et-vient*). In the Semitic languages a possessive noun is given a 'construct' form which attaches it closely to the name of thing possessed; there is a similar close association of the possessor and possessed in Pers. *kāghaz-e-mard* 'the man's letter'.

Juxtaposition and fusion cannot be distinguished when no change occurs, as in the typical Finnish compounds *sähkölamppu* 'electric lamp', *nerokas* 'wise', *epäsiveellinen* 'immoral'. Composition in

Malayo-Polynesian is of this sort; e.g. Samoan *matapeapea* 'greet', and in Quechua: *Pachacamac* 'creator of the world' (*Demiurge*). The inflected languages offer a higher degree of specialization in this respect because of their flexions. In a compound the bare stems appear and the flexion is added to the group. Thus the word within the fused group does not have the same aspect as when it stands alone, as in *hippopotamus*, *philanthropy*, *Archimedes*. Sometimes two words are given casual construction as in *Iphianassa* 'she who rules with might', *verisimilar* (*veri* gen. sg.). In Sp. *cazatorpedero* 'torpedo-boat destroyer' or *matasiete* 'swashbuckler' (kill seven) the verbs (*caza*, *mata*) might be abstract stems or in some finite form, but Sp. *correveidilo* 'tale-bearer' is certainly in a syntactic form with three imperatives (*corre, ve y dilo* 'run, see and tell it').

In the bureaucratic state of modern Russia a considerable number of new words have resulted not from the combination of other full words but from abbreviations and initials.[1] To what extent they may be regarded as established in the Russian language is not yet known. From time to time strong measures are taken to destroy them, but some may be ineradicable since they name organizations which will have at least a historical value. Some cannot be pronounced except by the aid of conventional vowels (*RKN*, *RSFSR*), others consist of initials only but have vowels (*VAI*, 'the old Russia association of engineers'), some are made from initial syllables (*narkom* 'people's commissar', *detkor* 'child correspondent') and yet others are mixed (*myzo* 'music department', *TRAM* 'theatre of working youths').

Derivation. By derivation a single basic stem is extended to form a family of related words. The methods are two: mutation of vowels and consonants and the use of affixes. The effect in each case is to create a family of words with a common basic sense and specific nuances indicated by conventional symbolization. A family exists *in esse* and *in posse*. Not all the symbols need be used; how many actually are employed depends on the use and wont of the given language. Those which exist *in posse* can be called into being to meet a temporary emergency. Whether they continue in use depends on whether they serve a generally felt want.

The device of mutation characterizes the Hamitic and Semitic languages but is especially developed in the latter. It is used along

---

[1] A. Bæcklund, *Die univerbierenden Verkürzungen der heutigen russischen Sprache*, Uppsala, 1940.

with affixation, but it excludes the possibility of composition and greatly restricts the need for, or feasibility of, borrowing foreign words. The arrangement of roots as formations of three consonants has been achieved with some arbitrariness, but the process has gone on for such a long time that it appears now to be the necessary way of analysing the Semitic lexicon. Given three consonants *f'l* the system is built up of vowel mutations such as *fa'l, fi'l, fu'l, fa'al, fā'il, fa'īl, af'al*, and consonant mutations like *fa''al, af'all*, together with the use of prefixes in *m '* and suffixes in *n '*. In addition there are verbal prefixes in *' t n 'st*, an infixed *t* and the tokens of the personal pronouns. There are 70 possible forms of the noun and 10 common and 6 less common forms of the verb, the latter complete with verbal nouns of agent, patient and action. The aorist and imperfect and passive forms of the verb differ by vowel mutation as if they were separate words, and 'broken' plurals (collectives) differ from the singulars in like manner. Some roots show little development: Arab. *sfk* exists in 2 verbal forms as I. *safaka* 'shed' VII. 'was shed', 1 verbal noun of the patient and 3 nominal forms 3 *sufk* 'hors d'œuvres', 25 *sufīk* 'poured out' (which is the verbal noun), and 28 *saffāk* 'shedder of blood, eloquent, liar'. From the last example it will be clear that shifts of meaning by metaphor or otherwise help to extend Arabic vocabulary. And in other instances it is far from obvious that a single basic sense is involved (e.g. *kalaba* 'spurred, said, barked like a dog'). From other stems, such as *frs*, a considerable number of forms are derived (7 verbs and 26 nouns or adjectives).

Mutation in the Indo-European tongues was based on an alternation of the vowels *e o* with the zero state of the root: **leip-/loip-/lip-*. The first represented continuous verbal activity, the second the act, and the third momentary action. Fom the second a perfect (past action resulting in a present state) was obtained by means of partial reduplication, and also new denominative verbs. These mutations seem to have come late in the common stage of these languages and to be opposed to more ancient and popular alternations such as *i/ī, u/ū*. They are associated with the rise of late thematic declensions and conjugations, i.e. those in which the stems end in *e/o*. Owing to the rapid evolution of Indo-European vowels these mutations remain recognizable only in Greek; elsewhere they give rise to irregularities of various sorts. The distinction between aspects of activity breaks down under the changes of vowel values;

in Slavonic, where conjugation continues to be based on verbal aspects, wide-reaching reorganization has occurred. In the end a new distinction has been effected by means of prefixes on the basis that the verb with prefix represents momentary activity. Some of these verbs answered to imperfective prefixless verbs; from perfective prefixed verbs new imperfectives were obtained by using the suffix -va-.

As for affixes they are either prefixed, suffixed, or infixed. Languages make highly characteristic use of these resources. There are only suffixes in Turkish to serve for derivation and grammatical relations. Comparatively few suffixes are used for the former purpose. In Quechua and Aymará (Bolivia) only suffixation is used alongside composition, but very elaborate word-families are built up.[1] In the Bantu languages a suffix -a with factitive value is probably to be seen in the final vowel of almost all verbs; it becomes -e in the subjunctive and -i in the habitual tense. In addition there are suffixes for aspects and moods, while persons and tenses are represented by prefixes. In the Indo-European languages prefixes and suffixes are employed with but one infix (-n- in Lat. iungo); it becomes a suffix in Old Bulg. dvignǫti 'move', Russ. dvinut' cf. dvigat'. The Indo-European prefixes were adverbial and could be used attached to the verb or separately. From the latter practice some of them developed into primary prepositions by becoming associated with nouns. Infixes are characteristic of the Caucasian languages, and in the Far East they are found as infixed consonants after the first consonant in Siamese (kam/klam, tan/tran). In Burmese a verb becomes transitive by aspirating an initial consonant: kruk 'fear'/ khruk 'frighten', and there must have been similar processes in prehistoric Chinese. There are agglutinative suffixes in Tibetan, which also employs mutation.

The basic word does not always agree in form with the derivative. This is especially true of English and other west European languages which have experienced the effects of the Latin Renaissance. The simple words belong to an older stratum and the derivatives have a Latinized appearance. Hence such families as faith, faithfulness, fealty, fidelity, and with the use of a synonym truth,

---

[1] J. M. Camacho, 'La lengua aymará', Boletín de la sociedad geográfica de La Paz, lvi, 1945, cites 44 formative particles in Aymará which give 51 derivatives of ayaña 'to carry a long object in one's hand', 48 of saraña 'give', and 60 of yatiña 'know'.

truthfulness, verity, verisimilitude, veracious. Cf. Sp. *fruto/fructífero, delito/delinquente.*

Affixes may be lively and productive, like *-ify, -ly, -ish*, or inert like *-wise, -ment.*

The original type of derivation which greatly increased the number of English verbs during the nineteenth century consisted of the postposition of a preposition. In this way *to get* produced different values in *get up, get at, get about, get on* and similar families of verbs sprang up around other simple verbs. The use of these postposed prepositions is carried further in American usage, as in *to meet up with a person, to visit with somebody.* The device is sometimes characterized as American, with little justification. If these creations are not redundant, they represent additional resources in our speech.

Shifts of meaning. The store of words is also increased by transactions which affect meaning.[1] Since the meanings of a given word form a kind of spectrum with a concentration in some region, it is possible for the concentration to shift, or for two words with approximately the same meanings to drift apart, or for meanings in one band to be transferred to another. Passive *cognitus* 'known' becomes active OFr. *cointes* 'knowing' and its range of meanings broadened out to 'knowledgeable, skilful, clever, wise, prudent, hidden, sly, artful, neat, brave, bold, courtly, fine, proud, keen, coquettish, impudent, lusty, cheerful, happy'. Eng. *quaint*, which still meant 'clever' for Shakespeare, has passed through 'prim, affectedly nice, fine' to 'unusual, odd, whimsical'.[2] Words are seen to descend in moral worth as Germ. *List* (from 'wisdom' to 'trickery'), Eng. *silly* (from 'happy, inoffensive' to 'foolish'), *valetudinarian* from *valetudo* 'health', Sp. *fortuna* 'tempest' from 'fortune'. But words also gain in stature, as *knight* from *cniht*, Germ. *Knecht* 'servant', *client* from 'servant' to the person who commands a service. A general sense may become restricted as *tectum* 'covering' > Fr. *toit* 'roof', Arm. *mart* 'man' = Gk. βροτός 'mortal'. MGk. ἄλογον 'horse' from 'speechless animal' (cf. Russ. *nemec* 'German', speechless person). Extension of meaning is equally common: *pecunia* (from *pecus* 'cattle') 'wealth' in general, Sp. *ganado* 'cattle', *ganar* 'win, gain' (from 'to pasture'). Concrete terms become

[1] M. Bréal, *Essai de sémantique*, Paris, 1897; A. Darmesteter, *La vie des mots*, Paris, 1946 (1885); A. Meillet, *Linguistique historique et linguistique générale*, Paris, 1948.
[2] K. Vossler, *Frankreichs Kultur und Sprache*, 2 ed., Heidelberg, 1929, pp. 75, 78.

abstract: *scruple* (which also retains its concrete sense as denoting a light weight), and abstract words become concrete: *charity*, *alms*, *address*, *lecture*. When two words occupy the same ground they tend to diverge by specialization: *love/charity*, *brotherly/fraternal*, *agreement/accord*, *homo/vir*, *mulier/femina*.

An important source of new words is metaphor. Notions not to be apprehended by our five senses must be approached by sensual analogies so that one expression stands for a concept in another order. MGk. ἐγὼ δὲν συμφωνῶ 'I do not agree' is metaphorically derived from symphony or agreement of sounds. *Concord* is another musical term which has added an abstract meaning. 'To find' is 'to come into', 'to step on', or 'to take the cover off' something. Words made too familiar by use do not seem vivid enough for the experience they are meant to convey.

Things also change and with them words shift their senses. The Quechua *tampu* was a posting-house on the imperial roads. From that came *tambo* 'an inn' or a shop, and by specialization a 'dairy'. With the use of *lechería* for an up-to-date kind of dairy, *tambo* came to mean shop of poor class. *Father*, *mother*, *sister*, *brother*, *son*, *daughter* are relatively stable terms, but all the other family names have been affected by the disuse of the exogamic table of relations with its insistence on the difference between the two branches of the family.

Various kinds of taboo affect vocabulary. An act by a Polynesian chief or an emperor of China is described in terms other than those used for the same act by a subject. There are words to be avoided for religious reasons and others for reasons of superstition or prudery or humour. When the notion of courtesy intrudes, pronouns for the second person become more elevated and those for the first person depressed. Both may disappear and give place to nouns, either substantives indicating the rank of the persons of the dialogue or adjectives implying superior or inferior status.

Complete phrases may be petrified into words: *hobson-jobson* < *Ya Hasan! Ya Husain* ('*Oh* Hasan, *oh* Husain'), the commonest names in a Moslem crowd; hence the derived sense of 'native festal excitement'.

Borrowing. Though all languages have borrowed from others, none has done so more freely than English. *Hand*, *toe*, *bone*, *wife*, *winter*, *sail*, *cliff*, *swim*, and many others are probably not Indo-European, but taken from older languages by all Germanic peoples.

The ancient Britons left a few words to the Anglo-Saxons (*brock* 'badger', *coomb*, *rock*). From Continental Latin come *fort*, *street*, *tile*, *chalk*, *wine*, *cherry*, *chestnut*; from the Latin of the early church *bishop*, *pope*, *priest*, *angel*, *devil*, *school*, *master*, *cross*, *shrine*, *rose*, *lily*. Norse contributed *call*, *cost*, *die*, *dwell*, *full*, *haven*, *husband*, *low*, *law*, *aloft*, *road*, *skin*, *take*, *witness*, *wrong*. For a while further borrowing was kept in check by the ease of composition in Old English, which included amongst other effects an antiquarian treatment of the days of the week, with Germanic gods in place of Latin (except for Saturn, for whom there was no satisfactory equivalent). With the Norman Conquest, however, the scholarship and authority needed for these translations ceased to be effective and even a certain aesthetic objection was felt towards the process of composition. From Norman-French at first and then from the French of Paris there came words which have all the signs of being English (e.g. *carry*, *prey*, *deny*, *ransom*, *blame*, *male*, *chief*, *grief*, *faith*, *strange*, *butcher*, *carpenter*, *pork*, *veal*) as well as abstract nouns in *-ty*, *-nee*, *-our*, *-tion*, which took longer to acclimatize. In due course the Latin Renaissance brought words directly from Latin, and this led to the re-spelling of older loan-words such as *avantage/advantage* and words using the group *-ct-*. The pronunciation was fitted to the revised spelling. The technical language of the nineteenth and twentieth centuries has added a still further Graeco-Latin hoard to our vocabulary, and new French terms have entered owing to the prestige of French literature, diplomacy, and military organization. At the same time our lexicon is evidence of our traffic with all nations: Dutch *skipper*, *buoy*, *deck*, *mart*; Italian *piano*, *monkey*, *bandit*, *caprice*; Spanish *alligator*, *don*, *sherry*, *ambuscade*, *cordillera*, *comrade*; High German *wiseacre*, *larch*; Norwegian *ski*; Russian *czar*, *verst*, *rouble*. It is from Spanish that the main body of early American words was obtained: *llama*, *potato*, *tomato*, *inca*, *banana*; but later loans result from direct contact with the North American Indian: *mugwamp*, *sqwaw*, *mocassin*, *tomahawk*, *wigwam*. From the East came Indian words such as *pundit*, *bungalow*, *jungle*; Arabic *cotton*, *islam*, *minaret*, *mosque*, *jehad*; from Malaya *orang-utan*, *go-down* (*gudang*), *compound* (*kampong*); from Polynesia *taboo*; from Australia *corrobboree*, *kangaroo*; from China *tea*, *sampan*, *mandarin*; from Japan *samurai*, *rikshaw*, *geisha*.

With regard to new objects the normal procedure is to take over the name with the thing, and in general languages show little reluctance to do so as long as the merely practical vocabulary is involved. Thus on the back pages of South American newspapers there is copious use of English sporting terms which do not appear on the centre literary pages. For literary acceptance there are two obstacles to surmount: the technical difficulty of grammatical adaptation and the aesthetic objection to a change of linguistic habit.

The grammatical difficulty is at its minimum in English. It arises when parts of speech have proper forms which new words cannot adopt at once. A period occurs in which the new words are regarded as foreign; they wear their foreign dress and sometimes retain all or some of their foreign pronunciation. In English this obstacle is found in two forms: insistence on foreign sounds as in *nuance*, *genre*, *milieu*, and maintenance of the foreign accent. The sign of full acclimatization is the retraction of the accent to or towards the first syllable, as from *natión* to *nátion*, *tyranníze* to *týrannize*, *objur-gáte*, *objúrgate*, and *óbjurgate*.[1] For Spanish the test lies in the application of customary suffixes, such as the *-o* and *-a* of nouns, together with facilities for derivation. The word is still strange, however, because of its non-Romance character.

The aesthetic objection to foreign words has been felt most keenly by Germans and Czechs. The thing or concept is foreign and there is no less borrowing than under the other system, but indebtedness is disguised by translation. Germ. *Mitleid* is a transla-tion of *sympathy*, *herausgeben* of *edit*, *Fürwort* of *pronoun*. Czech *listopad* 'fall of the leaf' = *November*; it is not a translation but a substitution, the calendar of twelve months itself is what is bor-rowed; *lidovláda* is a translation of the two parts of *democracy*. The aesthetic result of this procedure is the preservation of unity of the national tongue. It has a political value as well, since it excludes overt acknowledgement of a foreign debt. On the other hand, languages which have borrowed freely obtain considerable stylistic advantages while at the same time keeping contact with the vocabulary common to other civilized peoples. The rise of doublets in English has led to discrimination of synonyms: *love/charity*, *acknowledge/confess*, *prayer/supplication*, *heartily/cordially*. Passage from the Germanic to the Latin half of our vocabulary is not passage from one language to another but from one style to

---

[1] B. Danielson, *Studies on the accentuation of polysyllabic Latin, Greek and Romance Loan-words in English*, Stockholm, 1948.

another. The simpler style is to be used for simpler concepts and is more lucid. The richer Latinized has the qualities of dignity and sonority. The two styles may be kept apart as with Swift and Sir Thomas Browne or mixed as by Shakespeare, so as to follow effectively the movements of the poet's thought. A social distinction is also involved, since mastery of the Latin half of vocabulary is a product of education, and the uneducated demand that Latinized phrases be restated 'in English' or 'in words of one syllable'. This difficulty lies in the concepts more than in the words and is not really avoided by translation. The meanings of *Mitleid* or *listopad* are not self-evident but have to be learnt as part of an educational process.

STUDIES IN WORDS

It is only languages with fully organized vocabularies that are capable of the developments proper to civilization. They have reached a perfection of discipline which has completely changed their nature. Instead of being mere phases of action they become vehicles for conveying thought. Their logical aspect rises above the dynamic, and they invite analysis both on the score of propriety of terms and of arrangement. Thus philosophy, with its reiterated query 'What do we mean when we say such a word?', becomes possible, and to some extent inevitable; and logic also as an art of arranging words philosophically precise in such a way as to make valid statements. Distinctions between words are not only for precision but for emotive effect. The poet, the orator, and the man of letters explore these possibilities and, when the artist is gifted, produce effects which in turn enter into the body of language. Thus it is natural that the study of language, which began with that of the most copious and beautiful one (Greek), should have taken for basis the word, its classes, and its arrangements. It is only in comparatively recent times that we have had reason to think the word is no more than an abstraction from innumerable contexts, precarious in its origins and in its attachment to things.

A number of auxiliary linguistic sciences attach themselves to the definitive word, and of these the most comprehensive is Lexicography.[1] It is a co-ordination of all branches of linguistic science to determine the origin and meanings of each word, their dates and relations, and the use of the word in typical sentences. The Greeks and Romans did not envisage such works, but only the compilation

[1] J. Casares, *Introducción a la Lexicografía moderna*, Madrid, 1950.

of word-lists covering unusual, archaic, or provincial expressions employed by great writers. This was termed a lexicon (as that of Suidas), but in modern parlance a selective dictionary is more often entitled a 'glossary'. A 'vocabulary' is a list of the words appearing in some particular context, as in one book or in a dialect, particularly when totality is not envisaged. The term for totality was first *thesaurus* or 'treasure', and it was applied to theoretically complete statements about the words of the Greek, Latin, and Hebrew tongues. It was in these languages that the need was felt to explain 'common' words, and as the articles extended, it became clear that even in a vernacular language needs were not met by simply listing rare, archaic, and provincial terms. A direct relation between the classical and the modern type of dictionary was established by Antonio de Nebrija's Latin-Castilian *Vocabularium* (1492), which foreign humanists studied in reverse so as to obtain a knowledge of Spanish from the Latin they already knew.

Italian, French, and Spanish dictionaries began to appear in the seventeenth and eighteenth centuries, with certain characteristic restrictions. The motto of the Spanish Academy was 'cleanses, fixes and gives splendour'. The dictionary embraced all words and usages which could be admitted as belonging to the reputable part of the language, but by the same token it makes excisions from actual speech to mark its disapproval of many terms as base or impermanent. Such collections limp behind the vernacular even as used by persons of distinction, who do not always talk on an exalted or even cultured level. In excluding provincialisms, the criterion tended to exclude a great part of the legitimate vocabulary of Spanish America in the same way that English dictionaries record insufficiently legitimate 'Americanisms'. For the word and for each of its uses authority had to be cited (the Spanish Academy's effort was termed the *Diccionario de Autoridades*), and this authority was obtained from standard authors. The whole work was thus eminently literary and prescriptive.

It is scarcely possible to finish any dictionary without some principle of exclusion, but more modern works aim theoretically at recording the entire language. In the case of Latin, Greek, Old Norse, or any other historical phase this totality can be reached by coming to the end of the written record, but for a language still in use, and therefore still adding to and discarding from its stock, the fullest dictionary requires supplementation from time to time. The appeal to authority is necessarily literary, and what is recorded is rather more than any speaker would be allowed colloquially to use or even any writer write without apology. There is inevitably an editorial judgement concerning the licitude or permanence of some words or meanings, and this may be shown to be ill-founded by future developments. *The New English Dictionary*, begun by Sir J. A. H. Murray and completed by Sir W. A. Craigie and Dr. C. T. Onions, Webster's *American Dictionary of the English Language* (more hospitable to fluctuating usage), Craigie's *Dictionary of American English on Historical Principles* and his *Dictionary of the Older Scottish Tongue* (still in progress) are among the greatest achievements of lexicography.

In addition to the encyclopaedic dictionary there are those of particular techniques, such as scientific or military terms. These propose to give more precise definition of words and are directed towards action in the sense that the words will be used so as to secure advances in knowledge or industry or effective strategy and tactics. Slang and argot have their dictionaries, justified by the exclusion of their matter from standard works. A particularly important type of dictionary from the linguist's point of view is the etymological, since it is only on sound etymologies that historical analysis can be grounded. For very many languages such collections are impossible; for others they are comparatively unrewarding. But for the Indo-European group the service they render is all-important. Changes have been so numerous and complex, both in the form of words and in their senses, that only arduous research can establish their true relations. Since the Indo-European tongues are flexional the first step is to discount the flexions. This gives a 'stem', i.e. a word in a condition to take the flexions which will integrate it in a sentence. As a result of derivation by prefix, infix, and suffix, these stems are distinguished as primary and derived. The primary stem may contain a system of mutations (as in Russian *ber-/bor-/br-* 'take'), no one of which can be said to take precedence over the others. They are already subject to a grammatical discipline, inasmuch as they stand ready for flexions, and a further analysis reveals the 'root'. The root was at one time thought of as a kind of linguistic atom with a real existence, like Chinese monosyllables, but it is now deemed theoretic. In the studies of Meillet and Benveniste advantage has been taken of this theoretical conception of the root to push these studies far back into the realm of abstractions. By a parallel process of comparison and abstraction we reach 'root-meanings', from which, with some plausibility, all later senses may be shown to fan out.

Linguistic geography is also primarily, though not exclusively, grounded on words. Only the simplest phrases have the consistency necessary to make comparison over the points of a map fruitful. Variations of response to inquiries were found occasionally to involve variations of the things named. Thus the townsman has but one word for 'yoke', but Galician peasants have to deal with yokes attached to the horns and yokes resting on the necks of oxen, and they may be either plain or heavily ornamented. Differences of this sort are expressed by differences of name. This has led to the important branch of lexicography called 'words and things', which has a periodical of its own (*Wörter und Sachen*). Since the differences of things often reveal cultural progress and survivals, this branch of studies has an obvious importance for historians.

The naming of anything is arbitrary, but the naming of things unique by nature, such as persons and places, is such that, if the word be lost, it cannot by any means be reconstituted. If we forget John's name or that of the city of London, there is no process of language-forming by which we can recover them. On the other hand, many linguistic processes weigh especially heavily on names, and their history is unlike that of common nouns.

Personal names are subject to fluctuations of fashion. The simplest situation is that of a name built out of common materials so as to express some wish or expectation concerning the child. Thus *Isaac* ('laughter'), *Elisha* ('the Lord is saviour'), *Aristocles* ('of best fame'), *Nabu-kudur-utsur* ('Nebo, defend the landmark') express wishes, vows, expectations. Names once significant tend to become traditional, and then to be restricted to a certain list. Thus Spanish names of men are all either Gothic in origin or those of saints, and the greater number of women's names are attributes of the Virgin (*Dolores*, *Carmen*, *Rosario*, *Angustias*, &c.). The sudden celebrity of some name (like *Victoria* or *Elizabeth* or *George*) may give it a specially wide extension at some time, and other names fall into disuse for their archaism or singularity. *Henry*, *John*, *Robert*, *William*, and *Richard* increased from 38 per cent. of recorded men's names in the twelfth century to 64 per cent. in the fourteenth ; on the other hand, baby-forms diversify the same name, as *Molly* and *Polly* from *Mary*, *Will* and *Bill* from *William*.

Surnames may refer to more than one individual, but they are still of such a nature that, if forgotten, there is no way to reconstitute them. The most primitive type is to cite the father's name along with the child's, as *Dafydd ap Gwilym, Simon Bar Jonas, Henry Fitzwilliam, Lev Nikolaevič, Marcus Gaii f*(ilius), *Muhammad ibn 'Âlî*. The Arabic system allows also for a name acquired by paternity, as *Abû 'Umar Muhammad ibn 'Âlî*. A considerable number of ancestors may be named, followed by a tribal name, name of birthplace, and possibly a nickname. The Roman system included the personal name (*praenomen*), that of the family (*nomen*) and that of the branch (*cognomen*). There were also nicknames and honourable styles conceded to distinguished generals. Spanish surnames are patronymics and matronymics, and are given in that order: *Don Ramón Menéndez Pidal, Miguel de Cervantes Saavedra*. The official surname therefore is penultimate, but if the mother's name is more distinctive it is often preferred in use. English names include patronymics, local names, names of trades and professions, and nicknames, as *Wood, Hill, Birtwhistle, Attwater, Johnson, Jones, Hendry, Baker, Gardener, Fox, Peacock, Strong, Littlejohn, Grant, Noble*.[1] In a restricted French region (Nan-sous-Thil) in 1940 nicknames were found to arise in seven ways: from physical or moral qualities, allusions to geographical origin, a trade, baby-names, speech-habits, the analogy of some other name (as *Saragosse* in connexion with Victor by allusion to the Marshal Victor who took Saragossa), or anecdotes (as *Le Roc* applied to someone who did not know that *roquefort* is a cheese and asked someone if his *roc* was good as well as strong!).

The arbitrary nature of place-names exempts them from the operation of normal analogies while exposing them to popular speculation; it both hastens and retards, according to circumstances, the effects of wear and tear. Some of the earlier attempts to explain English names by purely phonological principles led to mistakes and gratuitous assumptions which Sir A. Mawer pointed out in his British Academy lecture.[2] The work of the English Place-Name Society has shown that this department of investigation is complex and requires the combination of historical, geographical and linguistic gifts. Owing to false analogy and the vagaries of

[1] E. G. Withycombe, *Oxford Dictionary of English Christian Names* (Oxford, 1943) and the article 'Names' in *Chambers's Encyclopaedia*; P. Lebel, *Les noms de personnes en France* (Paris, 1946).

[2] A. Mawer, *English Place-Name Study*, London, 1921.

spelling, the first step is always to discover the oldest documented forms. These may be fully intelligible, and then the problem is solved. Local propriety has also to be considered. It is no use proposing an *etymon* involving a hill for a place in a plain or valley bottom, and inspection of the site may at once indicate which of several possibilities to adopt. Old maps are of great value in explaining *toponymia minora*, which are of special linguistic value as being exempt from literary influence. These names of fields, corners, and parishes can be made to give evidence of vocabulary otherwise unknown, and of local dialect usages which have sunk beneath the lava-flood of the official language. In other cases the survival is that of a deceased language, as Celtic names in England, Etruscan in Italy outside Etruria, Gaulish in France, and Iberian in Spain. A notorious example is the *Illiberis* (Basque *iri berria* 'the new town') next to Granada across the whole breadth of Spain from the present Basque country; the Celtic names of the Rhine and Main in Germany; and the presence of the Iranian element *danu* 'water' in the names of rivers in southern Russia. The village-name *Ferreirola* still bears three signs of the lost Mozarabic dialect of Granada (Castilian *Herreruela*).

A continuous spoken evolution makes for wide discrimination between spelling and pronunciation in such cases as *Milngavie* [Mulgai], *Pontefract* [Pomfret], *Cirencester* [Sisister]. On the other hand, the pronunciation of some major town-names was apparently retarded by the Latin of medieval documents, so that *Córdoba*, *Mérida*, &c., show a cadence generally extinguished in Spanish. *London* shows an unexpected development of *Lóndiniis* (places were frequently expressed in the locative); French *Londres* (with dissimilation of *n*) retains the sign of the locative plural as *-es*. In *Lisbon*, *Lisbonne* English and French record the old Mozarabic pronunciation of the city now called *Lisboa*; medieval Spanish *Lisbona* was retained so long as the Portuguese word was occasionally nasalized (*Lisbõa*); but thereafter *Lisboa* was taken from the Portuguese. Names in *-ona* from *-one(m)* (as in *Barcelona*, *Tarragona*, *Lisboa*) contain a feminine suffix contributed by Arabic, and provide evidence of former Moorish occupation. The alternative *Mulhouse/Mülhausen* shows that the French have retained the older pronunciation of German *û* (*ū* > *au*).[1] Translation is fre-

---

[1] W. Meyer-Lübke, *Introducción al estudio de la lingüística românce*, Madrid, 1914, p. 299.

quent in names along the Franco–German frontier, and indicates
the common interests of a mixed population or the alternate pre-
ponderance of one or other element. More often a French and a
German variant exists for the same name, as *Cologne/Köln*, *Spire/
Speier*, *Aix-la-Chapelle/Aachen*, *Genève/Genf*, *Fribourg/Freiburg*,
Grisons/Graubünden. Place-names in Eire were anglicized when
railway-stations were built. They are now being re-Celticized, but,
it is said, on the basis of the English rendering. The inhabitants,
who have kept their Celtic pronunciation as a local habit, now learn
a new Celtic name from the station boards.

Place-names refer to the situation or manner of a settlement, as
Edgehill or *Oxford*, and often include elements implying building,
open or fortified space, enclosure, dwelling: *Murviedro* 'old wall',
Fresneda 'ash-grove', *Koblenz* and *Conflans* 'confluence', *Talavera*
(-*briga* Celtic settlement). Others refer to persons, as *Norman-
ton*, *Charlton* (*ceorl* 'freeman'), *Birmingham*. Comparing *Villaiza*
(Agiza's villa) with *Villadiego* and *Villa de Frades* ('friars' villa') we
find place-names rendering a chronology from the time when there
was a genitive case to the time when analytic forms were universal
in Romance. Names of saints imply the words *ecclesia*, *basilica*, or
church, which may be expressed as in *Kirkpatrick* or *Grijalva*
(*ecclesia alba*) or omitted, as *Santander* (*Sancti Emeteriani*), *St.
Jean*. *Monasterium* (*minster*), and sometimes *temple* and *convent*
also appear. Casual circumstances are also recorded in *Matanzas*
('murders'), *Homemmorto*, &c. Ancient history is revealed in *Paris*
(*Parisiis* 'among the Parisii'), *Alfurno* (*Alburnus mons*, with the
Sabellian *f* for *b*), *Rheims* (*Remis*), *Autun* (*Augustodunum*), *Zaragoza* (*Caesar Augusta*) and prehistory in *Vienna* (Celtic *Vindobona*),
Bohemia (*Boiohaemum*, the home of the Celtic Boii who preceded
the Germanic Marcomanni and Quadi, as these preceded the
Czechs; the Czech name is *Čechy*). The British-Roman *Eboracum*
became the Anglo-Saxon *Eoforwic*, modified by the Northmen to
Jorvik, whence *York*.

Recent name-giving does not offer the same opportunities for
mental exercise as these older examples, but it has the advantage
of better documentation. G. Stewart's *Names on the Land* is not a
linguistic but an historical study, and is a revelation in this respect.
He was able in very many cases to find direct testimony for the act
itself, giving the date and the circumstances. Thus he has been able
to distinguish the succession of fashions in place-names. The first

arrivals tried to see a New England in America (*New Plymouth*, *New London*, &c.) or emphasized their loyalty in such terms as *Virginia*, *Jamestown*, or *Charleston*. Another fashion—an idealistic dream—caused the giving of names like *Providence* and *Concord*. The later colonial period stressed relations with Britain (*Delaware*, *Baltimore*, *New York*, *Williamsburg*), and was followed by the glorification of the Revolution (*Washington*, *Jefferson*, *Madison*). The acquisition of French and Spanish places, like *St. Louis* and *Florida*, involved adopting French and Spanish names, but did not set a fashion until the burgeoning of pseudo-Spanish in California. French variants of Indian names are seen in *Illinois*, *Chicago*, *Michigan*. There were many old Indian names in American use, such as *Susquehanna*, *Penobscot*, or *Potomac*, but later an Indian fashion set in, to give such names as *Dakota*, *Idaho*. Sometimes a name indicates a class of settlers, as *New Amsterdam*, *New Berlin*; at other times the name is a fantasy, as *Rome*, *Cairo*, *Memphis*. The fashions were so strongly operative that the United States Post Office had to set limits to the use of a given name within a defined area.

IX

VALUES

It is not difficult to say where stylistics begins, though authorities differ concerning its terminus. It begins with the notion of value in speech. Grammar has been defined above as a system of relations within the sentence, but it is found that these relations may be expressed in several concurrent ways. They are grammatically indifferent, but in fact speakers prefer one way to another and hearers understand the speakers' intentions. There is thus a function of communicating something more than the mere logical relations of the parties and the event. What is additionally communicated is value, and the grammatically indifferent sentences are found to differ in affectivity or emotiveness. The range is, of course, from zero upwards, since the phrase may be constructed so as to include emotive substance, and it is possible that more than one statement of the same relations may have zero affective value. An expression totally devoid of emotion is abnormal in ordinary intercourse, but the degree of affectivity may be so low as to be virtually nil. The whole material of language has to be reconsidered from this new standpoint, since the effect may be due to choice of sounds or words or order and grammatical resources.

The difficulty about fixing the end of this study lies in different conceptions of the linguist's function. If we accept that his competence is restricted to *la langue*, the organized resources at the disposal of every speaker of a given language, then stylistics stops short of the additional resources of *la parole*. In particular, it would not investigate the personal styles of great authors. But great authors are not necessarily odd practitioners. Their claim to our attention lies at least partly in their ability to make the best use of the common resources. They are specialists in an art which we all practise, an art of words or *Wortkunst*. To describe a language fully we should be permitted to describe it as it is most expertly used. The great masters, therefore, according to some stylisticians, are proper subjects for these studies and, indeed, the most rewarding. The question will arise, however, concerning them whether their whole art is one of words. In so far as it can be traced by intelligible symbols the linguist's science may follow them, but if there is an element of communication beyond symbolization, the positive discipline no longer suffices and a more intuitive method is required.

One may write down three sentences:

> I must decide whether to kill myself or not.
> Kill myself?—That is the question.
> To be or not to be, that is the question.

The references and logical meanings are the same but the affective values are quite different. The first is bald and colourless. It is indeed so trite as to raise one's doubts about its being used, since a fully grammatical sentence is not needed when a man talks to himself. He would be more likely to mutter (if at all) a few disjointed words. The second form shows a certain striving for effect by the inverted order and the abstract phrasing of the second part. The third shows evasion, since the question is treated as wholly abstract though it is personal to Hamlet, and since he poses the problem as one of survival not suicide. This evasiveness continues throughout the speech in words like *sleep, quietus, consummation, take arms against a sea of troubles, shuffle off this mortal coil*, and even *die*, but the word *self-slaughter* is delayed for many lines. Though the third formula is by the greatest poet in the English language it does not contain any word or device which is not within the reach of any English speaker. It is merely the best possible choice and arrangement of words as they would be used by a sensitive mind driven to self-destruction but still seeking refuge in self-deception.

There is no closed frontier between stylistics and grammar. Grammar is recreated from style as the creative effort in speech loses its freshness and becomes commonplace. The cliché is a typical example of such a process. The 'life' of words begins with their maximum effectiveness, passes through a stage of vulgarization and ends when the word is too spent to be worth using. So the *fatal* of Racine ('fateful, fated') falls to the level of the *femme fatale*, and the *nice* ('exact, fastidious') of the Elizabethans becomes the universal *nice* of the Victorian schoolgirl. In the series

1. Balbus murum aedificat
2. Balbus aedificat murum
3. Murum aedificat Balbus
4. Aedificat murum Balbus

grammar uses four identical sets of references and treats the sentences *as if* they were identical. For stylistics they constitute four different affective orders. One or more than one may be normal and of zero affectivity. It is used then merely as a basis for measuring the effects of order in the other instances. The first and second were probably normal for classical Latin, but in late Latin the second had come to predominate and so passed into the Romance vernaculars. By the fourteenth century the postponement of the verb is identified as an artifice of Latin prose style and was applied in this sense to artistic prose. On the other hand in early Romance the second and fourth orders were normal as they are still to a large extent in Spanish and Portuguese. They differ in subject-matter (τὸ ὑποκείμενον) since the second stresses agency but the fourth activity. A series of sentences constructed on the fourth pattern, as in the prose of Blasco Ibáñez, gives an impression of strenuous physical activity, while a series in the second pattern seems to be a logical exposition. But both orders were normal, for instance, in the *Chanson de Roland* (*Dist li paiens* 'the pagan said', *Marsilie vient* 'Marsilie comes', *halt sunt li pui, et li val tenebrus* 'the hills are high, the valleys dark'); it was at a later time, and as a result of the increasing intellectualism of French words and thoughts, that the verbal sentence was rejected and only the nominal survived. The effects of the verbal sentence have to be obtained by using new formulas, notably those with *c'est*. The third phrase would be used only for emphasis on the object in either Latin or a modern Romance.

One may pronounce *indeed* with a level unemotional intonation or with a steeply rising tone as a sign of dissent or with a broken rise and fall to show scepticism. Though the tones are not marked in spelling they are none the less symbols of speech with a precise significance for the hearer. Or one may say *that's what* YOU *say* (with stress on 'you'); this stress, also unnoticed by orthography, is a commonly accepted sign of disagreement. What is accomplished by stress in English is effected by a grammatical device which allows a change of order in modern French: *je vous dis/c'est à vous que je parle* 'I am speaking to YOU'. *To run away* and *to take to one's heels* are logically the same, but different in affectivity. The Spanish idiom *tomar las de Villadiego* adds a proverbial twist to the expression. In *Le Gendre de M. Poirier* a young spendthrift is not called *prodigue* but *un panier percé*. The substitution of one term for the other adds an effect of tolerant ruefulness to censure. We might say that the *poor boy has an awful hole in his pocket*. The metaphor hints that the boy is not entirely to blame. These and many other examples show that there is an element of relativity in our expressions and that this relativity is expressed somehow by symbols intelligible to the listener. This is matter for stylistic investigation. 'Stylistics investigates the facts of expression in organized language from the standpoint of their affective content, i.e. the expression of facts of sensitivity by language and the action of language upon sensitivity'.[1]

In accordance with this definition it is arguable that there can be no stylistics save of one's native tongue and of the present time. It is of that usage alone, if of any, that we are masters and we are our own best witnesses as to its affective nuances. Provided that the expressions are such as are available to any speaker, we can draw them out of our practice and consider them to see wherein their effect lies. We know the range of resources in our own tongue; we know the intention behind our own choice and can watch its transmission to a listener; when someone else speaks we can estimate the effect of his choice of expression upon us. Thus we might regard (1) *Good night*, (2) *'Night*, (3) *Nighty-night*, (4) *I wish you good night*, (5) *I wish you a good night*. The first has no implications. The second is casual and offhand. The third slangy and implying familiarity, which would be an impertinence if the personal relations of the speakers did not warrant its use. The fourth is formal, possibly old-fashioned or frigid and, in some contexts, menacing. The fifth implies some reason to distinguish one night from another, such as in the case of an invalid. This we know concerning our own tongue at the present time, but we cannot apply the same sort of measure to past times. The magistrate of Las Órdenes (orders) in one of Condesa Pardo-Bazán's novels, who was wont to introduce himself with the formula *juez de las Órdenes y a las de usted* ('magistrate of orders and at yours'), used a formula that had become fulsome in his time but was once an elegant accomplishment. The older systems had their own different consistency. Old French *sun dragun portet a qui sa gent s'alient* ('he bears his dragoon flag and his followers rally to it') is a phrase within its own eleventh-century scheme of language and has no bearing on the emotive effect of any modern French instance of an object which precedes

---

[1] Ch. Bally, *Traité de stylistique française*, 2 ed., Heidelberg, 1921, i. 16.

the verb. 'One may well have a history of successive styles', says
E. Winkler,[1] 'but there is little chance of an historical stylistics as of
an historical psychology.'

In these studies a foreigner has the single advantage of surprise.
Every distinctive idiom of another tongue catches him unawares.
His astonishment, however, is directed by differences of idiom less
to what has affective value for the native than to common expressions which the native considers indifferent. Thus one may compare *you* = Fr. *vous* = Germ. *Sie* = Ital. *Lei* = Sp. *usted* (< *vuestra
merced*) = Ptg. *Vossa Excelência*. It would be possible to infer that
the Spanish and Portuguese forms are marks of a specially courteous
attitude. They were in fact at one time (sixteenth century) expressions from the *estilo cortesano* or language of the court and gentry,
but at present no one of these expressions has more emotive value
than the others. Owing to the decay of the second person pronouns,
verb forms implying *ustedes* ('your worships!') can be used to dogs
in the Spanish of Argentina, and in Brazil the term *Vossa Excelência*
is often replaced for courtesy's sake by a title, such as the almost
universal *senhor doutor*. Similarly Germ. *ich werde sagen* = Fr. *je
dirai* (< dicere habeo) are identical in effect. The first is based on
an auxiliary of becoming, the second on one of obligation or necessity, but their historical differences do not affect their present uses.
To make a mistake = Fr. *se tromper*, *to fight* = *se battre contre*, *to
die* = Sp. *morirse*: in these cases it is impossible not to note the
use of the reflexive pronoun in contexts alien to English usage and
not capable of a logical defence on English principles; but there is
nothing unusual about them from the French or Spanish standpoint. A stranger cannot judge the effects for a native except by
learning from a native, and he is liable to give a wrong interpretation if he attempts one untaught. But his astonishment is not lost.
It calls attention to the oddity of common idiom and quite possibly
also to some affective situation in past time. Common idiom was
uncommon in its birth but is quite likely to pass unquestioned
as a result of overfamiliarity. Statements on style, even by a
native, are valid only when qualified by reference to some precise
time.

Between 'an investigation of the facts of expression from the
standpoint of their affective content', according to the above
definition, and the traditional study of rhetoric there is a marked

[1] E. Winkler, *Grundlegung der Stilistik*, Bielefeld–Leipzig, 1929.

difference. Classical rhetoric classified certain devices of formal composition from *acyrologia* to *zeugma* and recommended their use or avoidance; it distinguished three levels of style and offered rules for effective discourse. But this was on a footing of precepts resulting from observation of particulars as they chanced to arise and had no scientific basis or unity. Modern stylistics aspires to rank as a science or body of verified knowledge, like the rest of the linguistic techniques. The distinction between observation and precept, however, is sometimes narrow. To observe the cacophony of *-pa-ra-bla-la-fla* in *comparable à la flamme* and the felicitous use of vowel glides in *une ondulation majestueuse et lente*[1] is not far removed from saying 'go thou and do likewise'. To define *elocuzione* as clarity, precision, conciseness, simplicity, naturalness, harmony, and euphony[2] is to condemn the emergence of the opposites of these qualities. The suggestion of precept is inevitably increased when the passages observed come from great authors; it is right that those who have accurate notions of style should indicate virtues to imitate and vices to avoid. The difference between classical rhetoric and modern stylistics lies rather in the systematic nature of the modern science. As the youngest of the linguistic disciplines, however, stylistics has not yet attained a method,[3] and its distinguishing quality is its empirical outlook and purpose of systematization.

We may approach stylistics through the proposition that expressivity extends throughout all parts of a language and that stylistics deserves a place on a par with phonetics, vocabulary, and grammar. It takes all these aspects into its field of observation in order to study expressive values. The divisions of stylistics will thus be the branches of linguistic science which are to be studied again from this special angle. J. Marouzeau's treatise on French stylistics is divided into *Les sons*, *La graphie*, *Le mot*, *Les catégories grammaticales*, *Construction de la phrase*, *Agencement de l'énoncé*, *L'énoncé versifié*. Migliorini and Chiappelli's work has chapters on grammar, literature, and versification as well as stylistics. The latter covers words, elocution in respect of choice and forms (figures of speech), the tone of the discourse, and the language of Italian classics.

[1] J. Marouzeau, *La linguistique*, Paris, 1921, p. 58.
[2] B. Migliorini and F. Chiappelli, *Lingua e stile*, 4 ed., Florence, 1948, pp. 110–14.
[3] J. Marouzeau, *Précis de stylistique française*, Paris, 1946, p. 15: 'C'est qu'en effet la stylistique est une science à créer.'

Arrangement by grammatical categories is used by Ch. Bally[1] to dress the synoptic table of terms and identifications, but not for his exposition of stylistics as a science. The latter is defined by him, as we have seen, as the study of the facts of expression in an organized language from the point of view of their affective content; it is upon these facts of expression and not upon the thing expressed that the science rests: 'son objet est l'expression parlée et non le fait pensé'. It is not denied that language is a system of relations between the mind and speech, so that every expression has its outer and inner facets; but the object of linguistics is positive knowledge of language and it is from the facts of expression that linguistic investigators must seek to win knowledge of motives. The facts of expression correspond to ideas (i.e. to the purely intellectual aspect of communication), sentiments of the speaker, and social implications due to the presence of a listener. The purely intellectual aspect is of zero affectivity, it is a system of intelligible references within the sentence and no more, and its place in stylistics is that of a basis for estimating emotive effects. This degree of neutrality is found in scientific or logical statements which are quite devoid of passion. It is found less absolutely in common talk. These zero states constitute norms from which it is possible to measure differences due to refinements of meaning, the presence or absence of affective characteristics, and the social factors involved. The norm is, even so defined, ideal rather than real, because it is never quite perfectly realized. A logical statement may have more than logical appeal. We are told, for instance, that mathematical formulas are justified by their beauty, and there are poets who have been obsessed by the aesthetic appeal of atomic physics (Lucretius), syllogisms (Calderón), mathematics (Dante), and botany (Erasmus Darwin). Since the norm is not quite steady, the stylistician's task requires a special instinct to determine in any given case what are the ruling facts and to infer the expressive value of those which come within the rubric of this part of linguistic science. On the other hand, since the investigator's attention is concentrated on the expressive phrase and not on the mental impression or cerebral processes, Bally holds that the stylistician's relations with mental science are external. An elementary knowledge of psychology and some notion of the tendencies which rule society are no more than secondary aids to his studies.

[1] Ch. Bally, *Traité de stylistique française*, Heidelberg, 1919, i. 128 and ii. 'Appendice'.

Ch. Bally then seeks to determine the facts of expression so as to identify them. This involves passing under review all the aspects of language which have already been mentioned in this book. Stylistics is coextensive with the other studies of sounds, orders, and words. What is not observed by emotional communication in any of these respects is available for style, and may be converted into intelligible symbols of value. When the special material of stylistics is thus identified, its characteristics are to be determined with regard to natural effects or effects of evocation. To arrive at the facts we have to take account of the values of words as revealed by their contexts, and the natural association of words and phrases; we have to attempt a classification of facts on a logical basis. The evocative effects are those which refer to special social milieux, such as frequency or rarity of words, customary and unusual usages, discourse proper to some special public, and that of a literary or scientific writer, expressions which imply familiarity or laxity or even criminality.

According to Bally this part of linguistics must avoid being automatic or mechanical, it must not aim at a formal analysis which would separate facts from their contexts and it must not rely upon historical or etymological explanations. It is not denied that now is a point in time and part of the march of history, but it is asserted that the speaker when he speaks is not conscious of this march. He is only aware of a system of resources in present time which corresponds to a state of the language. The same has been true of speakers at every moment of past time; it is possible to define the stylistics of any given language at any given date (provided that the evidence is sufficient), but it is not possible to develop an historical or comparative stylistics. All that can be done in this way is to compare different states of one language as states, or to notice that different languages have developed the same devices of style. There is, for instance, a European mind revealed by the parallel development of resources in languages as historically unconnected as Hungarian and German. Starting from different origins the peoples who speak these languages have lived together for a thousand years and the increasing resources of the one have extended to the other also. A word for word translation is much more tolerable between two modern European languages than between any one of them and an ancient or oriental tongue. Modern European stylistic-objectives are everywhere alike.

To collect all the stylistic devices of all languages is a task impossible to conclude and it would prove meaningless. Study must proceed on the basis of one language in its universally available forms. It will include the case of habitual individual responses to commonly occurring situations, but it excludes (according to Bally) the style of a writer or of an orator. A man of letters makes a voluntary and conscious use of language and he employs it for aesthetic purposes. 'His intention is to make beauty with words as a painter does with colours and a musician with sounds. This intention is almost always that of the artist and almost never that of a person spontaneously speaking his mother tongue. This alone suffices to separate for ever style and stylistics' (i. 19). Thus we may speak of the individual stylistics of Balzac or any other writer when we mean their individual reactions to common speech-situations, but we must not confound these spontaneous effects with the author's style. For Bally, therefore, the domain of stylistics is strictly delimited by the threshold of literary effectiveness.

The same limitation is accepted by E. Winkler.[1] According to him stylistics is concerned with the psychological worth or value of speech-forms beyond the purely intellectual plane; but style is the individual sum of characteristics of a particular speaker, writer or poet. It is not the business of stylistics to investigate the creative work of such speakers or writers. Starting from W. von Humboldt's remark that all language has an intellectual tendency since it seeks intelligible symbols for emotions as well as ideas, Winkler divides linguistic studies into (1) those of spoken thought (concepts with their comprehensions of phenomena or things and their mode of operation by syntax), (2) utterance (words and their making, flexion, sounds single or in rhythm), and (3) values as studied by stylistics. The third section reviews the other two. It deals with the value of concepts, of the mechanism of speech, of sounds, and of speech-forms in relation to their milieux. This arrangement of materials might seem to promise a study of concepts and the value of concepts alongside the objective facts of expression, but in the end it does not prove to do so. Concepts are defined as speech-concepts—the means of expressing thoughts—and the values of the concepts (Begriffswerte) are values created by dominant meanings within the total capacity for significance possessed by words, values that arise from *etyma* and modifying affixes, special effects

[1] E. Winkler, *Grundlegung der Stilistik*, Bielefeld–Leipzig, 1929.

that arise from the use of conjunctions or pronouns in special contexts, affective use of parts of speech, formulas, and transferences by metaphor, abstraction or concretion, and fancy. Thus Winkler's stylistics does not offer a set of conceptual correlatives to observed facts of emotive expression and is as empirical as that of Bally.

Since the greater number of studies on stylistics have been of highly civilized west European languages, it is worth while, by way of contrast, to interpolate here a note on the ingenious consonantal play of the Nootka Indians as reported by E. Sapir.[1] These are stylistic exercises motivated by a wish to give sensational impressions of the personages involved in a narrative. Thus verbs and their forms receive diminutive endings when spoken of or to children and augmentative endings for fat or large persons. Dwarfs, cross-eyed persons or squinters, hunchbacks, lame persons, left-handed people (including bears), circumcized males and cowards are similarly addressed or satyrized by means of diminutives expanded by affective consonants or syllables. The number of devices employed is striking but their range is less remarkable, since they are mostly extensions of augmentative or diminutive senses by way of the usual secondary implications of dislike, contempt, and affection. The emotive effects aimed at are strikingly concrete impressions of visible and audible situations. Stylistics extends to all languages, though its objectives may be strikingly different in civilized and savage conditions. To the present date, however, this youngest branch of linguistics has been applied successfully to French alone, i.e. to the west European language of most intellectual structure, in which affective causes and effects can be objectively estimated. The accuracy of similar measurements when applied to a more spontaneous mode of speech (such as English) might be open to question. It is still too soon to say that stylistics has evolved its own proper method, or that existing techniques have more than an *ad hoc* usefulness.

'CHARACTEROLOGY' OF SPEECH

German authorities have formulated other definitions of the sphere of stylistics which are either narrower or broader than those of Bally and Winkler. The basis of all is the notion of choice between various ways of attaining a given logical effect. In learning one's own or a foreign language at school exercises are used with

[1] E. Sapir, *Selected Writings*, University of California, 1949, pp. 181–5.

the practical or didactic objective of attaining a certain minimum of grace in handling words and phrases. Such operations, it is suggested, should not be termed stylistic but idiomatic. While purely routine in themselves, they have their scientific justification in a theory of the psychological values of speech-formations to be sought from stylistics. This insistence on psychological backing ('Wissenschaft von den seelischen Werten der sprachlichen Gebilde')[1] contrasts with the lack of systematic psychological support for these studies so far as they have yet been developed. The most that Bally expects is that observation of the details of usage will reveal certain tendencies though these may have no more than empirical range.

K. Vossler's[2] definition runs 'style is the individual use of speech as distinguished from the general'. Language itself he equated to expression of the mind, and the common features placed at the disposition of each speaker or writer he regarded as the results of individual creative activities; further creative effects must be won in despite of the conventional constitution of a language. All the lower kinds of grammatical explanation (phonology, morphology, syntax, and the like) 'must find their sole and true explanation in the capital discipline, namely stylistics. So-called grammar must dissolve into aesthetics, without leaving a trace.' Of the two persons of the dialogue only *Ego* has a place in this definition, which regards habits of speech as so many impediments to creative expression. But *Ego*'s power to express his sentiments does not reside in his simple will to do so. Tradition gives him certain resources not merely to be understood by *Tu* but also to define and illustrate his own thought. Thought cannot extend and develop without these aids; thought, word, and phrase come together in the mind and are uttered on condition of being understood. The tension between the search for expressive values and the social contract of speech exists at every moment in the dialogue. Linguistic 'positivism' overstressed the traditional residue; Vossler's 'idealism' exaggerates the individual creative urge. Nor is it to the advantage of the study of language if we dissolve all its existing parts in a new but undefined synthesis.

A more modest and practical definition is that of A. Tobler

---

[1] See the discussion in E. Winkler, *Grundlegung der Stilistik*, Bielefeld–Leipzig, 1929, and K. von Ettmayer, *Vademecum*.

[2] K. Vossler, *Positivismus und Idealismus in der Sprachwissenschaft*, Heidelberg, 1904, p. 15; Ital. trsl., Rome, 1907.

and F. Strohmeyer. Style is the *way*; by it the tempo and mood of thought find expression in speech. Of this *way* the student of stylistics seeks to form a picture, a characterization of facts of expression. The sum of such characteristics should offer the 'characterology' of a language.

A number of attempts have been made, chiefly in Germany and Denmark, to say what are the characteristics of selected languages. They range from brief essays to long monographs. For both the one and the other it is easy to show that the attempt is premature; but that languages have character is at least an impression so widely held as to require investigation. Failure to identify this character must lie either in the imperfect or ambiguous nature of the evidence adduced or in the extra-linguistic correlations or the absence of proved categories of reference. To make an intelligible portrait of a language, as of a person, some features must be selectively emphasized and others omitted or minimized, and the risk is of running into caricature. Without some such selection a picture lacks distinctive outline. But each language is designed to cope in every kind of way with the whole universe of experience. When selection has been made, it is not difficult to turn to passages, both in the works of standard authors and in common usage, which do not conform to the proposed pattern. If, for instance, we start with Viggo Brøndal's *Le français: langue abstraite*, it is far from difficult to show that the adjective is insufficient and that there are authors, like Victor Hugo or the makers of the *fabliaux*, who find vivid and concrete ways of using the French language.

The characteristics of a language acquire interest when they are correlated with social and historical factors, but there is always the risk of making a false correlation or one which has lost its validity. The abstract and intellectual quality of French (if we concede the thesis) may be associated with the intellectual prominence of the medieval university or with the role of Cartesianism in shaping more modern French usage or with some other historical trend. The association of a linguistic fact with a non-linguistic situation is necessary if we are to draw any but strictly linguistic conclusions. But when making the link we have to rely to a considerable extent on intuition. In the case in point it is possible to overestimate the effect of philosophical debate on a language used chiefly for other than academic purposes. French erudition may be a symptom, not a cause, of the nature of the French language.

One regrets also the lack of reliable categories for this kind of explanation. The word 'abstract' is drawn from the intellectual vocabulary, but characterization may be due to concrete and quotidian features also. The Slavonic tongues, for instance, have experienced successive sound-shifts from the normal to the palatal orders. The tendency is to divide vowels and consonants into two orders so that 'hard' (*a o u y*) vowels are preceded by normal consonants, while 'soft' (*i e*) vowels are preceded by palatal consonants. It is an aesthetic principle for which no term drawn from the spheres of the intellect or emotions is applicable. The new creation of three genders in Slavonic and their rationalization according to declensions are highly characteristic features originating in some sense of propriety, not intellectual or sentimental. The qualities of Spanish according to Lerch[1] are realism, impulsiveness, fantasy, courtesy, and stoicism. The terms all refer to abstract qualities and involve the usual difficulties of detail. 'Realism', for instance, is a troublesome term in literary criticism since the most literal realism often goes with outbursts of extravagant fancy. The two terms 'realism' and 'fantasy' imply a language in a state of tension between extremes. The courteousness of a given formula may not be the courtesy of today but of some past time. And the list of Spanish qualities does not include the characteristic trochaic rhythm, reimposed in the thirteenth century, nor the simplicity and even distribution of the vowel sounds.

The most elaborate of these attempts to characterize a language is K. Vossler's *Frankreichs Kultur und Sprache*.[2] The work has been described as premature and in effect 'more French than the French'. Like all other works of scholarship it will, no doubt, be slowly remade, but its function was to bring together a vast number of linguistic and social factors and to provide a plausible account of their relations. If speech serves a social purpose, it is surely proper to inquire what purpose or kinds of purposes have mostly been served. Other purposes have doubtless also found their expression

---

[1] E. Lerch, 'Spanische Sprache und Wesenart', in *Handbuch der Spanienkunde*, Frankfurt a. M., 1932.

[2] K. Vossler, *Frankreichs Kultur und Sprache*, 2 ed., Heidelberg, 1929. For German see R. Priebsch and W. E. Collinson, *The German Language* (ch. xi: 'The Genius of the German Language'), 3 ed., London, 1948, in which there is a discussion of the difficulty of this undertaking. The difficulties are inevitably greater when the investigator is a stranger, since he is liable to remark the least remarkable stylistic effects.

in language, but this sort of investigation must hold to a main line. *De minimis non curat lex.*

It is also possible to base one's study not on a sum of characteristic features but on individual traits such as impressionism,[1] expressionism, the baroque, the classical or symbolism. The investigation starts from a term presumed to be valid and seeks to discover the corresponding linguistic facts. The validity of these terms is the more convincing in as much as they frequently draw their origin from the visual arts. There is thus the evidence of our eyes to justify our assumptions. Attempts to verify them are not infrequently disconcerting. While impressionism, for instance, can be *seen* on the canvases of a school of painters and has been proclaimed as a creed by some writers with a distinctive style, it is found on inquiry that no less than eight different programmes are implied. Impressionism may be the style of authors so named, the language which covers an impressionist experience, language which stresses phenomena not causes, that which avoids regular construction of the phrase, that which is free from references to *Ego*, the expression of momentary sensation not deformed by reflection, predominantly fanciful expression, or objective expression. The results vary according to the evidence accepted as relevant, and especially on the admission or refusal of testimony from artists in words concerning a term originating among artists in paint.

THE STUDY OF STYLE

Bally excluded the study of the personal style of great authors from the domain of stylistics on two grounds; first, that their choice of expression is voluntary and conscious at all times, and second that they aim at aesthetic effects. It is possible that neither of these considerations is as important as appears at first sight. Granted that a writer or orator uses speech with full consciousness of effect, but so also does the newspaperman after his fashion or the conversationalist or the seller of vacuum-cleaners. In fact speech is always purposive, though it is not always used adequately for its purpose. Where the means are consciously proportioned to the end style exists, but one may distinguish between the ends in view.

---

[1] Ch. Bally, E. Richter, A. Alonso, and R. Lida, *El Impressionismo en el Lenguaje*, Buenos Aires, 1936. J. Marouzeau commends the study of some particular stylistic resort. See the studies of the definite article and diminutives in A. Alonso, *Estudios lingüísticos*, Madrid, 1951.

The journalist's style aims at immediately capturing, but not keeping, the reader's attention. The commercial traveller, like the orator, rises to a peroration, though he may be content if he attains his object (the sale of goods) by a mere spate of words. The conversationalist may, like Dr. Johnson, give memorable shape to his remarks or may be satisfied with the immediate effects of wit. But in all these and other aspects of the use of speech there is a voluntary element in the attainment of ends by available means, and if our habitual usage—which Bally describes too readily as spontaneous—is often inadequate, literary expressions are also of varying degrees of adequacy.

The discrimination then rests upon the aesthetic intention. Of this, too, one may offer a relative account, and one should not forget that aesthetics is of all divisions of philosophy the most intractable.[1] It is scarcely helpful to assert that its object is beauty or that its special kind of intuition is called taste, since beauty and taste also elude logical definition. If art be a relation between intuition and expression, there is no reason why this should not be fully attained in conversation, even in spontaneous speech (if there be any speech which is not the result of an acquired skill). Art may reveal itself in an instant as well as after long reflection, while failure to equate means and ends is often confessed by men of letters. Schiller's epigram would find many echoes:

Warum kann der lebendige Geist dem Geist nicht erscheinen?
Spricht die Seele, dann spricht, ach! schon die Seele nicht mehr.

The objective that the man of letters places before himself may not be merely the achievement of beauty. He may, like Hooker, demonstrate the rule of law, or like Dante pass judgement on the moral order of the world. The literary effect is then seen in the adequacy of the expression to the 'thing meant', and its beauty is incidental though fully intended. Only a small part of the world's literature, and that not usually the best, has been written primarily to impress upon readers a sense of verbal beauty.

To obtain the most satisfying examples of verbal means and ends it is usual to cite passages from great authors, as J. Marouzeau does for French. These passages stand not for what is peculiar in the style of the writer himself but for the sort of effects which are

---

[1] E. F. Carritt's *Introduction to Aesthetics*, London, s.d., is the latest treatment available to me. B. Croce, *Estetica, come scienza dell' espressione e linguistica generale*, 4 ed., Bari, 1922, places this subject within the 'linguistic' field.

achieved in ordinary speech, though rarely with the same economy and fullness. The writer is not an aberrant being but a practitioner of a common art distinguished only by his greater success. It is true that he may form for himself a language, like that of Milton or Góngora, which he does not intend to pass as vulgar coin, but on the other hand he may, like Shakespeare, attain the most exquisite and personal triumphs with everyday materials. Nothing is more Shakespearean than the famous description of Cleopatra's arrival by barge on the Cydnus. In it only one important word is absent from the corresponding passage of North's Plutarch. That word (*burned*) makes the passage, but belongs to common speech. It is used with supreme felicity, and it forms part of the expression of a poet who repeated such felicities. We must not, of course, confuse Shakespeare or any other great writer with Everyman, but we should not suppose him to be made of different clay.

At certain historical junctures authors' preferences are of importance not only for their own style but also to determine the common standard of the language. The most recent occasion of this sort has been, no doubt, the creation of a literary Mandarin Chinese by Hu-shih and his collaborators. On the rise of modern Russian in the stylistic preference of Pushkin there is an admirable study by V. V. Vinogradov. For both Pushkin and standard Russian it was necessary at the beginning of the nineteenth century to come to a decision about the relative proportions of the colloquial and the ecclesiastical elements. Pushkin's judgement varied but his final decision affected not only himself but also the national language. A much older and equally well-authenticated example is the creation of standard Italian by Dante as recorded in his *De Vulgari Eloquentia*. That this is a voluntary and personal act is made clear in that treatise and that it affected the whole language can be seen in the fact that there is still no other common Italian usage than the literary compromise he began to construct on the basis of the Florentine dialect. In conversation educated Italians use this language with more or less admixture of their local patois. No doubt the main lines of Dante's solution existed before him in the work of Cavalcanti, and after him Petrarca, Boccaccio, and Bembo took part in the determination of the Italian norm. But the whole effort was carried through by individuals on the basis of their own preferences, though not without support from public opinion; a single ready-made standard of colloquial expression existed nowhere.

The distinction between stylistics and studies of style (*Stilstudien*), if it be maintained in despite of etymology, does not remove from the scope of linguistics concern for the practice of the greatest experts in expression. Their methods are deliberate and can to a large extent be objectively noted. One may compare the means used with the ends attained. A question which arises, however, is whether this objective measurement suffices as literary criticism or whether there is not still a place for intuition of literary values outside the positive linguistic range.

Claims for the linguistic study of style have been put strongly by German and Austrian scholars in revolt against the total suppression of language and literature in their university curricula. K. Vossler and L. Spitzer begin with criticism of the limits imposed on Romance linguistics by the positivist philology of W. Meyer-Lübke and both insist that the traditional linguistics of the nineteenth century was not an account of language but a preliminary to the true discipline. The older positivist scholars avoided every mark of the subjective in their studies: 'linguistics was until recently anaesthetized against aesthetics'.[1] The exponents of these methods assert 'the ultimate unity of linguistics and literary history'. The latter term does not seem well chosen since the examples offered are not from the history of literature but are criticisms of individual styles: Rabelais, Cervantes, Proust, Péguy, &c. The equation must be between the study of language and literary criticism; as such, it is one of several claims to have established an absolute criterion for appreciating works of literary art. The investigators' aim is 'a more rigorously scientific definition of the individual style, the definition of a linguist which would replace the casual impressionistic remarks of literary critics'.

When a writer has, like Cervantes in the preface to his *Galatea*, stated his intentions, it would seem appropriate to begin by taking them into account, to attempt to reveal the means employed and to assess their efficacy. It happens that this line is not taken by either of the two linguistic investigators of his art; they rely in different measures upon their intuitions of style. The problem has

[1] L. Spitzer, 'Sprachwissenschaft und Stilkunst' and 'Wortkunst und Sprachwissenschaft', *Stilstudien*, ii, Munich, 1928; *Linguistics and Literary History*, Princeton, 1948. Work in this field is reviewed by H. Hatzfeld in *Romanic Philology*, 1948; for purposes of exemplification I rely on H. Hatzfeld, *Don Quijote als Wortkunstwerk*, Leipzig, 1927 (*El Quijote como obra de arte del lenguage*, Madrid, 1949), and L. Spitzer, 'Perspectivism in Don Quijote'.

to be solved either by a catalogue proposed by the researcher himself or by the discovery of some fulcrum. The catalogue is applied *ad hoc* to the author or work. Thus stylistic means at the service of ideas, at the service of epic technique and at the service of ideology and temperament, are placed by H. Hatzfeld on the same footing as analysis, unreal conditional sentences, euphemisms, paradox, the pastoral style, &c. This is a medley rather than a picture. The examples are massed, but their importance consists in supporting rubrics some of which might have been demonstrated on other grounds than language. Their want of homogeneousness prevents 'achieving what I would call an integration of the historical styles into one Cervantine style, in which the personality of the writer would manifest itself' (L. Spitzer). The literary critic, however casual, would be careful from the beginning to present some such unity of person.

The fulcrum method used by L. Spitzer is described by him thus:

in my reading of French novels, I had acquired the habit of underlining expressions which struck me as aberrant from general usage, and it often happened that the underlined passages, taken together, seemed to offer a certain consistency. I wondered if it would not be possible to establish a common denominator for all or most of these deviations; could not a common spiritual *etymon*, the psychological root, of several individual 'traits of style' in a writer be found, just as we have found an *etymon* common to various fanciful word-forms?

The investigator's hope is to produce a 'psychogram' of his author or book by a strict evaluation of facts of language. He works 'from the surface to the inward life centre' of the work of art; first observing details about the superficial appearance of the particular work (and the 'ideas' expressed by a poet are, also, only one of the superficial traits of a work of art); then, grouping these details and seeking to integrate them into a creative principle which may have been present in the soul of the artist; and, finally, making the return trip by other groups of observations in order to find whether the 'inward form' one has constructed gives an account of the whole. The result is a 'psychogram' of the artist obtained by a circular movement of thought: first the listing of some particulars, then the intuition of a general principle, then the corroboration of the principle by fresh observations. As a method this is sound enough. Pure induction—the listing of every particular before attempting any inference—is as obviously impossible in stylistics as in any other science. Inductive-deductive movement characterizes Darwin's thoughts on evolution and Bopp's concerning the Indo-European language family. The intuition or divination of some whole is necessary if any whole is to be reached.

Spitzer's method however has, in practice, one more intuitive feature, namely that each investigation is entered at one point only. His study of Rabelais depends on the creation of nonce-words and leads to a general estimate of Rabelais's style. That of *Don Quijote* rests on the insecurity of names of persons, an insecurity increased by Cervantes's ironical use of medieval processes of etymology. This is called 'linguistic perspectivism'—a term which would scarcely be understood outside the context of the article. The 'psychogram' is usually some such term, applicable once and once only. Among supporting evidence offered there is contrast between Turkish and Arabic words in an episodic passage of *Don Quijote*. The Turkish words are factual, narrowly descriptive and with no transcendental connotations ('for the Turks are excluded from the possibility of enlightenment by Grace'), but the Arabic words are nearly always connected with things spiritual. The inference is that those who distributed their words to the advantage of Arabic were Arabs. But spiritual words of Turkish are normally borrowed from Arabic; what they had to offer to anyone from their own hoard were official and military terms. The families referred to by Cervantes have since been identified by J. Oliver Asín as neither Turks nor Arabs but 'Arnauts' as Cervantes himself stated, i.e. renegades of mixed origin used by the Sultans to organize their armies and empire. Arabic words of high spiritual value had been borrowed in Spain between the time of the Moslem conquest and the fall of the Caliphate. Their use began to decline after the tenth century. To use linguistic material as a basis for criticism involves social correlations for which more than linguistic evidence is required.

A further danger lies in progress 'from the observed detail to ever-broadening units which rest, to an increasing degree, on speculation'. There is, of course, no objection to intuitions presented as intuitions, but if they are presented as the results of a 'more rigorously scientific definition of individual style', then it is necessary to ask for a valid relation between the facts observed and the conclusions adduced. A point may come where affirmations are no longer supported by factual evidence, but (if at all) by some other guarantee. From the observed fact that a writer is master of his characters[1] and that he may, if he pleases, etymologize their names, to the conclusion that the hero of *Don Quijote* is Cervantes himself—'the artist himself, who combines a critical and illusionistic art according to his free will . . . an almighty overlord is directing us, who leads us where he pleases . . . the artist is godlike but not divine'—is a step beyond the evidence. This conclusion is strangely unlike Cervantes's highly ironical appreciation of his own merits and fame. This genial intuition of the artist—'enthroned, an all-embracing creative self, naturelike, godlike, almighty, all-wise, all-good and benign'—must run its fortune with other intuitive appreciations formed with and without the aid of linguistics. Objective conclusions from language alone have a shorter range; between the creative writer and the recreative reader more immediate and humane relations must be established.

Critics of the school of Lanson,[2] not less objective in their methods than German students of *Wortkunst*, place their science outside the frontiers of linguistics. The structural and historical grammarian takes his place with the political and social historian and other external experts whose evidence is solicited when a work of literary art is to be assessed. Bibliography, textual criticism, archives, and letters are other components of a complex art which brings to bear on each line and word of a text the fullest range of illumination. The literary art is not merely an art of words, and the objective critic must prepare many lists besides the list of verbal aberrations. A. F. G. Bell's *Cervantes* (Oklahoma, 1947) lists phrases which define motions of the soul, descriptions of the cramping effect of poverty, suicide judged to be cowardice, &c., all of which are relevant to a complete understanding of this most complex of authors. Bell is, after all, an intuitive critic of Cervantes, but his numerous annotations show that the impressionistic remarks of literary critics are not, as above alleged, necessarily 'casual'. Even when the working is not shown, intensive critical work may have been done. The doctrine of Rudler, however, formally eschews intuition: 'Impressionism cannot be taught; by definition it escapes all method, if not all discipline.'

---

[1] In M. de Unamuno, *Niebla*, a character argues with the author whether the character creates the author or the author the character.

[2] G. Rudler, *L'explication française* and *Les techniques de la critique et de l'histoire littéraire*, Oxford, 1923.

Erudite and documentary criticism stands according to some within Linguistics, according to others just outside the border; but, to whichever side it may be adjudged, one may doubt whether erudition is a full and sufficient response to literature. It is rare indeed for works of art to be addressed to erudites, still less to critics. The critic is treated by the artist with insouciance. It is to the general reader that the literary masterpiece is addressed, and the critic is thanked not for what he may prove or disprove but for stimulating and enlivening the general reader's response. The relation wished for is between the creative mind and the receptive, recreative mind. As in the fundamental dialogue of *Ego et Tu*, *Tu* also is an artist, stimulated to a secondary energy of creation by the words of *Ego*. The necessary stimuli lie in the text, but their effects vary with the sensitiveness of the reader. A documented commentary may be helpful and become necessary for the understanding of long-dead authors; but its use is subordinate to the primary and direct relation between reader and author. The author's power lies in his verbal skill in evoking the impression of 'things', but it is 'things' that move the passions. Aristophanes weighed the 'things' of Aeschylus against those of Euripides in the scales of Dionysus, and found that the older poet's weighty lines sank down while the lightness of the younger caused his scale to kick the beam. Apart from the solemnity of a latinized vocabulary and syntax, the prose of Hooker is impressive by its evocation of universal Law. That evocation is made by words, but does not wholly reside within them; the reader is moved by the 'thing' behind the façade of context. The intuitive sympathy of poet and public may exist in a livelier degree in some individuals. These are the literary critics who, having this kind of mercurial sensitivity, enlighten and enliven more sluggish readers. Their impressions may be, and in some instances have been proved to be, erroneous, but their keenness, lucidity, and elevation give them an abiding value. It is for their freshness that one reads and reads again the Schlegels, Sainte-Beuve, Coleridge, and Bradley. Flaws are detected by unpitying Time, and not least in works of erudition, but in the commerce of lively minds there is something not wholly enclosed in words but lying between two intelligences as they severally appreciate the whole circumstance of discourse. Observation of language is an important aid to appreciation of literature, but there remains a field for intuitive criticism.

X

CLASSIFICATION, DESCRIPTION, AFFILIATION

FOR about a hundred years languages have been classified by the terms isolating, agglutinative, flexional, and semiflexional, analytic, synthetic and polysynthetic (including the incorporating class). Though not satisfactory in every respect, they have the advantage of easy illustration: a language is isolating like Chinese, agglutinative like Turkish, flexional like Sanskrit or Greek, semiflexional like Finnish, analytic like English, synthetic like Russian, polysynthetic like Eskimo, and incorporating like Mexican Nahuatl. The basis of classification lies in the handling of morphemes, units of grammatical relation attached to or formally modifying words. In an isolating language the word remains invariable. An agglutinative language employs semi-independent morphemes, i.e. such as have substantial form and meaning, though not used apart from other words. Inflexion employs fused morphemes and develops paradigms for both nouns and verbs. In a semi-inflected language the morphemes have a consistent form and sense, but they are not phonetically autonomous; they also tend to cohere in declensions and conjugations, of which the former are somewhat longer and looser than in an inflected tongue. An analytic language tends to reduce each significant unit of meaning and relation to a word. It thus resembles an isolating language in its reliance on word-order and auxiliaries, but differs by being analysis applied to an originally synthetic system. Synthesis is present in agglutination, flexion, and polysynthesis, which differ in degree and technique. Polysynthesis has been described as agglutination run mad; it involves not merely the association in one word of a principal concept and all its relational symbols, but the fusing of words into word-sentences and the massing of relational and derivative concepts. The word-sentence, when nothing is left over, might be described as due to holosynthesis. When the verb is a complex formed of the verb proper and its objects and adverbial complements, but the subject is distinguished, the language is described as incorporating.[1]

[1] Russian linguists use the term 'incorporation' for polysynthesis. From the languages of north-eastern Siberia, however, they supply examples of the word-

An important advantage of this set of terms, exploited by Henry Sweet in his *History of Language* (London, 1901), lies in its substantial agreement with geographical distribution. From the flexional and synthetic Indo-European tongues (analytic in some modern forms) there is a regular succession via the semi-inflexional Uralian (Finno-Ugric) languages to the agglutinative Turkish and the polysynthesis of the Behring Straits and Arctic Canada. The isolating languages also form a block cut off from the rest of Asia by the Kuen-luen and Himalayan ranges. One theory, grounded on the notion that highly developed paradigms represent the most expressive achievement of speech, builds upon isolated stems or roots loose agglutinative structures which are represented as finally hardening into declensions and conjugations, as in Sanskrit, Greek, and Latin. It is also possible to argue that language is most efficient when it identifies sense and symbol with all possible assurance, and that therefore the final goal of human speech is an isolating technique attained through analysis, i.e. English or Chinese. The second view overlooks the achievement of Turkish, in which sense and symbol are firmly welded without sacrificing the principle of subordinating relational to conceptual symbols. Nor, of course, is it at all certain that the isolating technique of Chinese is due to resolution by analysis of some prehistoric synthesis.

The term 'agglutinative' has too wide an extension in this scheme. Any synthesis may be a 'glueing together' of significant particles. When we illustrate agglutination by the structure of the Turkish language, we introduce implicitly notions of discipline and order. Subordinate elements of meaning are clearly distinct from principals in Turkish; they follow a prescribed order and consist only of suffixes. On the first count, this procedure differs from the 'amalgamation of units which are for the most part semantically self-sufficient' in Papuan and Australian languages[1]—a process I should prefer to call agglomerative. In them the stems fused into one verbal mass are grammatically unspecialized or imperfectly specialized. On the second count, Turkish agglutination by suffix only is marked off from the development of prefixes in the Bantu class-prefix languages. The use of infixes in Caucasian languages is striking enough to give them a distinctive character.

phrase and the phrase constituted by incorporating blocks (the subject-adjective group and the verb-complement).
[1] W. K. Matthews, *Languages of the U.S.S.R.*, Cambridge, 1951, p. 67 n.

Morphological classification has the advantage of referring to one basis of distinction—devices of relation within the sentence—but it excludes some features which provide useful labels. Thus Semito-Hamitic and Indo-European are two inflected language systems, which seem less alike the more they are scanned. If we transfer our attention from relational signs to the construction of basic stems, the three-consonant basis of Semitic, ancient Egyptian, Berber (and the two-consonant system of some Cushitic tongues) offers an instantly recognizable mark of distinction from Indo-European or any other language group. Chinese is not only isolating and invariable, but also monosyllabic; Malay is isolating, almost invariable, but predominantly dissyllabic. Chinese and Malay agree fairly well in expressing relations, but their basic stems are visibly different.

Now, the object of classification is to supply serviceable labels. If we consult exponents of another science, we find that the labels are useful rather than logically exclusive. If we care to do so, we can imagine a breast-fed monster walking on its head and breathing through gills—a lamellibranch, cephalopod mammal. It happens that there is no such creature, and that by using the term 'mammal' we do in fact, though not in words, exclude the notion of gills or walking on the head. On the other hand, 'mammal' goes in fact, though not verbally, with other less signal characteristics, such as terrestrial, vertebrate, hairy, and with convoluted brains. In like manner, to speak of class-prefixes marks off Bantu and semi-Bantu by a convenient label when the term agglutinative would lead to structural, historical and geographical confusion; and for Semitic the term triconsonantal (usually styled 'triliteral', but here distinguished from Benveniste's triliteral theory of Indo-European roots) is eminently distinctive. Both the class-prefixes and the three-consonant structure are probably relatively recent features of these languages; but they are eminently characteristic and therefore proper for use as labels.

One must remember, moreover, that language classes are unlike those of zoology, since there is no law against cross-breeding. No language is pure in one type. In Chinese there are a few genuine agglutinations, and traces of lost processes of derivation. There may even be signs of declension. The other Sino-Tibetan languages, though still predominantly monosyllabic and isolating, have many more signs of derivation, and agglutination. Turkish might be classed as an isolating language if we ignored the difference between principal and relational syllables and concentrated upon the invariability (save for vowel-harmony) of stems and suffixes. A grammar based on order without flexion is found in isolating and holosynthetic sentences alike; the distinction between two extreme linguistic types is minimized in this way. Languages rich in flexions may be construed according to word-order. Alongside flexions they are liable to show some agglutinations. The Indo-European parent language seems to have split while still in the making; its singular noun-flexions are more complete than those of the dual or plural, and the active voice than the passive or middle. The latter show agglutination and analysis where the former have fused flexions. It is an open question whether Finnish relational suffixes should be considered flexions or agglutinations, and whether the association of a principal stem with a confusing mass of determinative suffixes in Quechua and Algonquin should be considered as agglutinative, agglomerative, or polysynthetic. Though the use of word-sentences (holosynthesis) is commonly exemplified by examples taken from dialects of Eskimo, fully transcribed passages do not consist uniquely of word-sentences.

The labels are useful in a general way, but they are not consistent concerning human speech. This has always been a medium of intercourse between men of different mental and linguistic habits. As such, however, languages have been exposed as much to convergence as to divergence and, if we ignore minimal inconsistencies, there is a remarkable uniformity of linguistic type in broad geographical areas. One may construct a simplified world map thus:

NW.		NE.
EUROPE	*ASIA*	*AMERICA*
Semi-flexion	Agglutination	Polysynthesis
Flexion: (i) Triliteralism?	Isolation:	and
(ii) Infixation	(i) Monosyllabism	Incorporation
(iii) Triconsonantalism	(ii) Dissyllabism	
Class-prefixes	Agglomeration	
AFRICA	*AUSTRALIA*	
SW.		SE.

The 'triliteralism' of this scheme is that ascribed to Indo-European roots by E. Benveniste, and it is queried as not yet established beyond doubt. The isolating monosyllabic languages cover both the Sino-Tibetan and Mon-Khmer groups. Polysynthesis is found not only in the Americas but on the nearest shore of Asia.

Dissyllabic isolating languages extend from Madagascar to Easter Island.

SUMMARY DESCRIPTION

Discussing types of linguistic structure in his *Language* (Oxford, 1921), E. Sapir proposed a new principle of classification, which seems to me to lead rather to summary description. It was based on the expression of relations within the sentence and on the presence or absence of derivation. A language expressing relations by position and auxiliaries only was termed 'pure', and one using relational particles was termed 'mixed'. A 'non-deriving' language was called 'simple', and a 'deriving' language 'complex'. By juggling terms in this way four main types were established in two orders:

pure-relational languages which are	*A.*	Simple
	B.	Complex
mixed-relational languages which are	*C.*	Simple
	D.	Complex

The four types offer subdivisions according to the 'technique' of attaching secondary elements: (*a*) isolating, (*b*) agglutinative, (*c*) fusional, (*d*) symbolic. What is meant by 'symbolic' is the mutation of vowels or consonants as in *bid/bade* or *qatala/qattala*. By considering synthesis, three other terms emerge: analytic, synthetic, polysynthetic. Thus far the classification contains 4 × 4 × 3 possible divisions. To them we must add *plus* and *minus* signs, since language types are never pure. Thus we may speak of a language as 'agglutinative (with a symbolic tinge)' or 'mildly synthetic' or as representing relations mostly by concrete grammatical marks or only slightly as 'pure relations'. Brackets are used to distinguish less important from more important elements in structure. Cross-references are also made to I. concrete radical concepts, II. derived concepts, III. concrete relational concepts, IV. pure relational concepts.

Since these divisions are partly lettered and numbered, they offer two ways of classifying a language. Taking French and English as instances, we may state their conditions thus:

French. C, II. (*c*), III *c*, (*d*), IV. *a*, fusional, analytic (mildly synthetic);
English. D, II. *c*, III. *c*, *d*, IV. *a*, fusional, analytic.

Or we may write out in full these descriptions:

French. A simple mixed-relational language, which might nearly as well be described as complex mixed-relational, with a weak development of fused derivatives, a fairly strong body of fused concrete relational signs with some symbolic devices, generally fusional in technique, with an analytic (and sometimes mildly synthetic) kind of synthesis;

English. A complex mixed-relational language, with fused derivatives and fusional or symbolic relational symbols, isolating in its expressions of pure relation, fusional in technique, and analytic as to synthesis.

To Sapir's framework one must object in the first place that it makes a singularly unfortunate choice of terms. 'Pure' and 'mixed' mean nothing in themselves, nor do 'simple' and 'complex'. Relations within the sentence are not established in two, but in three ways: by order, auxiliary words, and morphemes. Probably all languages use at least two of these devices; some use all three. Among morphemes we must include permutations of consonants and vowels. They are no more 'symbolic' than the rest of language, which consists wholly of symbols, but they should be treated for what they are, viz. mutations of words. The business of the linguist is not with 'concepts' but with their expression in sound-symbols. He is concerned with the distinction between basic words or stems and derivatives. Some statement is required concerning the basic vocabulary of each language, though it may not always be possible to do more than state general phonetic conditions. Under I. ('concrete radical concepts' emended to 'stems') come statements concerning the triconsonantalism of Arabic and the monosyllabism of Chinese, both features of the most characteristic importance. All languages have devices for inferring secondary from primary vocabulary, and in this wide application 'non-derivational' is a term without application. It is taken as derivation by affix or mutation, but the process of inferring secondary words includes composition by juxtaposition and fusion and the use made of variations of meaning.

More than this, Sapir's classification, when extended into words, no longer provides a label. It gives, in fact, a summary description, imperfect in part, but useful as a guide once its terminology is broken down. This sort of description is necessarily less than a full statement of the synchronic system of a language. A full grammar of a language marks it off from all other languages and even from its own dialects. A summary description is selective, and is directed towards the comparison and differentiation on broad lines of various languages, not necessarily related. How far the account is pressed depends on the comparison envisaged. If English and Norwegian or Spanish and Portuguese are to be compared and distinguished, it is obvious that the statements will have to be very full. Spanish and Portuguese did not finally sever their links until intervocal *n* and *l* were lost to Portuguese in the tenth century; before that date, however, the two languages share a great many evolutionary features of Romance and of Ibero-Romance. In comparing standard Spanish with standard French the opposition of *hijo/fils* must be considered, but if the comparison includes Spanish and French dialects then Gascon *hilh*/Asturian *fillo* become relevant. It is not necessary for purposes of comparison that languages should be related. The resemblance between English and Chinese has been remarked more than once. The two summary accounts supporting such a comparison would naturally ignore specifically Indo-European or Sino-Tibetan features of the two languages. The value of the short accounts lies in its relevance to some specific purpose.

Upon a global basis, however, there are four things to learn concerning any language: (1) the constitution of its basic stems, (2) its resources of derivation, (3) the means of expressing relations within the sentence, and (4) what scheme of concords (if any) binds the discourse.

Basic stems. In considering the basic vocabulary of a language we deduct symbols of derivation and grammatical relations. What remains is the stem. In isolating languages stem and word are identical; in polysynthetic languages stems, rather than words, convey meaning, and they are relatively stable within the word-sentence. The stems of an agglutinative language are readily distinguished from affixes and they sometimes, as in Turkish nouns, may stand as words. In the fused inflexional tongues the final vowel of a stem is liable to be blurred, and if not restored to its pristine form, the stem proposed for consideration may be partly theoretical. Roots, which are wholly hypothetical, are not suitable as a base for comparison.

The summary description is synchronic. Historical considerations should be brought into the picture only when they simplify relations. If attempted of a highly evolved European language of the present day, it may be hard to state which stems should be deemed fundamental. Thus, *young* and *youth* are not obviously on different planes, though the dead suffix *-th* is seen in the light of *deep/depth, true/truth*. *Truth* offers support for *truthful, truthfulness, untruthful,* &c. *Faith, peace, view, bull, haven, leg, sly, happen* are all loan-words in English, but from the standpoint of the present day cannot be regarded as otherwise than basic. It would be hard to formulate a succinct account of such stems (or words) in contemporary English apart from some generalities about the phonetic basis (or 'phonematic structure') of our utterance: tendency of the stress accent towards the first syllable, absence of mixed vowels of the nature of *ü ö* and presence of many diphthongs in southern English, prominence of certain affricates and fricatives, use of tone for syntax and emphasis, &c. As compared with Latin, Italian, or Spanish, French vowels are thrown towards the front of the mouth and French rhythm is iambic, not trochaic. Russian and Gaelic divide vowels and consonants into two parallel orders determined by palatals; in Finnish the parallelism is due to tension. Loss of intervocalic consonants has led to long-vowel series in Samoan and, to a less extent, in Portuguese. In the Caucasian languages consonants are cluttered together; in Old Bulgarian consonants and vowels alternated. Initial consonant groups are not found in Arabic (though they occur in the Maghreb dialect through loss of intervening vowels), and there are two orders of velars. Which among these or other observations may be put forward depends upon the particular comparison envisaged, but some consideration of phonetic structure must be part of a summary description. Concerning meanings it may be possible to offer some brief statement, such as to remark on the rigidly concrete senses of Australian Arunta stems.

On the other hand, the structure of basic stems may in some instances provide highly characteristic marks. The triconsonantal basis of Semitic and north Hamitic is the classic example. It makes these languages recognizable at sight and carries by implication knowledge of the rest of their structure. This structural feature is as old as our documents, and yet may be regarded as relatively recent. On the one side, the triconsonantal structure may be supposed to have arisen from a biconsonantal type through the mediation of semivowels (*w y '*); on the other side, this biconsonantal form is reported as characteristic of the east Hamitic (Cushite) tongues spoken east of the Nile and as far south as Somaliland. It is not the quality of antiquity, but definiteness, that makes an item useful for summary description.

If the theories of E. Benveniste are accepted, we may offer almost as succinct an account of Indo-European stems. They consist of a triliteral root such as *sen* with a zero variant *sn*, followed by a suffix with the same sort of variation (say *ei/i*) which combines in full form with a zero root and in zero form with a full root, to which may be added an enlargement which has no alternatives. This process provides the stem *sn-ei-gh^w* or *sn-oi-gh^w* 'snow' (Russ. *sneg*, Lat. *nix*, Gk. *νύψ*, &c.). Concerning modern English or French we might say that, though no succinct account can be given of the structure of their basic stems at the present day, they are such as to rest historically upon stems as reconstructed by Benveniste.

Attention is required in some instances for the principles of monosyllabism and dissyllabism and for the use of closed as well as open syllables. The monosyllabic Chinese stem is an invariable word, without affix or mutation, and employed in an isolating technique. It has tone as an integral part of its structure. In Pekinese the tones are limited to four; the word consists of an end and generally a beginning. The end consists of a vowel or diphthong concluded by no other consonants than the nasals *n ng* (which tend to become nasalizations of the vowel); the single initial consonant, if any, is as aspirated or unaspirated voiceless consonant, though a slight voicing of the latter may be heard. Siamese monosyllables are not invariable, but show derivation by infix of a consonant immediately after the initial consonant. Tibetan monosyllables have affixes and also some mutation of vowels; they are also so complex as to require the unacknowledged aid of fugitive vowels to ease the pronunciation of groups of consonants. This is a link with dissyllabism, which could arise from monosyllabism by strengthening fugitive vowels. Turkish stems are normally monosyllabic, but correspond to two or more syllables in Mongolian parallel words.

That there is a dissyllabic principle is harder to show, since languages with stems of this sort are wont to possess monosyllabic particles and even some ancient monosyllabic substantive stems. The principle is displayed in Bantu. In this family of languages stems are normally dissyllabic in themselves; monosyllabic stems (other than particles) retain their class-prefixes when these are dropped by dissyllables, and thus continue to present a dissyllabic appearance. The dissyllabism of Malayo-Polynesian is strikingly contrasted with the monosyllabism of Sino-Tibetan and Mon-Khmer because of the general agreement of these languages in matters of grammar. There are, none the less, some Malayan substantive monosyllables. The Chinese monosyllables in Japanese are contrasted with the substantive dissyllables of the native vocabulary.

Japanese dissyllables and the monosyllables of some West African languages are typically open (i.e. not closed by a consonant). Chinese and Turkish monosyllables are more often than not closed. In Quechua there are dissyllables with some monosyllables; four-syllable words are derived, and three-syllable words are probably derived from two plus one. In a dissyllable, the first syllable may be open or closed, the second is usually open, so that the typical stem is of the nature of $xo(x)xo$. Initial consonants are frequently geminated, but not grouped. Neither grouped consonants nor closed syllables are characteristic of Tupi-Guaraní, the other great language of South America.

The case may also arise, as with the Arunta of Australia, that unsure and indifferent articulation makes no significant distinction between monosyllabic and dissyllabic stems. Thus *ltja altja iltja tja* are the same in significance. The tendency of the language is to avoid groups of consonants and to prefer open syllables, but in applying these principles in detail allowance has to be made for the fluctuating structure of stems.

Derivation. To make new words from old, languages use a number of devices: juxtaposition, fused composition, gemination, reduplication, affixation (with prefixes, infixes, and suffixes). In this sense Sapir's class of 'non-deriving' languages does not exist, nor can we use the word 'simple' with that implication. It seems that simple, tangible things and actions are *named*; they have basic words assigned to them, without any labour of association and inference, as *papa*, *mama*, *son*, *dog*, *cow*, *run*, *walk*, *swim*. I speak of these in the synchronic sense. Even when it may be shown that one of these words has its etymon, there is no consciousness of derivation in the language as spoken. But we soon find ourselves in a region of concepts which cannot be made clear except by some process of association with concrete basic terms. It is at this point that languages diverge. Some remain so close to the concrete level that they do not provide for derivation. Such an one is said to be Turkish, which is capable of such fusions as *son-teşrin* 'November', and affixations like *sönmek* 'to die out' or *merhamet-siz* 'pitiless', but is generally forced to find its vocabulary of ideas by borrowing from Arabic (as in *merhamet*) or European languages. There would seem to be a genuine poverty of resource in Turkish.

The case of Chinese is entirely opposite. Though Chinese is an isolating language, making no use of fusion, reduplication (other than gemination), or affixation (except for a very few particles which are represented as individual words), the language has not encountered any difficulty in keeping step with the most refined efforts of western philosophy or science. It only requires time for assimilation. The device used is juxtaposition, by which two or more words are habitually associated on condition that the joint meaning is not precisely that of any of the contributors. That these are new words is shown by special transactions with regard to tone, and, unless my memory is at fault, by the predominance of one stress. Whenever Chinese words come together within a breath-group, there are transactions between the tones,[1] and this is *a fortiori* true of customary juxtapositions. There is no tone in an unstressed syllable, such as those which I have described as virtual agglutinative affixes, but stressed syllables may have a principal stress, a secondary stress, or a level tension. The intimate connexion between tone and stress is too delicate for me to represent without authority, and authorities are usually content to mark tone only. The semantic principle, however, is clear in $t'iao^4$-pan^3 (jump/cross+plank) 'gangway', $t'iao$-^4lung-$^2mên^2$(jump+dragon+gate) 'to graduate'. Chinese is capable of such efforts as $shih$-^2li-^{4} chu-$^3i^4$ 'utilitarianism' and huo-^3lun-$^2ch'ê^1$ 'railway train or locomotive'. The condition is that there should be time enough to assimilate and analyse the novelty, and when that is not given (as in the instance of Buddhistic missionary work), Chinese borrows foreign vocabulary in terms of existing Chinese syllables.

The Semitic languages use mutation to provide for a vast number of contingencies, not all of which affect each basic word; but they also use prefixes, suffixes, and (rarely) infixes. Four-consonant words are usually the result of gemination of a consonant. Reduplication is akin to gemination, but the repetition is reduced to a convention, as in Greek τί-θημι 'I place'. The Indo-European languages rely on affixation principally, though there is little use of infixation (Latin *iugum* 'yoke', *iu-n-go* 'I yoke'), but they also use

---

[1] W. Simon, *Chinese*, i. 20 (Linguaphone Oriental Language Courses, s.d.).

fusion (*hippopotamus*) and the other devices. These fusions involve use of a bare stem in the first part. In Finnish there is no difference between a stem and a word, and there is no sign of adaptation to form compounds like *laulu-kunta* (song-assembly) 'concert', or *kiihottu-vaisuus* 'irritability'. Since the parts of a fused compound may be in a syntactical relation with each other, it is plain that Finnish has, in its fused compounds, as ample a resource as Chinese with its juxtapositions or Arabic with its permutations.

In Siamese it is evident that words are derived by means of sonants (*l n r*) infixed after the initial consonant. In Burmese the active verb is obtained by aspirating an initial consonant. From these hints it is possible to conclude that Chinese words now pronounced with different initials or tones may at one time have formed parts of derivational groups. Such a consideration cannot enter into a description of Chinese as it now is, where the words in question present themselves to the consciousness as distinct, though they are sometimes associated under one written sign. A description must be limited to a given time and region. Similarly, a summary description must ignore rare phenomena and confine itself to a statement about the principal derivational devices of a language. Thus the Vale of White Horse, the White House are, in fact, juxtapositions in English, but the device is so rare that one treats them as separate words, whereas the fused term Whitehaven is considered one word. Fusions are found in French or Spanish, but are admitted with such reluctance that we can say these languages do not characteristically admit them as compared with the numerous fusions of German or Russian. Even in a summary description it may not be possible to describe the derivational processes of a language by one term only, but it is highly characteristic if we can do so. Thus Chinese is characterized by its restriction to juxtaposition, Finnish by its predominant use of fused compounds, and Semitic by its use of permutation (eked out by some affixes). A considerable use of gemination, such as we find in Samoan and other Polynesian languages, also gives character to a language.

Relation. Relations of stems or words within the sentence are shown by order or auxiliaries ('empty words') or by affixes. There is some use of each of these devices in every language known to me, and I should be disinclined to describe any one language as 'pure'. But there is often enough a preponderant use of the first two or the last two, and even of the last alone.

In respect of order there is spontaneous order and several logical orders. Spontaneous order is that in which the various parts of an event present themselves to the speaker's mind. It seems to be the order of savage discourse, and in literary work it is usually found to be stylistically significant—the actual grammatical meaning being carried forward by auxiliaries and affixes. It has a certain lucidity, since it follows the order of interest which is felt by one person and may be shared by others, though it is not arranged so that the listener can hear certain parts of speech in certain places. Though the use of affixes may render unnecessary the grammatical use of order, the startling *hyperbata* of Latin verse are a highly sophisticated device. Old English is largely logical in its word-order, though capable of putting early the words of emotional interest; yet the grammatical meaning is carried forward by flexions.

If order alone is used by any language, it is presumably so within the word-sentence. We are told that Eskimo *takusariartorumagaluarnerpâ?* means 'pensez-vous que réellement il ait l'intention d'aller s'occuper de cela?'[1] That is possible on two conditions: (i) that the phrase contains intelligible parts (*takusar-iartor-uma-(g)aluar-ner-(p)â*) and (ii) that there is an intelligible order in 'il s'occupe de cela—il va à—il a l'intention de—il fait ainsi—mais—pensez-vous qu' il—(3rd person query)'. However, word-sentences are often quoted but rarely explained grammatically, so we must leave this one as it has been left to us. According to Marshman, cited with approval by S. Julien,[2] 'the whole of Chinese grammar depends on position', but this is an exaggeration. Chinese has a very few genuine suffixes (*la, mên, ti,* &c.), which happen to be represented as independent words, and are so in some uses. It also makes considerable use of 'empty words', that is of auxiliaries in the broad sense of the term, which includes prepositions as well as subordinate members of the verbal complex. It also builds up each sentence of word-groups which are sufficient to themselves in their syntax. For instance, *kei³ t'a¹-mên* is 'give them', but *wo³ kei³ t'a¹-mên mai³* means 'I bought for them'. The use of suffixes increases in the western Sino-Tibetan tongues, though still not to the point that they cease to be deemed isolating languages.

The logical or grammatical orders, as distinct from the spontaneous, are characterized by the place assigned to the verb with

---

[1] A. Meillet and M. Cohen, *Les langues du monde,* 1924, p. 597.
[2] S. Julien, *Syntaxe nouvelle de la langue chinoise,* i, 1869, p. viii.

respect to subject and object. They are SVO (as in English, French, or Chinese), VSO, or VOS (as in Spanish and Arabic verbal sentences), SOV (as in Japanese). Since varieties of position are so few, the sense must be eked out by auxiliaries or by affixes. Subsections of the above may be due to incorporation, as of the object within the verb in Nahuatl or of the conjugated (predicated) adjective in Japanese.

The auxiliaries include verbal auxiliaries, which denote tense, mood, aspect, &c., and nominal auxiliaries, such as prepositions or postpositions. The auxiliaries may be habitually placed before the noun or verb (as in English and Chinese), and in that case they usually retain their independence, or they may follow (as in Turkish). When they follow they can hardly be distinguished from other conjugational or declensional suffixes, and they are liable to fusion in inflected languages. Thus Homeric ᾽Ιλιόθι πρό 'before Ilium' contains in its second word a postposition, if it be not an adverb associated with the verb, but - θι may be explained as flexion, an agglutination or a postposition.

When position and auxiliaries are the only, or almost the only, relational devices used, a language is said to be isolating in type, if its sentences are distinguished by fully formed words. Where there is no such definition, one gets polysynthesis or word-sentences (as in Eskimo), or incorporation of objects and adverbs combined with distinction of subjects (as in Nahuatl), or of adjectives and the copula (as in Japanese), or agglomeration of a principal notion with a number of others (as in Arunta). Order seems to be the elucidating principle with these masses, but the order is liable to be spon-spontaneous rather than logical or grammatical.

Many languages have sought to provide for all contingencies by means of affixes, which may be prefixed, infixed, or suffixed. Prefixation seem to be an African characteristic, strict suffixation characterizes the Altaic languages, while Semitic uses a limited number of prefixes and suffixes. In Indo-European the number of prefixes is usually restricted and the number of suffixes more extensive. The use of infixation for grammatical purposes is a characteristic of Basque and Caucasian, at least in their present state. An important distinction is made when affixation ceases to be theoretically unlimited (as in Turkish), and is reduced to specified forms which can be tabulated in declensions and conjugations (as in Indo-European and Semitic). Thus agglutination differs from flexion. Between the two lie the Finno-Ugric or Uralian languages and the Basque nouns, which can be formed into declensions of about eleven to fifteen cases, but continue to cover other relations by postpositions, scarcely distinguishable from the more elaborate case-endings. The Indo-European cases are spatial, and have to be eked out by prepositions. One may distinguish between a condition, like that of Old Bulgarian or Homeric Greek, in which the relations are denoted by the cases and the nuance provided by the accompanying auxiliaries, and that state of language in which prepositions 'govern' cases. The effect is usually to make the case-signs otiose, and so cause their disappearance, as in Romance.

We may also include mutation among relational devices, since it provides plurals and tenses in Semitic and Indo-European.

Concord. The fourth factor in language is wont to be concord, that is the recognizable adaptation of some words or parts of words to suit others. The zero degree is found in Chinese, in which the word is invariable. Turkish and, in general, Altaic and Finno-Ugrian vowel-harmony is a concord established between the principal stem and its affixes, as in Turkish *değil mi-dir* 'is it not?', *soğuk mu-dur* 'is it cold?', and *bu süt mü-dür* 'is this milk?'[1] Vowel-harmony is also found in some African languages. In an attenuated form it is found in the metaphony, or adaptation of stem-vowels to finals, in Portuguese.

Concord of nouns and verbs arises from the tendency to represent at least the subject, and sometimes the object, within the verbal complex. This is accomplished by means of enclitic or proclitic pronouns. The latter distinguish person (i.e. *EGO et TU* from all the rest, who are pointed out), sometimes number, and less often gender. The effect in Indo-European and Semitic is to associate the subject and verb, in Bantu the subject and object with the verb, and in Basque the indirect object and parties interested in the discourse (ethic dative).

Reference to gender recalls another concord, chiefly shown between substantives and adjectives. Many languages assign substantives to classes, and give these classes a grammatical expression. In some the distinction is into animate and inanimate or masculine and feminine, or both, with further acknowledgement of number and case. Sometimes the class is not marked in the substantive itself, as in Khasi or Caucasian, but is revealed by the concords of

[1] A. C. Mowle, *The New Turkish*, 1942, p. 9.

the sentence. It is highly significant of language structure when, as in Bantu, all substantives are assigned to classes and these are denoted by prefixes, related prefixes being impressed on verbs and any other words associated with the subject. This amounts to a strict disciplining of the sentence under the regimen of the subject. On the other hand, Chinese, Malay, Japanese, and other Far Eastern languages use words which classify their substantives according to their general meaning, but base no concords on these classes.

It will be seen that these four aspects of language structure, with the distinctions to be made within each, serve as a sort of grid providing a summary description of specific tongues. It will be the business of the next chapter to apply these methods. Classification arises out of summary description whenever we are able to isolate some characteristic as eminently possessed by a language or group. Thus the triconsonantalism of Semitic is outstanding, and is associated with a number of other features less uniquely proper to Semitic, but which complete the whole picture. The terms selected as typical, however, may depend on the classifier's purpose. In a broad treatment like this one, it may be best first to note the inflected nature of Semitic, and use its triconsonantalism as a criterion of difference from the inflected Indo-European tongues.

AFFILIATION

To prove kinship of languages it is necessary to combine similarity of formal description with equations of basic stems. Languages are not necessarily related because their processes of construction are the same. A summary description is, as we have shown, necessarily selective, and might apply to unrelated tongues. Etymological equations, however, are rarely so secure as to serve alone to prove kinship. If they are very numerous and can be carried back over a great space of time, as in Indo-European, they have, of course, a high probatory value. The same may arise by the conservatism of a language-family such as the Uralian or the Altaic, or by conservatism combined with ancient and abundant records, as with Semitic. But, generally speaking, unsupported equations allow only shallow inferences, and do not greatly outdistance the historical record. There may be kinships which cannot be proved, nor even satisfactorily demonstrated as probable, simply because the equations have lost probatory force. On the other side, false equations have been so numerous that the evidence of etymology, without the evidence of structural identity, cannot safely be accepted as proof. Owing to religious reasons, for instance, speculative minds have toyed with the notions of connecting Chinese and the Oceanic languages with Semitic, especially as represented by Hebrew, and in older times a strenuous attempt was made to derive all languages from Hebrew. Though these are regarded as unscientific, there are also 'scientific' arguments so tenuously spun as to deserve scarcely more credit.

We have to resign ourselves to an admission of our ignorance. However much energy is devoted to investigating the relationships of some languages, it is unlikely that our positive gains will be more than plausible. The standard puzzle of the kind is provided by Basque, a language lodged in the western Pyrenees and completely unlike its present neighbours. It must, of course, have survived from an epoch before the latinization of the West, but its own records go back in bulk only to 1545, with brief word-lists in the fifteenth and twelfth centuries, and four verbs from the tenth. It is thus separated by a millennium or a millennium and a half from its presumable original, a dialect of the still undeciphered 'Iberian' tongue. The latter is recorded on inscriptions and has been transcribed into a modified Latin alphabet, but the transcriptions resist explanation, including explanation by known Basque words. With the aid of 105 basic words Hugo Schuchardt offered to prove kinship between Basque, Iberian, Berber, and African languages as far as the Upper Nile. It has been pointed out that the same evidence might be used to classify German as African; Berber is Hamitic; Basque is certainly not Hamitic. If, on the other hand, we pin our hopes upon formal description, supported only by the evidence of some suffixes, then the Basque dialects seem to resemble those of the Caucasus. We may add that there was a Caucasian Iberia, the modern Imeretia. Very elaborate hypothetical reconstructions have been offered to include Basque within a Japhetic or an Alarodian language-family. Etymological evidence is singularly poor, and as for grammatical form, we have seen that these systems are rarely exclusive. Basque *lezakiguzukete* 'they could see it for you' and Abkhaz *izleyp'ərxagaxarəzey* 'how will they oppose him?'[1]

---

[1] G. Dumézil, 'Caucasien du Nord et Basque', *Introduction à la grammaire comparée des langues caucasiennes du nord*, Paris, 1933, p. 148. Cf. also J. Karst's 'Asian-Mediterranean' parallels in *Geschichte der armenischen Philologie*, Heidelberg, 1930.

are doubtless both highly complex verbal forms which include various pronominal elements; but they are not more complex than Eng. *aigeftim*, which (because we have had a long history of literacy and grammatical analysis) we happen to write *I gave it him*. In transcribing Bantu words it is optional to write *wakikamatwa* 'if they are handled' as *wa ki ka matwa*, so far as the natives are concerned, since each element is significant and all make one whole. Since breath-groups are continuous emissions of breath, their analysis by words and morphemes is largely a matter of convention and tradition, and the different descriptive terms are not wholly unlike.

On the other hand, precisely those circumstances that make family identification difficult to affirm, prevent categorical denial. We can see only a little way into the history of human speech. In that period convergence is as common as divergence, and one language grows into another. Not only do languages not ramify outward for ever like the branches of a tree, but they are not isolated units like human beings. There is nothing to prevent a language of one sort being construed after the fashion of another, as in 'picin' English (English construed as Chinese) or the Creole dialects. Intermediate stages of convergence are due to symbiosis, as illustrated by the resemblance between Magyar and Indo-European (especially German) sentences.

The special obstacles created by monosyllabism prevent our establishing many etymological equations to support the formal resemblance of Chinese, Siamese, Burmese, and Tibetan. Arranged in that order they form a band extending from the almost totally isolating nature of Chinese to the semiagglutinative structure of Tibetan. A few equations corroborate this association. But whether Sino-Tibetan is akin to Miao and the Mon-Khmer monosyllabic languages, and whether both groups are linked to the dissyllabic, but isolating, Malayo-Polynesian is arguable, though not yet demonstrable. Advancing knowledge of North American Indian languages tends to reduce the number of their 'families' by means of plausible affiliations. Perhaps, too many distinct families have been recognized in South and Central America, and fuller knowledge might elicit more common features.

When a language is, like primitive Bantu, organized on a very distinctive pattern, it is easy to affirm that other languages are not Bantu, but hard to say that they are not akin to Bantu. The class-prefix system of concords has been imposed upon less coherent language-matter, probably at a fairly recent date, say, in the first century of our era. The dissyllabic stems of Bantu include some older and more comprehensive monosyllabic stems, which may once have been much more plentiful. If we discount the specifically Bantu organizational features, what remains is not unlike the stuff of other African languages which employ open syllables, chiefly in monosyllables or dissyllables. African languages have African characteristics; they may have African kinship.

A problem likewise not open to definitive solution is the relationship between the Indo-European and Uralian (Finno-Ugric) families. The former are demonstratively a kindred going back to virtual unity about 3000 B.C. The latter are even more obviously related, and their state of unity is conjecturally placed about 2000 B.C. The Finno-Ugrian languages have borrowed heavily from the Indo-European, not only in the present era, but even when the Aryan branch of Indians and Iranians was still established in south Russia. Thus equations between the two groups are both numerous and ancient and there is great similarity of structure in their declensions and conjugations. What is difficult is to discover an etymological equation which definitely excludes suspicion of borrowing. On the other side of the Urals, the ultimate kinship of Uralian and Altaic languages has been asserted and denied; positive proof is lacking because the comparative history of Turkish, Mongol, and Manchu is still insufficiently known. A dozen or more equations can be set up, extending from Lapland to Japan; the question we cannot answer is, how firm are they? More knowledge would probably show more family likeness, and ramifications might reach out towards the Hyperborean languages of north-east Asia, the ancient Sumerian, and the Dravidian Indian languages which once extended into lands now belonging to Iran and Turan.[1]

[1] Cf. H. Koppelmann's argument to associate all languages from Korea to Europe in *Die eurasische Sprachfamilie*, Heidelberg, 1933. The state of these researches is summarized by C. Tagliavini in his illuminating paper entitled 'La preistoria dell'indoeuropeo e le relazioni di questo con altre famiglie linguistiche'.

XI

LANGUAGES

THEORETICALLY any class or description of language might be encountered anywhere, but in practice it is not so. Individual features recur at great distances, but not only do types occupy vast areas, they shade into each other in a continuous shifting pattern. Monosyllabic Sino-Tibetan in its most westerly form (Tibetan) possesses a considerable number of agglutinative suffixes, which make for easy transition to agglutinative Turkish, which has predominantly monosyllabic basic stems. Though there is no single American family of languages, American features abound in all parts of the two continents. Australian tongues are assigned to branches of a single family, and those of Africa were, according to some theorists, originally one.[1] The consequences of the Indo-European alternation *e/o/-* are found all the way from the Atlantic to the Deccan, and the Semitic permutations of triconsonantal stems extend from Mesopotamia to Morocco. These great language-families share the peculiarity of flexion, and are cushioned against the agglutinative block by semi-inflected, semiagglutinative tongues.

It is true that there are exceptions. Basque is entirely surrounded by Romance speech and cannot be affiliated with any other tongue beyond peradventure. The associations of ancient Etruscan are uncertain, and even its nature is but slowly yielding to analysis. Sumerian remains an enigma, as do Burushaski and Lati farther east. Among the polysynthetic American tongues it is surprising to encounter the monosyllables of Hia-Hiu or Otomí. But these exceptions would not cause surprise if they did not stand out in high relief against a prevailing conformity. Were languages developed at random, disconformity should be normal. The exceptions stimulate investigators to find some place for them in a wider pattern. Intercourse requires a considerable degree of mutual intelligibility between neighbours and builds linguistic bridges (mixed dialects or bilingualism) over frontiers. If our efforts towards accommodation prove unrewarding, we must remember the

[1] 'Having lived to see the unity of Negro-African languages that was proclaimed by us in 1912 become a recognized fact', Mlle L. Homburger, *The Negro-African Languages*, 1949, p. 221.

shortness of our vision. Only in the rarest event do we have a view of 5,000 years of the 50–100,000 years of human speech. Generally the perspective is much shorter, and contracts to some 500 years for Basques and a generation or so for some American tongues. Since it is through history that we solve problems of kinship, we should be in a poor state to pose these questions were it not for the surprising uniformity of the language pattern and the gradual way in which one feature is displaced by another.

The linguistic map (Map I), unlike others, shows double tints in most of its areas. A very small number of international languages cover enormous spaces and serve many millions of human beings. At the same time there is often in the same areas a tight-woven tartan of insignificant dialects which serve only a few hundred or a few thousand speakers. Intermediate between the dozen or so great international languages and these tribal tongues there are some thirty languages which serve as vehicles of important national cultures. The latter are more easily defined than the international ones, since international use springs from various causes, official, commercial, cultural, auxiliary interpretation and so on. Each of these motives implies a different attitude towards local dialects or national languages. The maps of *Les langues du monde* show English restricted to a portion of the British Isles, with considerable areas in solid Celtic green, while the wastes of Canada are assigned to Athabascans and Algonkins, and all Australia to the Australian Blacks. Yet, in fact, Canada and Australia are predominantly English-speaking, just as Siberia (north of Aral and Balkash) has far more Russian-speakers than Buriats or Tunguses. English is not a national language of Holland and Scandinavia, where it is spoken admirably by large sections of the community; it is an administrative language in India and a commercial language from Suez to Hong Kong, but is used by a minority and often as a jargon. French is the *lingua franca* of the Levant, the administrative tongue of Morocco and Algeria, and the second language of most cultured Europeans and South Americans, but is at home only in France, eastern Canada, and Louisiana. Italian has a more than national appeal for people concerned with the arts, and German for those who deal in science and erudition. In short, the international role of languages is varied, and maps would be differently coloured for each criterion of use, but the fact of greatness is well enough established. There are a few languages used for wide communica-

MAP I

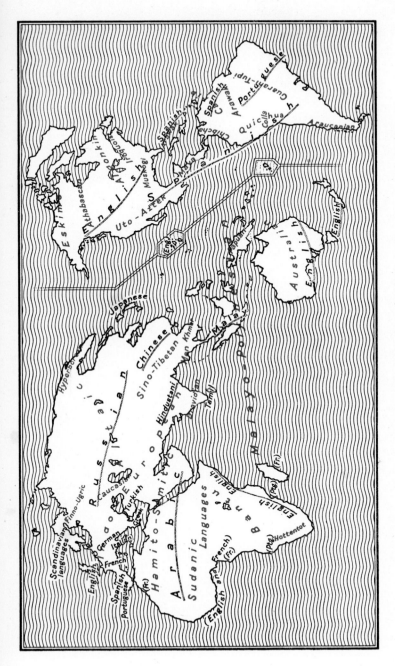

tions. They tend to become fewer and fewer, because civilization requires that the problem of Babel be simplified or eliminated. On the other hand, the immense majority of human speeches have much more modest prospects. Some have attained national status, but the vast majority of the 3,000 serve only restricted communities.

Nor is there anything new in this picture. The tablets of Tell-el-Amarna show the seventy peoples of Babel corresponding diplomatically in one language only: Babylonian. Later on, the commercial and administrative tongue of the Assyrian and Persian empires was Aramean, though the Bible and Herodotus speak of the many 'peoples' of these dominions. Latin, Greek, and Aramean, with Coptic restricted to Egypt, once served the *Oecumene* or inhabited world. The north Chinese of the Han and T'ang dynasties spread as far as Annam, Korea, and Japan in secondary uses. Modern Mandarin occupies three-fourths of the Chinese-speaking area, though Cantonese may be the more direct representative of T'ang. Under barbarous conditions one may find that a politically important language, such as Nahuatl and Quechua, has relatively little expansive force. The present extension of these languages owes rather more to Spanish missionaries than to the old emperors, who were content in Peru to limit instruction to the sons of chiefs. On the other hand, savage Athabascans and Algonkins covered enormous areas of the prairies with dialects of their two tongues. It is where movement is hampered, as in the tangles of the Amazon and of Central America, that languages become isolated and fragmentary.

From the uniformity of human speech some scholars have inferred its original unity.[1] But as to that, we cannot know more than a tenth or twentieth part of the story. The diversity of languages (say, in Asia Minor in the time of St. Paul) is no less remarkable than the overriding prevalence of one; and it is as easy to imagine a prehistoric process of levelling out by intercourse sporadic inventions as to envisage a single dramatic discovery of speech. Once launched on its way, a language is not fatally impelled to splinter into dialects which for ever draw away from each other; their history includes division and reunion and the elimination of weaker languages by stronger. Society tightens or relaxes its control of language according to its need of intercourse. Though mutability afflicts everything beneath the moon, there are some notable

[1] Notably A. Trombetti, *L'Unità dell'Origine del Linguaggio*, Bologna, 1905.

examples of linguistic stability. Evidently, on the other hand, nomads have little need of urban concepts nor savages of philosophy. Matriarchal groups, no doubt, had ways of speech unlike those of the succeeding families ruled by the paterfamilias.[1] One notes, for instance, that the practice of exogamy requires, in Arunta and Quechua, an exact terminology for family relations which distinguishes the paternal and maternal branches but confounds persons of the same degree of affinity on one side. At the other extreme of civilization various sorts of prestige—religion, conquest, superior refinement, commercial advantage, &c., have helped to spread the use of some languages and eliminate others. In sum, though there are many unresolved problems of affinity and type, it is possible to offer in simple form a pattern of the world's languages with types that shade into each other.[2]

While human speech itself is immensely old, it sometimes happens, as we have seen, that a particular family is relatively modern. One thinks of the Romance family, which was constituted by the break up of Latin between the fifth and tenth centuries of our era, or Slavonic, which had only begun to fissify about the year A.D. 1000. Polynesian dialects are still fairly homogeneous because we find that they spread over the Pacific only between the fifth and fourteenth centuries. The last tide of migrants from Malaya reached Madagascar in the sixteenth century. The Bantu languages unquestionably belong to our era, and as late as the fifteenth century they contested the region of the great African lakes with the Hottentots and Bushmen. At an earlier period these savages must have held Africa as far as the shores of the Red Sea. The Indo-European languages were one and enclosed within a relatively small geographical room about 3000 B.C. Finno-Ugric unity has been postulated for about 2000 B.C. (Map II). The pattern of languages which we behold is, at least in part, of relatively recent weaving,

---

[1] This anthropological aspect of language structure is described most amply by Father W. Schmidt, *Sprachfamilien und Sprachenkreise der Erde*, Heidelberg, 1926.

[2] Father Schmidt made seven geographical groups: I. Europe and west and north Asia, II. Africa, III. east and south Asia, IV. Austronesia and Australia, V. North America, VI. Mexico and Central America, VII. South America. Trombetti ignored the Americas and divided his continents into Africa, Eurasia, and Oceania, with ten groups of languages: I. Bantu, II. Hamito-Semitic, III. Caucasian, IV. Indo-European, V. Ural-Altaic, VI. Dravidian, VII. Indo-Chinese, VIII. Mon-Khmer, IX. Malayo-Polynesian, X. Papuan (Andamanese–Papuan–Australian).

MAP II

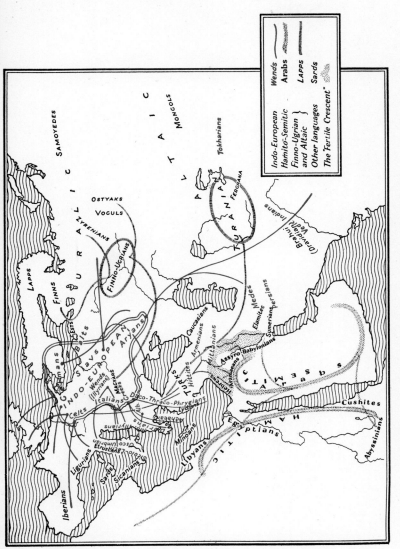

MAP TO ILLUSTRATE THE EXPANSION OF THE INDO-EUROPEAN, HAMITO-SEMITIC, FINNO-UGRIAN AND ALTAIC LANGUAGES

but if we were able to go back beyond our knowledge we might just find other broad patterns. The Mon-Khmer languages almost certainly are the fragments of what was once a vast linguistic community, and it has been argued that Caucasian languages fall, with Etruscan and Basque and lost languages of Asia Minor and the Mediterranean, into a Japhetic or Nostratic or Alarodian family shattered by the advancing Indo-Europeans. It is only in the Americas that efforts at reconstruction encounter insuperable obstacles, but even there scholars tend to reduce the number of language-families as knowledge increases.

I. AUSTRALIA

Tribal memories are too short to reconstruct the history of the Australian peoples, and there are several theories of their origin. One possibility is that they may be connected with the Veddas, Bhils, Gonds, and other primitive tribes of India, with the Andamanese and with scattered communities throughout the Indonesian islands and Papua (Map IV). The crossing was presumably made at Cape York, but there may have been landings farther west. Their languages are still insufficiently studied. Comparisons have been made on a lexical basis and are necessarily insecure. For what they may be worth, Trombetti[1] gives words for 'ear' which show likeness between some Andaman, English New Guinea, and Central Australian dialects. The extinct Tasmanians are said to have resembled 'Papuans' and Malays, but the first term is far from secure.

Within the Continent, the Northern languages are held by Father Schmidt to be distinct from the Southern, and the latter divide into a south-western and a south-eastern group. The easterly languages are much subdivided.

Protected by the stormy Timor Sea, the jungles of Papua, and the great coral barrier, with further obstacles on the inhospitable northern coast and the desert centre, the Australian tribes are to be found with their backs to the civilized world. Their racial affinities nowhere show a higher stage of civilization, so that we may take them as authentic modern representatives of Stone Age culture. Since all peoples have passed through a Stone Age, the primitive Australians give some sort of notion of the conditions of that life, and of the language created to serve it. It happens that

[1] *L'Unità dell' Origine del Linguaggio*, p. 14.

one of their tribes, the Arunta, has been described as a society by
Spencer and Gillen and as speakers by Strehlow and others. A
certain contradiction has arisen between the anthropologists, who
envisage a community with limited horizons, and the grammarians,
who interpret plurality of forms as due to an acute grammatical
sense. A Sommerfelt[1] has investigated this difficulty and has pointed
out that want of organization would give the same excess of forms,
and that the Arunta system is characterized by indifference to
many of the grammatical distinctions of other languages.

The basic stems of Arunta are often monosyllabic or dissyllabic,
but cannot be precisely determined owing to the interchangeability
of speech-sounds. The vowel *a* is most common, and *i* and *u* are
identified, though they may be interchangeable with *a* or with no
vowel. The voiceless occlusives (*p t k*) may become voiced without
change of sense. Thus *alpa alba ilba ulba lpa lba* are undifferentiated
and *lama illuma, lara larra laia ulara,* &c. The vowels *e o* seem secondary. Consonant groups, other than those (largely accidental) which
involve the sonants *l m n r*, are rare, and the most common phonetic
feature of the language is its regular alternation of consonants and
vowels, as in *gunama, laramanga, larakalberama*. Meanings are
always tangible and palpable; the Arunta have no capacity for
abstraction. Lacking a sense of personality, their 'personal' pronouns are rather indications of position in space. They have no
proper numerals or specialized parts of speech, but their stems are
gerundial, yielding nouns or verbs according to circumstances.

It is difficult to speak of derivation, though stems fuse easily and
suffixation is a normal procedure. The reason lies in the system of
relations, which is effected by agglomerations of suffixes and quali-
ficatives following the principal stem. A purely spontaneous order
of discourse, which does not necessarily imply a definite sentence,
moves from one concrete expression surrounded with its qualifica-
tives to the next. Suffixes operate less as grammatical signs than by
their own vague intrinsic force. Sommerfelt's texts are chants, and
thus submitted to a discipline of rhythm, but their spontaneous
sequence is illustrated by such lines as

> *nutupirkiljirkil nopanama*
> *keratja nuturka nopanama*

which he explains as 'ventre saillant — être assis constamment —

---

[1] *La langue et la société*, Oslo, 1938.

(creux) se trouvant sur la plaine — ventre court — être assis constamment'. This means 'the large-bellied opossum is there, the short-bellied animal is in the hollow of the plain'. The sentence can only be construed in sight of the animal or of the totemic ceremony itself. It has no definite form, but is composed of groups of notions as they present themselves to the speaker.

There has been no intellectual effort to rationalize experience by dividing nouns into classes or genders, and Arunta folk-tales show no understanding of the phenomena of sex, though obvious facts are noted. There is no basis for concord in Arunta grammar.[1]

2. AMERICA

The human associations of the Americas are with Asia and Oceania, not with Europe and Africa. The Atlantic became a barrier before the emergence of the great apes. During the period between the rise of the primates and the beginnings of Man the continents were presumably unoccupied. American Man entered with a number of skills, including the domestication of the dog and basket-making, but without domesticated cattle or horses or the wheel. Since these people are 'mongoliform', entry by the Alaskan bridge or the Behring Straits is generally favoured, but it is not impossible that the inhabitants of South America may have come, at least in part, drifting along the ocean currents from Polynesia. Parallel word-lists have been offered by P. Rivet for Hoka (Oregon-Tehuantepec) and Malayo-Polynesian (281 instances) and for Chon and Australian.[2]

Arctic America is associated with Kamchatka in such a way that the 'Hyperboreans' and the Eskimo-Aleuts are held to form one

---

[1] A map of the 'Post-Palaeolithic Cultural Invasions of South-East Asia' in *Chambers's Encyclopaedia*, 1950 (s. v. 'Asia'), vol. i, p. 685, shows two movements into Australia. One, the Microlithic, follows the line of the islands as far as Timor and enters Australia by Arnhem Land. The other is the Hoabhinian, and take the route Borneo–Celebes–Papua–Cape York. Papua itself is affected by three other movements.

The remoteness of Australia can be estimated by the fact that, even with modern seamanship, its discovery required over a century and a half: from Janszoon's sight of Cape York Peninsula in 1606 to Cook's anchoring in Botany Bay in 1770.

A summary grammar of south Narrinyeri (mouth of the Murray River) is given by E. Kieckers, *Die Sprachstämme der Erde*, Heidelberg, 1931, pp. 136–40, with parallels from other languages.

[2] *Les origines de l'homme américain*, pp. 303, 306, quoted by L. Pericot, *América Indígena*, 1926, vol. i, pp. 434–5.

linguistic group, the Palaeoarctic. It is below the Arctic that the real America begins. Estimates of the linguistic situation are:

Language families in	North	Middle	and South America (Map I)
(Rivet) . . .	25	20	77
(Schmidt) . . .	20	12	35
(Kieckers) . . .	22	27	45

P. Radin proposed a drastic reduction of the North American languages to three groups, but that is as yet an hypothesis beyond scientific verification. H. Hoijer regards the greater number of South American tongues as insufficiently described but singles out twenty as of particular importance. His Middle group is twenty-three, but north of Mexico he counts individual languages, not families, and reaches a total of fifty-three (apart from Eskimo-Aleut). Pericot's description refers primarily to peoples.[1]

It is plain that there is no American family of languages, though American features are found throughout them all. What chiefly characterizes this speech situation is the absence of linguistic hegemony and want of grammatical specialization. The sentence is still a matter of blocks of stems and particles, whether treated agglomeratively as in Delaware, or with incorporation as in Nahuatl (the noun-object being part of the verb) or Yana (conjugated adjectives), or agglutinatively and with an imperfect approximation to declension and conjugation as in Quechua. Complete holo-synthesis or the word-sentence, which implies definition of sentences or clauses, is attained in Eskimo, but polysynthesis is general in both continents. Monosyllabism occurs in Otomí and the Maya word seems normally very short.

As to the other characteristic of this area, the most advanced civilization was that of the Mayas. It was illiterate and completely self-regarding. One colony only was planted—on the Mexican coast near Vera Cruz. Nahuatl is one of a family which extends from Montana to Tehuantepec, but was only one of four used in the market-place of Tenochtitlan (Mexico City). Quechua was taught to the sons of subject princes in Cuzco, but the name of the empire,

---

[1] P. Rivet, Les langues du monde, Paris, 1924; W. Schmidt, Sprachfamilien, Heidelberg, 1926; E. Kieckers, Die Sprachstämme der Erde, Heidelberg, 1931; H. Hoijer's Introduction to Linguistic Structures of Native America, New York, 1946; L. Pericot, América Indígena, Madrid, 1936. I should like to take this opportunity of thanking the officers of the New York Viking Fund for their generosity in sending me the third of these works.

Ttahuantin-suyu 'Four Provinces', acknowledged its polyglot character. Spanish friars used Nahuatl and Quechua for missionary purposes, and Portuguese missionaries made one of the Tupi-Guaraní dialects serve as a *língua geral*. In this character these languages were supported by printed prayers and catechisms and even by a rudimentary literature, but in expanding their area they seem to have lost native vigour.

The three geographical divisions depend on obstacles to intercourse. The southern continent is cut off by the tangled jungles of Panamá, but has an easy outlet along the sickle of islands from Trinidad to Cuba. A similar region of entanglement occurs in southern Mexico, where the highlands plunge down to the Isthmus of Tehuantepec. Though it is customary to carry the term Middle America as far north as the Rio Grande, there is in fact no interruption of linguistic continuity as far south as the Mexican plateau endures. In its northern extension into the United States the same plateau ensures ease of movement and community of social conditions as far north as the Canadian border and forms a natural social area quite distinct from the prairies on the one side and the coastal fringe on the other. The prairies allow for the wide extension of a thinly spread population and account for the great space occupied by Athabascan, Algonkin, Iroquois, Muskogee, and other savage tongues. The west coast is broken into fragments occupied by many small tongues. Similarly, in South America, movement is favoured along the inter-Andine plateau, where life is quite different from that of the Pacific coast or the Amazon forests.

The principal indigenous language[1] of South America is Quechua (Kitšwa), which occupies the high plateaux between the Cordilleras from Quito in Ecuador to Tucumán. It is essentially an Andine

[1] In addition to the general surveys by Rivet, Pericot, Schmidt, and Kieckers, I have at hand C. Markham, *Quichua Grammar and Dictionary*, London, 1864; B. Jurado Palomino, *Catechismus Quichuensis*, ed. H. Galante (with grammar), Madrid, 1943; F. de Ávila, *De priscorum Huaruchiriensium origine et institutis*, ed. H. Galante, Madrid, 1942. P. M. Benvenutto Murrieta, *El Lenguaje Peruano*, Lima, vol. i, 1936 (for which I am indebted to the author); J. B. M. Farfán, *Clave de la Lengua Quechua*, Lima, 1940 (thanks to Dr. J. V. Harrison's kindness); *Catálogo de las voces usuales de Aimará*, Paris, s.d.; J. M. Camacho, 'La Lengua aymará', *Boletín de la Sociedad Geográfica*, La Paz, 1945; A. Tovar, 'Lengua guaraní', *Anales del Instituto de Lingüística*, Mendoza, 1950; M. A. Morínigo, *Hispanismos en el guaraní*, Buenos Aires, 1931; R. Lenz, in *Zeitschrift für romanische Philologie*, vol. xvii, for Mapuche, and his observations in *La Oración y sus Partes*, Madrid, 1925; C. H. de Goeje, 'Fünf Sprachfamilien Südamerikas', *Mededelingen d. k. Akad. v, Wetenschapen*, Amsterdam, 1935.

language since the coast belongs to Yunga and the eastern Peruvian forests to Amazonian tongues. South of Lake Titicaca there is an enclave of 600,000 Aimará-speaking Collas, and these people held the western Cordillera as far north as Central Peru at the time of the Conquest. General similarity of phonemes, stem structure, and grammar suggests that Aimará and Quechua may be related. Modern Aimará vocabulary uses the same names as Quechua for many common objects, but for others it appears markedly unlike (e.g. *checca/checa* 'truth', *charqui* 'jerked beef', *challhua* 'fish', but *cchaca/tullu* 'bone', *chaclla/guagua* 'child', *maya/uc* 'one' &c.).

There are two Quechua orthographies, one agreed by the congress of Americanists of 1939, and another developed by Spanish missionaries and used for a considerable number of religious works, chronicles, and even one play. The revised alphabet includes some English (American) digraphs and excludes some that are typically Spanish but does not seem conspicuously more faithful.

Quechua basic stems are gerundial in meaning, i.e. not specifically nouns or verbs. The fact that personal endings of the verb are the same as possessive suffixes of nouns bears witness to this degree of grammatical indifference. The common form of stem is dissyllabic: either *xóxo* or *xóxxo*, where *x* stands for any consonant, and *o* for any vowel. When the second syllable is closed, the final consonant may be a suffix: from *cama-* or *kama-* 'creation, creating', which gives *kamaq* (*camac*) 'creator' and *kamay* 'to create'. Derivation is by fusion (*Pachacamac* 'Demiurge, God'), reduplication (*runaruna* 'crowd, people', collective from *runa* 'man'). There may be many derivatives from one basic Quechua or Aimará stem. The voiceless consonants *p t ch(č) k q s sh(š)* are not paired with voiced consonants. Voicing occurs accidentally and is without significance, as also the pronunciation of *i u* as *e o*. Thus *tampu* gives Sp. *tambo* 'shop', *pampa* is found in *Urubamba* and *Cochabamba*, &c. The voiceless consonants may, however, apart from *ch* and *sh*, be accompanied by aspiration (*ph* &c.), or preceded by a glottal stop and made more explosive (*pp cch* &c.). Thus Quechua phonetics stand between those that are 'easy' and those that are 'difficult' for Europeans. There is a palatal *ll*[λ], but *l* is rare and is confused with fricative *r* (*Rimaq* > *Lima*).

Relations are defined by suffixes only, and these are not self-sufficient in formation. The noun's suffixes form a declension of eight or eleven cases, which merge into a general use of postpositions where we use prepositions. The qualifier precedes the thing qualified (adjective before substantive, adverb before adjective). There are absolute forms of pronouns, but these are mostly suffixed in abbreviated form to nouns or verbs. The first person plural has inclusive and exclusive forms. Verbs suffix subject pronouns, and a remarkable feature is the existence of four other conjugations to mark the transition of an action from a subject to another person. This is effected by combining pronominal suffixes, not by employing another set of subject pronouns as in Hungarian. Time and mood are indicated by suffixes, and there are plenty of participles. According to C. R. Markham the sentence order is object–verb–subject.

As nouns are not classified, there is no concord apart from number. A decimal system of numerals is used, and has 3, 5, 6, 10, 100, 1,000 in common with Aimará. There is a plural sign -*kuna*, but the notion of plurality does not seem fully established, and various realistic devices are employed.

Like most American languages Quechua is highly polysynthetic. Thus Professor Farfán cites *paykunaq yanapayachikunankupas chinkapunkus* as meaning 'their folk—who (they thought) would help them—have been lost'. This involves the analysis: *pay-kuna-q yana-pa-ya-chi-kuna-na-n-ku-pas chinka-pu-n-ku-s*, with three basic stems (*pay* 'he', *yana* 'aid', *chinka* 'lose'), thirteen suffixes, and one euphonic sign.

In contrast to Quechua, Tupí-Guaraní did not serve an empire but owed its extensive use as a *língua geral* in Paraguay, NE. Argentina, and Brazil to its simplicity of sounds and forms. The basic stems are, apparently, open monosyllables, but are extended by somewhat naïve processes of reduplication. The stress accent is on the last syllable: *guarāré* 'fall noisily' (*ai*)*põcãyorá* 'untie'. The six vowels (*a e i ï o u*) may be nasalized, but there are none of mixed type. The consonants are *g k t p, n ñ m, y ch[ĉ] r s*, fricative *b*, but no *l* or *ll*[λ]. *Mb* and *nd* are sounds of double formation. Oddly enough *ll* has been acquired from Spanish and is retained, though now unknown to Argentines, Uruguayans, and some Brazilians. A prefix *mbo* makes a neutral stem into a factitive verb, as *guëyi* 'descend'/*mbogüeyi* 'put down', *pú* 'sound'/*mbopú* 'cause to sound, play'. A suffix -*ucá* is causative: *mbopucá* 'cause someone to play'. Grammatical specialization is still rudimentary; phonemes may serve indifferently nouns and verbs. A number of particles express time, interrogation, exclamation, and different categories of action, and may be classed as adverbs. The final accent is used to give an 'Indianist' flavour to writing in Spanish and Portuguese. The language shows many agglomerations, and it is not certain, in the absence of a native criterion, whether to print these as groups or analytically as separate words.

The Tupies and Guaranies migrated by water, either along shores of Brazil or along the courses of eastern affluents of the the Amazon and Paraná rivers. Their language is still that of the market-place in Paraguay and was that of Brazil (except for administration) until the nineteenth century. They have enclosed on the east Brazilian massif the little-known Ge (* Že*) people or Tapuyas, who know themselves as Nan-manuc or Burús. Their language is said to tend towards isolation.

Quechua and Tupí-Guaraní are the two languages of international importance in South America. South of them, the Mapuche language of the Araucanian Indians is known from Lenz's careful descriptions. To it was wrongly ascribed the role of a cause in the evolution of Chilean pronunciation. It has the interesting feature of what Lenz calls 'pro-verbs', that is, symbols of person and time without the actual stem of some simple verbs. Puelche and Tehuelche are spoken on the Argentine plains, and Alacaluf, Yahgan, and Ona in the island fringe. The upper Amazon basin is occupied by a tangle of languages (Pano, Tucan, Katukina, &c.); it was out of this region that speakers of various dialects of Arawak emigrated. They descended the Orinoco in canoes and followed the sickle of the Antilles to Cuba and the Bahamas. Hence they were the first peoples encountered by Columbus, and gave to Europeans the names of typical American objects. The cannibal Caribs followed them from Venezuela along the Lesser Antilles, devouring the men and marrying the women, so that these islands were remarkable for their distinction between male and female languages. The Chibcha language of Colombia extends along the Panamá isthmus to Lake Nicaragua.

The Central American region, extending as far as the isthmus of Tehuantepec, is excessively complex. At its northern end is Maya, the language of the highest American semi-civilization, which was developed by city-states. Apart from the sudden and unexplained abandonment of their sites, the Maya people and their language showed little power of expansion. Though a polysynthetic

LANGUAGES 317

or incorporating language, Maya seems to be a language of organization. It has definite parts of speech and a consistent association of
form and sense.[1]

The Rio Grande is not an Indian frontier. More important for
them was the Chichimec or Barbarian frontier which runs west
from Tampico through Central Mexico. North of that line conditions of life are those of North American savages. South are many
barbaric or semi-civilized peoples with Central American affinities:
Otomi-Mangue, Zapotek, Mixtek, Mixe, &c. Into the midst of
them a North American speech-family has intruded, and has become the most important of all, viz. the Aztec and Toltek branches
of the Uto-Aztec family. Migration has been favoured by the inter-
mont plateaux which extend from Montana to Tehuantepec. The
Uto-Aztecs include the Shoshoni sub-family (to which the Utes
belong), the Sonorans of northern Mexico, and the Aztec (Nahuatl)
and Toltek (Nahuat) groups. It is on passing the Chichimec line
that these peoples pass from nomadic to settled conditions of life.
The Tolteks led the invasion, but were followed by the fiercer
Aztecs not long before the Spanish Conquest.

For Nahuatl or Aztec there are two orthographies: the old
Spanish transliterations, which have some support in missionary
propaganda, literature, and maps, and modern phonetic transcriptions.[2] This is the typical incorporating language, viz. one in which
the subject noun is distinguished, while the direct and indirect
object and adverbs remain within the verbal complex. The noun,
when isolated, has singulative and plural suffixes which depend on
its phonetic construction or on usage. The result is a set of discriminations analogous to declensions:

(From Sandoval)

Singular	Plural	
ichcatl	ichcamê	'sheep'
teotl	teteô	'god'
oquichtli	oquichtin	'man'

[1] S. G. Morley, *The Ancient Maya*, Stanford, 1947, pp. 18–20; an account of
Subtiaba is given by Kieckers, from Lehmann. Other languages of the area are
Lenka, Matagalpa, Miskito, Sumo, Khikake, Paya, &c.
[2] B. L. Whorf, 'The Milpa Alta Dialect of Aztec', in *Linguistic Structures of
Native America* (Viking Fund Publication), New York, 1944. Whorf's 'The
Hopi Language, Toreva dialect' refers to a language of the Shoshoni branch of
the family. For the older style of grammars I have at hand R. Sandoval, *Arte de
la Lengua mexicana*, Mexico, 1810.

totolin	totoltin/totolmê	'bird'
telpochtli	telpopochtin	'youth'
chihuatontli	chihuatotontin	'dog' (suffix -*ton*-)
tlatlacoanipal	tlatlacoanipopol	'sinner'

Nouns are not distributed among genders. Casual endings do not form a closed series, though it is possible to select some of the more common as cases. Whorf claims that there is a case system in Hopi. As for incorporation, the noun complement of the verb lies between the pronoun representing the subject and the verbal stem, as *ni-petla-chihua* 'I make mats' (or *nipeλačiwa*), but its sense derives from the context. Thus this incorporated noun may be an indirect object or an adverb of some sort, as *nicxochipepena in tomin* 'I select money like flowers' and *xochiquiponi in milli* 'millet grows like flowers' by the incorporation of *xochi-* (*šoči-*) 'flower', or *nixcocona* 'my eyes are sore' by the incorporation of *ix-* (*iš-*) 'eye' in a locative sense ('as to my eyes').[1]

Basic stems are of various lengths, and constructed without voiced occlusives or fricatives, with two laterals (*l ll/tl* = Whorf's λ) but no *r*, two nasals (*m n*), and four primary vowels (*a e i o*, with *u ε ɔ* as functional variants). Derivation is by fusion, reduplication, and suffixation. Casual relations are also shown by postpositions. The pronouns show their basic forms as prefixes of verbs or possessives of nouns (*no-cal* 'my house'), but have more elaborate forms when standing alone. Tense and aspect employ the same symbols, and there are aspects not referring to time, as the frequentative, transitive, causative, applicative, and respectful. Verbal nouns and verbal adjectives are readily formed by use of prefixes and suffixes, and take the place of nouns referring to actions, site, instrument, passivity, &c. (*no-tla-popolhui-lo-ca* 'my pardon' = 'my being pardoned': *tla . . . ca* being the combined prefix and suffix of passivity). It is easy to derive verb from verb or noun, and noun from noun or verb, and suffixes are readily piled on each other.

The languages of North America, and especially of the United States and Canada, have been studied meticulously by Brinton, Boas, Sapir, Bloomfield, Hoijer, and their associates. Many have disappeared, and some are almost extinct.[2] Under these circum-

---

[1] The indirect object or dative is indicated by the use of 'applicative' forms of the verb ('to do something for someone').

[2] Miss Mary Haas remarks that there is only one Tunica Indian (born *c.* 1870) 'who has the ability to speak his language with any degree of fluency'. See 'A Grammatical Sketch of Tunica' in *Linguistic Structures of Native America*, 1946,

stances it is natural that the method of linguistic analysis should not take account of social conditions. The number of separate families of languages is being reduced by American scholars, who are cautiously forming ever larger aggrupations. It is even possible to attempt a historical reconstruction when there are plenty of dialect variations, as in L. Bloomfield's reconstruction of 'Proto-Algonquian', based on a comparison of Fox, Cree, Menomini, and Ojibwa. Ease of movement on the eastern flank of the Rockies has given huge thinly occupied territories to the Athabascan languages in central and northern Canada and along the Rio Grande, to the Algonkins of eastern and south-central Canada, the Mississippi and the eastern seaboard of the United States (so as to enclose completely the Iroquois of the St. Lawrence, Erie, and Ontario), and to the Sioux of the Missouri and Arkansas lowlands). The Muscogi family, which includes the Creeks and Choctaws, has a considerable domain from Georgia to Louisiana. On the other hand, these wide-ranging peoples are thinly spread on the ground. The Uto-Azteks occupy most of the plateaux; and between the western ranges and the sea, there is an intricate pattern of local tongues, with intrusive elements from elsewhere.

These languages offer to American students a vast laboratory for the study of linguistic devices. Some have genders and the dual, others have not; some are highly polysynthetic or agglomerative, and others relatively simple; some are so fluid in phonetic structure that they imitate in sound the persons or animals introduced into a narrative. In Yana (North California) the adjective is conjugated as in Japanese. All these languages are without letters or the rudiments of civilization, and so offer conditions considered ideal by many linguists, viz., complete absence of interference in the spoken evolution by literary conventions. They use very different phonetic and grammatical resources, though the tendency to polysynthesis is most marked. Thus in Delaware (east Algonkin) *kpa-tama-ṭíhimo héč* means 'are you little fellows praying?', *enta-kəntká-ṭie-kw* means 'when you little fellows were dancing', *kaṭa-ləmskáhamo heč* 'do you fellows want to get going?'[1] They are also

---

p. 337. Some Californian languages are extinct. Similarly Mr. M. Swadesh says 'There is only one person who can speak the Chitimacha language among sixty or so who constitute the present population of the tribe on Bayou Teche in southern Louisiana', ibid., p. 312.

[1] C. F. Voegelin, 'Delaware', *Linguistic Structures of America*, New York, pp. 154–5.

remarkably concrete in expression. An action cannot always be expressed simply as an action; it must be made more realistic by indicating the position and character of the parties. Miss Haas, for Tunica, distinguishes between 'her dogs' (collective) and 'her dogs' (as individuals, male and female). She describes Tunica nouns as masculine or feminine in gender, with a cross-division into animate (human and non-human) and inanimate. The inanimates are integers like 'stone' or continuous like 'water'. The integers are mostly masculine in the singular and dual, but become feminine (continuous) in the plural, while continuous inanimates are feminine, but not dualized or pluralized. Visibility or invisibility is made part of the demonstrative pronoun in Tshimshian and Kwakiutl, and also in neighbouring Chinook and Salish dialects.[1] The speaker cannot at all withdraw his attention from the immediate occurrence. Taken as a whole, these languages give witness to the extraordinary variety of secondary concepts human beings have believed to be necessary for a complete expression, just as Chinese is proof that almost all may be intelligibly omitted.

3. AMERASIA

From Greenland to the Kolyma in Siberia, with some extensions as far as the Lena, there is a region of sea communications during summer and solid ice over land and sea during winter. In Asia its languages are known as Hyperborean (a merely geographical term) and are thinly spoken and excessively ill known. They show holosynthetic traits like the Eskimo dialects on America, though we cannot definitely prove kinship and constitute a Palaeoarctic speech area. Arguments have been put forward for considering Eskimo as one member of an enormous family embracing the Uralian, Altaic, Eskimo, Korean, and Japanese tongues. In this arrangement account is taken of the projection of Eskimo, through Aleutic, towards the northern Japanese islands, and the Hyperborean languages (if they do, in fact, form a family) are regarded as an enclave. The separation of Eskimo from American Indian languages is complete so far as affinity goes, but in respect of type it is no more than the perfection of the polysynthesis which most American tongues show to a greater or lesser degree. It may be relevant to note that the Arctic specialization of Eskimos or Inuits—a landward winter season in the snows of winter and a seaward summer hunting

[1] L. Bloomfield, *Language*, New York, 1946, p. 470.

season—draws them away from the nomad Athabascans. Eskimo life seems to imply great skill within a very limited sphere of possible achievement.[1]

The fact of Eskimo holosynthesis has been better illustrated than its nature and syntax. It is not that every sentence is a word-sentence, but that in a single word-group stems of equal importance are associated. Thus it is possible to deny that Algonkin (Fox) *ehkiwinamohtatiwach(i)* is truly holosynthetic on the ground that there is only one principal stem (*kiwi* 'movement') amid subordinate affixes (agglomeration). In so far as the word-sentence seems to imply recognition of the sentence as a structural unit, it may be considered an effort of specialization superior to, for instance, that of an incorporating language like Nahuatl. Within the word-sentence stems are related by position, and are also substantially invariable. Their syntax is thus not wholly incompatible with that of an isolating language. Standing separately, Eskimo stems have grammatical props and not necessarily the same vocalization that appears in the word-sentence. A different path of evolution is suggested by the presence of phenomenal elements, especially toward the end of the clause. This tends towards specializing an agglutinative verb at the end of the phrase, and so holosynthesis is capable of shading into agglutination. The Turkish verb is final. But in the typical form one may assert (as Meščaninov does) that all the stems in a word-sentence are nouns.[2] That is to say, they name things or activities, or things as activities; they are better described as gerunds. The Hyperborean languages show decomposition of the word-sentence with a tendency toward agglutination, i.e. towards the Altaic type of speech. They show the development of the final verb from final particles specialized to represent the phenomenal aspect of the phrase; but they also show verbs in middle position.

To exemplify: 'One entirely failed to find a resting place' and 'he has nothing fit for a special report' are both phrases composed of elements on the same plane of importance. Both are word-

---

[1] For the Hyperboreans I must rely chiefly on notes in I. I. Meščaninov, *Členy predloženija i časti reči*, Moscow, 1945, and *Glagol*, Moscow, 1949. For Eskimo, as well as study of some of W. Thalbitzer's writings, I have at hand the account in F. N. Finck, *Die Haupttypen des Sprachbaus*, 3 ed., 1936, and M. Swadesh, 'South Greenlandic', *Linguistic Structures of Native America*, New York, 1946.

[2] I. I. Meščaninov, *Glagol*, Moscow, 1949, p. 11.

sentences in south Greenland Eskimo. The former is *qasu-iiɣ-saɣ-βiɣ-ṣaɣ-si-ññit-luinaɣ-naɣ-puq* which is built up from 'tired+not to be = rest, +cause to+place of = resting-place, +find+not to = not to find a resting-place, +entirely+there is . . . -ing by someone = there is entirely a failing by someone to find a resting-place'.

In the Hyperborean languages one may trace, according to Meš-čaninov, the beginnings of analysis. The word-sentence exists in Koryat *tyjamajn'ylautytkynajkyplyg'e* 'I'll hit you hard on the head', or Chukchee *tymajn'yvaljamnarkyn* 'I am sharpening a big knife' (I big knife sharpen). The latter has the verb at the end, but a medial verb appears in *typeljarkynegyt* 'I'll leave you'. In each *rkyn* marks present time. In Chukchee adjectives are united with nouns, in Gilyak objects with predicates. Aleutic marks the third person subject or object, noun or verb, by the suffix *-h*, present time by *-ku-*, possibility by *-ka-*, and these phenomenal elements are massed at the end of the verbal complex in *ada-h ikja-h sigutasiga-ka-ku-h* (SOV) 'father is probably repairing the boat'. The repetition of the suffix gives a primitive concord of subject and verb. The same order—subject–object–verb—is found in Turkish and Japanese, which have the same massing of phenomenal elements at the end of the sentence.

4. ASIA ULTERIOR AND OCEANIA

The dramatic opposition between isolating and synthetic languages is set against the equally dramatic background of the highest mountain ranges of the earth. These begin to rise with the Stanovoi Mountains of Siberia and continue to increase in height along the Altai and T'ien Shan systems to culminate in the knot of the Pamirs. Then they turn abruptly eastward along the line of the Himalayas. Lastly there is a right-angled bend southward in a series of parallel ridges, which thrust south through Assam to Arakan, and along the spine of Indo-China to Malaya. Mountains are not a barrier in themselves, but commonly serve to distinguish highlanders from lowlanders. Thus there are Mongols on the steppes south of the Altai range, and Tibetan peoples south of the Himalayas. But the great Asiatic V is backed by forbidding wastes: the cold wet forests of the Amur, the Gobi and Takla-makan deserts, the barrens of western Tibet, and the hot wet forests of Arakan. The 'black water' of the Bay of Bengal has not prevented

MAP III

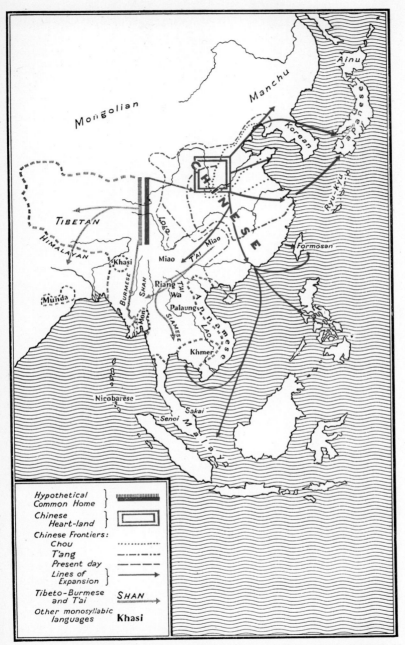

MAP TO ILLUSTRATE THE EXPANSION OF THE SINO-TIBETAN
LANGUAGES

PLATE III.

MAP TO ILLUSTRATE THE EXPANSION OF THE SINO-TIBETAN
LANGUAGES

Indian cultural influences from reaching the Far East, but has deterred Indian peoples from expansion overseas.

There is reason to place the focus of migration somewhere along the borders of China and Tibet (Map III). The southward turn of the gorges has led a series of migratory waves south along the Irrawaddy into Burma, or by the Salween into Siam. The head of the Red River valley of Tongking also touches this nucleus. The western side of the Malay peninsula takes sea-faring people to the islands of Indonesia, which sweep eastward to Papua and Australia and also north-eastward to the Philippines and Formosa. Micronesia forms an island bridge as far as Samoa and Tahiti. From Tahiti Polynesian voyagers have sailed to colonize Hawaii and New Zealand. The Pacific has proved to be an open road for a succession of migrations, including those of isolating languages of the dissyllabic type. From Java it has also proved possible to sail south of the monsoon belt to Madagascar, and even to plant linguistic colonies on the mainland of Africa (Map IV).

Mention has already been made of the early migrations of Negrito folk to Melanesia, Papua, and Australia. In the area we are now discussing there are three great language families: Sino-Tibetan, Austric or Munda-Nicobarese-Khasi-Mon-Khmer, and Austronesian or Malayo-Polynesian. The first two have a monosyllabic, the last a dissyllabic, base. They all resist analysis so far that it is not possible to affirm or deny their ultimate unity of origin. There are likenesses which may be due to affinity or to the effects of association; for instance, both Malay and the T'ai branch of Sino-Tibetan place the attribute after the noun, whereas the adjective is prefixed in Chinese.[1]

Chinese has had a tremendous influence on the grammar and vocabulary of Korean and Tibetan, but these appear to be basically distinct.

China has always been a way of living rather than a state or a linguistic unit, and in this sense its 'cradle land' seems to have been located in the great southern bend of the Yellow River. As a civilization it is probably autochthonous.[2] But the sharp division

---

[1] See especially, W. Schmidt, *Sprachfamilien*, Heidelberg, 1926; K. Wolff, *Über das Verhältnis des Mālāyo-polynesischen zum Indochinesischen*, Copenhagen, 1942.

[2] H. G. Creel, *The Birth of China*, London, 1936; maps of Chinese expansion in L. C. Goodrich, *A Short History of the Chinese People*, London, 1948, C. P. Fitzgerald, *China*, London, 1942.

between great and little men and the attribution of a life after death
to the souls (the character represents a skeleton) only of the great,
suggests that the Shangs (c. 1523–1027 B.C.) were victorious
intruders. The Chous (1027–265) came from the west by the Wei
river valley and were not regarded as wholly civilized, and the
Ch'ins (221–201) from farther west were semi-barbaric. There is
no reason to believe these invaders were not Chinese-speaking. It
follows that the earliest period shows a drift from some base
approximately in Kansu and Szechwan into the loess belt at the
bend of the Yellow River, and in this supposed original emplace-
ment Chinese-speakers would be in contact with the nomad
ancestors of the Tibetans. The T'ais formed a powerful kingdom
around Talifu in Yünnan between the sixth and ninth centuries
and began to infiltrate southward in the twelfth. The Burmese
kingdom of Pagan was established about A.D. 800, but the mouth
of the Irrawaddy is still in other hands. Actual linguistic proof of
Sino-Tibetan unity is difficult to obtain because of the singularly
resistant nature of the evidence. Monosyllables defy analysis into
parts. Chinese characters are designed to convey meaning (which
they do admirably) rather than sound, and it was only as a result
of association with Indian phoneticians that a phonetic account
was given of Chinese as it existed in the fifth–seventh centuries of
our era.[1] Medieval Chinese can be reconstructed and compared
with Tibetan, which is written in an alphabet of Indian origin true
for about the same period. This gives apparently related words for
woman, dog, silver, ear, I, day, die, fish, come, some pronouns, and
the numerals, and it is possible to make out a similar list for
Siamese.

Chinese is the typical isolating language, monosyllabic and invariable. Every concept or relation is expressed by a word, perfectly definite in form and meaning, and unalterable. Derivation
is possible only by juxtaposition, the convention being that two or
more words may be associated to give a meaning common to both
or due to their common factors. This device is used also to form
some Chinese characters, formed from simple pictographs. Thus
the signs for two bright objects (sun and moon) are combined in
$ming^2$ 'bright'. On the other hand $ming^2$ 'bright' and pai^2 'clear,
white' combine to give the new sense of 'understand'.

---

[1] These reconstructions are due primarily to B. Karlgren and H. Maspéro;
see R. D. Forrest, *The Chinese Language*, London, 1948.

MAP IV

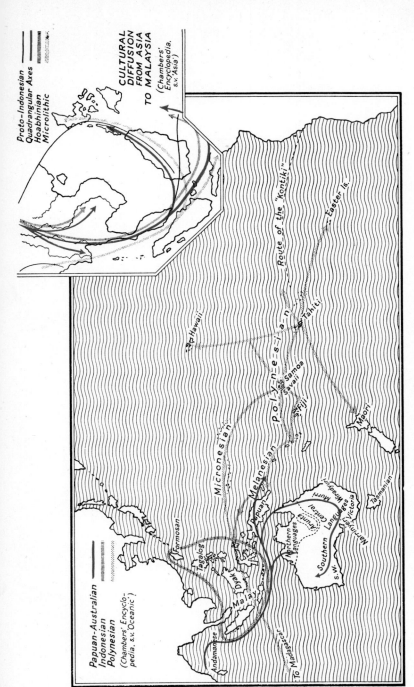

MAP TO ILLUSTRATE THE DIFFUSION OF PAPUAN-AUSTRALIAN AND
POLYNESIAN LANGUAGES

There is no formal distinction between parts of speech, but usage sets aside the pronouns, numerals, nouns, and verbs (though the latter extend to verbal nouns), and conjunctions. A common distinction is made between full and empty words, the latter being grammatical auxiliaries. But these also have full meanings, and within the word-group give a definite syntax. Thus $tsai^4$ means 'dwell', but $tsai^4$-$mien^4$-$shang^4$ 'dwell-face-up' means 'on the face'. Self-explanatory groups of this sort may be put into absolute construction so as to avoid too long a string of monosyllables before the clue to the general sense appears. Thus pa^4 'take hold of' is placed before an object which precedes the verb; the construction is 'take such-and-such, do so-and-so (with it)'. Otherwise there is a fixed order, subject–verb–object and qualifier-qualified. The sentence is further articulated by certain typical rhythmic patterns which group words that are especially closely associated, and its intelligibility is probably furthered by Chinese laconism. Everything that can be omitted within the circumstances is omitted, so that, for example, $ch'uan^2$ lai^2 may mean 'the steamer (huo^3-lun^2-$ch'uan^2$) is coming in to berth'. The literary style is based on systematic exploitation of this laconism, not only in word but also in thought, and is highly elliptic.

There is no concord in Chinese. A primitive philosophy divides all things between the male and female principles of good and evil, but it has no grammatical consequence. All nouns are particularized with the aid of fifty classifiers, which do not give rise to a grammatical class system. One says, for instance, i^1 $t'iao^2$-lu^4 'one length road' = 'a road', since roads are characterized by length. The classifier aids understanding by giving a general warning of the nature of the thing to be mentioned, and mitigates to that extent the excessive concentration of significance in monosyllables. The device is used in Pidgin English, in Malay, Japanese, and Korean, as well as in Sino-Tibetan, but it seems most fully developed in Chinese. It is duplicated in the Chinese written character of the so-called phonetic type. In such signs the first part is one of 214 radicals which give a general warning of the class of meaning; the second part is a sign associating the sound of the word with some sound already symbolized. Thus $mêng^3$ 'fierce, cruel' is in the category of despicable concepts (radical 'dog') though it has a sound like $mêng^4$ 'first, senior, superior'. The radical and the phonetic are combined in the sign for $mêng^3$.

Chinese is eminently a tonal language. The fact is universally true of Chinese dialects, but there are tone-shifts every few miles and three different arrangements within the Mandarin area alone. Words of the same constitution are differentiated by tones, which mark, for instance, the whole difference between 'devil' and 'honourable'. But owing to the tonal shifts the semantic importance of tones tends to be local. They form places in a local system, but understanding between strangers depends much more on visible circumstances and juxtaposed words. Historically, too, some tones may represent lost initials. South Chinese dialects and Siamese are more markedly tonal, but the use of tones is less well established for the Tibeto-Burman group. Burmese is said to be tonal, with three high-pitched and two low-pitched categories of sound. Earlier European grammars of Burmese ignored tone.

After the end of the archaic period of tribal movement from west to east (but from east to west as regards culture), Chinese has taken a southerly course along a main axis from the Po-yang and Tung-ting lakes to Si-kiang. One result of this advance is that Cantonese, on the whole, represents the language of medieval China better than the much evolved and impoverished Mandarin. Another effect was to encircle the Min region on the south-east coast and leave its full assimilation till later. Hence the modern Min dialect may contain a considerable pre-Chinese vocabulary. Expansion into Yünnan was in progress when Marco Polo visited the court of Kublai Khan, and south China was still regarded as foreign (Man) territory. The Han empire included the Red River basin of Annam, so that Annamese culture is heavily sinicized, though the language seems to be a mixture of Khmer and T'ai.

It has already been remarked that a polysynthetic language is composed of stems all on the same syntactic level, so that if Chuk-chee *tymyngyntorkyn* were written *ty myngy nto rkyn* 'I (my) hands take-out do' it would be an isolating phrase. Conversely, Chinese *ni³ pa³-chê⁴-shih²-chi³-ko-ch'ien² kei³-t'a¹* 'Give him these ten cash or so' might be written without pauses as *ni pachêshihchiko-ch'ien keit'a*. The difference lies in the Chinese consciousness of the word's autonomy within the sentence, a consciousness expressed and reinforced by the script. The Indian alphabets used for Tibetan, Burmese, and Siamese tend to disguise the monosyllabism of these languages, which is affirmed chiefly by the speakers' consciousness. However, it is at present enough to note that isolation and synthesis are relative terms within the possibilities afforded by language structure. Utterance in either is by breath-groups.

Chinese words are invariable. But there are cases in which one character covers two words, differing in tone or initial or otherwise. Even when characters differ along with pronunciation, there may still be reason to believe that the words belong to an original derivational family, as *chiang*[1] 'river', *chiang*[2] 'lagoon' and *ching*[1] 'underground stream'. In Siamese there are such families, formed by infixing a sonant after an initial consonant,[1] and in Burmese an active verb may be obtained by aspirating (infixing an aspirate after) an initial. In Tibetan verbs are variable for tense and capable of taking a prefix or suffix.[2]

Further than this, Chinese has a number of true agglutinations (*la*, *mên*, *ti*, and the end-words *a*, *pa*) distinguished for their loss of tone. In other groups there are transactions of tone or stress which are due to the grouping. In Burmese nouns there is a casual declension of suffixes, which suffer voicing of their initial consonant, as *lu* 'man', *lu-go* 'man' (acc.), *lu-i* 'of the man', *lu-do* 'men', &c. The Pali script shows voiceless consonants in these positions. In Tibetan the casual suffixes are more indefinite, but are more adapted to the phonetic condition of the noun (e.g. gen. suffixes *kyi*, *gyi*, *gi*, *'i*: *yul gyi rgyal-po* 'the country's king'). Tibetan is an isolating language half-way towards agglutination, or semi-agglutinative, with a tendency to fusion.

Medieval Chinese shows a complicated system of semivocalic glides, and was presumably in process of transmission from some other condition. The equivalence *Fo*[2] = *Buddha* shows that there were once voiced initials, but other glides may represent consonants lost in groups. There are consonant groups in Burmese and T'ai, and in Tibetan they are so complicated that they can only be pronounced with the aid of a fugitive vowel resembling Malay *ĕ*. But this practice bridges the distance between monosyllabism and dissyllabism, as in Malay *bĕgap*/Tibetan *b(ĕ)sgrubs*.[3]

---

[1] K. Wulff, *Chinesisch und Tai*, Copenhagen, 1934.

[2] J. Bacot, *Grammaire du tibétain littéraire*, Paris, 1946, p. 53, cites *slob-pa* 'teach', *bslabs* 'taught', *bslab* 'will teach'; Burmese *kruk* 'fear', *khruk* 'frighten'.

[3] K. Wulff's articles (*Über das Verhältnis des Malayo-polynesischen zum Indochinesischen*, Copenhagen, 1942) treat of 145 parallels in vocabulary. For example (73, 74), Mandarin *fa*[1] 'chastiser destroy' descends from Old Chinese *b'ĭŭt* < *b'ĭwät*, cf. Malay *tĕbas* 'fell, clear undergrowth' (*tobas, tĕbös, tevy, tĕwas, tabas* in other languages of the group), and Mandarin *fu*[2] < *p'ĭŭət* 'brush off, dust' (Siam.

The southerly advance of Burmese and Siamese (the latter including the Ahom of Assam and the Shans of Burma) covered a thousand years and was still in progress in the sixteenth century. It disrupted a linguistic community now composed of islets: the Khasi of Assam, the Mon of Pegu, the Karens of the Irrawaddy delta, the Khmers of Cambodia, and the Nicobarese, as well as (probably) the Mundas of India in the west and the Annamese (as to one part of their language) in the east. The original area was presumably continuous over Assam and Indo-China, and may have extended into China proper. There the Miao tribesmen are assigned by some authorities to the T'ai family, but by another to the Mon-Khmer.[1] They are relics of the original non-Chinese barbarians living on and south of the Yangtze. A name for the whole family is 'Austroasiatic' which leads easily to 'Austronesian' for what was formerly called Malayo-Polynesian and to 'Austric' as a common denominator. It is not impossible that both may have had some remote genetic association with Sino-Tibetan.

As exemplified by the somewhat archaic Khasi[2] of Assam, this family is monosyllabic like Tibeto-Burman, but not originally tonal. Derivation is often by prefixes: Khasi *lait* 'free', *pyl-lait* 'set free', *jing-pyl-lait* 'freedom'. There is also derivation by initial infix as in Siamese: Khmer *kăt* 'cut'/*k'năt* 'measure'. In Nicobarese prefixes may be vocalized: Nic. *kalang* 'eagle'/Khmer *k'leng*, Stieng *kleng*. In these respects Austroasiatic words are intermediate between monosyllabic Sino-Tibetan and dissyllabic Malayo-Polynesian. The adjective follows the substantive as in Siamese and Malay (and sometimes in Burmese), but is marked in Khasi by the prefix *ba-*. Khasi has articles (masc. sg. *u*, fem. sg. *ka*, diminutive sg. *i*, common pl. *ki*) which reveal the innate gender (sex or size) of nouns: *u lok* 'a friend', *ka lok* 'a female friend', *ki lok* 'friends', *u briw* 'a man', *i briw* 'a dwarf'. The noun itself is invariable. These articles are rather generic classifiers than either definite or indefinite. The article is often repeated before an adjective or a verb,

---

pat˜ Lao *pat'*, Shan *pat* 'turn') he connects with Malay *hapus* 'expunge, wipe out' (elsewhere *apus*, *hapos*, and *pas-pas*, *papas*, *fafa*).

[1] R. D. Forrest, *The Chinese Language*, London, 1948, p. 89. They call themselves Mhông. The Nosu or Lolo peoples are certainly Tibeto-Burman. There is a system of verbal derivation like that of Burmese in Nosu *da* 'drink'/ *ta* 'cause to drink', *du* 'go out'/*tu* 'cause to go out'. (Dr. A. Henry's notes cited by E. G. Kemp, *Chinese Mettle*, London, 1921, p. 128.)

[2] H. Roberts, *A Grammar of the Khassi Language*, London, 1891.

as *ka* in *ka miáw ka pah* 'the cat (it) mews' and *u* in *u mrád u barúnar* 'a cruel beast', *u barúnar u ksew* 'it is fierce, the dog = it is a fierce dog'. Such concords have no place in Sino-Tibetan or Malayo-Polynesian, but concords of genders denoting sex and importance are found in both Aryan and Dravidian languages of India.

Farther to the south there are peoples carried by earlier waves of the same general migratory movement from Asia. They are successively 'the Australoid, the Papua-Melanesoid, the Indonesian, and Proto-Malay (or Indo-Nesian cum Mongoloid), each overlapping and influencing one another'.[1] The peopling of Australia has already been discussed. The Papuan and Melanesoid movement or movements seem to have ended in Fiji, and to have been partly submerged by Polynesian from the east. The Polynesian languages probably spread along the bridge of the Carolines and Samoa is regarded as a centre of their diffusion. Tahiti was occupied in the fifth century of our era, Tonga and Fiji in the tenth, North Island of New Zealand in expeditions from the tenth to the fourteenth, and the occupation of Hawaii seems to have begun in the tenth century. The dates of these settlements are guaranteed by a rough chronology of 'generations' in Polynesian adventure histories. Movements among the great islands seem to have been much more complex, but included a curve north-eastward along Borneo to the Philippines, and including Formosa. Indonesian sailors are said to have reached the coast of India about 1000 B.C. The first stratum in Madagascar has Melanesian affinities, presumably due to voyages south of the monsoon belt in the early centuries of our era; the last arrivals were Malays in the sixteenth century. Malagasy is akin to Melanesian.

The migration of languages is much more simple than that of settlers. Austronesian or Malayo-Polynesian is manifestly one lan-

---

[1] Sir R. Winstedt, 'Malay Language' in *Chambers's Encyclopaedia*, 1950. See also s.v. 'Asia', 'Oceania', 'Fiji', 'Tonga', 'Hawaii'. I have at hand R. O. Winstedt, *Malay Grammar*, Oxford, 1913, and *Simple Malay*, London, 1938; H. Neffgen, *Die samoanische Sprache*, Vienna–Leipzig, s.d., with notes on Tahiti and Maori, and the account of Samoan in F. N. Finck, *Die Haupttypen des Sprachbaus*, Leipzig–Berlin, 3 ed., 1936; Anon. *Observaciones gramaticales sobre la lengua Tiruray*, Manila, 1892. There is an analysis based on Malay and Samoan in E. Kieckers, *Die Sprachstämme der Erde*, Heidelberg, 1931. D. Macdonald's *Oceanic Languages*, London, 1909, contains a rich comparative vocabulary, but is hard to disentangle from his thesis of the Semitic origin of these tongues.

guage family, though divided into many dialects of relatively recent formation. It is dissyllabic in its basic stems: Malay *pulau* 'island', *pulan* 'crisp', *punggok* 'small owl'. There are old monosyllables in Malay, and the presence of the neutral vowel *ĕ* (as in *bĕgap* 'robust') and of vowels of the same category (as in *belek* 'examining closely') make it possible to believe in a more extensive original monosyllabism, with initial consonant-groups. Now there are no initial groups, and medial groups result only from contact between syllables. In Polynesian final consonants are lost, and medial groups correspondingly reduced. The 18 Malay consonants are reduced to 9 in Samoan, 8 in Tahitian, and 10 in Maori. With the loss of middle and final consonants (Samoan *i'a* = Malay *ikan* 'fish') the Polynesian tongues have become highly vocalic: Samoan *'ua lātou nonofo ai i po e tele i Mulinu'u* 'they dwelt a long time in Mulinuu'. There was no original *f*, which is bilabial in Halmahera [ϕ], and reduced to *h* in Tahiti, Hawaii, and New Zealand (where it may also become *wh*): *alofa* = *aloha* 'greeting'. Similarly Samoan *s* becomes *h* in these regions (*Savaii* = *Hawaii*), and is a sign of settlement from Tahiti. The consonants *r l d* are somewhat unstable and interchangeable in the whole Malayo-Polynesian area: *dua* = *lua* = *rua, ruo* 'two'.

Derivation is by composition, fusion, and gemination, and to a slight extent by affixes (prefixes, infixes, and suffixes), which are most numerous in Melanesian. The use of gemination is highly characteristic, as Malay *orang-orang* 'all kinds of men', *kanak-kanak* 'very young children', *mata-mata* 'police' (*mata* 'eye'), Samoan *fulufulu* 'hair', *gase'ele'ele* 'eclipse of the moon'. Usage is liable to be impulsive and idiomatic, with syllables in Samoan which have only 'euphonic' value (as *ai* in the sentence cited). In principle, however, the Malayo-Polynesian word is virtually invariable and its syntax is that of an isolating language. Order and particles determine meaning. As in Siamese, the qualifier follows the qualified: Malay *rumah burok* 'a shabby house', *orang-liar* 'shy man = aboriginal savage'. By this rule there is no distinction between an adjective and a noun in the genitive. A predicated adjective follows after a slight pause: *rumah burok* 'the house is shabby'. The verb is neuter as in Sino-Tibetan, i.e. active or passive according to context, and it readily becomes the 'subject' of the sentence, the various nouns being in adverbial relations to a verb which signifies an activity that is the topic of the phrase.

Malay makes use of classifiers of nouns without grammatical consequences, and, like Chinese, omits unneeded words: *sudah habis*, *jangan dudok* 'if (such and such a work you know of) is finished, don't (you) sit down = don't sit down when you have finished your work'. There is no article in Malay, but a variety of articles variously used in the whole language group. In Melanesian languages there are marked Polynesian characteristics combined with others which seem to belong to a Papuo-Melanesoid substratum.[1]

5. EURASIA

Eurasia[2] and Eurafrica are defined by the crests of the great Asiatic mountains and the deserts of Arabia and Africa. They resemble a mouth facing west, with Libya, Egypt, and Arabia as the underslung jaw, articulating by the vast ball-and-socket joint of the 'Fertile Crescent'. The latter is the strip of fertile land which runs through Syria, Aram, and Mesopotamia, and which has been successfully held by Semitic settlers against the Indo-Europeans. There has been constant historical interaction between the peoples of these two stretches of the earth's surface, two branches of the Great White Race, and arguments have been made to support a theory of common Indo-European and Semitic origins. They are questionable. More likely is the argument for some original unity of Indo-Europeans and Ural-Altaic speakers. If there is such a connexion, it must be very remote in time. A nearer view envisages three foci of irradiation: one in central Europe, one between the great bend of the Volga and the Ob for the Uralic peoples, and another somewhere in central Asia for the Turks, Mongols, and Tunguzes. A characteristic of the Eurasian land-mass is the great freedom of movement offered by steppes and plains from the Amur to the Loire. Hence the migrations of Huns and Tatars from China to central Europe within historical times, and the seasonal wandering of Altaic peoples to this day. Conversely, from central Europe there are not only facilities for penetrating peninsular Europe (whereby Indo-European speakers have disrupted one or more older systems), but also across the Persian uplands to India. Asia Minor is accessible from both west and east; it has been occupied,

[1] D. Macdonald's comparative dictionary and grammar (*Oceanic Languages*, London, 1907) is based on the Melanesian tongue of Efate Island in the New Hebrides.

[2] There is a geographical term which comprises Europe and all Asia. The limitation proposed above seems valuable for linguistics.

amongst others, by Indo-European Hittites and Altaic Turks, though not systematically by Semites.

The peoples of Eurasia and Eurafrica speak synthetic languages. These are agglutinative in the east, semi-agglutinative (or semi-flexional) in the north-centre, and inflected in the west and south. Semitic and Indo-European are both inflected, but the former employs a unique organization of mutations. The languages which survive from one or more older systems (Japhetic, Alarodian, Mediterranean, or Alpine) commonly show, so far as we know them, an unusual reliance on infixation.

Since Japanese and Korean[1] are agglutinative and have highly disciplined grammars of suffixes, it seems reasonable to attach them to Eurasia. There is no actual barrier on the Yalu River, but there was at one time a human void due to the extreme sparsity of the Manchu tribesmen. Chinese colonization of Manchuria, apart from Liaotung, is very recent. Thus Korea and Japan form a peninsular and insular sub-continent, which reaches out in the north to Kamchatka and the Aleutians, and in the south towards the Philippines. The former fact has encouraged some to associate Eskimo, Japanese, and Korean with the Altaic, Uralic, and ultimately Indo-European groups in a vast prehistoric association of languages. As to the latter, Ryu-kyu islanders speak a tongue closely related to Japanese, and presumably represent insular languages rolled up by the Indonesian advance to the Philippines and Formosa. The sounds and forms of Japanese words (normally dissyllabic and without consonant-groups, with simple vowels and relatively few consonants) resemble those of Malayo-Polynesian, with which they have no actual affiliation. To prove kinship with Altaic languages is excessively difficult, and even to unite Korean and Japanese is hard. Though they are alike in type, they differ in means. A few ancient identities may be found among their words, but the correspondences cease almost at once. Among parallels cited by Eckardt are Kor. *kŏd* = Jap. *koto* 'thing', Kor. *kurŭm* = Ainu *Kuroro* = Jap. *kumo* 'cloud', Kor. *kŏmŏ-* = Ainu *kune* = Jap. *kuroi* 'black' (Turk. *kara*), Kor. *nophŭ-* = Ainu *nupure* = Jap. *noboru* 'high', Kor. *kui* 'ear' = Jap. *kiku* 'hear' (Turk. *kulak* 'ear').

---

[1] G. B. Sansom, *An historical Grammar of Japanese*, Oxford, 1928; H. Plaut, *Japanese Conversation-Grammar*, Heidelberg, 2 ed., 1926; W. M. McGovern, *Colloquial Japanese*, London, s.d.; A. Eckardt, *Koreanische Konversations-Grammatik*, Heidelberg, 1923.

The numerals, usually very conservative in their forms, have no points in common apart from the decimal basis. With regard to their general structure these languages agree in lack of gender or concord or a simple conception of plurality, in having noun-declensions of approximately the same number of cases (including an absolute case for isolating the noun in the sentence), and verbal conjugations which include considerations of politeness as well as time and mood, but exclude persons. They also conjugate their adjectives, with a few exceptions in Japanese. Thus Jap. *ashi* 'bad' gives *ashiki hito* 'a man who is bad', *ashikarishi hito* 'a man who was bad', *ashikaranu hito* 'a man who is not bad', but predicatively (without conjugation) *hito ashi* 'the man is bad'. But this predicative form has virtually disappeared from the colloquial, and one finds conjugated predicates like Jap. *bara wa akak'te* 'the rose is red' (*akai*). So Kor. *kŏmta* 'to be black', *kŏmso* 'is it black?', &c. Since the copula is a suffix in Turkish, adjectives used predicatively are in fact conjugated, as *ip-iyiyim* 'I am very well' (*ip-iyi* 'very good'). The position of the verb in Japanese, Korean, and Turkish is at the end of the phrase.

Both languages have felt the impact of Chinese and may be written partly in Chinese characters, but in Japanese the characters may represent either of two different old Chinese dialects (that of Wu and that of central or Han China). They may also be read in Japanese: thus *kōjin* = *yoki hito* 'good man'. One effect has been to isolate Japanese nouns, making them apparently invariable, since the noun is liable to be in Chinese character and the suffixes follow in Japanese script: *anata no chichi wa* 'your father' (*no* genitive, *wa* absolute), *anata ga watakushi wo miru* 'you see me' (*ga* nominative, *wo* accusative). Since Korean uses an efficient alphabet, the case-endings appear as suffixes: *sarǎ mi* 'the man', *sarǎmě* 'of the man', *sarǎměke* 'to the man', &c. On the other hand the agglutinative character of the verb is obvious in both languages. It starts from five bases in Japanese, as *suru* 'make, do' from *se* (or *shi*)/*shi*/*suru*/*sure*/*shi* (or *se*), and *kaku* 'write' from *kaka*/*kaki*/*kaku*/*kake*/*kakō*. With the polite suffix -*masŭ* this gives *shimasu* and the like. There are suffixes to indicate wish, likelihood, and purpose, and others to show time; the negation involves yet another conjugation. In Korean etiquette alone requires five verbal forms, and suffixes are extremely numerous and varied.

The Japanese syllabary takes into account five vowels, *a e i o u*, and shows that some consonants are merely functions of others: as *sh(i)* of *s*, *ch(i) ts(u)* of *t*, *f(u)[φ]* of *h*, *j(i)* of *z*, and *j(i) dz(u)* of *d*. *L* is wanting, but is found in Korean at the end of syllables and corresponding to initial or medial *r*. Korean script distinguishes *a/ya*, *e/ye*, *ŏ/yŏ*, *o/yo*, *u/yu*.

Since there are roughly ten times as many Turanians[1] (Turko-Tatars) as Mongols, and about as many more Mongols than Tunguses, it would seem proper to place the Altaic centre of gravity in western Asia. Nomad life follows a rhythm of three seasons, for which Ferghana gives an excellent opportunity: spring on the open steppe, summer in High Tatary, and winter in the sheltered westerly valleys. Such towns as there are tend to stand on the outlet from these valleys, equally accessible to the steppe and the high pastures. This life requires considerable skill within a narrow range of possibilities of development. As to language, Turkish is admirably organized, but seems to have little power of evolution.

This tardiness of evolution serves to compensate for want of early documents in establishing the unity of the Altaic family. Its members have suffered relatively little displacement. Though several of the most wide-ranging conquerors—Attila, Genghis Khan, Kublai, Batu, Akbar, Alp Arslan, and Timur—have been Huns, Mongols, or Turks, their followers have rarely been numerous and never superior in culture to their victims. The Tunguses remain in Manchuria and eastern Siberia, to the number of barely half a million. The Manchus, like the Mongols before them, were wholly absorbed by their Chinese subjects. The Buryat Mongols lie to the north of the Altai, other Mongols to the south, and only the Kalmuks have branches in Astrakhan and the Caucasus. Turanians are at home in south-west Siberia, with only one group (the Yakuts) in north-east Siberia, others in the Volga-Ural and Caucasus areas, and the Osmanli Turks in Asia Minor and Istanbul. The first are inconsiderable minorities, but the last represents a considerable mass.

Osmanli Turkish[2] basic stems tend to be monosyllabic and closed by a consonant: as *ev* 'house', *at* 'horse', *sev-* 'love', *yaş* 'wet, age', *il* 'province'. But there are also stems of more than one

---

[1] I use the term 'Turanian' for Turko-Tatar or Turkic at the suggestion of W. K. Matthews, *Languages of the U.S.S.R.*, Cambridge, 1951.

[2] C. S. Mundy, 'Turkish Language', *Chambers's Encyclopaedia*, 1950; A. C. Mowle, *The New Turkish*, London, 3 ed., 1942; and articles in *Les langues du monde*.

syllable, like *adam* 'man', *agaç* 'tree', *aslan* 'lion'. Comparison with Mongolian suggests that they derive from longer primitive stems. The language does not readily admit derivation, but adopted Persian and Arabic terms in the Middle Ages, and French and Italian today. Thus it has gained the intellectual and scientific vocabulary which the Turks did not require in their nomad state. Relations within the sentence are expressed by suffixes arranged in strictly prescribed orders. Though incapable of standing alone, they are sufficiently well-founded to keep their identity of form and meaning. The same principle of strict sequence applies to Mongolian, with some differences of order. Turkish and Mongolian, but not Tungusic, apply to these suffixes the principle of vowel harmony, so that suffixes are bound to their basic stem by agreement of vowels: *evler* 'houses', *adamlar* 'men'. Since the Ugric branch of Finno-Ugric (Uralian) makes the most elaborate use of harmony, the principle may have been borrowed or shared in the regions beyond the Ural mountains. Nouns and verbs are construed by suffixes, and have in common signs of plurality (*ler/lar*) and person (1. sg. *-im*, 2. *-in*, 1. pl. *-(im)iz*, 2. *-iniz*, &c.): *evim* 'my house', *im* 'I am', *siniz* 'you are', *güzelim* 'I am beautiful', *geliniz* 'come (ye)'. Cases, tenses and moods are also built up by suffixes; the most common casual suffixes can be made into a declension, and signs of tenses, moods, and persons into a conjugation. It is characteristic that upon a word with suffixes more suffixes can be piled; *evim* 'my house', *evimin* 'of my house', *evlerimden* 'from my houses'. These complexes reach extraordinary lengths like *yerleştirilemediğinden* 'owing to the fact that it was impossible for him to be placed' or *düsdüğümden yürüyemem* 'because I fell, I cannot walk'. Sentences are paratactic. Subordination is effected by participles and gerunds with appropriate case-endings and postpositions (instead of prepositions). The qualifier precedes the qualified: and the verb comes last: *o eski evlerimden geldiler* 'they came from my old houses' (old houses-my-from came they). The copula is suffixed: *soğuğum* 'I am cold' (*um* corresponds to *im* in vowel harmony), *bir kuştur* 'it is a bird' (*kuş+-dir*, with harmonious vowel and assimilation of consonant). The genitive is expressed by a possessive suffix after the thing possessed, as *adam işi* 'man's work' (*-i* 'his'), and more precise definition is given by suffixing the genitive case ending, as *adamin işi* 'the man's work'.

The Finno-Ugrian and Samoyede languages constitute a Uralian group, which many scholars have held to be linked by affinity to the Altaic. The proof is difficult and has been denied by other authorities. We know them as having been located in comparatively recent times (from the days of Herodotus to the beginning of our era) around the great bend of the Volga, across the Urals to the Ob. The Mordvinians occupy some of the original ground. Their way of life was shifting, but differed entirely from that of the Altaic peoples, since they were fishers and woodland hunters, not nomadic herdsmen. Their sparse land-tenure in due course made possible penetration by agricultural and fur-hunting Slavs. The Ugrians lay in western Siberia, and their principal feat was accomplished by the Magyars who cut a way across south Russia in the ninth century and settled in Hungary. Some tribes of both stocks migrated northward. Finns and Ests moved west to the Gulf of Finland towards the beginning of our era, and the Finns entered western Finland between A.D. 100 and 600. There has been a steady assimilation of Finns in Russia (both Moscow and Leningrad stand on originally Finnish ground), so that the surviving tribes are no more than relics of the original communities. Their antiquity in their old sites is demonstrated by borrowings from common Aryan, when the future Persians and Indians still inhabited south Russia (c. 2000 B.C.). Estonian differs from Finnish by scarcely more than dialect marks, so that one may say there are only two important cultural languages in this family: Finnish (with Estonian) and Magyar.

Finnish[1] stems are commonly dissyllabic, as *kala* 'fish', *kallio* 'rock', *isä* 'father', *ilma* 'air', *joki* 'river', *rakas* 'dear', *pitkä* 'long', &c. But some dissyllables can be analysed, like *saa-da* 'receive', *tä-mä/tää-llä* 'this/here' and there are basic monosyllables like *maa* 'earth', *jää* 'ice', as well as monosyllabic pronouns and other particles. Three- and four-syllable words are usually fused compounds, which may be made readily (*juomalasi* 'tumbler, glass', *kalastaa* 'to fish', *päinvastoin* 'on the contrary'. It is less easy to give an account of Hungarian stems, which were somewhat fuller when first recorded and show concessions due to the mixed Ugric-Turkish character of the Magyar invaders. The characteristic octo-

---

[1] J. Szinnyei, *Finnisch-ugrische Sprachwissenschaft*, Berlin-Leipzig, 1922; C. N. E. Eliot, *A Finnish Grammar*, Oxford, 1890; A. Sauvageot, *Esquisse de la langue finnoise*, Paris, 1949; P. J. Cook, *Estonian self-taught*, London, 1933; I. Kont, *Petite grammaire hongroise*, Heidelberg, 1926; L. Tóth, *La Lingua magiara*, Naples, 1939; and articles in *Chambers's Encyclopaedia*.

syllabic rhythm of Finnish folk-verse with melodic phrase of 4+4 notes admits words of one, two, three, or four syllables, but not often more than that. There is a lack of initial voiced occlusives or of consonant-groups within the syllable, and a fundamental distinction between tense and relaxed positions of consonants, which shows best in medial position. The consonant is tense when the following syllable is open, and relaxed when it is closed by a consonant. This gives a set of alternating phonemes: *kk/k k/O pp/p p/v tt/t t/d*, as in *vika/viat* 'fault(s)', *setä/sedät* 'uncle(s)', *kukka/kukat* 'flower(s)', *harppu/harput* 'harp(s)'. Initial consonants are tense, but this is not shown by doubling them. Vowels are doubled for length (*maa = mā* 'earth'). In addition they are distinguished into two series (*a/ä o/ö u/y* &c.) so as to support vowel-harmony, not only between stem and suffix, but also to a large extent within the stems: *näkymätön* 'invisible'/*loppumaton* 'endless'. This is to carry the principle further than in Turkish, where it is restricted to the concord of suffixes and stems. There have been more consonant-shifts in Hungarian than in Finnish, so that the consonantal alternances are not so clearly seen. In the earliest documents vowel harmony was less systematic than now in Magyar.

Finnish expresses relations by suffixes attached to noun or verb, as *kytä-ssä/stä/llä/ltä* 'in/out of/at/from the village', *tule-n/t/mme/tte* 'I/thou/we/you come' (cf. Indo-European *-m/-s/mes/te*), *tul-i-n* 'I was coming', *tul-isi-n* 'I would come', and has a conjugated negative *en/et/emme/ette tule* 'I/thou/we/you don't come'. Syntax is essentially paratactic, and this leads to a considerable development of the infinitive with various case-endings. The total number of cases may be set at sixteen, and they are mostly spatial (rest or movement to/in/from or from one thing to another, as well as instrument, lack, &c.). There are also postpositions. Hungarian seems to have a less definite paradigm of the noun, with a highly systematic arrangement of spatial notions by postpositions. Its suffixes are more evolved than those of Finnish. The verb shows by the choice of suffixed pronoun a distinction between actions complete in themselves and those which affect some object (indefinite and definite conjugations: *lát-ok* 'I see'/*lát-om* 'I see [something]'). The latter are in general agreement with the system of suffixed possessive pronouns. They are suffixed also to prepositions (as in Irish): *nekem* 'to me', *bennem* 'in me', *hozzám* 'towards me', &c. Magyar employs prefixes for verbal derivation and subordinating conjunctions, so that the actual structure of the phrase is not unlike that of the surrounding Indo-European tongues. The chief difference lies in the Magyar preference for postposition over preposition, as in *Péter szorgalmas-abb Pál-nál* 'Peter (is) industrious-more Paul-than' = 'Peter is more industrious than Paul'. The influence of Indo-European has been felt by Finnish for more than 2,000 years as to vocabulary, but only since about 1860 in the expression of a literary culture. Hence the continued occurrence of essentially paratactic constructions with the infinitive such as *Tuoni toisi tullessansa* 'Tuoni brought-would-have (thee) coming-in-his' = Tuoni would have brought thee when he came'. Subtle nuances of modification can be operated by the wealth of suffixes in Magyar; in Finnish alliteration combines with vowel harmonies to fill verse with echoes. Normal and palatal vowels can be made to follow each other in a scheme characterized by the alliteration of consonants, as in *vaka vanha Vänämöinen* 'Prudent old Vanamoinen'. Lack of these echoes distinguishes the verse of *Hiawatha* from its model, the *Kalevala*.

Indo-European languages are flexional as to class, and as a second criterion they use or formerly used the mutation $e/o/$- for both constructional and grammatical purposes. The first characteristic places each word in a paradigm such as *mensa, mensam mensae*, or *rego regis regit*, &c. The stem is fused with the flexion and conventional stems are cited (*mensa- reg-*); the flexion is a composite sign of declensional or conjugational class, number, and person or gender and case. The $e/o/$- mutation is a feature of late Indo-European which has been obliterated or mangled in most of the ensuing individual languages; but it is well illustrated by ancient Greek conjugations. Older mutations seem to have been in $i/\bar{\imath}$ and $u/\bar{u}$. In the centre of Indo-European territory, Baltic and Slavonic continue to present the appearance of highly inflected tongues, but English and modern Persian are analytic, and French and Hindustani slightly less so. In Baltic and Slavonic the eminently synthetic declensions are contrasted with the collapse of the original conjugations.

The main divisions of this family of languages are as follows:

Germanic	Baltic	Slavonic	Tokharian
Celtic	Italic	Illyrian	Armenian	Iranian
Latin	Greek	Hittite	Sanskrit

Knowledge of Tokharian and Hittite has been won in this century.

The 'Tokhari' were Iranian-speakers and their name has been used by way of a convenient misnomer for two dialects (A and B) which should probably be called Agnean and Kuchean. The first was the language of Karashahr (Agni in Sanskrit) and the other of the kingdom of Kucha (Kuci), north of the Taklamakan desert.[1] The most easterly of Indo-European languages, Tokharian, does not have certain characteristically 'eastern' features, namely the conversion of palatal occlusives into sibilants. In this respect and in the use of an *r*-passive it agrees with Hittite.[2] The decipherment of Hittite has vastly increased the age of our Indo-European records. Tokharian, on the other hand, was isolated at a very early date. Yet both show signs of marked evolution along with archaism and add new terms to the equations of the Indo-European family without bringing the original tongue materially into view. The limitation of gender in Hittite to animate and inanimate classes, for instance, though probably corresponding to a primitive condition of Indo-European itself, has been shown to arise through loss of the feminine by attrition (as in the modern Scandinavian languages). There seems little reason to put Hittite on the same plane as Indo-European and to refer them to a hypothetical 'Indo-Hittite original. The language is mixed with Asian elements, but its structure and much of its vocabulary is evolved Indo-European.

Armenian is a language of ancient date intermediate between Slavonic and Iranian. Its vocabulary is very mixed, and in both vocabulary and pronunciation it probably shows non-Indo-European, Caucasian features. According to Herodotus the Armenians came from Phrygia. Phrygian, Thracian, and Dacian constitute a sub-family which extended from an original home in the bend of the Carpathians into central Asia Minor, and (if Herodotus was right) to Armenia. But this group is excessively ill known. The same is true of Illyrian. No doubt modern Albanian is a representative of Illyrian, but hardly in the same sense as Venetic and Messapic have been claimed. There is also the view that Illyrian formed

[1] H. W. Bailey, 'Recent work in "Tokharian"', *Transactions of the Philological Society*, London, 1947; E. Sieg, W. Siegling, and W. Schulze, *Tocharische Grammatik*, Göttingen, 1931; H. Pedersen, *Tocharisch*, 2 ed., Copenhagen, 1949; A. J. van Windekens, *Morphologie comparée du Tokharien*, Louvain, 1944.
[2] E. H. Sturtevant, *Comparative Grammar of the Hittite Language*, Philadelphia, 1933, *Hittite Glossary*, Philadelphia, 1936 (2nd ed.); W. Couvreur, *Das hettitische Ḫ*, Louvain, 1937; H. Pedersen, *Hittitisch und die anderen indoeuropäischen Sprachen*, Copenhagen, 1938, *Lykisch und Hittitisch*, Copenhagen, 1945.

an Indo-European substratum over which subsequent waves of invaders passed. Thus the Celts who invaded Gaul drove Veneti into Armorica. The Slavs were called Venedi (Wends) by Tacitus on the faith of German informers, who gave them the name of older occupants of their land. When the Baltic is called the Wendish Gulf (Ptolemy), it means presumably that Slavs occupied, or had occupied, part of its southern shore, but the reference might have been to 'Illyrian' Veneti. The concept of Illyrian is thus probably an important one, but may be misleading. Its place is taken in evidence by Albanian, but one cannot be sure of the status and ancient history of this tongue, which, in its modern form, is so changed under Latin and Greek influence. It is, however, a language which turns palatal occlusives into sibilants according to a formula of its own, and was thus probably once lodged in a more easterly position than Greek.

The evidence of two or more disconnected branches suffices to refer an etymon to Indo-European.[1] An equation is formed and a solution reached, such as Eng. *fire* (OEng. *fȳr*) = Osco-Umbrian *pir* = Greek *πῦρ* = Arm. *hur* = Hitt. *pahhur* = Tokh. *por*, from which we infer initial Indo-European $*p$, final $*r$, and some difference in the vowels ($*\bar{u}$, $*e\partial u$). It is important to decide what value is attached to this solution. If the linguist considers it valid only in respect of its consequences, then there is nothing to stop him from proposing solutions which are improbable as elements of speech. It is the difficulty of attaching spoken significance to both Meillet's and Benveniste's Indo-European roots that keeps them rigorously on the plane of hypothesis. The concept 'Indo-European' itself takes on an abstract nature and may be represented as some sort of primordial egg in a diagram designed only to show general associations.

If, on the other hand, the solution is predicated of some community, though strictly unknowable, the picture of contiguities takes on the appearance of a map, and the interpretation follows to some extent the methods of linguistic geography. The map for 'fire' is approximately

teine, tan	fire, fȳr, fúir, fon		ugnis		ogoń	por
	pir	zjarr			hur	ātash, ātarš
	ignis		πῦρ			pahhur	Agnis

---

[1] On the principles of the comparative method see especially A. Meillet, *La méthode comparative en linguistique historique*, Oslo, 1925, and *Introduction à l'étude comparative des langues indo-européennes*, Paris, 1924.

Irish *teine*, Welsh *tan* is shown to be Indo-European by Avestic *tafnah*-'heat', and Albanian *zjarr* by Lithuanian *žarija* 'glowing coal'. They arise by shifts of meaning. Latin, Baltic, Slavonic, and Sanskrit agree upon a term which must be of equal or greater antiquity than that used by Germanic, Italic, Greek, Armenian, Hittite, and Tokharian. Persian *ātash* is a name for fire considered as a sacred principle.

A rigidly unified Indo-European language may never have existed, and certainly did not exist at the time indicated by the heads for our inferences. The above example gives evidence of two terms of 'fire' equally attributable to the mother tongue. The heads of inference are not necessarily contemporary. There is reason to think Latin contains some archaic elements of the parent language, and that the type *ignis* may belong to an older stratum than the type *fire*. Or, alternatively, it may answer to a different way of regarding the object, whether as a self-engendering destroyer or as something under human control. What we can envisage is determined not merely by the fact of entering into an equation, but by consistent differences in evolution. In the example chosen, the difference between the initials in *fire* and *pir* provides a cross-bearing in the remote past; identity would leave us uncertain how far back the inference might be carried. It follows that what we know is essentially a number of points of divergence, not necessarily contemporary, but attributable roughly to the period 3000–2000 B.C. It is also plausible to suppose that there are genuine relics from that period confined to a single language-group or language, as, for instance, *fieri* is restricted to Rumanian among Romance languages, though undoubtedly Latin. The equations cover only what can be proved, not all that was. They affect differently the different branches of language-study. They restrict the number of words by the difficulty of finding words even for primary concepts still in use. They increase the demand for conformity of morphemes, since, where forms are wanting, lack of evidence does not enter into the account; and the preferential treatment of Greek, Latin, and Sanskrit has probably given an impression of a more coherent language-system than ever existed at one time. In the study of the lexicon, comparison gives an advantage to general senses over specific ones.

Since the heads of inference reach back to different dates in the past the question arises whether there can be some sort of relative chronology, if not for the development of Indo-European as a whole, at least for specific features. At the time of separation the vowel and consonant scheme was distinctive, but the consideration of words by semantic areas suggests that speech-sounds were formerly interchangeable. The thematic declensions appear to be the last to arise in the common language; the use of *a*-stems as feminines is later than their use as collectives (neuter plurals); the declensions in *i* and *u* (and *ī ū*) are probably more ancient, but less so than those consonant-stems which add flexions without a final stem-vowel. The organization of the singular cases was virtually complete (apart from the instrumental, which has an agglutinative suffix), but the dual and plural were less well established. The passive was less distinct than the middle voice, and the middle voice was dependent on the active, and used more than one device (*-r*/diphthong for simple vowel). The western (*centum*) group of languages, including Tokharian, provides no evidence of a palatal *$*\hat{k}$; the eastern (or rather north to south-eastern, *satem* group) provides no evidence of a labialized *$*k^w$. It would seem that the *satem* group entered on a series of innovations after the severance of Tokharian while the western languages remained faithful to archaic standards. Comparison with Romance philology is instructive, since not only do we have the heads of inferences from the existing languages (Romance), but we have imperial Latin as well. Reconstituted Romance forms are valid for their consequences, but they not infrequently differ (in ways that can be explained) from attested Latin. They allow us to estimate the sureness and the element of doubt in the comparative method.

At the time of separation the Indo-European dialects were those of tribes who may never have known linguistic unity. They may, on the other hand, have not all originally spoken Indo-European, but have acquired it from some single tribe of high prestige. The non-Indo-European words in English, which apply to some fundamental concepts, may have been due to the conquest of some non-Indo-European substratum in north Germany and Denmark, or they may have been due to adoption of Indo-European peacefully by a non-Indo-European community. Both conquest and pacific penetration are ways of propagation attested by the more modern history of languages.

The Indo-European community, so far as it was united, lived

among oak-trees, birches, willows, and probably beeches, elms, and limes. Their animals were the ox, cow, horse, dog, sheep, pig, bear, wolf, duck, goose, eagle, and probably the fox, but definitely not the camel, elephant, lion, tiger, goat, or cat. Winter and snow were familiar, but not so certainly the sea. Their instruments were probably of stone, but with some use of metals; their dispersion on expeditions of conquest was due to copper, and later iron, weapons, but these were not metals of their original community. They reared cattle, drank milk, and used the hand-plough. The family was well organized, since the words for father, mother, sister, brother, son-in-law, daughter-in-law, father-in-law, and mother-in-law were common; the organization was presumably patriarchal. They counted on two hands up to ten, and knew ten tens (100). They had at least the rudiments of a nature religion, with a Sky-father and Earth-mother; they had chiefs (*rex, rajah*), though not in all tribes, and some sacerdotal institutions as represented by solemn compound nouns and compound proper names. Shifts of meaning, especially in the names of trees and animals, have made some of these identifications difficult. The proposed locations of the original Indo-European home have varied in consequence. South-west Asia, south Russia, the Carpathians, the central European plain, and even Scandinavia have been proposed, with various degrees of assent from scholars.

A somewhat different identification is that of the focus of dispersion. For this we have evidence either of history or of a state of affairs immediately previous to the emergence of Indo-European peoples as historical actors. The movements cover a period of some 3,000 years, and separation was not necessarily abrupt. Contact may have been made, as between Romance languages, while initial urges to change completed themselves separately in different areas. In general, however, diffusion presents a clear pattern. From a base-line extending from the Rhine along the Danube to the Don pressure has been outwards to the west, south-west, south, and south-east (Map II).

While we cannot account for the arrival of Indo-European speakers in the region of Turfan, the north to south-easterly line of the *satem* languages follows the highway of the Dniester from the central European plain to the bend of the Don. Baltic, Slavonic, Iranian, and Indian languages have in common the use of sibilants for ancient palatal occlusives (*$\hat{k}$ *$\hat{g}$ *$\hat{g}h$). In this they agree with

Armenian and less perfectly with Albanian. Slavonic and Indo-Iranian coincide also in modifying s to $ş$ (or a derivative of $ş$) in contact with the semivowels i and u, the vibrant r and the velar occlusive k. In the use of *Bogŭ* for 'god' and 'grain, wealth' Slavonic is especially associated with Iranian. If prehistoric movements were in the same direction as those at the dawn of history, we might suppose that the Indo-Iranian or Aryan branch was originally lodged at the head of the Dnieper road in the plains of Poland and eastern Germany. Their presence in the tract from the Danube to the Don is attested by the use of *danu* in river-names. Shakhmatov has also shown that the earliest Finno-Ugrian borrowings from their neighbours in south Russia show common Aryan, rather than specifically Iranian, traits. By 1200 B.C., however, the Indian branch of the family was already overlooking the plains of India. The Aryan dialect was approximately a unit; after the departure of the Indian branch Iranian dialects acquired their own characteristics, but never consolidated into one language. Some of the Scyths known to Herodotus, the Asii (Ossetes) of later geographers and the Sarmatians of the beginnings of the Christian era remained behind in Russia as the rear-guard of the Iranian migration; its advanced members began to appear above the Semitic Fertile Crescent about 800 B.C.

The comparative vocabulary of Baltic and Slavonic collected by R. Trautmann justifies the use of the term 'Balto-Slavonic'. The coincidences in evolution are too numerous not to imply community of intercourse. But the divergencies are also highly characteristic, though always in a subordinate degree. We know from Tacitus and Strabo that the contact of Balts and Slavs was disrupted by the thrusts south of Bastarnæ and Goths in the first two centuries of our era. Similar losses of contact at other times may account for the separate development given to so many common initial impulses.

From somewhere in the curve of the Danube the Dacians and Thracians advanced towards the Aegean and crossed into Asia Minor under the style of Phrygians. Hittites and Armenians may have followed the same track. Since Albanian is a *satem* language, it is to be presumed that the Shkipetars crossed the Balkan chain diagonally from the lower Danube. Albanian is often accepted as an offspring of ancient Illyrian. If forms like *Veneti* are names of Illysian peoples, they may be encountered in German *Wendland*,

Italian *Venice* and French *La Vendée*. From these data some infer that the Illyrians were the first Indo-Europeans to migrate westward and that their language must have formed part of the substratum of Latin and Gaulish, the tongues of later invaders. Farther west were, no doubt, the Greeks. Their south-south-easterly migration was in two main waves: that of the Achaeans via the Vardar to Thessalian Achaea and thence along the islands until they are recorded (*Ahhiyawâ*) upon Hittite inscriptions as raiding the south-western corner of Asia Minor. Later, the Dorians descended the spine of the Balkan Peninsula to the Morea and Crete. Both invasions seem to have by-passed Athens, whose writers boast that they belong to an autochthonous people. Attica did not fail thereby to be hellenized.

The base for Italian migrations may have been on the middle Danube. First the Latins, Ausones, and Sicules advanced into Illyria and crossed the Adriatic below the line Pescara–Rome. Next came the Osco-Umbrians, who lodged in the hilly spine of Italy, keeping clear of Tuscany and the Po Valley. Then Illyrian Veneti and Messapi entered north-east and south-east Italy, and last of all Albanian colonies crossed the sea at its narrowest point. The Osco-Umbrians have developed *p* from *kw* like some Hellenes, the Germans and a branch of the Celts, and are thus opposed to the Goidelic Celts and the Latins who retained *kw*. This throws doubt on the unity of the Italian languages in ancient times, some scholars holding that the similarity of Italic and Latin is to be explained by secondary movements of convergence.[1]

Celtic-speakers occupied a base from Vindobona (Vienna) to the Moenus (Main) and Rhine and extending into south-west Germany and Bohemia (the home of the Boii). This region can be identified by river- and place-names. It must have touched upon the original home of the Latins and Italians, since the resemblance between Celtic and Italic dialects is close enough to have suggested the hypothesis of an original Celto-Italic language. A feature in common was the *r*-passive, which has later been found in Phrygian, Hittite, and Tokharian. The hypothesis of unity of speech has receded in favour, but the marked similarity of development remains a fact, along with the division of both groups by P and Q (Osco-Umbrian *petora*, Welsh *pedwar* = Latin *quattuor*, Gaelic

---

[1] See G. Devoto, *Storia della Lingua di Roma*, Bologna, 1939; D. M. Jones, 'Relation of Latin to Osco-Umbrian', *Trans. Philological Soc.*, 1950.

ceithir). This *p* shifted to *f* in accordance with Germanic sound-laws (Gothic *fidwōr*, Eng. *four*). Thus Celtic as a whole has much in common with Germanic, but the P-Celts show signs of longer contact. The most archaic forms are found, as one would expect, on the circumference of the area of expansion. Migrations began somewhat later than those of the Italian tribes and continued into the last century before Christ. They have thus been partially recorded by Latin and Greek authors. France was occupied by successive waves of migrants, and Spain and Portugal were largely controlled by a Celtic dominant caste as early as the time of Herodotus. Britain and Cisalpine Gaul were reached by the usual radial movements, but the Celtic settlement in Galatia involved cutting across other Indo-European areas.

The last to move were the Germans and the Slavs. The Balts remain virtually in their original emplacements, though they have lost ground near the headwaters of the Volga and in east Prussia. The Slavonic expansion, ultimately the most imposing of all, was due to the evacuation of eastern Germany by Germanic peoples and the collapse of Attila's Hunnish empire. In the first instance its main axis was the Dnieper, running south-east. Southerly and easterly movements followed. Westward infiltration as far as the Elbe was due to the German vacuum, but was not dense enough to hold these lands when the Germans began their easterly expansion in the Middle Ages. The German movements are all recorded. They began in eastern Germany, and the most spectacular was the Gothic descent from Skåne (disrupting the Slavonic way of life and turning them into the brigands described by Tacitus) to the Dnieper, and then westerly by Mœsia and northern Italy to Spain. The western migrations were of Franks into northern France, English and Norsemen into England, and Norsemen to Iceland. In modern times the expansion of English, Spaniards, and Portuguese has brought vast oversea territories into the Indo-European area, and Russian has spread to Siberia.[1]

In their expansion radially from a focus on the central European plain, speakers of Indo-European tongues overran non-Indo-Europeans and even some of their own kinsmen. Of the earlier

---

[1] A summary of the present state of information about Indo-European is given by P. Noble in the article 'Indo-European languages', *Chambers's Encyclopaedia*, London, 1950; see also articles on individual languages there and in the 'Great Language' series.

communities it is not always possible to give an account, but there is a fringe of shattered languages along the southern frontier of the advance, protected from extinction by mountain fastnesses in some cases, and extending from the western Pyrenees to the Deccan. Whether these represent one or several language families is hard to determine upon the defective evidence. Basque, the three branches of the Caucasian tongues, and Dravidian survive; a good deal is known of ancient Sumerian; something of Etruscan; and little but the names of the ancient languages of Asia Minor and the heights above the Fertile Crescent. They have been combined in elaborate schemes of Japhetic, Nostratic, Mediterranean, and Alarodian languages, all of which extend from the Pyrenees to the Caucasus and some into Hither Asia. A further complication implied in the term Mediterranean lies in the probable intercourse of peoples on the northern shore with those of the southern, and in particular of the Iberians with the Berbers of Lybia. Since these speak a Hamitic language, their tongue is akin to ancient Egyptian and to the Cushitic languages between the Nile and the Red Sea and Indian Ocean. There have been Nubian impulses, no doubt, in the Nilotic languages and those of the Sudan. Thus the area of speculation concerning pre-Indo-European languages is immense, and it includes conjectures that some of them may have been, as it were, cousins of Indo-European itself. Identifications of vocabulary have often a certain plausibility, though they are far from conclusive. As for structure, there is infixation in Caucasian languages and in Basque, comprehensive verbal forms, and the use of an ergative case alongside a 'passive' nominative. In Etruscan, but not in Basque, consonants are massed as they are in Georgian and, by Caucasian influence probably, in Armenian. The search for affinities for Sumerian has covered most of the possibilities without success. The Dravidian languages of the Deccan have left behind them a solitary outpost in the Brahui of Baluchistan. They must have occupied this whole area before the irruption of the Indo-Europeans, who presumably cut them off from contact with Uralian or Altaic peoples.

A serious obstacle to identification lies in the fact that some necessary intermediate tasks have not been accomplished. The identification of Basque with 'Iberian' is plausible, at least as regards some particular Iberian dialect, but is held up by the impossibility of giving an account of the surviving Iberian inscriptions. There are plausibly Basque words in use in Sardinia,[1] and other words of the Pyrenean-Alpine region have been identified as Ligurian or Alpine. The Ligurians have been limited by some writers to the region from the Alps to the Pyrenees. There is, however, classical authority for the word in Britain and Spain. Among other possibilities there is the thesis that Ligurian is a primitive form of Celtic or a language sister to primitive Indo-European. Etruscan inscriptions have been deciphered, but afford only meagre lexical and grammatical information. It is still debated whether the Etruscans were at home in Tuscany or migrated, as some of the ancients held, from Asia Minor.[2] An Etruscan dialect was used in the island of Lemnos. If their associations were eastern, the question of their relations with the pre-Hellenic Leleges and with the ancient Lydians arises, and cannot be solved for lack of information apart from some formatives of place-names. The Caucasian languages are divided into three groups: north-west, north-east, and southern. The business of description is still uncompleted, and it is still uncertain whether they do or do not form one speech-family. *A fortiori* it is more difficult to assert that they are the central link of a speech-family extending over the northern shores of the Mediterranean into Hither Asia.

With regard to Basque,[3] it is a language of postpositions used with the noun, and some eleven of these may be joined together as a plausible declension. There is a suffixed definite article -a as in *gizona* 'the man'. This is the simple nominative; but the active nominative has a suffixed -k (*gizonak*), which recalls not only the Georgian ergative, but also the -s of Indo-European. The adjective follows, as *eche berria* 'the new house', and the definite article is suffixed to the entire relative clause, thus making it an adjective or noun in apposition to the substantive. The verbal complex includes prefixed patient, followed by dative or ethic dative, then the verbal stem, and lastly the suffixed agent. Thus *d-e-k* is entirely parallel to Sp. *lo ve-s* 'it seest thou' in the transitive verb. The distinction between agent and patient is irrelevant for the intransitive verb, and Basque has elected to treat the subject of an intransitive verb as the patient of the state or activity: *d-a* 'he is', *d-oa* 'he goes'.

[1] W. von Wartburg, *Die Entstehung der romanischen Völker*, 2 ed., Tübingen, 1951, p. 30.

[2] H. L. Stoltenberg, *Etruskische Sprachlehre*, Gießen, 1950.

[3] H. Gavel, *Grammaire basque*, Bayonne, 1929 ff.; B. de Arrigarai, *Euskera*, San Sebastian, s.d.

Thus transitive and intransitive conjugations differ in their subject pronouns, though not by the same mechanism as in Magyar and Quechua, and the transitive verb is 'passively' construed, as sometimes in Georgian. As there is only one voice, the distinction between active and passive is not strictly relevant, since the passive is a grammatical device to invert active order. The verbal complex is strangely fused in Basque, so that all forms have to be learned individually, and separately for each dialect and subdialect. Thus *izan* 'to have' is not readily recognizable in *baginduzek* 'if you had us' or *bau* 'if you have it'. By way of compensation, conjugation is applied only to a limited number of verbs, usually called 'auxiliaries', and the rest are treated analytically, with the help of *izan* 'to be'.

The Caucasian[1] languages develop the case system up to twenty-three places. Nouns are classified generically into between four and eight classes. The four-class system distinguished between rational and irrational. The former are divided into masculine (sg. *w* pl. *b*) and feminine (sg. *y* pl. *b*); the latter into individuals (sg. *b* pl. *r*) and collectives (sg. *r* pl. *r*). Among the collectives a further distinction can be made between collectives proper (*r*) and 'relatives' (*d*), and there are three other classes in Abkhazian. If the system is an essential and original part of the Caucasian languages, it cuts them off from Basque. On the other hand, one may note that Indo-European also distinguishes animates from inanimates, masculine from feminine animates (though with a tendency to less discrimination in the plural), and uses a collective suffix (-*a*) for the plural of its neuters. Classes like these occur again in Bantu. The most extraordinary feature of Georgian is the verb, which includes pronominal features and is much fused. As in Basque the verbal stem is sometimes hard to find. The verbal activity is expressed as affecting the subject in various ways: as the point of departure of the action (nominative), as actor (ergative), as person interested in the event (dative), and as agent in a passive construction (genitive with postposition -*gan* 'on the part of'). In the first instance the object or aim of the action is expressed in the dative, but in the other three it is in the nominative, since the actor's objective may reasonably be conceived as that from which

[1] G. Dumézil, *Introduction à la grammaire comparée des langues caucasiennes du nord*, 1933; F. N. Finck, 'Die georgische Sprache', *Die Haupttypen des Sprachbaus*, 1936; H. Vogt, *Esquisse d'une grammaire du géorgien moderne*, Oslo, 1936.

the whole action issues. These four constructions are bound up with the expression of voice, tense, and mood, so that comparison with the Basque 'passive' verb cannot pass beyond a very simple, and probably fallacious, stage.

Concerning ancient Etruscan,[1] some regard the language as indigenous and 'Mediterranean', others as an immigrant from Asia Minor (specifically from *Tirra*). Place-names in -*ss*- ranging from Italy to Asia give support to the ancient identification of Pelasgians and Etruscans, and that brings into sight the equally ancient distinction of Pelasgians and Leleges. The latter lead on to the complex of unknown Asian languages: Lydian, Carian, Lycian, &c., including possibly the non-Indo-European or 'Caucasian' elements of Armenian. Along the mountains above Mesopotamia were Cossæan and Elamite, and in the delta of the rivers was ancient Sumerian.[2] In this the greater number of stems are monosyllabic, and both noun and verb freely take on agglutinative particles, which have a fixed order of sequence. In these respects Sumerian appears to be an agglutinative tongue, like Altaic, but it does not use vowel-harmony or restrict itself to suffixation. Affiliation with any other language has still to be proved.

Finally, the Dravidian[3] languages of Peninsular India represent another victim of the Indo-European advance. The Brahui language, marooned in Baluchistan, is a witness to their former extension over all India, but it seems they themselves are invaders. Comparison of Tamil and Telegu words with Finno-Ugric renders affiliation highly plausible. As in Finnish there is no prefixing or infixing, but only the use of suffixes. The original consonant system was simple, and some peculiar modifications may have arisen on Indian soil. There is no gender in Brahui, which presumably represents an archaic condition of Dravidian, but in the languages of southern India there is a remarkable generic distinction between superior and inferior beings, crossed with sex. A number of different notions have been at work, and the results are variegated. In one instance, gods, men, and demons are deemed superior, and animals and inanimates inferior; goddesses and women are sometimes classed as inferior in the singular but superior in the plural,

---

[1] M. Pallottino, *La civilisation étrusque*, Paris, 1949.
[2] See the article 'Sumerian' in *Chambers's Encyclopaedia*, 1950, with bibliography.
[3] See 'Indian Languages' in *Chambers's Encyclopaedia*, 1950.

and in one language gender depends on the persons of the dialogue:
men speaking to men or women use the superior gender for females,
but women talking together use the inferior.

6. AFRASIA

The borders of Afrasia have already been defined by the deserts
of the south and the Mediterranean and Fertile Crescent in the
north. A single linguistic family of great antiquity, the Hamito-
Semitic, occupies the whole region.

Semitic movements have been recorded since about 2000 B.C.
They include the infiltration of the Akkadian Semites into Babylonia, that of the Hebrews and other tribes into Palestine, and lastly
the Aramæans into Syria and the region of Carchemish. These
have been the ancient migrations, which have given rise to important languages of civilization: Babylonian, the diplomatic tongue
of the second century B.C., Hebrew for religion and its congener
Phœnician for commerce, and Aramæan for the trade and administration of the Assyrian and Persian empires. In the early part
of the Christian era Himyarites (southern Arabs) migrated to
Abyssinia, carrying with them the Christian religion. Then, in the
seventh century the advent of Mohammed launched Arabic on a
career of extension from Persia to Spain. Many of the principal
Arabic thinkers and writers have been Spaniards and Persians, but
national reactions expelled the Arabic tongue from these territories,
though leaving behind a great store of words. It remains in use
from Morocco to Iraq, and as the language of the Quran it is
employed for religious purposes from Java to the Sudan.

Since Egypt has been thrice overrun by Semites in historical
times, it is not unreasonable to suppose one such invasion before
the rise of the First Dynasty. One may thus understand why
ancient Egyptian should show a marked degree of correspondence
with Semitic in vocabulary and organization, while at the same
time revealing some fundamental divergencies. The ancient Libyan
languages are represented now by Berber 'islands' within the
western Arabic of Morocco, Algiers, and Tunis.[1] These, too, show
a marked triconsonantalism. On the other hand, the other branch
of the Hamitic family, the Cushite of the region between the Nile

---

[1] G. Hanoteau, *Essai de grammaire kabyle*, Algiers, 1858; F. Newman, *Libyan
Vocabulary*, London, 1882; John, Marquess of Bute, *On the ancient language of
the natives of Tenerife*, London, 1891.

and Red Sea (disrupted by Abyssinian or Ethiopic), has a bicon-sonantal structure. It is possible that the oldest Egyptian stratum might have been of this nature, but that it was semiticized in pre-historic times, and that wave of influence spread steadily westward.

To what extent ancient Egyptian was triconsonantal is a matter of contention between experts, according as they prefer Asian or African parallels. The hieroglyphic orthography is often ambigu-ous. Some words are written by ideographs, which give no indica-tion of sound. Others are begun with ideographs, representing a letter or a syllable, and completed with alphabetical signs. The latter include no vowels, and it is most scholarly not to presume what they were. Since the sculptors were artists concerned to fill square spaces, they did not feel bound to include signs which spoiled their symmetry. Apart from the orthography of the word, there may be a sign determining its meaning as of some certain kind. As to the vowels, they may be inferred from Coptic, provided one allows for the very considerable, and in detail unknown, history of the Egyptian language over 4,000 years. Another device, which avoids writing down strings of consonants, is to employ *e* as repre-senting any vowel. Thus one may write *ntk* or *entek* 'thou', *nzm* or *nezem* 'sweet', *yb* or *yby* or **yîbew* 'heart' (taking into account Coptic *-êbi* and Semitic *libb*), *yt* or *yty* or **yô-têj* 'father' (Coptic *eiôt*). Owing to phonetic wastage the triconsonantalism of Coptic is much less marked than that of ancient Egyptian: *noute = neter* 'god', *nanu/nefer* 'good', *she = shet* 'hundred'. The Egyptian of the hieroglyphs was a sacred and monumental language, Coptic was that of the Christian minority and many of its terms as well as its whole alphabet were Greek.[1]

On the other hand, it is plain that strict triconsonantalism is a system imposed on the Semitic languages. Arabic *yad* 'hand' is one of a small number of simple words which have not been fitted into the system. The semivowels *w y* and ' (*alif* or soft breathing and pause) are reckoned as consonants to make up the required number of three, but they disappear in the mutations of words. Theory has been so strong that it reconstitutes each word-family on the basis of the third person singular of the aorist tense, as in *qatala* 'he

---

[1] A. H. Gardiner, *Egyptian Grammar*, 2 ed., Oxford, 1950; G. Farina, *Gram-matica della Lingua egiziana antica*, 2 ed., 1926, pp. 13–23, summarizes the correspondences between Egyptian and Semitic. For Coptic I have at hand Miss M. A. Murray, *Elementary Coptic (Sahidic) Grammar*, 1911.

killed', notwithstanding the fact that this form includes a suffix -*a*, possibly factitive. The basic stem cannot be *qatala*, but only *qatal-*, if it is not one of the simple nouns *qatl* or *qitl*. In theory, barking (*kalaba*) and rabies (*kaliba*) come before the dog (*kalb*), and the heart (*qalb*) would be recognized from an activity of turning over (*qalaba*). A few words have more than four consonants. They may be readily recognized as foreign or onomatopœic.

The word-maker has at his disposal, in Arabic, a rich system of consonants, with velar *k g* = *j* followed further down the throat by the gutturals ' (the glottal stop) *h ḥ kh gh*. *T d s z* are also duplicated further back by *ṭ ḍ ṣ ẓ*. Thus the whole enunciation is pushed backwards in the mouth and has the specially throaty quality which travellers so often remark. Ancient Egyptian, though simpler, is also relatively rich in gutturals. The first and second consonants may not stand together at the beginning of a word, but the second and third may form a group, and either may be doubled. This begins a series of permutations which is carried forward for Arabic nouns by three consonantal prefixes and two suffixes. Short vowels are not noted, but the permutations of *a*/*i*/*u*/O provide the simpler words. Long vowels and diphthongs (*ā ī ū ya wa ai au āi āü*) are marked by the semivocalic consonants *y w* ' (soft breathing at the beginning of a word, diæresis within). When vocalic and consonantal permutations are multiplied together, they give seventy possible models of nouns for each basic stem, and these are quite enough for all derivational purposes and some purposes of syntax. Thus simple and mutated forms are associated together arbitrarily to provide singulars and their corresponding collective plurals. These plurals have feminine concords, and the feminine -*at* was presumably first a collective. Nouns, whether substantives or adjectives, can also be recruited from verbs. The verbs distinguish active from passive and aorist from the continuous tense by mutations of the vowels *a i u*. Nine derived forms are obtained by doubling consonants, lengthening vowels, prefixing vowels, infixing *t*, and prefixing *ta*, *in*, *ista*. The correspondence of aorist and continuous tenses in the simple verb form is arbitrary, so that one might deem them separate words brought into association by usage. They differ also in persons, since the aorist is conjugated by suffixed pronouns (with distinction of gender for the 2nd and 3rd), but the continuous tense by prefixed pronouns with non-pronominal suffixes. Only the continuous tense has moods. The triconsonantal pattern is thus an immense effort towards foreseeing all likely demands of language, and it does so beyond actual requirements of the greater number of stems.

In respect of relations an important distinction is made between verbal and nominal sentences in Semitic and Hamitic. The verbal sentence is phenomenal, the nominal is judicial; that is, the verbal sentence expresses an event as happening, but the nominal equates a noun to some predicate. Thus Egyptian *sedem sekhtï kheru* 'hears the peasant a voice = the peasant hears a voice'/*ynuk neb ymat* 'I lord of graciousness = I am a gracious lord'. A mixed sentence is obtained by placing the subject first in absolute position and then forming a verbal sentence. The genitive relation between nouns is expressed by the construct, i.e. by associating the possessor with the thing possessed in a semi-fused construction.

In Coptic the Egyptian language shows drastic modification in an 'African' sense. The gutturals are much reduced. Phonetic decay has left in the language many open monosyllables or dissyllables: *na* 'mercy', *nub* 'gold', *nobe* 'sin', *nute* 'god', *nanu* 'beautiful', *me* 'truth', *kah* 'earth', *rôme* 'man', *neef* 'sailor', *eiôt* 'father', *kô* 'lay', &c. There is a grammatical shift from predominant suffixation to predominant prefixation. Though nouns are classed as masculine and feminine, some derivational prefixes indicate agent, act, pertinence ('man of' *r̄m*-), negation, place, and abstraction. Articles and demonstratives are prefixed, and thus singular and plural are distinguished by prefix in *urôme* 'a man', *prôme* 'the man'/*henrôme* 'men'. The personal pronoun is suffixed to prepositions and in verbs. In the latter instance it is suffixed only to a few old verbs, but most verbs are conjugated by suffixing the pronoun to prefixes of time, mood, relation, condition, or negation. Thus the grammatical distinctions in *sah-f-sotm̄* 'he is accustomed to hear' are presented before the verbal stem is reached. The noun-subject is also suffixed to these auxiliary prefixes (*share-prôme hobs̄* '[The] man is wont to be clothed'), and the object, whether noun or pronoun, is suffixed to the verb, which then takes a shortened (construct) form. Thus a considerable part of the Coptic sentence is fused together. True adjectives are rare, and the relation is expressed either as possession or more often as a predicated relative: *tsheere nsabê* 'the wise daughter (*n* = 'of'), *pran etuaab* 'the name which (*et-*) is holy = the holy name'.

7. AFRICA

Beneath the belt of deserts and swamps lies Africa proper. The oldest of its cultures is that of the Pygmies of the Congo forests.[1] They have been completely absorbed into the Bantu linguistic area, and culturally are enclosed within the West African culture of forest-dwellers and matriarchal Bantu tribes. The latter form the bulk of the Bantu-speaking peoples, but it was not with them that the grammatical organization of Bantu originated. The latter is found at its best between the Victoria and Albert Lakes, and shows a main thrust southward along the Great Rift valley. This thrust disrupts into two groups the east Hamitic culture of the Cushitic Hamites on the horn of Africa and the Bushmen and Hottentot tribes in the south-western deserts. They are joined and largely included in the way of life of hunters of the steppes. In the fifteenth century Hottentot tribes were still fighting against Bantu invaders in the Rift valley, and at the beginning of our era people of that sort were lodged as far north as the Red Sea. The east Hamitic culture is quite unconnected with that of Egypt and Barbary, though linguistically Somali, Galla, Bilin, Bedauye, and the like form the Cushitic branch of a family which included formerly all Egypt and Libya. Mlle Homburger has pointed out that Nubians are shown on ancient Egyptian monuments unaccompanied by interpreters.

A second main road of penetration extends from the Bahr-al-Ghazal to the Shari river and Lake Chad; thence it follows the Benue to its confluence with the Niger, and ascends the Niger towards its source. A short land-traverse leads to the Senegal, and so to the Atlantic Ocean. This east–west axis is that of the West African forest-dwellers, of the Neo-Sudanese culture and, in part of the Paleo-Negritic. It is the axis of the Sudanic languages, i.e. of those of the Nilotic tribes, inhabitants of the Sudan, and West Africans. The corresponding languages have been referred to a number of family-groups (seven according to Kieckers) or considered as of one origin in the Nilotic area, from which Bantu also descended. The southerly extension of the Paleo-Negritic area corresponds to that of the Bantu tongues, and the Rhodesian culture approximately to the realm of Monomotapa, of which the Portuguese venturers heard news. It is with the Paleo-Negros, as

[1] H. Baumann and D. Westermann, *Les peuples et les civilisations de l'Afrique*, Paris, 1948. (Map V.)

it would seem, that Bantu grammatical organization should be associated, possibly under impulse of members of a white race from further north. Mlle Homburger is willing to identify this impulse with late ancient Egyptian mediated through Nubian. There are Nubian texts from the eighth to eleventh centuries. Sir H. H. Johnston, taking into account the Bantuoid or Semi-Bantu languages of the Niger Bend and Sierra Leone, preferred to suppose a common focus in the Chad region, with a specifically Bantu centre of diffusion in the region of the Victoria Nyanza.

The Mediterranean culture of the Barbary states crossed the Sahara via Tibesti and Chad, and directly to the great bend of the Niger at Timbuktu. The Berber Tawarek extend so far to the south, and their neighbours the Hausa speak a language with a Sudanic basis and a considerable degree of Hamitic organization.

West African languages include such as Wolof, Mandingo, Mende,[1] Fula, Ibo, Yoruba, Ewe, Fante, &c. They tend to have a monosyllabic base (Mende *pa* 'a coming', *nja* 'water', *pu* 'cave', *nje* 'goat'), with open syllables and various tones. There are also dissyllables, generally with open syllables unless closed by a nasal (Mende *kenya* 'uncle', *fombo* 'spread', *kulu* 'receive', *sani* 'bottle'). Consonants in Mende are divided into two orders, strong and weak; the strong consonants are pronounced with greater tension which is sometimes shown in their being voiceless (k/g, kp/gb, t/l, f/v, p/w, s/j) and sometimes by double formation in the mouth (mb/b, nd/l, ng/y, w, nj/y). There is no one notion of plurality, but three, which indicate indefinite, definite and collective notions. Tenses are formed by suffixes. A notable feature of Mende is that place is conceived as a relation to the body of the speaker, so that locative postpositions are classed with parts of the body. There is no grammatical gender.

In Hausa[2] there are two genders, masculine and feminine, as in Hamitic languages, and these are marked for the second and third persons. The pronouns precede the verb and are fused with signs for tense and mood (as in Coptic), so that it is the pronoun which seems to be conjugated: *yanâ tafê* 'he is coming', *yâ tafi* 'he has gone'. Nouns are related to each other by means of a construct state: *sarkin Kano* 'the chief of Kano'. There are few true adjectives. Those that exist precede the noun as attributes, but follow

[1] K. H. Crosby, *An Introduction to the Study of Mende*, Cambridge, 1944.
[2] F. W. Taylor, *Hausa Grammar*, Oxford, 1923.

MAP V

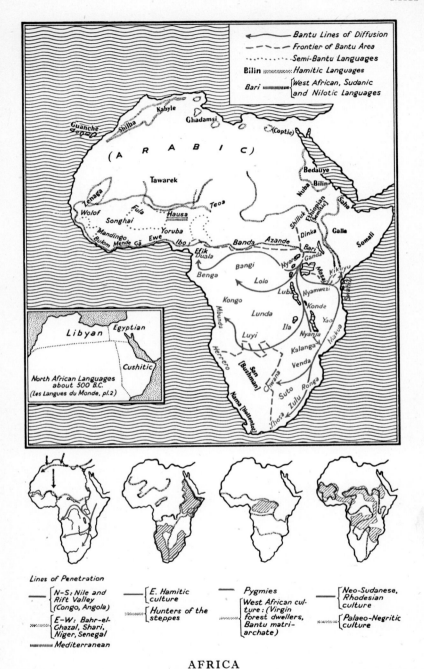

AFRICA

AFRICAN CIVILIZATIONS (adapted from H. Baumann and D. Westermann, *Les Peuples et les Civilisations de l'Afrique*, Paris, 1948)

AFRICA

AFRICAN CIVILIZATIONS (adapted from H. Baumann and D. Westermann, *Les Peuples et les Civilisations de l'Afrique*, Paris, 1948)

as predicates. In general quality is expressed as a possession or lack (*mai* 'having', *rasa* 'lacking'), as *mai-rôwa* 'having meanness = mean'. On the other hand, Hausa is African in its monosyllabic and dissyllabic basis, without triconsonantalism, and in its avoidance of consonant-groups.

The languages of the central Sudan and the upper Nile are described by Mlle Homburger in a linguistic appendix to Baumann and Westermann's work already cited, and in other works.[1] The open monosyllables of West Africa answer to generally closed monosyllables in East Africa. Hottentot (Nama) and Bushman (San) perhaps should be attached to the Hamitic of the horn of Africa.

Bantu[2] languages appear to have been organized in the vicinity of the Equatorial lakes and to have penetrated southward in two main thrusts, the one by way of the chain of lakes to Natal and Cape Agulhas, the other to the coast at Zanzibar and thence coastwise to the south. Westerly extensions follow the northward curve of the Congo or its principal southern affluents, or cross the high ground towards Angola. The Semi-Bantu languages extend north of the Bantu line in West Africa as far as Sierra Leone, and show affinity with Bantu in organization. Bantu itself has a predominantly 'African' basis, upon which has been rivetted a highly characteristic organization into classes of nouns by means of class-prefixes. Plurality answers to class, and the whole phrase is placed under the regimen of the subject by pronominal class-prefixes attached to the verb or other significant elements. Some of the Bantu languages also use pre-prefixes.

There are some Bantu monosyllabic stems, such as *li* 'with', and

---

[1] L. Homburger, *Le langage et les langues*, Paris, 1951; *The Negro-African Languages*, London, 1949; A. Werner, *The Language-Families of Africa*, London, 1915.

[2] Sir H. H. Johnston, *Comparative Study of the Bantu and Semi-Bantu Languages*, Oxford, 1922; works by Mlle Homburger and Miss Werner cited above: C. Meinhof, *Lautlehre der Bantusprachen*, 2 ed., Berlin, 1910; L. Homburger, *Étude sur la phonétique historique du Bantou*, Paris, 1914; C. M. Doke, *Bantu* (bibliography), London, 1945, *Bantu Linguistic Terminology*, London, 1935; A. V. Madan, *Living Speech in Africa*, Oxford, 1911. I have at hand C. M. Doke, *Zulu Grammar*, 4 ed., London, 1947; E. O. Ashton, *Swahili Grammar*, 2 ed., London, 1947; T. Price, *Elements of Nyanja*, Blantyre (Nyasaland), 1947; A. W. McGregor, *Grammar of the Kikuyu Language*, London, 1905. I cite Swahili forms as being the simplest to understand. For Sir H. H. Johnston's great work I am indebted to the Delegates of the Clarendon Press, and to Mr. C. S. S. Higham of Messrs. Longmans for several others.

'be', *pa* 'give', *ti* 'say', composed of consonant and vowel, but these stems are wont to be highly indeterminate in meaning, and by a special provision of grammar they may not appear without prefix in places where other stems drop their prefixes. The greater number of stems are dissyllabic, and of the form *xoxo* (where *x* is any consonant and *o* any vowel). Some of these stems may have been built up from monosyllables, and so may serve to show a link between monosyllabic Sudan languages and Bantu, but the majority are clearly dissyllabic. Before the second consonant there may be a nasal, less often before the first. Verbs end in *-a*, with few exceptions. This probably represents a factitive suffix, which becomes *-e* (commonly resulting from *-ai*) in the subjunctive, and *-i* occurs in general negation: Swahili *ataka* 'he wants'/*hataki* 'he does not want'. There are also some verbs in *-i* in addition to the primitive *li* and *ti*, such as *rudi* 'return' and *zidi* 'increase'. Probably such a word as *fa* 'die' should be analysed as *fa-a*, but in other cases the vowel suppressed may not be known. A final *-o* denotes the noun of action. Thus the dissyllabic stems are not invariable, but significant mutations. To derive verbal aspects from the simple verbal stem a number of suffixes are available: Swahili *zidi* 'increase'/ *zidisha* 'cause to increase', *fuata* 'follow'/*fuatia* 'follow after', *ita* 'call'/*itwa* 'be called', *la* 'eat'/*liwa* 'be eaten', *pata* 'get'/*patikana* 'be procurable'. Noun stems remain invariable, however, and derivation is by fusion: Swahili *mwanamke* 'woman', *mwanamume* 'man'.

The system of speech-sounds is very simple. The vowels are *a i u*; *e* and *o* result from *ai* and *au*. The Swahili consonants *p t ch k* are pronounced on the outgoing breath, but *b dj g* on the incoming breath (implosively), except after a nasal. *S z sh f v l r w y* are used, and the nasals are *m n ny ng'*. Other consonants are used to render the numerous Arabic words in Swahili. In Zulu *b* is implosive, but clicks have been borrowed from Hottentot, and the whole articulation is more difficult. The normal Bantu practice is primitive in the sense that it rests on the three primitive vowels, and shows disconformity between voiceless and voiced occlusives. Labial sounds are very prominent in Bantu sentences.

The most remarkable feature of Bantu is the distribution of its nouns into classes (twenty-one according to Meinhof) marked by prefixes, and the subordination of the whole sentence to the noun-subject by means of pronominal prefixes. Tense and negation are also represented by prefixes, so that there is a prefix-conjugation. The grammar relies on prefixes as markedly as Turkish on suffixes, and the order of sequence is prescribed in each case. A prescribed sequence of prefixes is also characteristic of Sumerian.

It is easy to wax too lyrical in praise of Bantu classes. They are not logically discriminated, but they do represent a conscious, if somewhat fanciful and magical, ordering of experience. Distinctions like these occur in Caucasian and even in Indo-European, though not always with grammatical effect. There is no dual, but plural prefixes differ from singular, and there are rather fewer plural prefixes than singular ones, showing that the importance of classification is less in the plural. That is so, for instance, also in Russian. There is a rational class, as in Caucasian, for persons: Swahili *m/wa-*, as *mtoto* 'child' / *watoto* 'children'. But small and dear persons may be relegated to the category of things: Sw. *kitoto* 'infant', cf. Gk. μειράκιον 'stripling', Russ. *Danilo*. Irrational, though animate, are animals: Swahili *(n)/(n)-*, *ndovu* 'elephant(s)', *mbwa* 'dog(s)'. The prefix is commonly lost before *ch f k m n p s t*, though *p t ch k* acquire a considerable degree of aspiration: *kuku* 'chicken(s)', *fisi* 'hyena(s)'. But this class is very widely applied to common objects, foreign words, and monosyllabic stems. The class in *ki/vi-* is of things that can be distinguished: as Sw. *kikapu* 'basket' / *vikapu* 'baskets'. *M/mi-* commonly refers to living things which are not animate, and so to trees, plants, &c., and the notion of 'living' is anything that spreads or extends: Sw. *mguu* 'foot', *moto* 'fire', *mkeka* 'mat', *mlima* 'mountain', *mtego* 'trap', *mwaka* 'year', *mwendo* 'journey'. A *(ji)/ma-* class, with the *ji-* sometimes reduced to *j* and sometimes absent, refers to things which may occur in quantities but also be thought of singly, and to constituent parts of things: *jani/majani* 'leaf/leaves'. There are two *u*-classes in Swahili. One in *u/n-* representing an original *lu-* refers to composite wholes which are not usually thought of in detail, as Sw. *unywele/ nywele* 'hair(s)'. The other *u-* is from *bu-*, has no plural and refers to abstract qualities, states, or countries: Sw. *utoto* 'childhood', *Uganda*. *Ku-* is an abstract of action and corresponds to our infinitive, and there are locative prefixes *ku- pa- mu-*: Nyanja *paphiri* 'on the hill', *kuMlanje* 'over at Mlanje', *KwaLiwonde* 'Liwonde's village'.

To all these prefixes there correspond pronominal prefixes in the verbal complex. They refer both to subject and object, but to subject first and always. They are usually different from the noun prefixes, though not always, and they occur with adverbs, demonstratives, interrogatives, and possessives as well as with verbs. The order of verbal prefixes is: negative, subject (or subject, negative), relative *o*, object, verb, verbal suffixes. The tenses denote aspects of time, as *wagonjwa wamelala* 'the sick folk have fallen asleep' or 'are asleep' (*-me-* of past action and present state). So Sw. *kazi i-na-yo-m-faa* 'work it-now-which-him-suits = work that suits him'. There are only about fifty pure adjectives, which are expressed appositively after the substantive, using that substantive's prefixes: Sw. *mtu mvivu* 'a lazy man (*un homme paresseux*)'. Otherwise adjectives are either regarded as qualities possessed by their substantive or as predicated of them by means of a relative clause. This treatment has already been noticed in Coptic. It is to be noted that concords hold also with the locative prefixes: Nyanja *KwaLiwonde ku-tenta* 'At Liwonde's it is hot'.

The Bantu languages are, strictly speaking, only oral, and to write them down is to give them a rigidity improper to them. They are eminently naïve. This appears particularly in the 'ideophone', which has been admirably described by C. M. Doke. The ideophone is not a word in the sense of uniting a definite form to a definite meaning, nor, on the other hand, is it a simple imitation of something in sound. It conveys an impression, not a meaning, and 'describes a predicate in respect to manner, colour, sound, or action'. To this extent it resembles an adverb, but has not the grammatical precision of an adverb. Those used in Zulu extend from one to five syllables, and can all be supposed to function with the verb *ukuthi* 'to express, act, demonstrate, manifest'. The 160 ideophones listed by Doke are all sensual, but not all concerned with sound. They include such impressions as of the gait of fat persons, hitting on the back or ribs, pressing something soft, sniggering, putting away carefully, stealthy gait, stirring porridge, appearing suddenly, issuing in numbers, walking as a chameleon, guilty looks, lying on the stomach watching for something, a short stout young girl. The impressions are the more satisfying as being total, and not analysed into words.

The Zulu and Kaffir (Xhosa) languages show adoption of some features of Bushman and Hottentot, particularly in the matter of clicks. These consist of double attachments of the tongue to areas of the roof of the mouth, so as to suck out air and make a vacuum.

When the tongue is detached, there is a sharp explosion.[1] The click in Zulu may be made on the teeth, on the palate or gums, or on one side of the mouth, and they may be normal, aspirated, voiced, or nasal. No less than nine tones enter into the making of Zulu words; in Swahili tone belongs to syntax.

[1] On Hottentot and Bushman there are some notes in L. Homburger, *The Negro-African Languages*, App. to ch. xi, 1949.

INDEX

PRINTED IN
GREAT BRITAIN
AT THE
UNIVERSITY PRESS
OXFORD
BY
CHARLES BATEY
PRINTER
TO THE
UNIVERSITY